SHAKESPEARE
as a Dramatic Artist

A POPULAR ILLUSTRATION OF
THE PRINCIPLES OF SCIENTIFIC CRITICISM

BY 1344

RICHARD G. MOULTON

WITH A NEW INTRODUCTION BY
ERIC BENTLEY

Dover Publications, Inc., New York

This Dover edition, first published in 1966, is an unabridged and unaltered republication of the third revised and enlarged edition published by the Clarendon Press, Oxford, in 1893.

This edition also contains a new Introduction by Eric Bentley and is published by special arrangement with Oxford University Press.

Library of Congress Catalog Card Number: 66-14556

Manufactured in the United States of America

Dover Publications, Inc.
180 Varick Street
New York, N. Y. 10014

INTRODUCTION TO THE DOVER EDITION

IN sixteenth-century England, a new form of drama was invented, and Shakespeare showed the world what it was capable of. Or did he? The French decided, as early as the seventeenth century, that Elizabethan drama was barbaric and formless. Their own classical tragedy provided the civilized and "well-made" alternative, the "well-made plays" of the nineteenth century being a popular and perhaps somewhat decadent version of the genre. And it is the French who decide the world's taste —in theatre as well as in ladies' fashions. Though Romantic poets—even French ones like Victor Hugo and Alfred de Musset—tried to reverse the trend and positively worshipped Shakespeare, the popular theatre held to the well-made pattern.

During the nineteenth century, it is true, Shakespeare's powers in some departments were praised and even over-praised. It was now well known that he created Real Human Beings and not Types. It was well known that he provided wonderful Purple Patches for the anthologists to quote. He understood Human Nature and he was a Poet.

26998

But what about playwriting? Did he know anything about that? To read the manuals on the subject—and at the end of the nineteenth century more and more manuals on playwriting began to appear—you wouldn't think so. Mostly the authors of these manuals were students and advocates of the French method. William Archer himself, who wrote one of the best manuals, and who was no lover of the Commercial Theatre, brought out his *The Old Drama and the New*, in which the method of Sir Arthur Wing Pinero is represented as a vast improvement on that of the Elizabethans.

I say "that of the Elizabethans" rather than "that of Shakespeare" because Archer made of Shakespeare an exception. Shakespeare was good in spite of his method, not with the help of it. *The Old Drama and the New* is a book everyone should read because it expresses everyone's prejudices—or what till recently were everyone's prejudices—with less cant and confusion than perhaps anyone else would have brought to their defense. Wrongheaded as can be, Archer was intelligent, bold, learned, and clear.

After all, who had ever shown that Shakespeare's method *was* any good?

I can recall looking around for some helpful comment on, for example, the shape of Shakespeare's plots, and concluding that A. C. Bradley had made a beginning in the second of his Shakespeare lectures, "Construction in Shakespeare's Tragedies."

Worth more to me in the end than Bradley's whole

chapter was a footnote to it which begins: "The famous critics of the Romantic Revival seem to have paid very little attention to this subject. Mr. R. G. Moulton has written an interesting book on *Shakespeare as a Dramatic Artist*." It is hard to believe that Bradley ever read the "interesting book," as he never refers to it again, and even in the footnote proceeds to say a great deal more about a greatly less distinguished student of the drama, Gustav Freytag.

Bradley had, in fact, no need to "make a beginning," as a beginning had already been made by Moulton whose book first appeared in 1885. It was indeed much more than a beginning, and in 1965 it remains the only notable book on Shakespeare's handling of plot. As such it is one of the most valuable of all books on Shakespeare to the student of today.

To such a student, let me add a warning: do not be put off by Moulton's outlook and terminology. The sub-title (A Popular Illustration of the Principles of Scientific Criticism) almost causes one never to read this book, as does the title of the Introduction (Plea for an Inductive Science of Literary Criticism). Moulton, one gathers, was a crank. But many a crank is a better critic than many a non-crank. A book, as I. A. Richards once put it, is a machine to think with. Moulton built such a machine. So long as it works—and it still does—do not jib at some of the Victorian eccentricities of its design.

There is a twentieth-century book called *The Theatre of Tomorrow* in which the author condemns what I've been calling the French method and exalts the Greeks and even Shakespeare. But note the terms on which Shakespeare is admitted to the theatre of tomorrow: "compared with the intricate arrangements of the well-built three-act play, [the Shakespearean drama] seems almost formless." Even in turning against the French view of dramaturgy, our modern prophet retains the French view of Shakespeare! Here one's sympathies turn to the French, who at least do not regard formlessness as a good thing.

But my point is that such a mistake about Shakespeare could not be made by anyone who has read Moulton. May I refer the men of tomorrow to a critic of yesterday?

ERIC BENTLEY

Wellfleet, Massachusetts
1965

PREFACE TO THE THIRD EDITION

————

THE present edition is distinguished by two features. In the first place, the list of plays treated in Part First has been enlarged by three,—*Othello, Love's Labour's Lost,* and *As You Like It.* The Study of *Othello* has been made No. XI, to associate it with previous Studies of *Julius Cæsar* and *Lear,* since it connects Character and Plot as these had connected Passion and Movement. The Studies of *Love's Labour's Lost* and *As You Like It* (Nos. XIV, XV) are placed after those on *The Tempest,* and carry further the topics of Central Ideas and Dramatic Colouring. The new matter is the substance of papers read at various times before the New Shakspere Society of London.

Such additions to Part First involve, according to the plan of the whole work, additions of detail and restatements of various points in Part Second. But besides these there is a change of a more general character in Part Second, which makes the other main feature of this edition. It has always been my contention that the Science of Dramatic Criticism admits at present of no systematisation other than a digest of critical topics, and such a digest must always be provisional. One of the most difficult problems in this science is the proper treatment of Dramatic Movement, to determine whether its relations with Passion or with Plot are the closer, or whether indeed it does not constitute a fundamental division of Drama by itself. In previous editions I have treated this problem by making a compromise, which separated Motive Force from Motive Form, associating the former with Passion and the latter with Plot. Further experience has led me to think that it is more accurate—as it is certainly simpler—to treat the whole of Movement as a division of Plot, leaving Passion-Movement to be represented by successions of Tone. A glance at the Table of Topics on page 398 will make the new scheme clear.

December, 1892.

PREFACE TO THE SECOND EDITION

IN this edition two new Studies, Nos. XI and XII, have been added to Part First, dealing with *The Tempest*, and bringing the treatment in that portion of the book, which has for its purpose to illustrate master-pieces of dramatic art in particular plays of Shakespeare, to a natural climax in the discussion of Central Ideas. The new Studies are the substance of a paper read before the New Shakspere Society of London in

January, 1887.   Such addition to Part First carries with
it, according to the plan of the whole work, additions of
detail and restatement of various points in Part Second.
A few verbal corrections and alterations have been
made in other parts of the book.

July, 1888.

PREFACE TO THE FIRST
EDITION

I HAVE had three objects before me in writing this
book.   The first concerns the general reader.   No one
needs assistance in order to perceive Shakespeare's
greatness ; but an impression is not uncommonly to
be found, especially amongst English readers, that
Shakespeare's greatness lies mainly in his deep knowledge of human nature, while, as to the technicalities
of Dramatic Art, he is at once careless of them
and too great to need them.   I have endeavoured
to combat this impression by a series of Studies of
Shakespeare as a Dramatic Artist.   They are chiefly
occupied with a few master-strokes of art, sufficient to
illustrate the revolution Shakespeare created in the
Drama of the world—a revolution not at once per-
ceived simply because it had carried the Drama at a
bound so far beyond Dramatic Criticism that the
appreciation of Shakespeare's plays was left to the

uninstructed public, while the trained criticism that ought to have recognised the new departure was engaged in clamouring for other views of dramatic treatment, which it failed to perceive that Shakespeare had rendered obsolete.

While the earlier chapters are taken up with these Studies, the rest of the work is an attempt, in very brief form, to present Dramatic Criticism as a regular Inductive Science. If I speak of this as a new branch of Science I am not ignoring the great works on Shakespeare-Criticism which already exist, the later of which have treated their subject in an inductive spirit. What these still leave wanting is a *recognition* of method in application to the study of the Drama : my purpose is to claim for Criticism a position amongst the Inductive Sciences, and to sketch in outline a plan for the Dramatic side of such a Critical Science.

A third purpose has been to make the work of use as an educational manual. Shakespeare now enters into every scheme of liberal education ; but the annotated editions of his works give the student little assistance except in the explanation of language and allusions ; and the idea, I believe, prevails that anything like the discussion of literary characteristics or dramatic effect is out of place in an educational work— is, indeed, too 'indefinite' to be 'examined on.' Ten years' experience in connection with the Cambridge University Extension, during which my work has been to teach literature apart from philology, has confirmed my impression that the subject-matter of literature, its exposition and analysis from the sides of science, history, and art, is as good an educational discipline as it is intrinsically valuable in quickening literary appreciation.

There are two special features of the book to which I may here draw attention. Where practicable, I have appended in the margin references to the passages of Shakespeare on which my discussion is based. (These references are to the Globe Edition.) I have thus hoped to reduce to a minimum the element of personal opinion, and to give to my treatment at least that degree of definiteness which arises when a position stands side by side with the evidence supporting it. I have also endeavoured to meet a practical difficulty in the use of Shakespeare-Criticism as an educational subject. It is usual in educational schemes to name single plays of Shakespeare for study. Experience has convinced me that methodical study of the subject-matter is not possible within the compass of a single play. On the other hand, few persons in the educational stage of life can have the detailed knowledge of Shakespeare's plays as a whole which is required for a full treatment of the subject. The present work is so arranged that it assumes knowledge of only five [1] plays—*The Merchant of Venice, Richard III, Macbeth, Julius Cæsar*, and *King Lear*. Not only in the Studies, but also in the final review, the matter introduced is

---

[1] A sixth play, *The Tempest*, is added in the Second Edition, and three more in the third Edition, viz.—*Othello, Love's Labour's Lost*, and *As You Like It*.

confined to what can be illustrated out of these five plays. These are amongst the most familiar of the Shakespearean Dramas, or they can be easily read before commencing the book ; and if the arrangement is a limitation involving a certain amount of repetition, yet I believe the gain will be greater than the loss. For the young student, at all events, it affords an opportunity of getting what will be the best of all introductions to the whole subject—a thorough knowledge of five plays.

In passing the book through the press I have received material assistance from my brother, Dr. Moulton, Master of the Leys School, and from my College friend, Mr. Joseph Jacobs. With the latter, indeed, I have discussed the work in all its stages, and have been under continual obligation to his stores of knowledge and critical grasp in all departments of literary study. I cannot even attempt to name the many friends—chiefly fellow-workers in the University Extension Movement—through whose active interest in my Shakespeare teaching I have been encouraged to seek for it publication.

RICHARD G. MOULTON.

April, 1885.

CONTENTS

———◆———

INTRODUCTION

*PLEA FOR AN INDUCTIVE SCIENCE
OF LITERARY CRITICISM*

INTRODUCTION.

IN the treatment of literature the proposition which seems *Proposi-*
to stand most in need of assertion at the present *tion.*
moment is, *that there is an inductive science of literary criticism.*
As botany deals inductively with the phenomena of vegetable
life and traces the laws underlying them, as economy reviews and systematises on inductive principles the facts of
commerce, so there is a criticism not less inductive in character which has for its subject-matter literature.

The presumption is clearly that literary criticism should *Presump-*
follow other branches of thought in becoming inductive. *tion in*
favour of
Ultimately, science means no more than organised thought; *inductive*
and amongst the methods of organisation induction is the *literary*
criticism.
most practical. To begin with the observation of facts ; to
advance from this through the arrangement of observed
facts ; to use *à priori* ideas, instinctive notions of the fitness
of things, insight into far probabilities, only as side-lights for
suggesting convenient arrangements, the value of which is
tested only by the actual convenience in arranging they
afford ; to be content with the sure results so obtained as
'theory' in the interval of waiting for still surer results based
on a yet wider accumulation of facts : this is a regimen for
healthy science so widely established in different tracts of
thought as almost to rise to that universal acceptance which
we call common sense. Indeed the whole progress of
science consists in winning fresh fields of thought to the
inductive methods.

Current conceptions of criticism coloured by notions other than inductive.

Yet the great mass of literary criticism at the present moment is of a nature widely removed from induction. The prevailing notions of criticism are dominated by the idea of *assaying*, as if its function were to test the soundness and estimate the comparative value of literary work. Lord Macaulay, than whom no one has a better right to be heard on this subject, compares his office of reviewer to that of a king-at-arms, versed in the laws of literary precedence, marshalling authors to the exact seats to which they are entitled. And, as a matter of fact, the bulk of literary criticism, whether in popular conversation or in discussions by professed critics, occupies itself with the merits of authors and works; founding its estimates and arguments on canons of taste, which are either assumed as having met with general acceptance, or deduced from speculations as to fundamental conceptions of literary beauty.

Criticism judicial and inductive. The two distinguished.

It becomes necessary then to recognise two different kinds of literary criticism, as distinct as any two things that can be called by the same name. The difference between the two may be summed up as the difference between the work of a *judge* and of an *investigator*. The one is the enquiry into what ought to be, the other the enquiry into what is. Judicial criticism compares a new production with those already existing in order to determine whether it is inferior to them or surpasses them; criticism of investigation makes the same comparison for the purpose of identifying the new product with some type in the past, or differentiating it and registering a new type. Judicial criticism has a mission to watch against variations from received canons; criticism of investigation watches for new forms to increase its stock of species. The criticism of taste analyses literary works for grounds of preference or evidence on which to found judgments; inductive criticism analyses them to get a closer acquaintance with their phenomena.

Let the question be of Ben Jonson. Judicial criticism

starts by holding Ben Jonson responsible for the decay of the English Drama.

Inductive criticism takes objection to the word 'decay' as suggesting condemnation, but recognises Ben Jonson as the beginner of a new tendency in our dramatic history.

But, judicial criticism insists, the object of the Drama is to pourtray human nature, whereas Ben Jonson has painted not men but caricatures.

Induction sees that this formula cannot be a sufficient definition of the Drama, for the simple reason that it does not take in Ben Jonson; its own mode of putting the matter is that Ben Jonson has founded a school of treatment of which the law is caricature.

But Ben Jonson's caricatures are palpably impossible.

Induction soon satisfies itself that their point lies in their impossibility; they constitute a new mode of pourtraying qualities of character, not by resemblance, but by analysing and intensifying contrasts to make them clearer.

Judicial criticism can see how the poet was led astray; the bent of his disposition induced him to sacrifice dramatic propriety to his satiric purpose.

Induction has another way of putting the matter: that the poet has utilised dramatic form for satiric purpose; thus by the 'cross-fertilisation' of two existing literary species he has added to literature a third including features of both.

At all events, judicial criticism will maintain, it must be admitted that the Shakespearean mode of pourtraying is infinitely the higher: a sign-painter, as Macaulay points out, can imitate a deformity of feature, while it takes a great artist to bring out delicate shades of expression.

Inductive treatment knows nothing about higher or lower, which lie outside the domain of science. Its point is that science is indebted to Ben Jonson for a new species; if the new species be an easier form of art it does not on that account lose its claim to be analysed.

The critic of merit can always fall back upon taste : who would not prefer Shakespeare to Ben Jonson?

But even from this point of view scientific treatment can plead its own advantages. The inductive critic reaps to the full the interest of Ben Jonson, to which the other has been forcibly closing his eyes; while, so far from liking Shakespeare the less, he appreciates all the more keenly Shakespeare's method of treatment from his familiarity with that which is its antithesis.

The two criticisms confused : It must be conceded at once that both these kinds of criticism have justified their existence. Judicial criticism has long been established as a favourite pursuit of highly cultivated minds ; while the criticism of induction can shelter itself under the authority of science in general, seeing that it has for its object to bring the treatment of literature into the circle of the inductive sciences. It is unfortunate, however, *conception of critical method limited to judicial method.* that the spheres of the two have not been kept distinct. In the actual practice of criticism the judicial method has obtained an illegitimate supremacy which has thrown the other into the shade; it has even invaded the domain of the criticism that claims to be scientific, until the word *criticism* itself has suffered, and the methodical treatment of literature has by tacit assumption become limited in idea to the judicial method.

Partly a survival of Renaissance influence : Explanation for this limited conception of criticism is not far to seek. Modern criticism took its rise before the importance of induction was recognised : it lags behind other branches of thought in adapting itself to inductive treatment chiefly through two influences. The first of these is connected with the revival of literature after the darkness of the middle ages. The birth of thought and taste in modern Europe was the Renaissance of classical thought and taste ; by Roman and Greek philosophy and poetry the native powers of our ancestors were trained till they became strong enough to originate for themselves. It was natural for their earliest criticism to take the form of applying the classical standards to their own imitations : now we have *and its testing by classical models.* advanced so far that no one would propose to test exclusively by classical models, but nevertheless the idea of *testing* still lingers as the root idea in the treatment of literature.　Other branches of thought have completely shaken off this attitude of submission to the past : literary criticism differs from the rest only in being later to move.　This is powerfully suggested by the fact that so recent a writer as Addison couples science in general with criticism in his estimate of probable progress ; laying down the startling proposition that 'it is impossible for us who live in the later ages of the world to make observations in criticism, in morality, *or in any art or science,* which have not been touched upon by others ' !

And even for this lateness a second influence goes far to *Partly that methods of journalism have invaded systematic criticism.* account.　The grand literary phenomenon of modern times is journalism, the huge apparatus of floating literature of which one leading object is to review literature itself.　The vast increase of production consequent upon the progress of printing has made production itself a phenomenon worthy of study, and elevated the sifting of production into a prominent literary occupation ; by the aid of book - tasters alone can the ordinary reader keep pace with production.　It is natural enough that the influence of journalism should pass beyond its natural sphere, and that the review should tend to usurp the position of the literature for which reviewing exists.　Now in journalism testing and valuation of literary work have a real and important place.　It has thus come about that in the great preponderance of ephemeral over permanent literature the machinery adapted to the former has become applied to the latter : methods proper to journalism have settled the popular conception of systematic treatment ; and the bias already given to criticism by the Renaissance has been strengthened to resist the tendency of all kinds of thought towards inductive methods.

*The limita-
tion de-
fended :
theory of
taste as con-
densed ex-
perience.*

History will thus account for the way in which the criticism of taste and valuation tends to be identified with criticism in general : but attempts are not wanting to give the identification a scientific basis. Literary appreciation, it is said, is a thing of culture. A critic in the reviewer's sense is one who has the literary faculty both originally acute and developed by practice : he thus arrives quickly and with certainty at results which others would reach laboriously and after temporary misjudgments. Taste, however arbitrary in appearance, is in reality condensed experience ; judicial criticism is a wise economy of appreciation, the purpose of which is to anticipate natural selection and universal experience. He is a good critic who, by his keen and practised judgment, can tell you at once the view of authors and works which you would yourself come to hold with sufficient study and experience.

*The theory
examined.
The judi-
cial spirit a
limit on ap-
preciation.*

Now in the first place there is a flaw in this reasoning : it omits to take into account that the judicial attitude of mind is itself a barrier to appreciation, as being opposed to that delicacy of receptiveness which is a first condition of sensibility to impressions of literature and art. It is a matter of commonest experience that appreciation may be interfered with by prejudice, by a passing unfavourable mood, or even by uncomfortable external surroundings. But it is by no means sufficient that the reader of literature should divest himself of these passive hindrances to appreciation : poets are pioneers in beauty, and considerable activity of effort is required to keep pace with them. Repetition may be necessary to catch effects—passages to be read over and over again, more than one author of the same school to be studied, effect to be compared with kindred effect each helping the other. Or an explanation from one who has already caught the idea may turn the mind into a receptive attitude. Training again is universally recognised as a necessity for appreciation, and to train is to make receptive.

Beyond all these conditions of perception, and including *On the* them, is yet another. It is a foundation principle in art- *other hand* *sympathy* culture, as well as in human intercourse, that *sympathy is the the great* *grand interpreter :* secrets of beauty will unfold themselves to *interpreter.* the sunshine of sympathy, while they will wrap themselves all the closer against the tempest of sceptical questionings. Now a judicial attitude of mind is highly unreceptive, for it necessarily implies a restraint of sympathy : every one, remarks Hogarth, is a judge of painting except the connoisseur. The judicial mind has an appearance of receptiveness, because it seeks to shut out prejudice : but what if the idea of judging be itself a prejudice ? On this view the very consciousness of fairness, involving as it does limitation of sympathy, will be itself unfair. In practical life, where we have to act, the formation of judgments is a necessity. In art we can escape the obligation, and here the judicial spirit becomes a wanton addition to difficulties of appreciation already sufficiently great ; the mere notion of condemning may be enough to check our receptivity to qualities which, as we have seen, it may need our utmost effort to catch. So that the judicial attitude of mind comes to defeat its own purpose, and disturbs unconsciously the impression it seeks to judge ; until, as Emerson puts it, 'if you criticise a fine genius the odds are that you are out of your reckoning, and instead of the poet are censuring your caricature of him.'

But the appeal made is to experience : to experience let *The theory* it go. It will be found that, speaking broadly, *the whole refuted by* *experience :* *history of criticism has been a triumph of authors over critics : the history* so long as criticism has meant the gauging of literature, so *of criticism* long as its progress has consisted in the reversal of critical *of authors* *a triumph* judgments by further experience. I hesitate to enlarge upon *over critics.* this part of my subject lest I be inflicting upon the reader the tedium of a thrice-told tale. But I believe that the ordinary reader, however familiar with notable blunders of criticism, has little idea of that which is the essence of my argument—the degree of regularity, amounting to absolute law, with which criticism, where it has set itself in opposition to freedom of authorship, has been found in time to have pronounced upon the wrong side, and has, after infinite waste of obstructive energy, been compelled at last to accept innovations it had pronounced impossible under penalty of itself becoming obsolete.

Case of the Shakespearean Drama: retiring waves of critical opposition.

Shakespeare-criticism affords the most striking illustration. Its history is made up of wave after wave of critical opposition, each retiring further before the steady advance of Shakespeare's fame. They may almost be traced in the varying apologetic tones of the successive *Variorum* editors, until Reed, in the edition of 1803, is content to leave the poet's renown as established on a basis which will 'bid defiance to the caprices of fashion and the canker of time.'

1. *Unmeasured attack.*

The first wave was one of unmeasured virulent attack. Rymer, accepted in his own day as the champion of 'regular' criticism, and pronounced by Pope one of the best critics England ever had, says that in Tragedy Shakespeare appears quite out of his element:

> His brains are turned; he raves and rambles without any coherence, any spark of reason, or any rule to control him or set bounds to his phrensy.

The shouting and battles of his scenes are necessary to keep the audience awake, 'otherwise no sermon would be so strong an opiate.' Again:

> In the neighing of an horse, or in the growling of a mastiff, there is a meaning, there is as lively an expression, and, may I say, more humanity, than many times in the tragical flights of Shakespeare.

The famous Suggestion Scene in *Othello* has, in Rymer's view, no point but 'the mops, the mows, the grimace, the grins, the gesticulation.' On Desdemona's

> O good Iago,
> What shall I do to win my lord again?

he remarks that no woman bred out of a pig-stye would talk so meanly. Speaking of Portia he says, 'she is scarce one remove from a natural, she is own cousin-german, of one piece, the very same impertinent flesh and blood with Desdemona.' And Rymer's general verdict of *Othello*— which he considers the best of Shakespeare's tragedies— is thus summed up :

> There is in this play some burlesque, some humour and ramble of comical wit, some show and some mimicry to divert the spectators : but the tragical part is plainly none other than a bloody farce, without salt or savour.

In the eighteenth century Lord Lansdowne, writing on 'Unnatural Flights in Poetry,' could refuse to go into the question of Shakespeare's soliloquies, as being assured that 'not one in all his works could be excused by reason or nature.' The same tone was still later kept up by Voltaire, who calls Shakespeare a writer of monstrous farces called tragedies ; says that nature had blended in him all that is most great and elevating with all the basest qualities that belong to barbarousness without genius ; and finally proceeds to call his poetry the fruit of the imagination of an intoxicated savage.—Meanwhile a second wave of opinion had arisen, *2. The* not conceiving a doubt as to the total inadmissibility of the *Shake-spearean* Shakespearean Drama, yet feeling its attraction. This is *Drama* perhaps most exactly illustrated in the forgotten critic *held inad-missible,* Edwards, who ruled that 'poor Shakespeare'—the expression *yet attrac-* is his own—must be excluded from the number of good *tive.* tragedians, yet 'as Homer from the Republic of Plato, with marks of distinction and veneration.' But before this the more celebrated dramatists of the Restoration had shown the double feeling in the way they reconstructed Shakespeare's plays, and turned them into 'correct' dramas. Thus Otway made the mediæval Capulets and Montagus presentable by giving them a classical dress as followers of Marius and Sulla ; and even Dryden joined in a polite version of *The*

Tempest, with an original touch for symmetry's sake in the addition to the heroine Miranda, a maid who had never seen a man, of a suitable hero, a man who had never seen a

3. The Shakespearean Drama admitted with excuses.

maid.—Against loud abuse and patronising reconstruction the silent power of Shakespeare's works made itself more and more felt, and we reach a third stage when the Shakespearean Drama is accepted as it stands, but with excuses. Excuse is made for the poet's age, in which the English nation was supposed to be struggling to emerge from barbarism. Heywood's apology for uniting light and serious matter is allowed, that 'they who write to all must strive to please all.' Pope points out that Shakespeare was dependent for his subsistence on pleasing the taste of tradesmen and mechanics ; and that his 'wrong choice of subjects' and 'wrong conduct of incidents,' his 'false thoughts and forced expressions' are the result of his being forced to please the lowest of the people and keep the worst of company. Similarly Theobald considers that he schemed his plots and characters from romances simply for want

4. The Shakespearean Drama not felt to need defence as a whole, but praised and blamed in its parts.

of classical information.—With the last name we pass to yet another school, with whom Shakespeare's work as a whole is not felt to need defence, and the old spirit survives only in their distribution of praise and blame amongst its different parts. Theobald opens his preface with the comparison of the Shakespearean Drama to a splendid pile of buildings, with 'some parts finished up to hit the taste of a connoisseur, others more negligently put together to strike the fancy of a common beholder.' Pope—who reflects the most various schools of criticism, often on successive pages— illustrates this stage in his remark that Shakespeare has excellences that have elevated him above all others, and almost as many defects; 'as he has certainly written better so he has perhaps written worse than any other.' Dr. Johnson sets out by describing Shakespeare as 'having begun to assume the dignity of an ancient'—the highest commendation in his eyes. But he goes on to point out the inferiority of Shakespeare's Tragedy to his Comedy, the former the outcome of skill rather than instinct, with little felicity and always leaving something wanting; how he seems without moral purpose, letting his precepts and axioms drop casually from him, dismissing his personages without further care, and leaving the examples to operate by chance; how his plots are so loosely formed that they might easily be improved, his set speeches cold and weak, his incidents imperfectly told in many words which might be more plainly described in few. Then in the progress of his commentary, he irritates the reader, as Hallam points out, by the magisterial manner in which he dismisses each play like a schoolboy's exercise.—At last comes a revolution in criticism and a new order of things arises; with Lessing to lead the way in Germany and Coleridge in England, a school of critics appear who are in complete harmony with their author, who question him only to learn the secrets of his art. The new spirit has not even yet leavened the whole of the literary world; but such names as Goethe, Tieck, Schlegel, Victor Hugo, Ulrici, Gervinus suggest how many great reputations have been made, and reputations already great have been carried into a new sphere of greatness, by the interpretation and unfolding of Shakespeare's greatness: not one critic has in recent years risen to eminence by attacking Shakespeare.

5. Finally criticism comes round entirely to Shakespeare.

And the Shakespearean Drama is only the most illustrious example of authors triumphing over the criticism that attempted to judge them. It is difficult for a modern reader to believe that even Rymer could refer to the *Paradise Lost* as 'what some are pleased to call a poem'; or that Dr. Johnson could assert of the minor poems of Milton that they exhibit 'peculiarity as distinguished from excellence,' 'if they differ from others they differ for the worse.' He says of *Comus* that it is 'inelegantly splendid and tediously

Other examples.

Milton.

instructive'; and of *Lycidas*, that its diction is harsh, its rhymes uncertain, its numbers unpleasing, that 'in this poem there is no nature for there is no truth, there is no art for there is nothing new,' that it is 'easy, vulgar, and therefore disgusting,'—after which he goes through the different parts of the poem to show what Milton should have done in each. Hallam has pointed out how utterly impotent Dr. Johnson has been to fix the public taste in the case of these poems; yet even Hallam could think the verse of the poet who wrote *Paradise Lost* sufficiently described by the verdict, 'sometimes wanting in grace and almost always in ease.' In the light of modern taste it is astonishing indeed to find Steevens, with his devotion of a lifetime to Shakespeare, yet omitting the Sonnets from the edition of 1793, 'because the strongest Act of Parliament that could be framed would not compel readers into their service.' It is equally astonishing to find Dryden speaking of Spenser's 'ill choice of stanza,' and saying of the *Faerie Queene* that if completed it might have been more of a piece, but it could not be perfect, because its model was not true: an example followed up in the next century by a 'person of quality,' who translated a book of the *Faerie Queene* out of its 'obsolete language and manner of verse' into heroic couplets. I pass over the crowd of illustrations, such as the fate of Gray at the hands of Dr. Johnson, of Keats at the hands of monthly and quarterly reviewers, or of the various Waverley Novels capriciously selected by different critics as examples of literary suicide. But we have not yet had time to forget how Jeffrey —one of the greatest names in criticism—set in motion the whole machinery of reviewing in order to put down Wordsworth. Wordsworth's most elaborate poem he describes as a 'tissue of moral and devotional ravings,' a 'hubbub of strained raptures and fantastical sublimities': his 'effusions on . . . the physiognomy of external nature' he characterises as 'eminently fantastic, obscure, and affected.' Then, to

Shakespeare's Sonnets.

Spenser.

Gray.
Keats.
Waverley Novels.

Wordsworth.

find a climax, he compares different species of Wordsworth's poetry to the various stages of intoxication : his Odes are 'glorious delirium' and 'incoherent rapture,' his Lyrical Ballads a 'vein of pretty deliration,' his *White Doe* is 'low and maudlin imbecility.' Not a whit the less has the influence of Wordsworth deepened and solidified ; and if all are not yet prepared to accept him as the apostle of a new religion, yet he has tacitly secured his place in the inner circle of English poets. In fine, the work of modern criticism is seriously blocked by the perpetual necessity of revising and reversing what this same Jeffrey calls the 'impartial and irreversible sentences' of criticism in the past. And as a set-off in the opposite scale only one considerable achievement is to be noted : that journalism afforded a medium for Macaulay to quench the light of Robert Montgomery, which, on Macaulay's own showing, journalism had puffed into a flame. *Robert Mont-gomery.*

It is the same with the great literary questions that have from time to time arisen, the pitched battles of criticism : as Goldsmith says, there never has been an unbeaten path trodden by the poet that the critic has not endeavoured to recall him by calling his attempt an innovation. Criticism set its face steadily from the first against blank verse in English poetry. The interlocutors in Dryden's *Essay on the Drama* agree that it is vain to strive against the stream of the people's inclination, won over as they have been by Shakespeare, Ben Jonson, Beaumont and Fletcher ; but, as they go on to discuss the rights of the matter, the most remarkable thing to a modern reader is that the defence of blank verse is made to rest only on the colloquial character of dramatic poetry, and neither party seems to conceive the possibility of non-dramatic poetry other than in rhyme. Before Dryden's *Essay on Satire* the *Paradise Lost* had made its appearance ; but so impossible an idea is literary novelty to the 'father of English criticism' that Dryden in this Essay *Defeat of criticism in the great literary questions.* *Blank verse.*

refuses to believe Milton's own account of the matter, saying that, whatever reasons Milton may allege for departing from rhyme, 'his own particular reason is plainly this, that rhyme was not his talent, he has neither the ease of doing it nor the graces of it.' To one so steeped in French fashions as Rymer, poetry that lacks rhyme seems to lack everything; many of Shakespeare's scenes might, he says, do better without words at all, or at most the words set off the action like the drone of a bagpipe. Voltaire estimates blank verse at about the same rate, and having to translate some of Shakespeare's for purposes of exact comparison, he remarks that blank verse costs nothing but the trouble of dictating, that it is not more difficult to write than a letter. Dr. Johnson finds a theoretic argument in the unmusical character of English poetry to prove the impossibility of its ever adapting itself to the conditions of blank verse, and is confident enough to prophesy: 'poetry may subsist without rhyme, but English poetry will not often please.' Even Byron is found only one degree more tolerant than Dryden: he has the grace to except Milton from his dictum that no one ever wrote blank verse who could rhyme. Thus critical taste, critical theory, and critical prophecy were unanimous against blank verse as an English measure: for all that it has become the leading medium of English poetry, and a doubter of to-day would be more likely to doubt the permanence of *The 'three* English rhyme than of English blank verse. As to the *unities':* famous 'three unities,' not only the principles themselves, but even the refutation of them has now become obsolete. Yet this stickling for the unities has been merely the chief amongst many examples of the proneness the critical mind has exhibited towards limiting literary appreciation and pro-*and limita-* duction by single standards of taste. The same tone of *tions by* mind that contended for the classical unities had in an *still nar-* *rower* earlier generation contended for the classical languages as *classical* *standards.* the sole vehicle of literary expression, and the modern lan-

guages of Europe had to assert their rights by hard fighting.
In Latin literature itself a more successful attempt has been
made to limit taste by the writers of a single period, the
Augustan age, and so construct a list of Latin poets which
omits Lucretius. And for a short period of the Renaissance
movement the limitation was carried further to a single one
of the Augustan writers, and 'Ciceronianism' struggled hard
against the freedom of style it chose to nickname 'Apu-
leianism,' till it fell itself before the laughter of Erasmus. It *Criticism*
would seem almost to be a radical law of the critical tem- *failing to*
distinguish
perament that admiration for the past paralyses faith in the *the per-*
future; while criticism proves totally unable to distinguish *manent*
and tran-
between what has been essential in the greatness of its idols *sitory.*
and what has been as purely accidental as, to use Scott's
illustration, the shape of the drinking-glass is to the flavour
of the wine it contains. And if criticism has thus failed in
distinguishing what is permanent in past literature, it has
proved equally mistaken in what it has assumed to be accidental and transitory. Early commentators on Shakespeare,
whatever scruples they may have had upon other points, had
no misgivings in condemning the irregularities of his English
and correcting his grammar. This was described as obsolete by Dryden half a century after the poet's death; while it
is delicious to hear Steevens, in the Advertisement to his
edition of 1766, mentioning that 'some have been of opinion
that even a particular syntax prevailed in the time of Shakespeare '—a novel suggestion he promptly rejects. If the two
could have lived each a century later, Dryden would have
found Malone laying down that Shakespeare had been the
great purifyer and refiner of our language, and Steevens
would have seen Shakespeare's grammar studied with the
same minuteness and reduced to the same regular form as
the grammar of his commentators and readers; while one of
the most distinguished of our modern grammarians, insti-
tuting a comparison between Elizabethan and nineteenth-

century English, fancies the representative of the old-
fashioned tongue characterising current speech in the words
of Sebastian:

> Surely
> It is a sleepy language!

Critical works where inductive retain their force, where judicial have become obsolete.   The critics may themselves be called as chief witnesses
against themselves. Those parts of their works in which
they apply themselves to analysing and interpreting their
authors survive in their full force: where they judge, find
fault, and attempt to regulate, they inevitably become obsolete. Aristotle, the founder of all criticism, is for the
most part inductive in his method, describing poetry as it
existed in his day, distinguishing its different classes and
elements, and tabulating its usages: accordingly Aristotle's
treatise, though more than two thousand years old, remains
the text-book of the Greek Drama. In some places, however, he diverges from his main purpose, as in the final
chapter, in which he raises the question whether Epic or
Tragic is more excellent, or where he promises a special
treatise to discuss whether Tragedy is yet perfect: here he
has for modern readers only the interest of curiosity. Dr.
Johnson's analysis of 'metaphysical poetry,' Addison's development of the leading effects in *Paradise Lost*, remain as
true and forcible to-day as when they were written: Addison
constructing an order of merit for English poets with Cowley
and Sprat at the head, Dr. Johnson lecturing Shakespeare
and Milton as to how they ought to have written—these are
to us only odd anachronisms. It is like a contest with
atomic force, this attempt at using ideas drawn from the past
to mould and limit productive power in the present and
future. The critic peers into the dimness of history, and is
found to have been blind to what was by his side: Boileau
strives to erect a throne of Comedy for Terence, and never
suspects that a truer king was at hand in his own personal
friend Molière. It is in vain for critics to denounce, their

denunciation recoils on themselves: the sentence of Rymer that the soul of modern Drama was a brutish and not a reasonable soul, or of Voltaire, that Shakespeare's Tragedy would not be tolerated by the lowest French mob, can harm none but Rymer and Voltaire. If the critics venture to prophesy, the sequel is the only refutation of them needed; if they give reasons, the reasons survive only to explain how the critics were led astray; if they lay down laws, literary greatness in the next generation is found to vary directly with the boldness with which authors violate the laws. If they assume a judicial attitude, the judgment-seat becomes converted into a pillory for the judge, and a comic side to literary history is furnished by the mockery with which time preserves the proportions of things, as seen by past criticism, to be laid side by side with the true perspective revealed by actual history. In such wise it has preserved to us the list of 'poets laureate' who preceded Southey : Shadwell, Tate, Rowe, Eusden, Cibber, Whitehead, Warton, Pye. It reveals Dryden sighing that Spenser could only have read the rules of Bossu, or smitten with a doubt whether he might not after all excuse Milton's use of blank verse 'by the example of Hannibal Caro'; Rymer preferring Ben Jonson's *Catiline* to all the tragedies of the Elizabethan age, and declaring Waller's *Poem on the Navy Royal* beyond all modern poetry in any language; Voltaire wondering that the extravagances of Shakespeare could be tolerated by a nation that had seen Addison's *Cato*; Pope assigning three-score years and ten as the limit of posthumous life to 'moderns' in poetry, and celebrating the trio who had rescued from the 'uncivilised' Elizabethan poetry the 'fundamental laws of wit.' These three are Buckingham, Roscommon, and Walsh: as to the last of whom if we search amongst contemporary authorities to discover who he was, we at last come upon his works described in the *Rambler* as 'pages of inanity.'

But in the conflict between judicial criticism and science

In actual practice criticism is found to have gradually approached induction. the most important point is to note how the critics' own ideas of criticism are found to be gradually slipping away from them. Between the Renaissance and the present day criticism, as judged by the methods actually followed by critics, has slowly changed from the form of laying down laws to authors into the form of receiving laws from authors.

Five stages. *1. Idea of judging solely by classical standards.* The process of change falls into five stages. In its first stage the conception of criticism was bounded by the notion of comparing whatever was produced with the masterpieces and trying it by the ideas of Greek and Roman literature. Boileau objected to Corneille's tragedies, not because they did not excite admiration, but because admiration was not one of the tragical passions as laid down by Aristotle. To Rymer's mind it was clearly a case of classical standards or no standards, and he describes his opponents as 'a kind of stage-quacks and empirics in poetry who have got a receipt to please.' And there is a degree of *naïveté* in the way in which Bossu betrays his utter unconsciousness of the possibility that there should be more than one kind of excellence, where, in a passàge in which he is admitting that the moderns have as much spirit and as lucky fancies as the ancients, he nevertheless calls it 'a piece of injustice to pretend that our new rules destroy the fancies of the old masters, and that they must condemn all their works who could not foresee all our humours.' Criticism in this spirit is notably illustrated by the Corneille incident in the history of the French Academy. The fashionable literary world, led by a Scudéry, solemnly impeach Corneille of originality, and Richelieu insists on the Academy pronouncing judgment ; which they at last do, unwillingly enough, since, as Boileau admitted, all France was against them. The only one that in the whole incident retained his sense of humour was the victim himself ; who, early in the struggle, being confronted by critics recognising no merit but that of obedience to rules, set himself to write his *Clitandre* as a play which should obey all the rules of Drama and yet have nothing in it: 'in which,' he said, 'I have absolutely succeeded.'—But this reign of simple faith began to be disturbed by sceptical doubts: it became impossible entirely to ignore merit outside the pale of classical conformity. Thus we get a Dennis unable to conceal his admiration for the daring of Milton, as a man who knew the rules of Aristotle, 'no man better,' and yet violated them. Literature of the modern type gets discussed as it were under protest. Dr. Johnson, when he praises Addison's *Cato* for adhering to Aristotle's principles 'with a *scrupulousness* almost unexampled on the English stage,' is reflecting the constant assumption throughout this transitional stage, that departure from classical models is the result of carelessness, and that beauties in such offending writers are lucky hits. The spirit of this period is distinctly brought out by Dr. Johnson where he 'readily allows' that the union in one composition of serious and ludicrous is 'contrary to the rules of criticism,' but, he adds, 'there is always an appeal open from criticism to nature.'—Once admitted to examination the force of modern literature could not fail to assert its equality with the literature of the ancients, and we pass into a third stage of criticism when critics grasp the conception that there may be more than one set of rules by which authors may be judged. The new notion made its appearance early in the country which was the main stronghold of the opposite view. Perrault in 1687 instituted his 'Parallels' between the ancients and the moderns to the advantage of the latter; and the question was put in its naked simplicity by Fontenelle, the 'Nestor of literature,' when he made it depend upon another question, 'whether the trees that used to grow in our woods were larger than those which grow now.' Later, and with less distinctness, English criticism followed the lead. Pope, with his happy indifference to consistency, after illustrating the first stage where he advises to write ' as

2. Recognition of modern as illegitimate merit.

3. Modern standards of judging side by side with ancient.

if the Stagirite o'erlooked each line,' and where he contends
that if the classical writers indulge in a licence that licence
becomes a law to us, elsewhere lays down that to apply
ancient rules in the treatment of modern literature is to try
by the laws of one country a man belonging to another. In
one notable instance the genius of Dr. Johnson rises
superior to the prejudices of his age, and he vindicates in
his treatment of Shakespeare the conception of a school of
Drama in which the unities of time and place do not apply.
But he does it with trembling: 'I am almost frightened at
my own temerity; and when I estimate the fame and the
strength of those who maintain the contrary opinion, am

4. Concep- ready to sink down in reverential silence.'—Criticism had set
tion of
criticism out with judging by one set of laws, it had come to judge by
as judging two: the change began to shake the notion of *judging* as the
begins to
waver ; function of criticism, and the eyes of critics came to be
turned more to the idea of literary beauty itself, as the end
for which the laws of literary composition were merely
means.   Addison is the great name connected with this
further transitional stage.   We find Addison not only arguing
negatively that ' there is sometimes a greater judgment
shown in deviating from the rules of art than in adhering to them,' but even laying down as a positive theory

changing to that the true function of a critic is ' to discover the concealed
the search
for beau- beauties of a writer'; while the practical illustration of his
ties ; theory which he gave in the case of the *Paradise Lost* is
supposed to have revolutionised the opinion of the fashion-

5. and able reading-public.—Addison was removed by a very little
finally to
investiga- from the final stage of criticism, the conception of which is
tion of laws perhaps most fully brought out by Gervinus, where he de-
in litera-
ture as it clares his purpose of treating Shakespeare as the 'revealing
stands. genius' of his department of art and of its laws.   Thus
slowly and by gradual stages has the conception of criticism
been changing in the direction of induction : starting from
judgment by the laws of the ancient classics as standard

beyond which there is no appeal, passing through the transitional stage of greater and greater toleration for intrinsic worth though of a modern type, to arrive at the recognition of modern standards of judgment side by side with ancient; again passing through a further transitional stage of discrediting judgment altogether as the purpose of criticism in favour of the search for intrinsic worth in literature as it stands, till the final conception is reached of analysing literature as it stands for the purpose of discovering its laws in itself. The later stages do not universally prevail yet. But the earlier stages have at all events become obsolete; and there is no reader who will not acquiesce cheerfully in one of the details Addison gives out for his ideal theatre, by which Rymer's tragedy *Edgar* was to be cut up into snow to make the Storm Scene in Shakespeare's *Lear*.

It may be well to recall the exact purpose to which the present argument is intended to lead. The purpose is not to attack journalism and kindred branches of criticism in the interests of inductive treatment. *Separateness of the two criticisms.* It would be false to the principles of induction not to recognise that the criticism of taste has long since established its position as a fertile branch of literature. Even in an inductive system journalism would still have place as a medium for fragmentary and tentative treatment. Moreover it may be admitted that induction in its formal completeness of system can never be applied in practical life; and in the intellectual pursuits of real life trained literary taste may be a valuable acquisition. What is here attacked is the mistake which has identified the criticism of taste and valuation with the conception of criticism as a whole; the intrusion of methods belonging to journalism into treatment that claims to be systematic. So far from being a standard of method in the treatment of literature, criticism of the reviewer's order is outside science altogether. It finds its proper place on the creative side of literature, as a branch *Criticism of taste belongs to creative literature:*

in which literature itself has come to be taken as a theme for literary writing; it thus belongs to the literature treated, not to the scientific treatment of it. Reviews so placed may be regarded almost as the lyrics of prose: like lyric poems they have their completeness in themselves, and their interest lies, not in their being parts of some whole, but in their flashing the subjectivity of a writer on to a variety of isolated topics; they thus have value, not as fragments of literary science, but as fragments of Addison, of Jeffrey, of Macaulay. Nor is the bearing of the present argument that commentators should set themselves to eulogise the authors they treat instead of condemning them (though this would certainly be the safer of two errors). The treatment aimed at is one independent of praise or blame, one that has nothing to do with merit, relative or absolute. The contention is for a branch of criticism separate from the criticism of taste; a branch that, in harmony with the spirit of other modern sciences, reviews the phenomena of literature as they actually stand, enquiring into and endeavouring to systematise the laws and principles by which they are moulded and produce their effects. Scientific criticism and the criticism of taste have distinct spheres: and the whole of literary history shows that the failure to keep the two separate results only in mutual confusion.

as the lyrics of prose.

Our present purpose is with inductive criticism. What, by the analogy of other sciences, is implied in the inductive treatment of literature?

Application of induction to literary subject-matter.

The inductive sciences occupy themselves directly with facts, that is, with phenomena translated by observation into the form of facts; and soundness of inductive theory is measured by the closeness with which it will bear confronting with the facts. In the case of literature and art the facts are to be looked for in the literary and artistic productions themselves: the dramas, epics, pictures, statues, pillars, capitals, symphonies, operas—the details of these are the phenomena which the critical observer translates into facts.

A picture is a title for a bundle of facts: that the painter has united so many figures in such and such groupings, that he has given such and such varieties of colouring, and such and such arrangement of light and shade. Similarly the *Iliad* is a short name implying a large number of facts characterising the poem: that its principal personages are Agamemnon and Achilles, that these personages are represented as displaying certain qualities, doing certain deeds, and standing in certain relations to one another.

Here, however, arises that which has been perhaps the greatest stumbling-block in the way of securing inductive treatment for literature. Science deals only with ascertained facts: but the details of literature and art are open to the most diverse interpretation. They leave conflicting impressions on different observers, impressions both subjective and variable in themselves, and open to all manner of distracting influences, not excepting that of criticism itself. Where in the treatment of literature is to be found the positiveness of subject-matter which is the first condition of science? *Difficulty: the want of positiveness in literary impressions.*

In the first place it may be pointed out that this want of certainty in literary interpretation is not a difficulty of a kind peculiar to literature. The same object of terror will affect the members of a crowd in a hundred different ways, from presence of mind to hysteria; yet this has not prevented the science of psychology from inductively discussing fear. Logic proposes to scientifically analyse the reasoning processes in the face of the infinite degrees of susceptibility different minds show to proof and persuasion. It has become proverbial that taste in art is incapable of being settled by discussion, yet the art of music has found exact treatment in the science of harmony. In the case of these well-established sciences it has been found possible to separate the variable element from that which is the subject-matter of the science: such a science as psychology really covers two distinct branches of thought, the psychology that discusses formally *The difficulty not confined to literature.*

the elements of the human mind, and another psychology, not yet systematised, that deals with the distribution of these elements amongst different individuals. It need then be no barrier to inductive treatment that in the case of literature and art the will and consciousness act as disturbing forces, refracting what may be called natural effects into innumerable effects on individual students. It only becomes a question of practical procedure, in what way the interfering variability is to be eliminated.

It is precisely at this point that *à priori* criticism and in-duction part company. The *à priori* critic gets rid of uncertainty in literary interpretation by confining his atten-tion to effects produced upon the best minds : he sets up *taste* as a standard by which to try impressions of literature which he is willing to consider. The inductive critic cannot have recourse to any such arbitrary means of limiting his materials; for his doubts he knows no court of appeal ex-cept the appeal to the literary works themselves. The astronomer, from the vast distance of the objects he observes, finds the same phenomenon producing different results on different observers, and he has thus regularly to allow for personal errors : but he deals with such discrepancies only by fresh observations on the stars themselves, and it never occurs to him that he can get rid of a variation by ab-stract argument or deference to a greater observer. In the same way the inductive critic of literature must settle his doubts by referring them to the literary productions them-selves ; to him the question is not of the nobler view or the view in best taste, but simply what view fits in best with the details as they stand in actual fact. He quite recognises that it is not the objective details but the subjective impressions they produce that make literary effect, but the objective de-tails are the *limit* on the variability of the subjective impres-sions. The character of Macbeth impresses two readers differently : how is the difference to be settled ? The *à priori*

The variable ele-ment to be eliminated by reference not to taste ;

but to the objective details of the litera-ture itself.

critic contends that his conception is the loftier; that a hero should be heroic; that moreover the tradition of the stage and the greatest names in the criticism of the past bear him out; or, finally, falls back upon good taste, which closes the discussion. The inductive critic simply puts together all the sayings and doings of Macbeth himself, all that others in the play say and appear to feel about him, and whatever view of the character is consistent with these and similar facts of the play, that view he selects; while to vary from it for any external consideration would seem to him as futile as for an astronomer to make a star rise an hour earlier to tally with the movements of another star.

We thus arrive at a foundation axiom of inductive literary criticism: *Interpretation in literature is of the nature of a scientific hypothesis, the truth of which is tested by the degree of completeness with which it explains the details of the literary work as they actually stand.* That will be the true meaning of a passage, not which is the most worthy, but which most nearly explains the words as they are; that will be the true reading of a character which, however involved in expression or tame in effect, accounts for and reconciles all that is represented of the personage. The inductive critic will interpret a complex situation, not by fastening attention on its striking elements and ignoring others as oversights and blemishes, but by putting together with business-like exactitude all that the author has given, weighing, balancing, and standing by the product. He will not consider that he has solved the action of a drama by some leading plot, or some central idea powerfully suggested in different parts, but will investigate patiently until he can find a scheme which will give point to the inferior as well as to the leading scenes, and in connection with which all the details are harmonised in their proper proportions. In this way he will be raising a superstructure of exposition that rests, not on authority however high, but upon a basis of indisputable fact.

Foundation axiom of the inductive criticism: Interpretation of the nature of an hypothesis.

Practical objection: Did the authors intend these interpretations? In actual operation I have often found that such positive analysis raises in the popular mind a very practical objection: that the scientific interpretation seems to discover in literary works much more in the way of purpose and design than the authors themselves can be supposed to have dreamed of. Would not Chaucer and Shakespeare, it is asked, if they could come to life now, be greatly astonished to hear themselves lectured upon? to find critics knowing their purposes better than they had known them themselves, and discovering in their works laws never suspected till after they were dead, and which they themselves perhaps would need some effort to understand? Deep designs are traced in Shakespeare's plots, and elaborate combinations in his characters and passions: is the student asked to believe that Shakespeare really *intended* these complicated effects?

Answer: changed meaning of 'design' in science. The difficulty rests largely upon a confusion in words. Such words as 'purpose,' 'intention,' have a different sense when used in ordinary parlance from that which they bear when applied in criticism and science. In ordinary parlance a man's 'purpose' means his conscious purpose, of which he is the best judge; in science the 'purpose' of a thing is the purpose it actually serves, and is discoverable only by analysis. Thus science discovers that the 'purpose' of earthworms is to break up the soil, the 'design' of colouring in flowers is to attract insects, though the flower is not credited with foresight nor the worm with disinterestedness. In this usage alone can the words 'purpose,' 'intention,' be properly applied to literature and art: science knows no kind of evidence in the matter of creative purpose so weighty as the thing it has actually produced. This has been well put by Ulrici:

> The *language* of the artist is poetry, music, drawing, colouring: there is no other form in which he can express himself with equal depth and clearness. Who would ask a philosopher to paint his ideas in colours? It would be equally absurd to think that because a poet cannot say with perfect philosophic certainty in the form of reflection and pure thought what it was that he wished and intended to produce,

that he never thought at all, but let his imagination improvise at random.

Nothing is more common than for analysis to discover design in what, so far as consciousness is concerned, has been purely instinctive. Thus physiology ascertains that bread contains all the necessary elements of food except one, which omission happens to be supplied by butter : this may be accepted as an explanation of our 'purpose' in eating butter with bread, without the explanation being taken to imply that all who have ever fed on bread and butter have consciously *intended* to combine the nitrogenous and oleaginous elements of food. It is the natural order of things that the practical must precede the analytic. Bees by instinct construct hexagonal cells, and long afterwards mensuration shows that the hexagon is the most economic shape for such stowage ; individual states must rise and fall first before the sciences of history and politics can come to explain the how and why of their mutations. Similarly it is in accordance with the order of things that Shakespeare should produce dramas by the practical processes of art-creation, and that it should be left for others, his critics succeeding him at long intervals, to discover by analysis his ' purposes' and the laws which underlie his effects. The poet, if he could come to life now, would not feel more surprise at this analysis of his ' motives' and unfolding of his unconscious 'design' than he would feel on hearing that the beating of his heart—to him a thing natural enough, and needing no explanation— had been discovered to have a distinct purpose he could never have dreamed of in propelling the circulation of his blood, a thing of which he had never heard.

There are three leading ideas in relation to which inductive and judicial criticism are in absolute antagonism : to bring out these contrasts will be the most effective way of describing the inductive treatment.

The first of these ideas is order of merit, together with the

Three points of contrast between judicial and inductive criticism.

1.
Compari-
sons of
merit :
these out-
side science.

kindred notions of partisanship and hostility applied to individual authors and works. The minds of ordinary readers are saturated with this class of ideas; they are the weeds of taste, choking the soil, and leaving no room for the purer forms of literary appreciation. Favoured by the fatal blunder of modern education, which considers every other mental power to stand in need of training, but leaves taste and imagination to shift for themselves, literary taste has largely become confused with a spurious form of it: the mere taste for competition, comparison of likes and dislikes, gossip applied to art and called criticism. Of course such likes and dislikes must always exist, and journalism is consecrated to the office of giving them shape and literary expression; though it should be led by experience, if by nothing else, to exercise its functions with a double reserve, recognising that the judicial attitude of mind is a limit on appreciation, and that the process of testing will itself be tried by the test of vitality. But such preferences and comparisons of merit must be kept rigidly outside the sphere of science. Science knows nothing of competitive examination: a geologist is not heard extolling old red sandstone as a model rock-formation, or making sarcastic comments on the glacial epoch. Induction need not disturb the freedom with which we attach ourselves to whatever attracts our individual dispositions: individual partisanship for the wooded snugness of the Rhine or the bold and bracing Alps is unaffected by the adoption of exact methods in physical geography. What is to be avoided is the confusion of two different kinds of interest attaching to the same object. In the study of the stars and the rocks, which can inspire little or no personal interest, it is easy to keep science pure; to keep it to 'dry light,' as Heraclitus calls it, intelligence unclouded by the humours of individual sentiment, as Bacon interprets. But when science comes to be applied to objects which can excite emotion and inspire affection, then confusion arises, and the scientific student of political economy finds his treatment of pauperism disturbed by the philanthropy which belongs to him as a man. Still more in so emotional an atmosphere as the study of beauty, the student must use effort to separate the *beauty* of an object, which is a thing of art and perfectly analysable, from his personal *interest* in it, which is as distinctly external to the analysis of beauty as his love for his dog is external to the science of zoology. The possibility of thus separating interest and perception of beauty without diminishing either may be sufficiently seen in the case of music—an art which has been already reduced to scientific form. Music is as much as any art a thing of tastes and preferences; besides partialities for particular masters one student will be peculiarly affected by melody, another is all for dramatic effect, others have a special taste for the fugue or the sonata. No one can object to such preferences, but the science of music knows nothing about them; its exposition deals with modes of treatment or habits of orchestration distinguishing composers, irrespective of the private partialities they excite. Mozart and Wagner are analysed as two items in the sum of facts which make up music; and if a particular expositor shows by a turn in the sentence that he has a leaning to one or the other, the slip may do no harm, but for the moment science has been dropped.

There is, however, a sort of difference between authors and works, the constant recognition of which would more than make up to cultured pleasure for discarding comparisons of merit. Inductive treatment is concerned with *differences of kind* as distinguished from differences of degree. Elementary as this distinction is, the power of firmly grasping it is no slight evidence of a trained mind: the power, that is, of clearly seeing that two things are different, without being at the same time impelled to rank one above the other. The confusion of the two is a constant obstacle in the way of literary appreciation. It has been said, by way of comparison between two

Inductive treatment concerned with differences of kind, not of degree.

great novelists, that George Eliot constructs characters, but Charlotte Brontë creates them. The description (assuming it to be true) ought to shed a flood of interest upon both authoresses; by perpetually throwing on the two modes of treatment the clear light of contrast it ought to intensify our appreciation of both. As a fact, however, the description is usually quoted to suggest a preference for Charlotte Brontë on the supposed ground that creation is 'higher' than construction; and the usual consequences of preferences are threatened—the gradual closing of our susceptibilities to those qualities in the less liked of the two which do not resemble the qualities of the favourite. Yet why should we not be content to accept such a description (if true) as constituting a difference of kind, and proceed to recognise 'construction' and 'creation' as two parallel modes of treatment, totally distinct from one another in the way in which a fern is distinct from a flower, a distinction allowing no room for preferences because there is no common ground on which to compare? This separateness once granted, the mind, instead of having to choose between the two, would have scope for taking in to the full the detailed effects flowing from both modes of treatment, and the area of mental pleasure would be enlarged. The great blunders of criticism in the past, which are now universally admitted, rest on this inability to recognise differences of kind in literature. The Restoration poets had a mission to bring the heroic couplet to perfection: poetry not in their favourite measure they treated, not as different, but as bad, and rewrote or ignored Spenser and Milton. And generations of literary history have been wasted in discussing whether the Greek dramatists or Shakespeare were the higher: now every one recognises that they constitute two schools

Distinc-
tions of
kind a pri- different in kind that cannot be compared.
mary ele-
ment in ap-   It is hardly going too far to assert that this sensitiveness to
preciation. differences of kind as distinguished from differences of degree
is the first condition of literary appreciation. Nothing can be

more essential to art-perception than receptiveness, and receptiveness implies a change in the receptive attitude of mind with each variety of art. To illustrate by an extreme case. Imagine a spectator perfectly familiar with the Drama, but to whom the existence of the Opera was unknown, and suppose him to have wandered into an opera-house, mistaking it for a theatre. At first the mistake under which he was labouring would distort every effect : the elaborate overture would seem to him a great ' waste ' of power in what was a mere accessory; the opening recitative would strike him as ' unnaturally' delivered, and he would complain of the orchestral accompaniment as a 'distraction'; while at the first aria he would think the actor gone mad. As, however, arias, terzettos, recitatives succeeded one another, he must at last catch the idea that the music was an essential element in the exhibition, and that he was seeing, not a drama, but a drama translated into a different kind of art. The catching of this idea would at once make all the objectionable elements fall into their proper places. No longer distracted by the thought of the ordinary Drama, his mind would have leisure to catch the special effects of the Opera : he would feel how powerfully a change of passion could move him when magnified with all the range of expression an orchestra affords, and he would acknowledge a dramatic touch as the diabolic spirit of the conspirator found vent in a double D. The illustration is extreme to the extent of absurdity : but it brings out how expectation plays an important part in appreciation, and how the expectation has to be adapted to that on which it is exercised. The receptive attitude is a sort of mental focus which needs adjusting afresh to each variety of art if its effects are to be clearly caught; and to disturb attention when engaged on one species of literature by the thought of another is as unreasonable as to insist on one microscopic object appearing definite when looked at with a focus adjusted to another object. This will be acknowledged in reference to the great

Each author a separate species.

divisions of art : but does it not apply to the species as well as the genera, indeed to each individual author ?   Wordsworth has laid down that each fresh poet is to be tried by fresh canons of taste : this is only another way of saying that the differences between poets are differences of kind, that each author is a ' school ' by himself, and can be appreciated only by a receptive attitude formed by adjustment to himself alone.

Second axiom of inductive criticism: its function in distinguishing literary species.

In a scientific treatment of literature, at all events, an elementary axiom must be : *That inductive criticism is mainly occupied in distinguishing literary species.*   And on this view it will clearly appear how such notions as order of merit become disturbing forces in literary appreciation : unconsciously they apply the *qualitative* standard of the favourite works to works which must necessarily be explained by a different standard.   They are defended on the ground of pleasure, but they defeat their own object : no element in pleasure is greater than variety, and comparisons of merit, with every other form of the judicial spirit, are in reality arrangements for appreciating the smallest number of varieties.

II.
The ' laws of art': confusion between law external and scientific.

The second is the most important of the three ideas, both for its effect in the past and for the sharpness with which it brings judicial and inductive criticism into contrast.   It is the idea that there exist 'laws' of art, in the same sense in which we speak of laws in morality or the laws of some particular state—great principles which have been laid down, and which are binding on the artist as the laws of God or his country are binding on the man; that by these, and by lesser principles deduced from these, the artist's work is to be tried, and praise or blame awarded accordingly.   Great part of formal criticism runs on these lines; while, next in importance to comparisons of merit, the popular mind considers literary taste to consist in a keen sensitiveness to the 'faults' and 'flaws' of literary workmanship.

This attitude to art illustrates the enormous misleading

power of the metaphors that lie concealed in words. The word 'law,' justly applicable in one of its senses to art, has in practice carried with it the associations of its other sense; and the mistake of metaphor has been sufficient to distort criticism until, as Goldsmith remarks, rules have become the greatest of all the misfortunes which have befallen the commonwealth of letters. Every expositor has had to point out the widespread confusion between the two senses of this term. Laws in the moral and political world are external obligations, restraints of the will; they exist where the will of a ruler or of the community is applied to the individual will. In science, on the other hand, law has to do not with what ought to be, but with what is; scientific laws are facts reduced to formulæ, statements of the habits of things, so to speak. The laws of the stars in the first sense could only mean some creative fiat, such as 'Let there be lights in the firmament of heaven'; in the scientific sense laws of the stars are summaries of their customary movements. In the act of getting drunk I am violating God's moral law, I am obeying his law of alcoholic action. So scientific laws, in the case of art and literature, will mean descriptions of the practice of artists or the characteristics of their works, when these will go into the form of general propositions as distinguished from disconnected details. The key to the distinction is the notion of external authority. There cannot be laws in the moral and political sense without a ruler or legislative authority; in scientific laws the law-giver and the law-obeyer are one and the same, and for the laws of vegetation science looks no further than the facts of the vegetable world. In literature *The 'laws* and art the term 'law' applies only in the scientific sense; *of art' are scientific* the laws of the Shakespearean Drama are not laws imposed *laws.* by some external authority upon Shakespeare, but laws of dramatic practice derived from the analysis of his actual works. Laws of literature, in the sense of external obligations limiting an author, there are none: if he were voluntarily to

*The word
'fault'
meaning-
less in in-
ductive
treatment.*

bind himself by such external laws, he would be so far cur-
tailing art; it is hardly a paradox to say the art is legitimate
only when it does not obey laws.   What applies to the term
'law' applies similarly to the term 'fault.'   The term is
likely always to be used from its extreme convenience in art-
training; but it must be understood strictly as a term of education and discipline.   In inductive criticism, as in the other
inductive sciences, the word 'fault' has no meaning.   If an
artist acts contrary to the practice of all other artists, the
result is either that he produces no art-effect at all, in which
case there is nothing for criticism to register and analyse, or
else he produces a new effect, and is thus extending, not
breaking, the laws of art.   The great clash of horns in
Beethoven's Heroic Symphony was at first denounced as a
gross fault, a violation of the plainest laws of harmony; now,
instead of a 'fault,' it is spoken of as a 'unique effect,' and
in the difference between the two descriptions lies the whole
difference between the conceptions of judicial and inductive
criticism.   Again and again in the past this notion of faults
has led criticism on to wrong tracks, from which it has had
to retrace its steps on finding the supposed faults to be in
reality new laws.   Immense energy was wasted in denouncing
Shakespeare's 'fault' of uniting serious with light matter in
the same play as a violation of fundamental dramatic laws;
experience showed this mixture of passions to be the source
of powerful art-effects hitherto shut out of the Drama, and the
'fault' became one of the distinguishing 'laws' in the most
famous branch of modern literature.   It is necessary then to
insist upon the strict scientific sense of the term 'law' as
used of literature and art; and the purging of criticism from
the confusion attaching to this word is an essential step in its
elevation to the inductive standard.   It is a step, moreover,
in which it has been preceded by other branches of thought.
At one time the practice of commerce and the science of
economy suffered under the same confusion: the battle of

'free trade' has been fought, the battle of 'free art' is still
going on. In time it will be recognised that the practice
of artists, like the operations of business, must be left to its
natural working, and the attempt to impose external canons
of taste on artists will appear as futile as the attempt to
effect by legislation the regulation of prices.

Objections may possibly be taken to this train of argument *Objection*
on very high grounds, as if the protest against the notion of *as to the*
law-obeying in art were a sort of antinomianism, Literature, *moral pur-*
it may be said, has a moral purpose, to elevate and refine, and *pose of*
no duty can be higher than that of pointing out what in it is *literature:*
elevating and refining, and jealously watching against any
lowering of its standard. Such contention may readily be *this outside*
granted, and yet may amount to no more than this: that *inductive*
there are ways of dealing with literature which are more im- *treatment,*
portant than inductive criticism, but which are none the less *though in-*
outside it. Jeremy Collier did infinite service to our Restora- *trinsically*
tion Drama, but his was not the service of a scientific critic. *portant.*
The same things take different ranks as they are tried by the
standards of science or morals. An enervating climate may
have the effect of enfeebling the moral character, but this
does not make the geographer's interest in the tropical zone
one whit the less. Economy concerns itself simply with the
fact that a certain subsidence of profits in a particular trade
will drive away capital to other trades. But the details of
human experience that are latent in such a proposition: the
chilling effects of unsuccess and the dim colour it gives to the
outlook into the universe, the sifting of character and separation between the enterprising and the simple, the hard
thoughts as to the mysterious dispensations of human prosperity, the sheer misery of a wage-class looking on plenty and
feeling starvation—this human drama of failing profits may
be vastly more important than the whole science of economy,
but economy none the less entirely and rightly ignores it.

To some, I know, it appears that literature is a sphere in

Objection: Art as an arbitrary product not subject to law. which the strict sense of the word 'law' has no application : that such laws belong to nature, not to art. The essence, it is contended, of the natural sciences is the certainty of the facts with which they deal. Art, on the contrary, is creative ; it does not come into the category of objective phenomena at all, but is the product of some artist's will, and therefore purely arbitrary. If in a compilation of observations in natural history for scientific use it became known that the compiler had at times drawn upon his imagination for his details, the whole compilation would become useless ; and any scientific theories based upon it would be discredited. But the artist bases his work wholly on imagination, and caprice is a leading art-beauty : how, it is asked, can so arbitrary a subject-matte₁ be reduced to the form of positive laws ?

Third axiom of inductive criticism: art a part of nature. In view of any such objections, it may be well to set up a third axiom of inductive criticism : *That art is a part of nature.* Nature, it is true, is the vaguest of words : but this is a vagueness common to the objection and the answer. The objection rests really on a false antithesis, of which one term is 'nature,' while it is not clear what is the other term ; the axiom set up in answer implies that there is no real distinction between 'nature' and the other phenomena which are the subject of human enquiry. The distinction is supposed to rest upon the degree to which arbitrary elements of the mind, such as imagination, will, caprice, enter into such *Other arbi-* a thing as art-production. But there are other things in *trary pro-ducts sub-ject to inductive treatment.* which the human will plays as much part as it does in art, and which have nevertheless proved compatible with inductive treatment. Those who hold that 'thought is free' do not reject psychology as an inductive science ; actual politics are made up of struggles of will, exercises of arbitrary power, and the like, and yet there is a political science. If there is an inductive science of politics, men's voluntary actions in the pursuit of public life, and an inductive science of economy, men's voluntary actions in pursuit of wealth, why should there not be an inductive science of art, men's voluntary actions in pursuit of the beautiful? The whole of human action, as well as the whole of external nature, comes within the jurisdiction of science; so far from the productions of the will and imagination being exempted from scientific treatment, will and imagination themselves form chapters in psychology, and caprice has been analysed.

It remains to notice the third of the three ideas in relation to which the two kinds of criticism are in complete contrast with one another. It is a vague notion, which no objector would formulate, but which as a fact does underlie judicial criticism, and insensibly accompanies its testing and assaying. It is the idea that the foundations of literary form have reached their final settlement, the past being tacitly taken as a standard for the present and future, or the present as a standard for the past. Thus in the treatment of new literature the idea manifests itself in a secret antagonism to variations from received models; at the very least, new forms are called upon to justify themselves, and so the judicial critic brings his least receptive attitude to the new effects which need receptiveness most. In opposition to this tacit assumption, inductive criticism starts with a distinct counter-axiom of the utmost importance: *That literature is a thing of development.* This axiom implies that the critic must come to literature as to that in which he is expecting to find unlimited change and variety; he must keep before him the fact that production must always be far ahead of criticism and analysis, and must have carried its conquering invention into fresh regions before science, like settled government in the wake of the pioneer, follows to explain the new effects by new principles. No doubt in name literary development is recognised in all criticism; yet in its treatment both of old literature and new the *à priori* criticism is false to development in the scientific sense of the term. Such systems are apt to begin by laying down that ' the object of literature is so and

III. Testing by fixed standards inconsistent with inductive treatment.

Fourth axiom of inductive criticism: literature a thing of development.

Ignoring of development in new literature:

so,' or that ' the purpose of the Drama is to pourtray human nature ' ; they then proceed to test actual literature and dramas by the degree in which they carry out these fundamental principles. Such procedure is the opposite of the inductive method, and is a practical denial of development in

' purpose' in literature continually modifying.

literature. Assuming that the object of existing literature were correctly described, such a formula could not bind the literature of the future. Assuming that there was ever a branch of art which could be reduced to one simple purpose, yet the inherent tendency of the human mind and its productions to develop would bring it about that what were at first means towards this purpose would in time become ends in themselves side by side with the main purpose, giving us in addition to the simple species a modified variety of it ; external influences, again, would mingle with the native characteristics of the original species, and produce new species compound in their purposes and effects. The real literature would be ever obeying the first principle of development and changing from simple to complex, while the criticism that tried it by the original standard would be at each step removed one degree further from the only standard by which the literature could be explained. And if judicial criticism

Development in past literature confused with improvement.

fails in providing for development in the future and present, it is equally unfortunate in giving a false twist to development when looked for in the past. The critic of comparative standards is apt to treat early stages of literature as elementary, tacitly assuming his own age as a standard *up to* which previous periods have developed. Thus his treatment of the past becomes often an assessment of the degrees in which past periods have approximated to his own, advancing from literary pot-hooks to his own running facility. The clearness of an ancient writer he values at fifty per cent. as compared with modern standards, his concatenation of sentences is put down as only forty-five. But what if a certain degree of mistiness be an essential element in the phase of literary development to which the particular writer belongs, so that in him modern clearness would become, in judicial phrase, a fault? What if Plato's concatenation of sentences would simply spoil the flavour of Herodotus's story-telling, if Jeremy Taylor's prolixity and Milton's bi-lingual prose be simply the fittest of all dresses for the thought of their age and individual genius? In fact, the critic of fixed standards confuses development with *improvement :* a parallel mistake in natural history would be to understand the statement that man is higher in the scale of development than the butterfly as implying that a butterfly was God's failure in the attempt to make man. The inductive critic will accord to the early forms of his art the same independence he accords to later forms. Development will not mean to him education for a future stage, but the perpetual branching out of literary activity into ever fresh varieties, different in kind from one another, and each to be studied by standards of its own : the ' individuality ' of authors is the expression in literary parlance which corresponds to the perpetual ' differentiation' of new species in science. Alike, then, in his attitude to the past and the future, the inductive critic will eschew the temptation to judgment by fixed standards, which in reality means opposing lifeless rules to the ever-living variety of nature. He will leave a dead judicial criticism to bury its dead authors and to pen for them judicious epitaphs, and will himself approach literature filled equally with reverence for the unbroken vitality of its past and faith in its exhaustless future.

To gather up our results. Induction, as the most uni- *Summary.* versal of scientific methods, may be presumed to apply wherever there is a subject-matter reducible to the form of fact ; such a subject-matter will be found in literature where its effects are interpreted, not arbitrarily, but with strict reference to the details of the literary works as they actually stand. There is thus an inductive literary criticism, akin in

†

spirit and methods to the other inductive sciences, and distinct from other branches of criticism, such as the criticism of taste. This inductive criticism will entirely free itself from the judicial spirit and its comparisons of merit, which is found to have been leading criticism during half its history on to false tracks from which it has taken the other half to retrace its steps. On the contrary, inductive criticism will examine literature in the spirit of pure investigation; looking for the laws of art in the practice of artists, and treating art, like the rest of nature, as a thing of continuous development, which may thus be expected to fall, with each author and school, into varieties distinct in kind from one another, and each of which can be fully grasped only when examined with an attitude of mind adapted to the special variety without interference from without.

To illustrate the criticism thus described in its application to Shakespeare is the purpose of the present work.

The scope of the book is limited to the consideration of Shakespeare in his character as the great master of the Romantic Drama; and its treatment of his dramatic art divides itself into two parts. The first applies the inductive method in a series of Studies devoted to particular plays, and to single important features of dramatic art which these plays illustrate. One of the purposes of this first part is to bring out how the inductive method, besides its scientific interest, has the further recommendation of assisting more than any other treatment to enlarge our appreciation of the author and of his achievements. The second part will use the materials collected in the first part to present, in the form of a brief survey, Dramatic Criticism as an inductive science; enumerating, so far as its materials admit, the leading topics which such a science would treat, and arranging these topics in the logical connection which scientific method requires.

PART FIRST

———✦———

SHAKESPEARE

CONSIDERED AS A

DRAMATIC ARTIST

IN FIFTEEN STUDIES

I.

The Two Stories Shakespeare borrows for his Merchant of Venice.

A Study in the Raw Material of the Romantic Drama.

THE starting-point in the treatment of any work of literature is its position in literary history: the recognition of this gives the attitude of mind which is most favourable for extracting from the work its full effect. The division of the universal Drama to which Shakespeare belongs is known as the 'Romantic Drama,' one of its chief distinctions being that it uses the stories of Romance, together with histories treated as story-books, as the sources from which the matter of the plays is taken; Romances are the *raw material* out of which the Shakespearean Drama is manufactured. This very fact serves to illustrate the elevation of the Elizabethan Drama in the scale of literary development: just as the weaver uses as his raw material that which is the finished product of the spinner, so Shakespeare and his contemporaries start in their art of dramatising from Story which is already a form of art. In the exhibition, then, of Shakespeare as an Artist, it is natural to begin with the raw material which he worked up into finished masterpieces. For illustration of this no play could be more suitable than *The Merchant of Venice*, in which two tales, already familiar in the story form, have been woven together into a single plot: the Story of the Cruel Jew, who entered into a bond with his enemy of which the forfeit was to be a pound of this enemy's own flesh, and the Story of the Heiress and the Caskets. The present study will deal with the stories themselves, considering them as if with the eye of a dramatic artist to catch the points in which they lend themselves to dramatic effect; the next will show how Shakespeare handles the stories in telling them, increasing their dramatic force by the very process of working them up; a third study will point out how, not content with two stories, he has added others in the development of his plot, making it more complex only in reality to make it more simple.

Story of the Jew. In the Story of the Jew the main point is its special capability for bringing out the idea of *Nemesis*, one of the simplest and most universal of dramatic motives. Described *Nemesis as a dramatic idea.* broadly, Nemesis is retribution as it appears in the world of art. In reality the term covers two distinct conceptions: in ancient thought Nemesis was an artistic bond between excess and reaction, in modern thought it is an artistic bond between sin and retribution. The distinction is part of the general difference between Greek and modern views of life. *Ancient conception : artistic connection between excess and reaction.* The Greeks may be said to be the most artistic nation of mankind, in the sense that art covered so large a proportion of their whole personality: it is not surprising to find that they projected their sense of art into morals. Aristotle was a moral philosopher, but his system of ethics reads as an artistically devised pattern, in which every virtue is removed at equal distances from vices of excess and defect balancing it on opposite sides. The Greek word for law signifies proportion and distribution, *nomos*; and it is only another form of it that expresses *Nemesis* as the power punishing violations of proportion in things human. Distinct from Justice, which was occupied with crime, Nemesis was a companion deity to Fortune; and as Fortune went through the world distributing the good things of life heedlessly without regard to merit, so Nemesis followed in her steps, and, equally without regard to merit, delighted in cutting down the

prosperity that was high enough to attract attention. Poly- CHAP. I.
crates is the typical victim of such Nemesis : cast off by his
firmest ally for no offence but an unbroken career of good
luck, in the reaction from which his ally feared to be involved ; essaying as a forlorn hope to propitiate by voluntarily
throwing in the sea his richest crown-jewel ; recognising
when this was restored by fishermen that heaven had refused
his sacrifice, and abandoning himself to his fate in despair.
But Nemesis, to the moral sense of antiquity, could go even
beyond visitation on innocent prosperity, and goodness itself
could be carried to a degree that invited divine reaction.
Heroes like Lycurgus and Pentheus perished for excess of
temperance ; and the ancient Drama startles the modern
reader with an Hippolytus, whose passionate purity brought
down on him a destruction prophesied beforehand by those
to whom religious duty suggested moderate indulgence in
lust.

Such malignant correction of human inequalities is not *Modern*
a function to harmonise with modern conceptions of Deity. *conception*
Yet the Greek notion of Nemesis has an element of per- *artistic*
manency in it, for it represents a principle underlying human *between sin*
life. It suggests a sort of elasticity in human experience, a *bution.*
tendency to rebound from a strain ; this is the equilibrium of
the moral world, the force which resists departure from the
normal, becoming greater in proportion as departure from
the normal is wider. Thus in commercial speculation there
is a safe medium certain to bring profit in the long run ; in
social ambition there is a certain rise though slow : if a man
hurries to be rich, or seeks to rise in public life by leaps and
bounds, the spectator becomes aware of a secret force that
has been set in motion, as when the equilibrium of physical
bodies has been disturbed, which force threatens to drag the
aspirant down to the point from which he started, or to
debase him lower in proportion to the height at which he
rashly aimed. Such a force is ' risk,' and it may remain risk,

but if it be crowned with the expected fall the whole is recognised as 'Nemesis.' This Nemesis is deeply embedded in the popular mind and repeatedly crops up in its proverbial wisdom. Proverbs like 'Grasp all, lose all,' 'When things come to the worst they are sure to mend,' exactly express moral equilibrium, and the 'golden mean' is its proverbial formula. The saying 'too much of a good thing' suggests that the Nemesis on departures from the golden mean applies to good things as well as bad; while the principle is made to apply even to the observation of the golden mean itself in the proverb 'Nothing venture, nothing have.' Nevertheless, this side of the whole notion has in modern usage fallen into the background in comparison with another aspect of Nemesis. The grand distinction of modern thought is the predominance in it of moral ideas: they colour even its imagination; and if the Greeks carried their art-sense into morals, modern instincts have carried morals into art. In particular the speculations raised by Christianity have cast the shadow of Sin over the whole universe. It has been said that the conception of Sin is unknown to the ancients, and that the word has no real equivalent in Latin or Classical Greek. The modern mind is haunted by it. Notions of Sin have invaded art, and Nemesis shows their influence: vague conceptions of some supernatural vindication of artistic proportion in life have now crystallised into the interest of watching morals and art united in their treatment of Sin. The link between Sin and its retribution becomes a form of art-pleasure; and no dramatic effect is more potent in modern Drama than that which emphasises the principle that whatsoever a man soweth that shall he also reap.

Dramatic Nemesis latent in the Story of the Jew.

Now for this dramatic effect of Nemesis it would be difficult to find a story promising more scope than the Story of the Cruel Jew. It will be seen at once to contain a double nemesis, attaching to the Jew himself and to his

victim. The two moreover represent the different conceptions
of Nemesis in the ancient and modern world; Antonio's
excess of moral confidence suffers a nemesis of reaction in
his humiliation, and Shylock's sin of judicial murder finds a
nemesis of retribution in his ruin by process of law. The
nemesis, it will be observed, is not merely two-fold, but
double in the way that a double flower is distinct from two
flowers: it is a nemesis *on* a nemesis; the nemesis which
visits Antonio's fault is the crime for which Shylock suffers
his nemesis. Again, in that which gives artistic character
to the reaction and the retribution the two nemeses differ.
Let St. Paul put the difference for us: 'Some men's sins
are evident, going before unto judgment; and some they
follow after.' So in cases like that of Shylock the nemesis
is interesting from its very obviousness and the impatience
with which we look for it; in the case of Antonio the
nemesis is striking for the very opposite reason, that he of
all men seemed most secure against it.

Antonio must be understood as a perfect character: for
we must read the play in the light of its age, and intolerance
was a mediæval virtue. But there is no single good quality
that does not carry with it its special temptation, and the
sum of them all, or perfection, has its shadow in self-
sufficiency. It is so with Antonio. Of all national types
of character the Roman is the most self-sufficient, alike
incorruptible by temptation and independent of the softer
influences of life: we find that 'Roman honour' is the
idea which Antonio's friends are accustomed to associate
with him. Further the dramatist contrives to exhibit Antonio
to us in circumstances calculated to bring out this drawback to his perfection. In the opening scene we see the
dignified merchant-prince suffering under the infliction of
frivolous visitors, to which his friendship with the young
nobleman exposes him: his tone throughout the interview is
that of the barest toleration, and suggests that his courtesies

*Antonio;
perfection
and self-
sufficiency,
the Nemesis
of Sur-
prise.*

iii. ii. 297.

CHAP. I.   are felt rather as what is due to himself than what is due to
────────   those on whom they are bestowed.   When Salarino makes
i. i. 60–64. flattering excuses for taking his leave, Antonio replies, first
with conventional compliment,

> Your worth is very dear in my regard,

and then with blunt plainness, as if Salarino were not worth
the trouble of keeping up polite fiction :

> I take it, your own business calls on you
> And you embrace the occasion to depart.

i. i. 8.   The visitors, trying to find explanation for Antonio's seriousness, suggest that he is thinking of his vast commercial
speculations ; Antonio draws himself up :

i. i. 41.
> Believe me, no : I thank my fortune for it,
> My ventures are not in one bottom trusted,
> Nor to one place ; nor is my whole estate
> Upon the fortune of this present year :
> Therefore my merchandise makes me not sad.

Antonio is saying in his prosperity that *he* shall never be
moved.   But the great temptation to self-sufficiency lies in
his contact, not with social inferiors, but with a moral outcast such as Shylock : confident that the moral gulf between
the two can never be bridged over, Antonio has violated
dignity as well as mercy in the gross insults he has heaped
upon the Jew whenever they have met.   In the Bond Scene
i. iii. 99,   we see him unable to restrain his insults at the very moment
&c.   in which he is soliciting a favour from his enemy ; the effect
i. iii. 107–   reaches a climax as Shylock gathers up the situation in a
130.   single speech, reviewing the insults and taunting his op-
pressor with the solicited obligation :

> Well then, it now appears you need my help :
> Go to, then ; you come to me, and you say,
> 'Shylock, we would have moneys' : you say so ;
> You, that did void your rheum upon my beard
> And foot me as you spurn a stranger cur
> Over your threshold ; moneys is your suit.

There is such a foundation of justice for these taunts that

for a moment our sympathies are transferred to Shylock's CHAP. I.
side. But Antonio, so far from taking warning, is betrayed ——
beyond all bounds in his defiance; and in the challenge
to fate with which he replies we catch the tone of infatuated
confidence, the *hybris* in which Greek superstition saw the
signal for the descent of Nemesis.

> I am as like to call thee so again, i. iii. 131.
> To spit on thee again, to spurn thee too.
> If thou wilt lend this money, lend it not
> As to thy friends . . . .
> *But lend it rather to thine enemy,*
> *Who, if he break, thou may'st with better face*
> *Exact the penalty.*

To this challenge of self-sufficiency the sequel of the story
is the answering Nemesis: the merchant becomes a bankrupt, the first citizen of Venice a prisoner at the bar, the
morally perfect man holds his life and his all at the mercy of
the reprobate he thought he might safely insult.

So Nemesis has surprised Antonio in spite of his perfect- *Shylock:*
ness: but the malice of Shylock is such as is perpetually *malignant justice, the*
crying for retribution, and the retribution is delayed only *Nemesis of*
that it may descend with accumulated force. In the case of *Measure for*
this second nemesis the Story of the Jew exhibits dramatic *Measure.*
capability in the opportunity it affords for the sin and the
retribution to be included within the same scene. Portia's iv. i.
happy thought is a turning-point in the Trial Scene on the
two sides of which we have the Jew's triumph and the Jew's
retribution; the two sides are bound together by the principle of measure for measure, and for each detail of vindic-
tiveness that is developed in the first half of the scene there
is a corresponding item of nemesis in the sequel. To begin *Charter v.*
with, Shylock appeals to the charter of the city. It is one of *statute.*
the distinctions between written and unwritten law that no compare
flagrant injustice can arise out of the latter. If the analogy 102, 219.
of former precedents would seem to threaten such an
injustice, it is easy in a new case to meet the special

CHAP. I.   emergency by establishing a new precedent; where, however,
the letter of the written law involves a wrong, however great,
it must, nevertheless, be exactly enforced.   Shylock takes
his stand upon written law; indeed upon the strictest of all
compare   kinds of written law, for the charter of the city would seem
iii. iii. 26–   to be the instrument regulating the relations between citizens
31.
and aliens—an absolute necessity for a free port—which
could not be superseded without international negotiations.
But what is the result?   As plaintiff in the cause Shylock
would, in the natural course of justice, leave the court, when
judgment had been given against him, with no further
mortification than the loss of his suit.   He is about to do so
when he is recalled:

It is enacted in the laws of Venice, &c.

Unwittingly, he has, by the action he has taken, entangled
iv. i. 314.   himself with an old statute law, forgotten by all except the
learned Bellario, which, going far beyond natural law, made
the mere attempt upon a citizen's life by an alien punishable
to the same extent as murder.   Shylock had chosen the
letter of the law, and by the letter of the law he is to suffer.
Humour v.   Again, every one must feel that the plea on which Portia
quibble.   upsets the bond is in reality the merest quibble.   It is appropriate enough in the mouth of a bright girl playing the
lawyer, but no court of justice could seriously entertain it for
a moment: by every principle of interpretation a bond that
could justify the cutting of human flesh must also justify the
shedding of blood, which is necessarily implied in such
cutting.   But, to balance this, we have Shylock in the earlier
part of the scene refusing to listen to arguments of justice,
iv. i. 40–   and taking his stand upon his 'humour': if he has a whim,
62.
he pleads, for giving ten thousand ducats to have a rat
poisoned, who shall prevent him?   The suitor who rests his
cause on a whim cannot complain if it is upset by a quibble.
Similarly, throughout the scene, every point in Shylock's

justice of malice meets its answer in the justice of nemesis.   CHAP. I.
He is offered double the amount of his loan :

Offer of
double v.
refusal of
principal.

> If every ducat in six thousand ducats
> Were in six parts, and every part a ducat,

he answers, he would not accept them in lieu of his bond.   **iv.** i. 318,
The wheel of Nemesis goes round, and Shylock would   336.
gladly accept not only this offer but even the bare principal;
but he is denied, on the ground that he has refused it in open
court.   They try to bend him to thoughts of mercy :

Complete
security v.
total loss.

> How shalt thou hope for mercy, rendering none ?

He dares to reply :

> What judgement shall I dread, doing no wrong ?

The wheel of Nemesis goes round, and Shylock's life and all
lie at the mercy of the victim to whom he had refused mercy
and the judge to whose appeal for mercy he would not
listen.   In the flow of his success, when every point is   *Exultation*
being given in his favour, he breaks out into unseemly   v. *irony.*
exultation :

> A Daniel come to judgement ! yea, a Daniel !   **iv.** i. 223,

The ebb comes, and his enemies catch up the cry and turn   246, 250,
it against him :   301, 304.

> A Daniel, still say I, a second Daniel !   **iv.** i. 313,
> I thank thee, Jew, for *teaching* me that word.   317, 323,
    333, 340.

Such then is the Story of the Jew, and so it exhibits
nemesis clashing with nemesis, the nemesis of surprise with
the nemesis of equality and intense satisfaction.

In the Caskets Story, which Shakespeare has associated   *The Cas-*
with the Story of the Jew, the dramatic capabilities are of a   *kets Story.*
totally different kind.   In the artist's armoury one of the
most effective weapons is Idealisation : inexplicable touches   *Idealisa-*
throwing an attractiveness over the repulsive, uncovering   *tion :*
the truth and beauty which lie hidden in the commonplace,
and showing how much can be brought out of how little

CHAP. I.

*the exhibi-
tion of a
common-
place ex-
perience in
a glorified
form.*
with how little change. A story will be excellent material, then, for dramatic handling which contains at once some experience of ordinary life, and also the surroundings which can be made to exhibit this experience in a glorified form : the more commonplace the experience, the greater the triumph of art if it can be idealised. The point of the Caskets Story to the eye of an artist in Drama is the opportunity it affords for such an idealisation of the commonest problem in everyday experience—what may be called the Problem of Judgment by Appearances.

*Problem of
Judgment
by Appear-
ances.*
In the choice between alternatives there are three ways in which judgment may be exercised. The first mode, if it can be called judgment at all, is to accept the decision of chance—to cast lots, or merely to drift into a decision. An opposite to this is purely rational choice. But rational choice, if strictly interpreted as a logical process, involves great complications. If a man would choose according to the methods of strict reason, he must, first of all, purge himself of all passion, for passion and reason are antagonistic. Next, he must examine himself as to the possibility of latent prejudice ; and as prejudice may be unconsciously inherited, he must include in the sphere of his examination ancestral and national bias. Then, he must accumulate all the evidence that can possibly bear upon the question in hand, and foresee every eventuality that can result from either alternative. When he has all the materials of choice before him, he must proceed to balance them against one another, seeing first that the mental faculties employed in the process have been equally developed by training. All such preliminary conditions having been satisfied, he may venture to enquire on which side the balance dips, maintaining his suspense so long as the dip is undecided. And when a man has done all this he has attained only that degree of approach to strictly rational choice which his imperfect nature admits. Such pure reason has no place in real life : judgment in practical affairs

is something between chance and this strict reason; it
attempts to use the machinery of rational choice, but only so
far as practical considerations proper to the matter in hand
allow. This medium choice is what I am here calling Judgment by Appearances, for it is clear that the antithesis
between appearance and reality will obtain so long as the
materials of choice are scientifically incomplete; the term
will apply with more and more appropriateness as the
divergence from perfect conditions of choice is greater.

Judgment by Appearances so defined is the only method *This ideal-*
of judgment proper to practical life, and accordingly an *ised : a*
maximum
exalted exhibition of it must furnish a keen dramatic interest. *in the issue,*
How is such a process to be glorified? Clearly Judgment by
Appearances will reach the ideal stage when there is the
maximum of importance in the issue to be decided and the
minimum of evidence by which to decide it. These two
conditions are satisfied in the Caskets Story. In questions
touching the individual life, that of marriage has this unique
importance, that it is bound up with wide consequences which
extend beyond the individual himself to his posterity. With
the suitors of Portia the question is of marriage with the
woman who is presented as supreme of her age in beauty, in
wealth and in character; moreover, the other alternative is *ii. i. 40,*
a vow of perpetual celibacy. So the question at issue in the *&c.*
Caskets Story concerns the most important act of life in the
most important form in which it can be imagined to present
itself. When we turn to the evidence on which this question *and a*
is to be decided we find that of rational evidence there is ab- *minimum*
in the evi-
solutely none. The choice is to be made between three *dence.*
caskets distinguished by their metals and by the accompanying inscriptions:

> Who chooseth me shall gain what many men desire.   *ii. vii. 5-9.*
> Who chooseth me shall get as much as he deserves.
> Who chooseth me must give and hazard all he hath.

However individual fancies may incline, it is manifestly impossible to set up any train of *reasoning* which should discover a ground of preference amongst the three. And it is worth noting, as an example of Shakespeare's nicety in detail, that the successful chooser reads in the scroll which announces his victory,

iii. ii. 132.
>   You that choose not by the view,
>   Chance *as* fair, and choose *as* true:

Shakespeare does not say '*more* fair,' '*more* true.' This equal balancing of the alternatives will appear still clearer
i. ii. 30–36. when we recollect that it is an intentional puzzle with which we are dealing, and accordingly that even if ingenuity could discover a preponderance of reason in favour of any one of the three, there would be the chance that this preponderance had been anticipated by the father who set the puzzle. The case becomes like that of children bidden to guess in which hand a sweetmeat is concealed. They are inclined to say the right hand, but hesitate whether that answer may not have been foreseen and the sweetmeat put in the left hand; and if on this ground they are tempted to be sharp and guess the left hand, there is the possibility that this sharpness may have been anticipated, and the sweetmeat kept after all in the right hand. If then the Caskets Story places before us three suitors, going through three trains of intricate reasoning for guidance in a matter on which their whole future depends, whereas we, the spectators, can see that from the nature of the case no reasoning can possibly avail them, we have clearly the Problem of Judgment by Appearances drawn out in its ideal form; and our sympathies are attracted by the sight of a process, belonging to our everyday experience, yet developed before us in all the force artistic setting can bestow.

Solution of the problem: the characters of the But is this all? Does Shakespeare display before us the problem, yet give no help towards its solution? The key to the suitors' fates is not to be found in the trains of reasoning they go through. As if to warn us against looking for it in

this direction, Shakespeare contrives that we never hear the CHAP. I.
reasonings of the successful suitor. By a natural touch *choosers*
Portia, who has chosen Bassanio in her heart, is re- *determine*
presented as unable to bear the suspense of hearing him *their fates.*
deliberate, and calls for music to drown his meditations; it is iii. ii, from
43; esp. 61.
only the conclusion to which he has come that we catch as
the music closes. The particular song selected on this
occasion points dimly in the direction in which we are to
look for the true solution of the problem :

> Tell me where is fancy bred, iii. ii. 63.
> Or in the heart or in the head?

'Fancy' in Shakespearean English means 'love'; and the
discussion, whether love belongs to the head or the heart, is
no inappropriate accompaniment to a reality which consists
in this—that the success in love of the suitors, which they
are seeking to compass by their reasonings, is in fact being
decided by their characters.

To compare the characters of the three suitors, it will be
enough to note the different form that pride takes in each.
The first suitor is a prince of a barbarian race, who has ii. i, vii.
thus never known equals, but has been taught to consider
himself half divine ; as if made of different clay from the rest
of mankind he instinctively shrinks from 'lead.' Yet modesty ii. vii. 20.
mingles with his pride, and though he feels truly that, so far ii. vii. 24-
30.
as the estimation of him by others is concerned, he might
rely upon 'desert,' yet he doubts if desert extends as far as
Portia. What seizes his attention is the words, 'what many ii. vii, from
36.
men desire'; and he rises to a flight of eloquence in pictur-
ing wildernesses and deserts become thoroughfares by the
multitude of suitors flocking to Belmont. But he is all the
while betraying a secret of which he was himself unconscious : he has been led to seek the hand of Portia, not
by true love, but by the feeling that what all the world is
seeking the Prince of Morocco must not be slow to claim.
Very different is the pride of Arragon. He has no regal ii. ix.

CHAP. I. position, but rather appears to be one who has fallen in

compare social rank ; he makes up for such a fall by intense pride of

ii. ix. 47–9. family, and is one of those who complacently thank heaven
that they are not as other men. The 'many men' which
had attracted Morocco repels Arragon :

ii. ix. 31.
> I will not choose what many men desire,
> Because I will not jump with common spirits,
> And rank me with the barbarous multitudes.

ii. ix, from He is caught by the bait of ' desert.' It is true he almost

36. deceives us with the lofty tone in which he reflects how the
world would benefit if dignities and offices were in all cases
purchased by the merit of the wearer ; yet there peeps
through his sententiousness his real conception of merit—the
sole merit of family descent. His ideal is that the 'true seed
of honour' should be ' picked from the chaff and ruin of the
times,' and wrest greatness from the ' low peasantry ' who
had risen to it. He accordingly rests his fate upon desert :
and he finds in the casket of his choice a fool's head. Of
Bassanio's soliloquy we hear enough to catch that his pride
iii. ii, from is the pride of the soldier, who will yield to none the post of

73. danger, and how he is thus attracted by the ' threatening ' of

compare

i. ii. 124. the leaden casket :
> thou meagre lead,
> Which rather threatenest than dost promise aught,
> Thy paleness moves me more than eloquence.

Moreover, he is a lover, and the threatening is a challenge
to show what he will risk for love : his true heart finds its
natural satisfaction in ' giving and hazarding ' his all. This
is the pride that is worthy of Portia ; and thus the ingenious
puzzle of the ' inspired ' father has succeeded in piercing
through the outer defence of specious reasoning, and carrying its repulsion and attraction to the inmost characters
General of the suitors.

principle :

character Such, then, is Shakespeare's treatment of the Problem of

as an ele- Judgment by Appearances : while he draws out the problem

ment in

judgment. itself to its fullest extent in displaying the suitors elaborating

trains of argument for a momentous decision in which we see that reason can be of no avail, he suggests for the solution that, besides reason, there is in such judgments another element, character, and that in those crises in which reason is most fettered, character is most potent. An important solution this is; for what is character? A man's character is the shadow of his past life; it is the grand resultant of all the forces from within and from without that have been operating upon him since he became a conscious agent. Character is the sandy footprint of the commonplace hardened into the stone of habit; it is the complexity of daily tempers, judgments, restraints, impulses, all focussed into one master-passion acting with the rapidity of an instinct. To lay down then, that where reason fails as an element in judgment, character comes to its aid, is to bind together the exceptional and the ordinary in life. In most of the affairs of life men have scope for the exercise of commonplace qualities, but emergencies do come where this is denied them; in these cases, while they think, like the three suitors, that they are moving voluntarily in the direction in which they are judging fit at the moment, in reality the weight of their past lives is forcing them in the direction in which their judgment has been accustomed to take them. Thus in the moral, as in the physical world, nothing is ever lost: not a ripple on the surface of conduct but goes on widening to the outermost limit of experience. Shakespeare's contribution to the question of practical judgment is that by the long exercise of commonplace qualities we are building up a character which, though unconsciously, is the determining force in the emergencies in which commonplace qualities are impossible.

How Shakespeare Manipulates the
Stories in Dramatising Them.

A Study in Dramatic Workmanship.

CHAP. II.

Two points of Dramatic Mechanism.

IN treating Story as the raw material of the Romantic Drama it has already been shown, in the case of the stories utilised for *The Merchant of Venice*, what natural capacities these exhibit for dramatic effect. The next step is to show how the artist increases their force for dramatic purposes in the process of working them up. Two points will be illustrated in the present study: first, how Shakespeare meets the difficulties of a story and reduces them to a minimum; secondly, how he adds effectiveness to the two tales by weaving them together so that they assist one another's effect.

Reduction of difficulties specially important in Drama.

The avoidance or reduction of difficulties in a story is an obvious element in any kind of artistic handling; it is of special importance in Drama in proportion as we are more sensitive to improbabilities in what is supposed to take place before our eyes than in what we merely hear of by narrative. This branch of art could not be better illustrated than in the Story of the Jew: never perhaps has an artist had to deal with materials so bristling with difficulties of the greatest magnitude, and never, it may be added, have they been met with greater ingenuity. The host of improbabilities gathering about such a detail as the pound of flesh must strike every mind. There is, however, preliminary to these, another difficulty of more general application: the difficulty of painting a character bad enough to be the hero of the

First difficulty: monstrosity of the

story. It might be thought that to paint excess of badness
is comparatively easy, as needing but a coarse brush. On the
contrary, there are few severer tests of creative power than *Jew's character.*
the treatment of monstrosity. To be told that there is
villainy in the world and tacitly to accept the statement may
be easy; it is another thing to be brought into close contact
with the villains, to hear them converse, to watch their actions
and occasionally to be taken into their confidence. We realise
in Drama through our sympathy and our experience : in real
life we have not been accustomed to come across monsters
and are unfamiliar with their behaviour ; in proportion then
as the badness of a character is exaggerated it is carried outside the sphere of our experience, the naturalness of the
scene is interrupted and its human interest tends to decline.
So, in the case of the story under consideration, the dramatist
is confronted with this dilemma : he must make the character
of Shylock absolutely bad, or the incident of the bond will
appear unreal; he must not make the character extraordinarily bad, or there is danger of the whole scene appearing unreal.

Shakespeare meets a difficulty of this kind by a double *Its re-*
treatment. On the one hand, he puts no limits to the *pulsiveness counter-*
blackness of the character itself; on the other hand, he *acted by*
provides against repulsiveness by giving it a special attraction *sympathy with his*
of another kind. In the present case, while painting Shylock *wrongs.*
as a monster, he secures for him a hold upon our sympathy
by representing him as a victim of intolerable ill-treatment
and injustice. The effect resembles the popular sympathy
with criminals. The men themselves and their crimes are
highly repulsive ; but if some slight irregularity occurs in the
process of bringing them to justice—if a counsel shows
himself unduly eager, or a judge appears for a moment one-
sided, a host of volunteer advocates espouse their cause.
These are actuated no doubt by sensitiveness to purity of
justice ; but their protests have a ring that closely resembles

CHAP. II.   sympathy with the criminals themselves, whom they not
———   unfrequently end by believing to be innocent and injured.
e.g. in iii. In the same way Shakespeare shows no moderation
i, iii ; iv.
i ; ii. v.   in the touches of bloodthirstiness, of brutality, of sordid
            meanness he heaps together in the character of Shylock ;
            but he takes equal pains to rouse our indignation at the
e.g. iii. i ; treatment he is made to suffer.   Personages such as Gratiano,
iv. i, &c.
            Salanio, Salarino, Tubal, serve to keep before us the medi-
            æval feud between Jew and Gentile, and the persecuting
            insolence with which the fashionable youth met the money-
i. iii. 107– lenders who ministered to their necessities.   Antonio
138.
            himself has stepped out of his natural character in the
iii. i. 57, grossness of his insults to his enemy.   Shylock has been
133 ;
iii. iii. 22 ; injured in pocket as well as in sentiment, Antonio using his
and i. iii.   wealth to disturb the money-market, and defeat the schemes
45.
            of the Jew ; according to Shylock Antonio has hindered
            him of half-a-million, and were he out of Venice the usurer
            could make what merchandise he would.   Finally, our sense
            of deliverance in the Trial Scene cannot hinder a touch
            of compunction for the crushed plaintiff, as he appeals
            against the hard justice meted out to him :—the loss of his
            property, the acceptance of his life as an act of grace, the
            abandonment of his religion and race, which implies the
            abandonment of the profession by which he makes his living.

iv. i. 374.   Nay, take my life and all ; pardon not that :
                       You take my house when you do take the prop
                       That doth sustain my house ; you take my life
                       When you do take the means whereby I live.

            By thus making us resent the harsh fate dealt to Shylock the
            dramatist recovers in our minds the fellow-feeling we have
Dramatic   lost in contemplating the Jew himself.   A name for such
Hedging.
            double treatment might be ' Dramatic Hedging ' : as the better
            covers a possible loss by a second bet on the opposite side,
            so, when the necessities of a story involve the creation of a
            monster, the dramatic artist ' hedges ' against loss of attrac-

tiveness by finding for the character human interest in some Chap. II.
other direction. So successful has Shakespeare been in
the present instance that a respectable minority of readers
rise from the play partisans of Shylock.

We pass on to the crop of difficulties besetting the pound *Difficulties*
of flesh as a detail in the bond. That such a bond should be *connected*
proposed, that when proposed it should be accepted, that it *pound of*
should be seriously entertained by a court of justice, that if *flesh.*
entertained at all it should be upset on so frivolous a pretext
as the omission of reference to the shedding of blood : these
form a series of impossible circumstances that any dramatist
might despair of presenting with even an approach to
naturalness. Yet if we follow the course of the story as
moulded by Shakespeare we shall find all these impossibilities
one after another evaded.

At the end of the first scene Antonio had bidden Bassanio *Proposal of*
go forth and try what his credit could do in Venice. Armed *the bond.*
with this blank commission Bassanio hurries into the city. *i. i. 179.*
As a gay young nobleman he knows nothing of the commercial world except the money-lenders ; and now proceeds
to the best-known of them, apparently unaware of what any
gossip on the Rialto could have told him, the unfortunate compare
relations between this Shylock and his friend Antonio. At *i. iii. 1–40.*
the opening of the Bond Scene we find Bassanio and Shylock
in conversation, Bassanio impatient and irritated to find that
the famous security he has to offer seems to make so little
impression on the usurer. At this juncture Antonio himself *i. iii. 41.*
falls[1] in with them, sees at a glance to what his rash friend

---

[1] No commentator has succeeded in making intelligible the line
   How like a fawning publican he looks !   *i. iii. 42.*
as it stands in the text at the opening of Shylock's soliloquy. The
expression 'fawning publican' is so totally the opposite of all the
qualities of Antonio that it could have no force even in the mouth of
a satirist. It is impossible not to be attracted by the simple change in
the text that would not only get over this difficulty, but add a new
effect to the scene : the change of assigning this single line to Antonio,

CHAP. II. has committed him, but is too proud to draw back in sight of his enemy. Already a minor difficulty is surmounted, as to how Antonio comes to be in the position of asking an obligation of Shylock. Antonio is as impatient as dignity will permit to bring an awkward business to a conclusion. Shylock, on the contrary, to whom the interview itself is a triumph, in which his persecutor is appearing before him in the position of a client, casts about to prolong the conversation to as great a length as possible. Any topic would serve his purpose; but what topic more natural than the question at the root of the feud between the two, the question of lending money on interest? It is here we reach the very heart of our problem, how the first mention of the pound of flesh is made without a shock of unreality sufficient to ruin the whole scene. Had Shylock asked for a forfeiture of a million per cent., or in any other way thrown into a commercial form his purpose of ruining Antonio, the old feud and the present opportunity would be explanation sufficient: the real difficulty is the total incongruity between such an idea as a pound of human flesh and commercial transactions

The proposal led up to by the of any kind. This difficulty Shakespeare has met by one of his greatest triumphs of mechanical ingenuity; his leading

reserving, of course, the rest of the speech for Shylock. The passage would then read thus [the stage direction is my own] :

Enter ANTONIO.

Bass. This is Signior Antonio.

Ant. [*Aside*]. How like a fawning publican he looks—

[BASSANIO *whispers* ANTONIO *and brings him to* SHYLOCK.

Shy. [*Aside*]. I hate him, for he is a Christian,
But more, &c.

Both the terms 'fawning' and 'publican' are literally applicable to Shylock, and are just what Antonio would be likely to say of him. It is again a natural effect for the two foes on meeting for the first time in the play to exchange scowling defiance. Antonio's defiance is cut short at the first line by Bassanio's running up to him, explaining what he has done, and bringing Antonio up to where Shylock is standing ; the time occupied in doing this gives Shylock scope for his longer soliloquy.

up to the proposal of the bond by the discussion on interest. CHAP. II.
The effect of this device a modern reader is in danger of *discourse*
losing: we are so familiar with the idea of interest at the *on interest.*
present day that we are apt to forget what the difficulty was i. iii, from 69.
to the ancient and mediæval mind, which for so many generations kept the practice of taking interest outside the pale
of social decency. This prejudice was one of the confusions
arising out of the use of a metal currency. The ancient
mind could understand how corn put into the ground would
by the agency of time alone produce twentyfold, thirtyfold,
or a hundredfold; they could understand how cattle left to
themselves would without human assistance increase from a
small to a large flock: but how could metal grow? how
could lifeless gold and silver increase and multiply like
animals and human beings? The Greek word for interest,
tokos, is the exact equivalent of the English word *breed*, and
the idea underlying the two was regularly connected with
that of interest in ancient discussions. The same idea is
present throughout the dispute between Antonio and Shylock.
Antonio indignantly asks:

> when did friendship take i. iii. 134.
> A *breed* for *barren metal* of his friend?

Shylock illustrates usury by citing the patriarch Jacob and his i. iii. 72.
clever trick in cattle-breeding; showing how, at a time when
cattle were the currency, the natural rate of increase might
be diverted to private advantage. Antonio interrupts him:

> Is your gold and silver ewes and rams? i. iii. 96.

Shylock answers:

> I cannot tell; I make it *breed* as fast;

both parties thus showing that they considered the distinction
between the using of flesh and metal for the medium of
wealth to be the essential point in their dispute. With this
notion then of flesh *versus* money floating in the air between
them the interview goes on to the outbursts of mutual hatred
which reach a climax in Antonio's challenge to Shylock to do

CHAP. II.   his worst; this challenge suddenly combines with the root
            idea of the conversation to flash into Shylock's mind the sug-
i. iii, from   gestion of the bond.   In an instant he smoothes his face and
138.   proposes friendship.   He will lend the money without interest,
            in pure kindness, nay more, he will go to that extent of good
            understanding implied in joking, and will have a merry bond;
            while as to the particular joke (he says in effect), since you
            Christians cannot understand interest in the case of money
            while you acknowledge it in the case of flesh and blood,
            suppose I take as my interest in this bond a pound of your
            own flesh.   In such a context the monstrous proposal sounds
            almost natural.   It has further been ushered in in a manner
            which makes it almost impossible to decline it.   When one
            who is manifestly an injured man is the first to make ad-
            vances, a generous adversary finds it almost impossible to
            hold back.   A sensitive man, again, will shrink from nothing
            more than from the ridicule attaching to those who take serious
            precautions against a jest.   And the more incongruous Shy-
            lock's proposal is with commercial negotiations the better
            evidence it is of his non-commercial intentions.   In a word,
            the essence of the difficulty was the incongruity between
            human flesh and money transactions: it has been surmounted
            by a discussion, flowing naturally from the position of the
            two parties, of which the point is the relative position of
            flesh and money as the medium of wealth in the past.

Difficulty   The bond thus proposed and accepted, there follows the
of legally   difficulty of representing it as entertained by a court of
recognising
the bond   justice.   With reference to Shakespeare's handling of this
evaded: point it may be noted, first, that he leaves us in doubt
iv. i. 104.   whether the court would have entertained it: the Duke is
            intimating an intention of adjourning at the moment when
            the entrance of Portia gives a new turn to the proceedings.
iv. i. 17.   Again, at the opening of the trial, the Duke gives expression
            to the universal opinion that Shylock's conduct was intel-
            ligible only on the supposition that he was keeping up to the

last moment the appearance of insisting on his strange terms, CHAP. II.
in order that before the eyes of the whole city he might
exhibit his enemy at his mercy, and then add to his ignominy
by publicly pardoning him : a fate which, it must be admitted,
was no more than Antonio justly deserved. This will explain
how Shylock comes to have a hearing at all : when once he
is admitted to speak it is exceedingly difficult to resist the
pleas Shakespeare puts into his mouth. He takes his stand iv. i. 38.
on the city's charter and the letter of the law, and declines
to be drawn into any discussion of natural justice ; yet even as
a question of natural justice what answer can be found when iv. i. 90.
he casually points to the institution of slavery, which we
must suppose to have existed in Venice at the period? Shylock's only offence is his seeking to make Antonio's life a
matter of barter : what else is the accepted institution of
slavery but the establishment of power over human flesh and
blood and life, simply because these have been bought with
money, precisely as Shylock has given good ducats for his
rights over the flesh of Antonio? No wonder the perplexed
Duke is for adjourning.

There remains one more difficulty, the mode in which, *Difficulty*
according to the traditional story, the bond is upset. It is *as to the traditional*
manifest that the agreement as to the pound of flesh, if it is *mode of*
to be recognised by a court of justice at all, cannot without *upsetting the bond*
the grossest perversion of justice be cancelled on the ground *met.*
of its omitting to mention blood. Legal evasion can go
to great lengths. It is well known that an Act requiring
cabs to carry lamps at night has been evaded through the
omission of a direction that the lamps were to be lighted ;
and that importers have escaped a duty on foreign gloves at
so much the pair by bringing the right-hand and left-hand
gloves over in different ships. But it is perfectly possible to
carry lamps without lighting them, while it is a clear impossibility to cut human flesh without shedding blood. Nothing
of course would be easier than to upset the bond on rational

grounds—indeed the difficulty is rather to imagine it receiving rational consideration at all; but on the other hand no solution of the perplexity could be half so dramatic as the one tradition has preserved. The dramatist has to choose between a course of procedure which shall be highly dramatic but leave a sense of injustice, and one that shall be sound and legal but comparatively tame. Shakespeare contrives to secure both alternatives. He retains the traditional plea as to the blood, but puts it into the mouth of one known to his audience to be a woman playing the lawyer for the nonce ;

iv. i. 314, and again, before we have time to recover from our surprise
347. and feel the injustice of the proceeding, he follows up the brilliant evasion by a sound legal plea, the suggestion of a real lawyer. Portia has come to the court from a conference with her cousin Bellario, the most learned jurist of Venice.

iii. iv. 47 ; Certainly it was not this doctor who hit upon the idea of the
iv. i. 143. blood being omitted. His contribution to the interesting consultation was clearly the old statute of Venice, which every one else seems to have forgotten, which made the mere attempt on the life of a citizen by an alien punishable with death and loss of property: according to this piece of statute law not only would Shylock's bond be illegal, but the demand of such security constituted a capital offence. Thus Shakespeare surmounts the final difficulty in the story of the Jew in a mode which retains dramatic force to the full, yet does this without any violation of legal fairness.

The interweaving of the two stories. The second purpose of the present study is to show how Shakespeare has added to the effectiveness of his two stories by so weaving them together that they assist one another's effect.

First, it is easy to see how the whole movement of the play rises naturally out of the union of the two stories. One of the main distinctions between the progress of events in real life or history and in Drama is that the movement of a drama falls into the form technically known as Complication

and Resolution. A dramatist fastens our attention upon some CHAP. II.
train of events: then he sets himself to divert this train of ——
events from its natural course by some interruption; this *Complication and*
interruption is either removed, and the train of events returns *Resolution.*
to its natural course, or the interruption is carried on to some
tragic culmination. In *The Merchant of Venice* our interest
is at the beginning fixed on Antonio as rich, high-placed, the
protector and benefactor of his friends. By the events following upon the incident of the bond we see what would seem
the natural life of Antonio diverted into a totally different
channel; in the end the whole course is restored, and Antonio
becomes prosperous as before. Such interruption of a train
of incidents is its Complication, and the term Complication
suggests a happy Resolution to follow. Complication and
Resolution are essential to dramatic movement, as discords
and their ' resolution ' into concords constitute the essence of
music. The Complication and Resolution in the story of the *The one*
Jew serve for the Complication and Resolution of the drama *story com-plicated*
as a whole ; and my immediate point is that these elements of *and re-*
movement in the one story spring directly out of its connec- *solved by the other.*
tion with the other. But for Bassanio's need of money and i. i, from
his blunder in applying to Shylock the bond would never have 122 ; i. iii.
been entered into, and the change in Antonio's fortunes would
never have come about : thus the cause for all the Complication
of the play (technically, the Complicating Force) is the happy
lover of the Caskets Story. Similarly Portia is the means by
which Antonio's fortunes are restored to their natural flow :
in other words, the source of the Resolution (or Resolving
Force) is the maiden of the Caskets Story. The two leading
personages of the one tale are the sources respectively of the
Complication and Resolution in the other tale, which carry
the Complication and Resolution of the drama as a whole.
Thus simply does the movement of the whole play flow from
the union of the two stories.

One consequence flowing from this is worth noting ; that *The whole play symmetrical about its central scene.*

the scene in which Bassanio makes his successful choice of the casket is the Dramatic Centre of the whole play, as being the point at which the Complicating and Resolving Forces meet. This Dramatic Centre is, according to Shakespeare's favourite custom, placed in the exact mechanical centre of the drama, covering the middle of the middle Act. There is again an amount of poetic splendour lavished upon this scene which throws it up as a poetic centre to the whole. More than this, it is the real crisis of the play. Looking philosophically upon the whole drama as a piece of history, we must admit that the true turning-point is the success of Bassanio; the apparent crisis is the Trial Scene, but this is in reality governed by the scene of the successful choice, and if Portia and Bassanio had not been united in the earlier scene no lawyer would have interposed to turn the current of events in the trial. There is yet another sense in which the same scene may be called central. Hitherto I have dealt with only two tales; the full plot however of *The Merchant of Venice* involves two more, the Story of Jessica and the Episode of the Rings : it is to be observed that all four stories meet in the scene of the successful choice. This scene is the climax of the Caskets Story. It is connected with the

iii. ii, from 221.

catastrophe in the Story of the Jew : Bassanio, at the moment of his happiness, learns that the friend through whom he has been able to contend for the prize has forfeited his life to his foe as the price of his liberality. The scene is connected with the Jessica Story : for Jessica and her husband are the messengers who bring the sad tidings, and thus link together the bright and gloomy elements of the play. Finally, the Episode of the Rings, which is to occupy the end of the

iii. ii. 173– 187.

drama, has its foundation in this scene, in the exchange of the rings which are destined to be the source of such ironical perplexity. Such is the symmetry with which the plot of *The Merchant of Venice* has been constructed : the incident which is technically its Dramatic Centre is at once its mechanical

centre, its poetic centre, and, philosophically considered, its
true turning-point; while, considering the play as a Romantic
drama with its union of stories, we find in the same central
incident all the four stories dovetailed together.

These points may appear small and merely technical. But *Shake-*
it is a constant purpose with me in the present exposition of *speare as*
Shakespeare as a Dramatic Artist to combat the notion, so *of Plot.*
widely prevalent amongst ordinary readers, that Shakespeare,
though endowed with the profoundest grasp of human
nature, is yet careless in the construction of his plots: a
notion in itself as improbable as it would be that a sculptor
could be found to produce individual figures exquisitely
moulded and chiselled, yet awkwardly and clumsily grouped.
It is the minuter points that show the finish of an artist; and
such symmetry of construction as appears in *The Merchant
of Venice* is not likely to characterise a dramatist who sacrifices plot to character-painting.

There remains another point, which no one will consider *The union*
small or technical, connected with the union of the two *of a light*
stories: the fact that Shakespeare has thus united a light and *serious*
a serious story, that he has woven together gloom and bright- *story.*
ness. This carries us to one of the great battlefields of
dramatic history; no feature is more characteristic of the
Romantic Drama than this mingling of light and serious in
the same play, and at no point has it been more stoutly
assailed by critics trained in an opposite school. I say
nothing of the wider scope this practice gives to the dramatist, nor the way in which it brings the world of art nearer
to the world of reality; my present purpose is to review the
dramatic effects which flow from the mingling of the two
elements in the present play.

In general human interest the stories are a counterpoise *Dramatic*
to one another, so different in kind, so equal in the degree *effects*
of interest their progress continues to call forth. The inci- *of this*
dents of the two tales gather around Antonio and Portia *union.*

respectively; each of these is a full and rounded character, and they are both centres of their respective worlds. The stories seem to start from a common point. The keynote to the story of the Jew is the strange 'sadness'—the word implies no more than seriousness—which overpowers Antonio, and which seems to be the shadow of his coming trouble. Compare with this the first words we hear of Portia:

> By my troth, Nerissa, my little body is aweary of this great world.

Such a humorous languor is a fitting precursor to the excitement and energy of the scenes which follow. But from this common starting-point the stories move in opposite directions; the spectator's sympathies are demanded alternately for two independent chains of circumstances, for the fortunes of Antonio sinking lower and lower, and the fortunes of Portia rising higher and higher. He sees the merchant and citizen become a bankrupt prisoner, the lordly benefactor of his friends a wretch at the mercy of his foe. He sees Portia, already endowed with beauty, wealth, and character, attain what to her heart is yet higher, the power to lay all she has at the feet of the man she loves. Then, when they are at the climax of their happiness and misery, when Portia has received all that this world can bestow, and Antonio has lost all that this world can take away, for the first time these two central personages meet face to face in the

Trial Scene. And if from general human interest we pass on to the machinery of plot, we find this also governed by the same combination: a half-serious frolic is the medium in which a tragic crisis finds its solution.

But it is of course passion and emotional interest which are mainly affected by the union of light and serious: these we shall appreciate chiefly in connection with the Trial Scene, where the emotional threads of the play are gathered into a knot, and the two personages who are the embodiments of the light and serious elements face one another as judge and

prisoner. In this scene it is remarkable how Portia takes CHAP. II.
pains to prolong to the utmost extent the crisis she has come
to solve; she holds in her fingers the threads of the tangled
situation, and she is strong enough to play with it before she
will consent to bring it to an end. She has intimated her 178.
opinion that the letter of the bond must be maintained, she 184-207.
has made her appeal to Shylock for mercy and been refused,
she has heard Bassanio's appeal to wrest the law for once to 214-222.
her authority and has rejected it; there remains nothing but
to pronounce the decree. But at the last moment she asks 225.
to see the bond, and every spectator in court holds his
breath and hears his heart beat as he follows the lawyer's eye
down line after line. It is of no avail; at the end she can 227-230.
only repeat the useless offer of thrice the loan, with the effect
of drawing from Shylock an oath that he will not give way.
Then Portia admits that the bond is forfeit, with a needless 230-244.
reiteration of its horrible details; yet, as if it were some evenly
balanced question, in which after-thoughts were important,
she once more appeals to Shylock to be merciful and bid
her tear the bond, and evokes a still stronger asseveration
from the malignant victor, until even Antonio's stoicism begins to give way, and he begs for a speedy judgment. Portia 243.
then commences to pass her judgment in language of legal
prolixity, which sounds like a recollection of her hour with
Bellario :

> For the intent and purpose of the law
> Hath full relation to the penalty,
> Which here appeareth due upon the bond, &c.

Next she fads about the details of the judicial barbarity, 255-261.
the balance to weigh the flesh, a surgeon as a forlorn hope;
and when Shylock demurs to the last, stops to argue that he
might do this for charity. At last surely the intolerable
suspense will come to a termination. But our lawyer of 263.
half-an-hour's standing suddenly remembers she has forgotten to call on the defendant in the suit, and the pathos is

iv. i, from 225.

CHAP. II. intensified by the dying speech of Antonio, calmly welcom-
ing death for himself, anxious only to soften Bassanio's remorse, his last human passion a rivalry with Portia for the
love of his friend.

iv. i. 276.
                        Bid her be judge
            Whether Bassanio had not once a love.

iv. i, from When the final judgment can be delayed no longer its open-
299.
ing sentences are still lengthened out by the jingling repeti-
tions of judicial formality,

            The law allows it, and the court awards it, &c.

Only when every evasion has been exhausted comes the
thunderstroke which reverses the whole situation. Now it is
clear that had this situation been intended to have a tragic
termination this prolonging of its details would have been
impossible; thus to harrow our feelings with items of agony
would be not art but barbarity. It is because Portia knows
what termination she is going to give to the scene that she
can indulge in such boldness; it is because the audience
have recognised in Portia the signal of deliverance that the
lengthening of the crisis becomes the dramatic beauty of
suspense. It appears then that, if this scene be regarded only
as a crisis of tragic passion, the dramatist has been able to
extract more *tragic* effect out of it by the device of assisting
the tragic with a light story.

reaction   Again, it is a natural law of the human mind to pass
and comic   from strain to reaction, and suspense relieved will find vent
effect;
in vehement exhilaration. By giving Portia her position in
the crisis scene the dramatist is clearly furnishing the means
for a reaction to follow, and the reaction is found in the
iv. i, from Episode of the Rings, by which the disguised wives entangle
425.
their husbands in a perplexity affording the audience the
bursts of merriment needed as relief from the tension of the
Trial Scene. The play is thus brought into conformity with
the laws of mental working, and the effect of the reaction

is to make the serious passion more keen because more CHAP. II.
healthy.

Finally, there are the effects of mixed passion, neither *effects of*
wholly serious nor wholly light, but compounded of the two, *mixed*
which are impossible to a drama that can admit only a *passion.*
single tone. The effect of Dramatic Irony, which Shakespeare inherited from the ancient Drama, but greatly
modified and extended, is powerfully illustrated at the most
pathetic point of the Trial Scene, when Antonio's chance iv. i. 273–
reference to Bassanio's new wife calls from Bassanio and 294.
his follower agonised vows to sacrifice even their wives
if this could save their patron—little thinking that these
wives are standing by to record the vow. But there is an
effect higher than this. Portia's outburst on the theme of iv. i. 184–
mercy, considered only as a speech, is one of the noblest in 202.
literature, a gem of purest truth in a setting of richest
music. But the situation in which she speaks it is so framed
as to make Portia herself the embodiment of the mercy she
describes. How can we imagine a higher type of mercy,
the feminine counterpart of justice, than in the bright
woman, at the moment of her supreme happiness, appearing
in the garb of the law to deliver a righteous unfortunate
from his one error, and the justice of Venice from the in-
soluble perplexity of having to commit a murder by legal
process? And how is this situation brought about but by the
most intricate interweaving of a story of brightness with a
story of trouble?

In all branches then of dramatic effect, in Character, in
Plot and in Passion, the union of a light with a serious story
is found to be a source of power and beauty. The fault
charged against the Romantic Drama has upon a deeper view
proved a new point of departure in dramatic progress; and
by such combination of opposites the two tales have increased
the sum of their individual effectiveness by the added effect
of their union in a drama.

III.

How Shakespeare makes his plot more Complex in order to make it more Simple.

A Study in Underplot.

Chap. III.

───

Paradox of simplicity by means of increased complexity.

THE title of the present study is a paradox : that Shakespeare makes a plot more complex [1] in order to make it more simple. It is however a paradox that finds an illustration from the material world in every open roof. The architect's problem has been to support a heavy weight without the assistance of pillars, and it might have been expected that in solving the problem he would at least have tried every means in his power for diminishing the weight to be supported. On the contrary, he has increased this weight by the addition of massive cross-beams and heavy iron-girders. Yet, if these have been arranged according to the laws of construction, each of them will bring a supporting power considerably greater than its own weight; and thus, while in a literal sense increasing the roof, for all practical purposes they may be said to have diminished it. Similarly a dramatist of the Romantic school, from his practice of uniting more than one story in the same plot, has to face the

───

[1] It is a difficulty of literary criticism that it has to use as technical terms words belonging to ordinary conversation, and therefore more or less indefinite in their significations. In the present work I am making a distinction between 'complex' and 'complicated': the latter is applied to the diverting a story out of its natural course with a view to its ultimate 'resolution'; 'complex' is reserved for the interweaving of stories with one another. Later on 'single' will be opposed to 'complex,' and 'simple' to 'complicated.'

difficulty of complexity. This difficulty he solves not by seeking how to reduce combinations as far as possible, but, on
the contrary, by the addition of more and inferior stories ;
yet if these new stories are so handled as to emphasise
and heighten the effect of the main stories, the additional
complexity will have resulted in increased simplicity. In the
play at present under consideration, Shakespeare has interwoven into a common pattern two famous and striking tales ;
his plot, already elaborate, he has made yet more elaborate
by the addition of two more tales less striking in their
character—the story of Jessica and the Episode of the Rings.
If it can be shown that these inferior stories have the effect *The Jessica*
of assisting the main stories, smoothing away their difficulties *Story and*
the Rings
and making their prominent points yet more prominent, it *Episode*
will be clear that he has made his plot more complex only in *assist the*
main
reality to make it more simple. The present study is de- *stories.*
voted to noticing how the Stories of Jessica and of the Rings
minister to the effects of the Story of the Jew and the
Caskets Story.

To begin with : it may be seen that in many ways the *The Jessica*
mechanical working out of the main stories is assisted by the *Story. It*
serves as
Jessica Story. In the first place it relieves them of their *Underplot*
superfluous personages. Every drama, however simple, must *for me-*
chanical
contain 'mechanical' personages, who are introduced into *personages.*
the play, not for their own sake, but to assist in presenting
incidents or other personages. The tendency of Romantic
Drama to put a story as a whole upon the stage multiplies
the number of such mechanical personages : and when
several such stories come to be combined in one, there is a
danger of the stage being crowded with characters which
intrinsically have little interest. Here the Underplots become of service and find occupation for these inferior personages. In the present case only four personages are essential to the main plot—Antonio, Shylock, Bassanio, Portia.
But in bringing out the unusual tie that binds together

a representative of the city and a representative of the nobility, and upon which so much of the plot rests, it is an assistance to introduce the rank and file of gay society and depict these paying court to the commercial magnate. The high position of Antonio and Bassanio in their respective spheres will come out still clearer if these lesser social personages are graduated. Salanio, Salerio, and Salarino are mere parasites; Gratiano has a certain amount of individuality in his wit; while, seeing that Bassanio is a scholar as well as a nobleman and soldier, it is fitting to give prominence amongst his followers to the intellectual and artistic Lorenzo. Similarly the introduction of Nerissa assists in presenting Portia fully; Shylock is seen in his relations with his race by the aid of Tubal, his family life is seen in connection with Jessica, and his behaviour to dependants in connection with Launcelot; Launcelot himself is set off by Gobbo. Now the Jessica Story is mainly devoted to these inferior personages, and the majority of them take an animated part in the successful elopement. It is further to be noted that the Jessica Underplot has itself an inferior story attached

to it, that of Launcelot, who seeks scope for his good nature by transferring himself to a Christian master, just as his mistress seeks a freer social atmosphere in union with a Christian husband. And, similarly, side by side with the Caskets Story, which unites Portia and Bassanio, we have a

faintly-marked underplot which unites their followers, Nerissa and Gratiano. In one or other of these inferior stories the mechanical personages find attachment to plot; and the multiplication of individual figures, instead of leaving an impression of waste, is made to minister to the sense of Dramatic Economy.

*It assists
mechanical
develop-
ment:
occupying
the three*
Again : as there are mechanical personages so there are mechanical difficulties—difficulties of realisation which do not belong to the essence of a story, but which appear when the story comes to be worked out upon the stage. The Story of

the Jew involves such a mechanical difficulty in the interval CHAP. III.
of three months which elapses between the signing of the
bond and its forfeiture. In a classical setting this would be *months'*
interval,
avoided by making the play begin on the day the bond falls
due; such treatment, however, would shut out the great
dramatic opportunity of the Bond Scene. The Romantic
Drama always inclines to exhibiting the whole of a story; it
must therefore in the present case *suppose* a considerable
interval between one part of the story and another, and such
suppositions tend to be weaknesses. The Jessica Story con-
veniently bridges over this interval. The first Act is given
up to bringing about the bond, which at the beginning of the
third Act appears to be broken. The intervening Act consists
of no less than nine scenes, and while three of them carry
on the progress of the Caskets Story, the other six are
devoted to the elopement of Jessica: the bustle and activity
implied in such rapid change of scene indicating how an
underplot can be used to keep the attention of the audience
just where the natural interest of the main story would flag.

The same use of the Jessica Story to bridge over the *and so*
three months' interval obviates another mechanical difficulty *breaking*
gradually
of the main plot. The loss of all Antonio's ships, the *the news of*
Antonio's
supposition that all the commercial ventures of so prudent a *losses.*
merchant should simultaneously miscarry, is so contrary to
the chances of things as to put some strain upon our sense
of probability; and this is just one of the details which, too
unimportant to strike us in an anecdote, become realised
when a story is presented before our eyes. The artist, it
must be observed, is not bound to find actual solutions for
every possible difficulty; he has merely to see that they do
not interfere with dramatic effect. Sometimes he so arranges
his incidents that the difficulty is met and vanishes; sometimes it is kept out of sight, the portion of the story which
contains it going on behind the scenes; at other times he
is content with reducing the difficulty in amount. In the

CHAP. III. present instance the improbability of Antonio's losses is les-
sened by the gradual way in which the news is broken to us,
distributed amongst the numerous scenes of the three months'
ii. viii. 25. interval. We get the first hint of it in a chance conversation between Salanio and Salarino, in which they are
chuckling over the success of the elopement and the fury of
the robbed father. Salanio remarks that Antonio must look
that he keep his day; this reminds Salarino of a ship he has
just heard of as lost somewhere in the English Channel:

> I thought upon Antonio when he told me;
> And wish'd in silence that it were not his.

iii. i. In the next scene but one the same personages meet, and
one of them, enquiring for the latest news, is told that the
rumour yet lives of Antonio's loss, and now the exact place
of the wreck is specified as the Goodwin Sands; Salarino
adds: 'I would it might prove the end of his losses.'
Before the close of the scene Shylock and Tubal have been
added to it. Tubal has come from Genoa and gives Shylock
the welcome news that at Genoa it was *known* that Antonio
had lost an argosy coming from Tripolis; while on his
journey to Venice Tubal had travelled with creditors of
Antonio who were speculating upon his bankruptcy as a
iii. ii. certainty. Then comes the central scene in which the full
news reaches Bassanio at the moment of his happiness : all
Antonio's ventures failed—

> From Tripolis, from Mexico and England,
> From Lisbon, Barbary, and India,

iii. iii. not one escaped. In the following scene we see Antonio in
custody.

The Jessica   These are minor points such as may be met with in any
Story   play, and the treatment of them belongs to ordinary Dra-
assists
Dramatic matic Mechanism. But we have already had to notice that
Hedging in the Story of the Jew contains special difficulties which belong
regard to
Shylock. to the essence of the story, and must be met by special

devices. One of these was the monstrous character of the CHAP. III.
Jew himself; and we saw how the dramatist was obliged to
maintain in the spectators a double attitude to Shylock,
alternately letting them be repelled by his malignity and
again attracting their sympathy to him as a victim of wrong.
Nothing in the play assists this double attitude so much as
the Jessica Story. Not to speak of the fact that Shylock
shows no appreciation for the winsomeness of the girl who
attracts every one else in the drama, nor of the way in which
this one point of brightness in the Jewish quarter throws up
the sordidness of all her surroundings, we hear the Jew's
own daughter reflect that his house is a 'hell,' and we see ii. iii. 2.
enough of his domestic life to agree with her. A Shylock e.g. ii. v.
painted without a tender side at all would be repulsive; he
becomes much more repulsive when he shows a tenderness
for one human being, and yet it appears how this tenderness
has grown hard and rotten with the general debasement of
his soul by avarice, until, in his ravings over his loss, his iii. i, from
ducats and his daughter are ranked as equally dear. 25.

> I would my daughter were dead at my foot, and the jewels in iii. i. 92.
> her ear ! Would she were hearsed at my foot, and the ducats in her
> coffin !

For all this we feel that he is hardly used in losing her.
Paternal feeling may take a gross form, but it is paternal
feeling none the less, and cannot be denied our sympathy;
bereavement is a common ground upon which not only high
and low, but even the pure and the outcast, are drawn
together. Thus Jessica at home makes us hate Shylock;
with Jessica lost we cannot help pitying him. The perfection of Dramatic Hedging lies in the equal balancing of
the conflicting feelings, and one of the most powerful
scenes in the whole play is devoted to this twofold display of
Shylock. Fresh from the incident of the elopement, he is
encountered by the parasites and by Tubal : these amuse
themselves with alternately 'chaffing' him upon his losses,

CHAP. III. and 'drawing' him in the matter of the expected gratification of his vengeance, while his passions rock him between

Jessica Shakespeare's compensation to Shylock. extremes of despair and fiendish anticipation. We may go further. Great creative power is accompanied by great attachment to the creations and keen sense of justice in disposing of them. Looked at as a whole, the Jessica Story is Shakespeare's compensation to Shylock. The sentence on

iv. i. 348–394. Shylock, which the necessities of the story require, is legal rather than just; yet large part of it consists in a requirement that he shall make his daughter an heiress. And, to put it more generally, the repellent character and hard fate of the father have set against them the sweetness and beauty of the daughter, together with the full cup of good fortune which her wilful rebellion brings her in the love of Lorenzo and the protecting friendship of Portia. Perhaps the dramatist, according to his wont, is warning us of this compensating treatment when he makes one of the characters early in the

ii. iv. 34. play exclaim:

> If e'er the Jew her father come to heaven,
> It will be for his gentle daughter's sake.

The Jessica Story explains Shylock's unyieldingness. The other main source of difficulty in the Story of the Jew is, as we have seen, the detail concerning the pound of flesh, which throws improbability over every stage of its progress. In one at least of these stages the difficulty is directly met by the aid of the Jessica Story: it is this which explains Shylock's resolution not to give way. When we try in imagination to realise the whole circumstances, common sense must take the view taken in the play itself by the Duke:

iv. i. 17.
> Shylock, the world thinks, and I think so too,
> That thou but lead'st this fashion of thy malice
> To the last hour of act; and then 'tis thought
> Thou'lt show thy mercy and remorse more strange
> Than is thy strange apparent cruelty.

A life-long training in avarice would not easily resist an offer of nine thousand ducats. But further, the alternatives between which Shylock has to choose are not so simple as

the alternatives of Antonio's money or his life. On the one CHAP. III.
hand, Shylock has to consider the small chance that either
the law or the mob would actually suffer the atrocity to be
judicially perpetrated, and how his own life would be likely
to be lost in the attempt. Again, turning to the other alternative, Shylock is certainly deep in his schemes of vengeance, and the finesse of malignity must have suggested to
him how much more cruel to a man of Antonio's stamp it
would be to fling him a contemptuous pardon before the
eyes of Venice than to turn him into a martyr, even supposing this to be permitted. But at the moment when the
choice becomes open to Shylock he has been maddened by
the loss of his daughter, who, with the wealth she has stolen,
has gone to swell the party of his deadly foe. It is fury, not
calculating cruelty, that makes Shylock with a madman's
tenacity cling to the idea of blood, while this passion is
blinding him to a more keenly flavoured revenge, and risking
the chance of securing any vengeance at all [1].

From the mechanical development of the main plot and *The Jessica*
the reduction of its difficulties, we pass to the interweaving of *Story as-*
sists the
the two principal stories, which is so leading a feature of the *interweav-*
play. In the main this interweaving is sufficiently provided *ing of the*
main
for by the stories themselves, and we have already seen how *stories.*
the leading personages in the one story are the source of the
whole movement in the other story. But this interweaving
is drawn closer still by the affair of Jessica: technically *It is thus*
described the position in the plot of Jessica's elopement is *a Link*
Action,
that of a Link Action between the main stories. This

---

[1] This seems to me a reasonable view notwithstanding what Jessica
says to the contrary (iii. ii. 286), that she has often heard her father
swear he would rather have Antonio's flesh than twenty times the
value of the bond. It is one thing to swear vengeance in private, another
thing to follow it up in the face of a world in opposition. A man of
overbearing temper surrounded by inferiors and dependants often utters
threats, and seems to find a pleasure in uttering them, which both he
and his hearers know he will never carry out.

CHAP. III. linking appears in the way in which Jessica and her suite are in the course of the drama transferred from the one tale to the other. At the opening of the play they are personages in the Story of the Jew, and represent its two antagonistic sides, Jessica being the daughter of the Jew and Lorenzo a friend and follower of Bassanio and Antonio. First the contrivance of the elopement assists in drawing together these opposite sides of the Jew Story, and aggravating the feud on which it turns. Then, as we have seen, Jessica and

iii. ii, from her husband in the central scene of the whole play come into
221.
contact with the Caskets Story at its climax. From this point they become adopted into the Caskets Story, and settle down

helping to in the house and under the protection of Portia. This
restore the
balance be- transference further assists the symmetry of interweaving by
tween the helping to adjust the balance between the two main stories.
main
stories, In its *mass*, if the expression may be allowed, the Caskets tale, with its steady progress to a goal of success, is over-weighted by the tale of Antonio's tragic peril and startling deliverance: the Jessica episode, withdrawn from the one and added to the other, helps to make the two more equal. Once more, the case, we have seen, is not merely that of a union between stories, but a union between stories opposite in kind, a combination of brightness with gloom.

and a bond The binding effect of the Jessica Story extends to the union
between
their bright between these opposite tones. We have already had occasion
and dark to notice how the two extremes meet in the central scene, how
climaxes. from the height of Bassanio's bliss we pass in an instant to the total ruin of Antonio, which we then learn in its fulness for the first time: the link which connects the two is the arrival of Jessica and her friends as bearers of the news.

Character So far, the points considered have been points of Mechan-
effects.
Character ism and Plot; in the matter of Character-Interest the Jessica
of Jessica. episode is to an even greater degree an addition to the whole effect of the play, Jessica and Lorenzo serving as a foil to Portia and Bassanio. The characters of Jessica and Lorenzo

are charmingly sketched, though liable to misreading unless CHAP. III.
carefully studied. To appreciate Jessica we must in the first
place assume the grossly unjust mediæval view of the Jews as
social outcasts. The dramatist has vouchsafed us a glimpse
of Shylock at home, and brief as the scene is it is remark- ii. v.
able how much of evil is crowded into it. The breath of
home life is trust, yet the one note which seems to pervade
the domestic bearing of Shylock is the lowest suspiciousness.
Three times as he is starting for Bassanio's supper he draws 12, 16, 36.
back to question the motives for which he has been invited.
He is moved to a shriek of suspicion by the mere fact of his
servant joining him in shouting for the absent Jessica, by the 7.
mention of masques, by the sight of the servant whispering 28, 44.
to his daughter. Finally, he takes his leave with the words

> Perhaps I will return immediately,   52.

a device for keeping order in his absence which would be
a low one for a nurse to use to a child, but which he is not
ashamed of using to his grown-up daughter and the lady of
his house. The short scene of fifty-seven lines is sufficient
to gives us a further reminder of Shylock's sordid house-
keeping, which is glad to get rid of the good-natured
Launcelot as a 'huge feeder'; and his aversion to any form 3, 46.
of gaiety, which leads him to insist on his shutters being put 28.
up when he hears that there is a chance of a pageant in
the streets. Amidst surroundings of this type Jessica has
grown up, a motherless girl, mingling only with harsh men
(for we nowhere see a trace of female companionship for
her): it can hardly be objected against her that she should
long for a Christian atmosphere in which her affections might ii. iii. 20.
have full play. Yet even for this natural reaction she feels
compunction:

> Alack, what heinous sin is it in me   ii. iii. 16.
> To be ashamed to be my father's child!
> But though I am a daughter to his blood,
> I am not to his manners.

CHAP. III. Formed amidst such influences it would be a triumph to a character if it escaped repulsiveness; Jessica, on the contrary, is full of attractions. She has a simplicity which stands to her in the place of principle. More than this she has a high degree of feminine delicacy. Delicacy will be best brought out in a person who is placed in an equivocal situation, and we see Jessica engaged, not only in an elopement, but in an ii. iv. 30. elopement which, it appears, has throughout been planned by herself and not by Lorenzo. Of course a quality like feminine delicacy is more conveyed by the bearing of the actress than by positive words; we may however notice the impression which Jessica's part in the elopement scenes makes upon ii. iv. 30– those who are present. When Lorenzo is obliged to make a 40. confidant of Gratiano, and tell him how it is Jessica who has planned the whole affair, instead of feeling any necessity of apologising for her the thought of her childlike innocence moves him to enthusiasm, and it is here that he exclaims:

> If e'er the Jew her father come to heaven,
> It will be for his gentle daughter's sake.

ii. vi. In the scene of the elopement itself, Jessica has steered clear of both prudishness and freedom, and when after her pretty confusion she has retired from the window, even Gratiano breaks out:

ii. vi. 51.   Now, by my hood, a Gentile and no Jew;

while Lorenzo himself has warmed to see in her qualities he had never expected:

ii. vi. 52.
> Beshrew me but I love her heartily;
> For she is wise, if I can judge of her,
> And fair she is, if that mine eyes be true,
> And true she is, as she has proved herself,
> And therefore, like herself, wise, fair, and true,
> Shall she be placed in my constant soul.

So generally, all with whom she comes into contact feel ii. iii. 10. her spell: the rough Launcelot parts from her with tears he iii. i. 41. is ashamed of yet cannot keep down; Salarino—the last of

men to take high views of women—resents as a sort of blas- CHAP. III.
phemy Shylock's claiming her as his flesh and blood ; while
between Jessica and Portia there seems to spring in an iii. iv, v;
v. i.
instant an attraction as mysterious as is the tie between
Antonio and Bassanio.

Lorenzo is for the most part of a dreamy inactive nature, *Character*
as may be seen in his amused tolerance of Launcelot's *of Lorenzo.*
iii. v. 44-
word-fencing—word-fencing being in general a challenge 75.
which none of Shakespeare's characters can resist ; similarly,
Jessica's enthusiasm on the subject of Portia, which in reality iii. v. 75-
he shares, he prefers to meet with banter : 89.

> Even such a husband
> Hast thou of me as she is for a wife.

But the strong side of his character also is shown us in the
play : he has an artist soul, and to the depth of his passion
for music and for the beauty of nature we are indebted for v. i. 1-24,
some of the noblest passages in Shakespeare. This is the 54-88.
attraction which has drawn him to Jessica, her outer beauty
is the index of artistic sensibility within : 'she is never merry v. i. 69, 1-
when she hears sweet music,' and the soul of rhythm is 24.
awakened in her, just as much as in her husband, by the
moonlight scene. Simplicity again, is a quality they have
in common, as is seen by their ignorance in money- iii. i. 113,
matters, and the way a valuable turquoise ring goes for a 123.
monkey—if, at least, Tubal may be believed : a carelessness
of money which mitigates our dislike of the free hand Jessica
lays upon her father's ducats and jewels. On the whole,
however, Lorenzo's dreaminess makes a pretty contrast to
Jessica's vivacity. And Lorenzo's inactivity is capable of
being roused to great things. This is seen by the elopement
itself : for the suggestion of its incidents seems to be that esp. ii. iv.
Lorenzo meant at first no more than trifling with the pretty 20, 30 ; ii.
vi. 30, &c.
Jewess, and that he rose to the occasion as he found and
appreciated Jessica's higher tone and attraction. Finally,
we must see the calibre of Lorenzo's character through the

Jessica and Lorenzo a foil to Portia and Bassanio.

eyes of Portia, who selects him at first sight as the representative to whom to commit her household in her absence, of which commission she will take no refusal.

So interpreted the characters of Jessica and Lorenzo make the whole episode of the elopement an antithesis to the main plot. To a wedded couple in the fresh happiness of their union there can hardly fall a greater luxury than to further the happiness of another couple; this luxury is granted to Portia and Bassanio, and in their reception of the fugitives what picturesque contrasts are brought together! The two pairs are a foil to one another in kind, and set one another off like gold and gems. Lorenzo and Jessica are negative characters with the one positive quality of intense capacity for enjoyment; Bassanio and Portia have everything to enjoy, yet their natures appear dormant till roused by an occasion for daring and energy. The Jewess and her husband are distinguished by the bird-like simplicity that so often goes with special art-susceptibility; Portia and Bassanio are full and rounded characters in which the whole of human nature seems concentrated. The contrast is of degree as well as kind: the weaker pair brought side by side with the stronger throw out the impression of their strength. Portia has a fulness of power which puts her in her most natural position when she is extending protection to those who are less able to stand by themselves. Still more with Bassanio: he has so little scope in the scenes of the play itself, which from the nature of the stories present him always in situations of dependence on others, that we see his strength almost entirely by the reflected light of the attitude which others hold to him; in the present instance we have no difficulty in catching the intellectual power of Lorenzo, and Lorenzo looks up to Bassanio as a superior. And the couples thus contrasted in character present an equal likeness and unlikeness in their fortunes. Both are happy for ever, and both have become so through a bold stroke. Yet

in the one instance it is blind obedience, in face of all temptations, to the mere whims of a good parent, who is dead, that
has been guided to the one issue so passionately desired; in
the case of the other couple open rebellion, at every practical
risk, against the legitimate authority of an evil father, still
living, has brought them no worse fate than happiness in
one another, and for their defenceless position the best of
patrons.

It seems, then, that the introduction of the Jessica Story is
justified, not only by the purposes of construction which it
serves, but by the fact that its human interest is at once a
contrast and a supplement to the main story, with which
it blends to produce the ordered variety of a finished
picture.

A few words will be sufficient to point out how the effects *The Rings*
of the main plot are assisted by the Rings Episode, which, *Episode*
though rich in fun, is of a slighter character than the Jessica *mechanism*
Story, and occupies a much smaller space in the field of view. *of the main*
The dramatic points of the two minor stories are similar. *stories,*
Like the Jessica Story the Rings Episode assists the mechanical working out of the main plot. An explanation
must somehow be given to Bassanio that the lawyer is Portia
in disguise; mere mechanical explanations have always an
air of weakness, but the affair of the rings utilises the explanation in the present case as a source of new dramatic
effects. This arrangement further assists, to a certain extent,
in reducing the improbability of Portia's project. The point
at which the improbability would be most felt would be, not
the first appearance of the lawyer's clerk, for then we are
engrossed in our anxiety for Antonio, but when the explanation of the disguise came to be made; there might be
a danger lest here the surprise of Bassanio should become
infectious, and the audience should awake to the improbability of the whole story: as it is, their attention is at the
critical moment diverted to the perplexity of the penitent

husbands. The Story of the Rings, like that of Jessica, assists the interweaving of the two main stories with one another, *and their interweaving;* its subtlety suggesting to what a degree of detail this interlacing extends. Bassanio is the main point which unites the Story of the Jew and the Caskets Story; in the one he occupies the position of friend, in the other of husband. iv. i. 425-454. The affair of the rings, slight as it is, is so managed by Portia that its point becomes a test as between his friendship and his love; and so equal do these forces appear that, though his friendship finally wins and he surrenders his betrothal ring, yet it is not until after his wife has given him a hint against herself:

> And if your wife be not a mad-woman,
> And know how well I have deserved the ring,
> She would not hold out enemy for ever
> For giving it to me.

The Rings Episode, even more than the Jessica Story, assists in restoring the balance between the main tales. The chief inequality between them lies in the fact that the Jew Story is complicated and resolved, while the Caskets Story is a simple progress to a goal; when, however, there springs from the latter a sub-action which has a highly comic complication and resolution the two halves of the play become dramatically on a par. And the interweaving of the dark and bright elements in the play is assisted by the fact that the Episode of the Rings not only provides a comic reaction to relieve the tragic crisis, but its whole point is a Dramatic Irony in which serious and comic are inextricably mixed.

and assists in the development of Portia's character. Finally, as the Jessica Story ministers to Character effect in connection with the general ensemble of the personages, so the Episode of the Rings has a special function in bringing out the character of Portia. The secret of the charm which has won for Portia the suffrages of all readers is the perfect balance of qualities in her character: she is the meeting-point of brightness, force, and tenderness. And, to crown the

union, Shakespeare has placed her at the supreme moment of <small>CHAP. III.</small>
life, on the boundary line between girlhood and womanhood,
when the wider aims and deeper issues of maturity find
themselves in strange association with the abandon of youth.
The balance thus becomes so perfect that it quivers, and dips
to one side and the other.　Portia is the saucy child as she <small>i. ii. 39.</small>
sprinkles her sarcasms over Nerissa's enumeration of the
suitors: in the trial she faces the world of Venice as a
heroine.　She is the ideal maiden in the speech in which she <small>iii. ii. 150.</small>
surrenders herself to Bassanio : she is the ideal woman as
she proclaims from the judgment seat the divinity of mercy. <small>iv. i. 184.</small>
Now the fourth Act has kept before us too exclusively one
side of this character.　Not that Portia in the lawyer's gown
is masculine : but the dramatist has had to dwell too long on
her side of strength.　He will not dismiss us with this impression, but indulges us in one more daring feat surpassing
all the madcap frolics of the past.　Thus the Episode of the
Rings is the last flicker of girlhood in Portia before it merges
in the wider life of womanhood.　We have rejoiced in a great
deliverance wrought by a noble woman : our enjoyment rises
higher yet when the Rings Episode reminds us that this
woman has not ceased to be a sportive girl.

It has been shown, then, that the two inferior stories in
The Merchant of Venice assist the main stories in the most
varied manner, smoothing their mechanical working, meeting
their special difficulties, drawing their mutual interweaving
yet closer, and throwing their character effects into relief :
the additional complexity they have brought has resulted in
making emphatic points yet more prominent, and the total
effect has therefore been to increase clearness and simplicity.
Enough has now been said on the building up of dramas out
of stories, which is the distinguishing feature of the Romantic
Drama ; the studies that follow will be applied to the more
universal topics of dramatic interest, Character, Plot, and
Passion.

A PICTURE OF IDEAL VILLAINY IN
RICHARD III.

A Study in Character-Interpretation.

CHAP. IV.

Villainy as a subject for art-treatment.

I HOPE that the subject of the present study will not be considered by any reader forbidding. On the contrary, there is surely attractiveness in the thought that nothing is so repulsive or so uninteresting in the world of fact but in some way or other it may be brought under the dominion of art-beauty. The author of *L'Allegro* shows by the companion poem that he could find inspiration in a rainy morning; and the great master in English poetry is followed by a great master in English painting who wins his chief triumphs by his handling of fog and mist. Long. ago the masterpiece of Virgil consecrated agricultural toil; Murillo's pictures have taught us that there is a beauty in rags and dirt; rustic commonplaces gave a life passion to Wordsworth, and were the cause of a revolution in poetry; while Dickens has penetrated into the still less promising region of low London life, and cast a halo around the colourless routine of poverty. Men's evil passions have given Tragedy to art, crime is beautified by being linked to Nemesis, meanness is the natural source for brilliant comic effects, ugliness has reserved for it a special form of art in the grotesque, and pain becomes attractive in the light of the heroism that suffers and the devotion that watches. In the infancy of modern English poetry Drayton found a poetic side to topography and maps, and Phineas Fletcher idealised anatomy; while of the two

greatest imaginations belonging to the modern world Milton CHAP. IV.
produced his masterpiece in the delineation of a fiend, and
Dante in a picture of hell. The final triumph of good over
evil seems to have been already anticipated by art.

The portrait of Richard satisfies a first condition of ide- *The*
ality in the scale of the whole picture. The sphere in which he *villainy of*
Richard
is placed is not private life, but the world of history, in which *ideal in its*
moral responsibility is the highest : if, therefore, the quality *scale,*
of other villainies be as fine, here the issues are deeper. As *and in its*
another element of the ideal, the villainy of Richard is pre- *fulness of*
develop-
sented to us fully developed and complete. Often an artist *ment.*
of crime will rely—as notably in the portraiture of Tito
Melema—mainly on the succession of steps by which a character, starting from full possession of the reader's sympathies,
arrives by the most natural gradations at a height of evil which
shocks. In the present case all idea of growth is kept outside the field of this particular play; the opening soliloquy
announces a completed process :

> I am determined to prove a villain. i. i. 30.

What does appear of Richard's past, seen through the
favourable medium of a mother's description, only seems to
extend the completeness to earlier stages :

> A grievous burthen was thy birth to me : iv. iv. 167.
> Tetchy and wayward was thy infancy ;
> Thy school-days frightful, desperate, wild, and furious,
> Thy prime of manhood daring, bold, and venturous,
> Thy age confirm'd, proud, subtle, bloody, treacherous,
> More mild, but yet more harmful, kind in hatred.

So in the details of the play there is nowhere a note of the
hesitation that betrays tentative action. When even Buckingham is puzzled as to what can be done if Hastings should
resist, Richard answers :

> Chop off his head, man; somewhat we will do. iii. i. 193.

His choice is only between different modes of villainy, never
between villainy and honesty.

CHAP. IV.

It has no sufficient motive.

Othello:
i. iii. 392,
&c.

Lear: i. ii.
1–22.
Again, it is to be observed that there is no suggestion of impelling motive or other explanation for the villainy of Richard. He does not labour under any sense of personal injury, such as Iago felt in believing, however groundlessly, that his enemies had wronged him through his wife; or Edmund, whose soliloquies display him as conscious that his birth has made his whole life an injury. Nor have we in this case the morbid enjoyment of suffering which we associate with Mephistopheles, and which Dickens has worked up into one of his most powerful portraits in Quilp. Richard never turns aside to gloat over the agonies of his victims; it is not so much the details as the grand schemes of villainy, the handling of large combinations of crime, that have an interest for him: he is a strategist in villainy, not a tactician. Nor can we point to ambition as a sufficient motive. He is ambitious in a sense which belongs to all vigorous natures; he has the workman's impulse to rise by his work. But ambition as a determining force in character must imply more than this; it is a sort of moral dazzling, its symptom is a fascination by ends which blinds to the ruinous means leading up to these ends. Such an ambition was Macbeth's; but in Richard the symptoms are wanting, and in all his long soliloquies he is never found dwelling upon the prize in view. A nearer approach to an explanation would be Richard's sense of bodily deformity. Not only do all who come in contact with him shrink from the 'bottled spider,' but he

i. iii. 242,
228; iv. iv.
81, &c.
himself gives a conspicuous place in his meditations to the thought of his ugliness; from the outset he connects his criminal career with the reflection that he 'is not shaped for

i. i. 14.
sportive tricks':

> Deform'd, unfinish'd, sent before my time
> Into this breathing world, scarce half made up,
> And that so lamely and unfashionable
> That dogs bark at me as I halt by them;
> Why, I, in this weak piping time of peace,
> Have no delight to pass away the time,

Unless to spy my shadow in the sun
And descant on mine own deformity.

Still, it would be going too far to call this the motive of his crimes: the spirit of this and similar passages is more accurately expressed by saying that he has a morbid pleasure in contemplating physical ugliness analogous to his morbid pleasure in contemplating moral baseness. *esp. i. ii. 252–264.*

There appears, then, no sufficient explanation and motive for the villainy of Richard: the general impression conveyed is that to Richard villainy has become an end in itself needing no special motive. This is one of the simplest principles of human development—that a means to an end tends to become in time an end in itself. The miser who began accumulating to provide comforts for his old age finds the process itself of accumulating gain firmer and firmer hold upon him, until, when old age has come, he sticks to accumulating and foregoes comfort. So in previous plays Gloster may have been impelled by ambition to his crimes: by the time the present play is reached crime itself becomes to him the dearer of the two, and the ambitious end drops out of sight. This leads directly to one of the two main features of Shakespeare's portrait: Richard is an *artist in villainy*. What form and colour are to the painter, what rhythm and imagery are to the poet, that crime is to Richard: it is the medium in which his soul frames its conceptions of the beautiful. The gulf that separates between Shakespeare's Richard and the rest of humanity is no gross perversion of sentiment, nor the development of abnormal passions, nor a notable surrender in the struggle between interest and right. It is that he approaches villainy as a thing of pure intellect, a religion of moral indifference in which sentiment and passion have no place, attraction to which implies no more motive than the simplest impulse to exercise a native talent in its natural sphere. *Villainy has become to Richard an end in itself.* *compare 3 Henry VI: iii. ii. 165–181.* *Richard an artist in villainy.*

Of the various barriers that exist against crime, the most powerful are the checks that come from human emotions. It *Richard lacks the emotions*

is easier for a criminal to resist the objections his reason
interposes to evildoing than to overcome these emotional
restraints: either his own emotions, woven by generations of
hereditary transmission into the very framework of his
nature, which make his hand tremble in the act of sinning;
or the emotions his crimes excite in others, such as will
cause hardened wretches, who can die calmly on the scaffold,
to cower before the menaces of a mob. Crime becomes
possible only because these emotions can be counteracted by
more powerful emotions on the other side, by greed, by thirst
for vengeance, by inflamed hatred. In Richard, however,
when he is surveying his works, we find no such evil emotions
raised, no gratified vengeance or triumphant hatred. The
reason is that there is in him no restraining emotion to be
overcome. Horror at the unnatural is not subdued, but
absent; his attitude to atrocity is the passionless attitude of
the artist who recognises that the tyrant's cruelty can be set

i. ii.   to as good music as the martyr's heroism. Readers are
shocked at the scene in which Richard wooes Lady Anne
beside the bier of the parent he has murdered, and wonder
that so perfect an intriguer should not choose a more favourable time. But the repugnance of the reader has no place in
Richard's feelings: the circumstances of the scene are so
many *objections*, to be met by so much skill of treatment. A
single detail in the play illustrates perfectly this neutral attitude to horror. Tyrrel comes to bring the news of the
princes' murder; Richard answers:

iv. iii. 31.   Come to me, Tyrrel, soon at after supper,
And thou shalt tell the process of their death.

Quilp could not have waited for his gloating till after supper;
other villains would have put the deed out of sight when done;
the epicure in villainy reserves his *bonbouche* till he has leisure
to do it justice. Callous to his own emotions, he is equally
callous to the emotions he rouses in others. When Queen
Margaret is pouring a flood of curses which make the inno-

cent courtiers' hair stand on end, and the heaviest curse of CHAP. IV.
all, which she has reserved for Richard himself, is rolling on
to its climax,

i. iii. 216–
239.

> Thou slander of thy mother's heavy womb!
> Thou loathed issue of thy father's loins!
> Thou rag of honour! thou detested—

he adroitly slips in the word 'Margaret' in place of the
intended 'Richard,' and thus, with the coolness of a schoolboy's small joke, disconcerts her tragic passion in a way that
gives a moral wrench to the whole scene. His own mother's iv. iv, from
136.
curse moves him not even to anger; he caps its clauses with
bantering repartees, until he seizes an opportunity for a pun,
and begins to move off: he treats her curse, as in a previous
scene he had treated her blessing, with a sort of gentle im- ii. ii. 109.
patience as if tired of a fond yet somewhat troublesome
parent. Finally, there is an instinct which serves as resultant
to all the complex forces, emotional or rational, which sway
us between right and wrong; this instinct of conscience is
formally disavowed by Richard :

> Conscience is but a word that cowards use, v. iii. 309.
> Devised at first to keep the strong in awe.

But, if the natural heat of emotion is wanting, there is, on *But he regards
villainy
with the
intellectual
enthusiasm
of the
artist.*
i. iii, from
324.
the other hand, the full intellectual warmth of an artist's
enthusiasm, whenever Richard turns to survey the game he is
playing. He reflects with a relish how he does the wrong
and first begins the brawl, how he sets secret mischief
abroach and charges it on to others, beweeping his own
victims to simple gulls, and, when these begin to cry for
vengeance, quoting Scripture against returning evil for evil,
and thus seeming a saint when most he plays the devil. The
great master is known by his appreciation of details, in the
least of which he can see the play of great principles : so the
magnificence of Richard's villainy does not make him in-
sensible to commonplaces of crime. When in the long

CHAP. IV. usurpation conspiracy there is a moment's breathing space
———   just before the Lord Mayor enters, Richard and Buckingham
iii. v. 1-11. utilise it for a burst of hilarity over the deep hypocrisy with
which they are playing their parts; how they can counterfeit
the deep tragedian, murder their breath in the middle of a
world, tremble and start at wagging of a straw:—here we
have the musician's flourish upon his instrument from very
wantonness of skill.   Again:

i. i. 118.
> Simple, plain Clarence! I do love thee so
> That I will shortly send thy soul to heaven—

is the composer's pleasure at hitting upon a readily workable
theme.   Richard appreciates his murderers as a workman
appreciates good tools:

i. iii. 354.
> Your eyes drop millstones, when fools' eyes drop tears:
> I like you, lads.

i. ii, from   And at the conclusion of the scene with Lady Anne we have
228.   the artist's enjoyment of his own masterpiece:

> Was ever woman in this humour woo'd?
> Was ever woman in this humour won? . . .
> What! I, that kill'd her husband and his father,
> To take her in her heart's extremest hate,
> With curses in her mouth, tears in her eyes,
> The bleeding witness of her hatred by;
> Having God, her conscience, and these bars against me,
> And I nothing to back my suit at all,
> But the plain devil and dissembling looks,
> And yet to win her, all the world to nothing!

The tone in this passage is of the highest: it is the tone of a
musician fresh from a triumph of his art, the sweetest point
in which has been that he has condescended to no adven-
titious aids, no assistance of patronage or concessions to
popular tastes; it has been won by pure music.   So the artist
in villainy celebrates a triumph of *plain devil !*

The   This view of Richard as an artist in crime is sufficient to
villainy   explain the hold which villainy has on Richard himself; but
ideal in

ideal villainy must be ideal also in its success; and on this Chap. IV.
side of the analysis another conception in Shakespeare's
portraiture becomes of first importance. It is obvious enough *success: a*
that Richard has all the elements of success which can be *fascination*
reduced to the form of skill: but he has something more. *of irresistibility in
Richard.*
No theory of human action will be complete which does not
recognise a dominion of will over will operating by mere contact, without further explanation so far as conscious influence
is concerned. What is it that takes the bird into the jaws of
the serpent? No persuasion or other influence on the bird's
consciousness, for it struggles to keep back; we can only
recognise the attraction as a force, and give it a name,
fascination. In Richard there is a similar fascination of
irresistibility, which also operates by his mere presence, and
which fights for him in the same way in which the idea of
their invincibility fought for conquerors like Napoleon, and
was on occasions as good to them as an extra twenty or thirty
thousand men. A consideration like this will be appreciated
in the case of *tours de force* like the Wooing of Lady Anne,
which is a stumblingblock to many readers—a widow beside
the bier of her murdered husband's murdered father wooed
and won by the man who makes no secret that he is the
murderer of them both. The analysis of ordinary human
motives would make it appear that Anne would not yield at
points at which the scene represents her as yielding; some
other force is wanted to explain her surrender, and it is found
in this secret force of irresistible will which Richard bears about
with him. But, it will be asked, in what does this fascination
appear? The answer is that the idea of it is furnished to us
by the other scenes of the play. Such a consideration illustrates the distinction between real and ideal. An ideal incident is not an incident of real life simply clothed in beauty of
expression; nor, on the other hand, is an ideal incident
divorced from the laws of real possibility. Ideal implies that
the transcendental has been made possible by treatment: that

——

an incident (for example) which might be impossible in itself
becomes possible through other incidents with which it is associated, just as in actual life the action of a public personage
which may have appeared strange at the time becomes
intelligible when at his death we can review his life as a
whole. Such a scene as the Wooing Scene might be impossible as a fragment; it becomes possible enough in the
play, where it has to be taken in connection with the rest of
the plot, throughout which the irresistibility of the hero is
prominent as one of the chief threads of connection. Nor is
it any objection that the Wooing Scene comes early in the
action. The play is not the book, but the actor's interpretation on the stage, and the actor will have collected even from
the latest scenes elements of the interpretation he throws
into the earliest: the actor is a lens for concentrating the
light of the whole play upon every single detail. The fascination of irresistibility, then, which is to act by instinct in
every scene, may be arrived at analytically when we survey
the play as a whole—when we see how by Richard's
innate genius, by the reversal in him of the ordinary relation
of human nature to crime, especially by his perfect mastery of the successive situations as they arise, the dramatist steadily builds up an irresistibility which becomes
a secret force clinging to Richard's presence, and through
the operation of which his feats are half accomplished by
the fact of his attempting them.

*The fasci-
nation is to
be conveyed
in the
acting.*

To begin with: the sense of irresistible power is brought
out by the way in which the unlikeliest things are continually drawn into his schemes and utilised as means. Not
to speak of his regular affectation of blunt sincerity, he
makes use of the simple brotherly confidence of Clarence as
an engine of fraticide, and founds on the frank familiarity existing between himself and Hastings a plot by
which he brings him to the block. The Queen's compunction at the thought of leaving Clarence out of the

*The irre-
sistibility
analysed.
Unlikely
means.*

i. i, from
42.
iii. iv; esp.
76 com-
pared with
iii. i. 184.

general reconciliation around the dying king's bedside is the CHAP. IV.
fruit of a conscience tenderer than her neighbours' : Richard
adroitly seizes it as an opportunity for shifting on to the ii. i, from
73; cf. 134.
Queen and her friends the suspicion of the duke's murder.
The childish prattle of little York Richard manages to sug- iii. i. 154.
gest to the bystanders as dangerous treason; the solemnity
of the king's deathbed he turns to his own purposes by out- ii. i. 52–72.
doing all the rest in Christian forgiveness and humility; and
he selects devout meditation as the card to play with the iii. v. 99,
Lord Mayor and citizens. On the other hand, amongst &c.
other devices for the usurpation conspiracy, he starts a
slander upon his own mother's purity; and further—by one iii. v. 75–
of the greatest strokes in the whole play—makes capital 94.
in the Wooing Scene out of his own heartlessness, de- i. ii. 156–
scribing in a burst of startling eloquence the scenes of 167.
horror he has passed through, the only man unmoved to
tears, in order to add :

> And what these sorrows could not thence exhale,
> Thy beauty hath, and made them blind with weeping.

There are things which are too sacred for villainy to touch,
and there are things which are protected by their own foulness : both alike are made useful by Richard.

Similarly it is to be noticed how Richard can utilise the *The sensa-*
very sensation produced by one crime as a means to bring *tion pro-*
duced by
about more ; as when he interrupts the King's dying moments *one crime*
to announce the death of Clarence in such a connection as *made to*
bring about
must give a shock to the most unconcerned spectator, and *others.*
then draws attention to the pale faces of the Queen's friends ii. i, from
as marks of guilt. He thus makes one crime beget another 77 ; cf. 134.
without further effort on his part, reversing the natural law
by which each criminal act, through its drawing more suspicion to the villain, tends to limit his power for further
mischief. It is to the same purpose that Richard chooses *Richard's*
sometimes instead of acting himself to foist his own schemes *own plans*
foisted on
on to others ; as when he inspires Buckingham with the *to others.*

CHAP. IV.　idea of the young king's arrest, and, when Buckingham
seizes the idea as his own, meekly accepts it from him :

ii. ii. 112–
154 ; esp.
149.

> I, like a child, will go by thy direction.

There is in all this a dreadful *economy* of crime : not the
economy of prudence seeking to reduce its amount, but the
artist's economy which delights in bringing the largest
number of effects out of a single device.　Such skill opens
up a vista of evil which is boundless.

No signs of　The sense of irresistible power is again brought out by his
effort in
Richard :　perfect imperturbability of mind : villainy never ruffles his
imperturb-　spirits.　He never misses the irony that starts up in the
ability of
mind ;　circumstances around him, and says to Clarence :

i. i. 111.

> This deep disgrace in brotherhood
> *Touches* me deeply.

While taking his part in entertaining the precocious King
he treats us to continual asides—

iii. i. 79,
94.

> So wise so young, they say, do never live long—

showing how he can stop to criticise the scenes in which
he is an actor.　He can delay the conspiracy on which his
iii. iv. 24.　chance of the crown depends by coming late to the council,
and then while waiting the moment for turning upon his
iii. iv. 52.　victim is cool enough to recollect the Bishop of Ely's straw-
humour ;　berries.　But more than all these examples is to be noted
Richard's *humour*.　This is *par excellence* the sign of a
mind at ease with itself : scorn, contempt, bitter jest belong
to the storm of passion, but humour is the sunshine of the
soul.　Yet Shakespeare has ventured to endow Richard
with unquestionable humour.　Thus, in one of his earliest
i. i. 151–　meditations, he prays, ' God take King Edward to his
156.　mercy,' for then he will marry Warwick's youngest daughter :

> What though I killed her husband and her father !
> The readiest way to make the wench amends
> Is to become her husband and her father !

e. g. i. i.　And all through there perpetually occur little turns of lan-
118 ; ii. ii.

26998

guage into which the actor can throw a tone of humorous CHAP. IV.
enjoyment; notably, when he complains of being 'too
childish-foolish for this world,' and where he nearly ruins the
effect of his edifying penitence in the Reconciliation Scene,
by being unable to resist one final stroke :

109; iv. iii.
38, 43; i.
iii. 142; ii.
i. 72; iii.
vii. 51-54,
&c.

> I thank my God for my humility!

Of a kindred nature is his perfect frankness and fairness to *freedom*
his victims: villainy never clouds his judgment. Iago, *from pre-judice.*
astutest of intriguers, was deceived, as has been already
noted, by his own morbid acuteness, and firmly believed—
what the simplest spectator can see to be a delusion—that
Othello has tampered with his wife. Richard, on the contrary, is a marvel of judicial impartiality; he speaks of King
Edward in such terms as these—

> If King Edward be as true and just i. i. 36.
> As I am subtle, false and treacherous;

and weighs elaborately the superior merit of one of his
victims to his own :

> Hath she forgot already that brave prince, i. ii, from
> Edward, her lord, whom I, some three months since, 240.
> Stabb'd in my angry mood at Tewksbury?
> A sweeter and a lovelier gentleman,
> Framed in the prodigality of nature,
> Young, valiant, wise, and, no doubt, right royal,
> The spacious world cannot again afford :
> And will she yet debase her eyes on me,
> That cropped the golden prime of this sweet prince,
> And made her widow to a woful bed?
> On me, whose all not equals Edward's moiety?

Richard can rise to all his height of villainy without its
leaving on himself the slightest trace of struggle or even
effort.

Again, the idea of boundless resource is suggested by an *A reckless-ness sug-*
occasional recklessness, almost a slovenliness, in the details *gesting*
of his intrigues. Thus, in the early part of the Wooing *boundless resources.*

Scene he makes two blunders of which a tyro in intrigue might be ashamed.   He denies that he is the author of Edward's death, to be instantly confronted with the evidence of Margaret as an eye-witness.   Then a few lines further on he goes to the opposite extreme :

> *Anne.* Didst thou not kill this king?
> *Glouc.*   I grant ye.
> *Anne.* Dost grant me, hedgehog?

The merest beginner would know better how to meet accusations than by such haphazard denials and acknowledgments.   But the crack billiard-player will indulge at the beginning of the game in a little clumsiness, giving his adversaries a prospect of victory only to have the pleasure of making up the disadvantage with one or two brilliant strokes.   And so Richard, essaying the most difficult problem ever attempted in human intercourse, lets half the interview pass before he feels it worth while to play with caution.

General character of Richard's intrigue: inspiration rather than calculation.   The mysterious irresistibility of Richard, pointed to by the succession of incidents in the play, is assisted by the very improbability of some of the more difficult scenes in which he is an actor.   Intrigue in general is a thing of reason, and its probabilities can be readily analysed ; but the genius of intrigue in Richard seems to make him avoid the caution of other intriguers, and to give him a preference for feats which seem impossible.   The whole suggests how it is not by calculation that he works, but he brings the *touch* of an artist to his dealing with human weakness, and follows whither his artist's inspiration leads him.   If, then, there is nothing so remote from evil but Richard can make it tributary ; if he can endow crimes with power of self-multiplying ; if he can pass through a career of sin without the taint of distortion on his intellect and with the unruffled calmness of innocence ; if Richard accomplishes feats no other would attempt with a carelessness no other reputation would risk, even slow reason may well believe him irresistible.   When,

further, such qualifications for villainy become, by unbroken CHAP. IV.
success in villainy, reflected in Richard's very bearing ; when
the only law explaining his motions to onlookers is the law-
lessness of genius whose instinct is more unerring than the
most laborious calculation and planning, it becomes only
natural that the *opinion* of his irresistibility should become
converted into a mystic *fascination*, making Richard's very
presence a signal to his adversaries of defeat, chilling with
hopelessness the energies with which they are to face his
consummate skill.

The two main ideas of Shakespeare's portrait, the idea of
an artist in crime and the fascination of invincibility which
Richard bears about with him, are strikingly illustrated in
the wooing of Lady Anne. For a long time Richard will not i. ii.
put forth effort, but meets the loathing and execration hurled
at him with repartee, saying in so many words that he regards
the scene as a ' keen encounter of our wits.' All this time 115.
the mysterious power of his presence is operating, the more
strongly as Lady Anne sees the most unanswerable cause
that denunciation ever had to put produce no effect upon
her adversary, and feels her own confidence in her wrongs
recoiling upon herself. When the spell has had time to from 152.
work then he assumes a serious tone : suddenly, as we have
seen, turning the strong point of Anne's attack, his own
inhuman nature, into the basis of his plea—he who never
wept before has been softened by love to her. From this
point he urges his cause with breathless speed ; he presses a 175.
sword into her hand with which to pierce his breast, knowing
that she lacks the nerve to wield it, and seeing how such
forbearance on her part will be a starting-point in giving
way. We can trace the sinking of her will before the un-
conquerable will of her adversary in her feebler and feebler from 193.
refusals, while as yet very shame keeps her to an outward
defiance. Then, when she is wishing to yield, he suddenly
finds her an excuse by declaring that all he desires at this

moment is that she should leave the care of the King's funeral

> To him that hath more cause to be a mourner.

By yielding this much to penitence and religion we see she has commenced a downward descent from which she will never recover.   Such consummate art in the handling of human nature, backed by the spell of an irresistible presence, the weak Anne has no power to combat.   To the last *iv.* i. 66– she is as much lost in amazement as the reader at the way 87.   it has all come about :

> Lo, ere I can repeat this curse again,
> Even in so short a space, my woman's heart
> Grossly grew captive to his honey words.

Ideal v. *real villainy.*

To gather up our results.   A dramatist is to paint a portrait of ideal villainy as distinct from villainy in real life.   In real life it is a commonplace that a virtuous life is a life of effort ; but the converse is not true, that he who is prepared to be a villain will therefore lead an easy life.   On the contrary, 'the *way* of transgressors is hard.'   The metaphor suggests a path, laid down at first by the Architect of the universe, beaten plain and flat by the generations of men who have since trodden it : he who keeps within this path of rectitude will walk, not without effort, yet at least with safety ; but he who 'steps aside' to the right or left will find his way beset with pitfalls and stumblingblocks.   In real life a man sets out to be a villain, but his mental power is deficient, and he remains a villain only in intention.   Or he has stores of power, but lacks the spark of purpose to set them aflame.   Or, armed with both will to plan and mind to execute, yet his efforts are hampered by unfit tools.   Or, if his purpose needs reliance alone on his own clear head and his own strong arm, yet in the critical moment the emotional nature he has inherited with his humanity starts into rebellion and scares him, like Macbeth, from the half-

accomplished deed. Or, if he is as hardened in nature as
corrupt in mind and will, yet he is closely pursued by a
mocking fate, which crowns his well-laid plans with a mysterious succession of failures. Or, if there is no other
limitation on him from within or from without, yet he may
move in a world too narrow to give him scope : the man
with a heart to be the scourge of his nation proves in fact
no more than the vagabond of a country side.—But in
Shakespeare's portrait we have infinite capacity for mischief,
needing no purpose, for evil has become to it an end in
itself; we have one who for tools can use the baseness of his
own nature or the shame of those who are his nearest kin,
while at his touch all that is holiest becomes transformed
into weapons of iniquity. We have one whose nature in the
past has been a gleaning ground for evil in every stage of
his development, and who in the present is framed to look
on unnatural horror with the eyes of interested curiosity.
We have one who seems to be seconded by fate with a
series of successes, which builds up for him an irresistibility
that is his strongest safeguard ; and who, instead of being
cramped by circumstances, has for his stage the world of
history itself, in which crowns are the prize and nations the
victims. In such a portrait is any element wanting to arrive
at the ideal of villainy ?

The question would rather be whether Shakespeare has *Ideal*
not gone too far, and, passing outside the limits of art, ex- *villainy*
v. mon-
hibited a monstrosity. Nor is it an answer to point to the *strosity.*
'dramatic hedging' by which Richard is endowed with un-
daunted personal courage, unlimited intellectual power, and
every good quality not inconsistent with his perfect villainy.
The objection to such a portrait as the present study presents
is that it offends against our sense of the principles upon which
the universe has been constructed ; we feel that before a
violation of nature could attain such proportions nature must
have exerted her recuperative force to crush it. If, however,

the dramatist can suggest that such reassertion of nature is actually made, that the crushing blow is delayed only while it is accumulating force : in a word, if the dramatist can draw out before us a *Nemesis* as ideal as the villainy was ideal, then the full demands of art will be satisfied. The Nemesis that dominates the whole play of *Richard III* will be the subject of the next study.

RICHARD III: HOW SHAKESPEARE WEAVES NEMESIS INTO HISTORY.

A Study in Plot.

I HAVE alluded already to the dangerous tendency, which, as it appears to me, exists amongst ordinary readers of Shakespeare, to ignore plot as of secondary importance, and to look for Shakespeare's greatness mainly in his conceptions of character. But the full character effect of a dramatic portrait cannot be grasped if it be dissociated from the plot; and this is nowhere more powerfully illustrated than in the play of *Richard III.* The last study was devoted exclusively to the Character side of the play, and on this confined view the portrait of Richard seemed a huge offence against our sense of moral equilibrium, rendering artistic satisfaction impossible. Such an impression vanishes when, as in the present study, the drama is looked at from the side of Plot. The effect of this plot is, however, missed by those who limit their attention in reviewing it to Richard himself. These may feel that there is nothing in his fate to compensate for the spectacle of his crimes: man

must die, and a death in fulness of energy amid the glorious stir of battle may seem a fate to be envied. But the Shakespearean Drama with its complexity of plot is not limited to the individual life and fate in its interpretation of history; and when we survey all the distinct trains of interest in the play of *Richard III*, with their blendings and mutual influence, we shall obtain a sense of dramatic satisfaction

Chap. V. amply counterbalancing the monstrosity of Richard's villainy. Viewed as a study in character the play leaves in us only an intense craving for Nemesis : when we turn to consider the plot, this presents to us the world of history transformed into an intricate design of which the recurrent pattern is Nemesis.

The under-plot: a set of separate Nemesis Actions. This notion of tracing a pattern in human affairs is a convenient key to the exposition of plot. Laying aside for the present the main interest of Richard himself, we may observe that the bulk of the drama consists in a number of minor interests—single threads of the pattern—each of

Clarence. which is a separate example of Nemesis. The first of these trains of interest centres around the Duke of Clarence. He has betrayed the Lancastrians, to whom he had solemnly sworn

i. iv. 50, 66. fealty, for the sake of the house of York; this perjury is his bitterest recollection in his hour of awakened conscience, and is urged home by the taunts of his murderers ; while his only defence is that he did it all for his brother's love. Yet his

ii. i. 86. lot is to fall by a treacherous death, the warrant for which is signed by his brother, the King and head of the Yorkist house,

i. iv. 250. while its execution is procured by the bulwark of the house,

The King. the intriguing Richard. The centre of the second nemesis is the King, who has thus allowed himself in a moment of suspicion to be made a tool for the murder of his brother,

ii. i. 77–133. seeking to stop it when too late. Shakespeare has contrived that this death of Clarence, announced as it is in so terrible a manner beside the King's sick bed, gives him a shock from which he never rallies, and he is carried out to die with the words on his lips :

> O God, I fear Thy justice will take hold
> On me, and you, and mine, and yours, for this.

The Queen and her kindred. In this nemesis on the King are associated the Queen and her kindred. They have been assenting parties to the measures against Clarence (however little they may have contemplated the bloody issue to which those measures have

been brought by the intrigues of Gloster). This we must CHAP. V.
understand from the introduction of Clarence's children, ii. ii. 62–
who serve no purpose except to taunt the Queen in her 65
bereavement :

> *Boy.* Good aunt, you wept not for our father's death ;
>   How can we aid you with our kindred tears ?
> *Girl.* Our fatherless distress was left unmoan'd ;
>   Your widow-dolour likewise be unwept !

The death of the King, so unexpectedly linked to that of
Clarence, removes from the Queen and her kindred the sole ii. ii. 74,
bulwark to the hated Woodville family, and leaves them at &c.
the mercy of their enemies. A third Nemesis Action has *Hastings.*
Hastings for its subject. Hastings is the head of the court- i. i. 66 ; iii.
faction which is opposed to the Queen and her allies, and he ii. 58, &c.
passes all bounds of decency in his exultation at the fate
which overwhelms his adversaries :

> But I shall laugh at this a twelvemonth hence,
> That they who brought me in my master's hate,
> I live to look upon their tragedy.

He even forgets his dignity as a nobleman, and stops on his
way to the Tower to chat with a mere officer of the court, in iii. ii. 97.
order to tell him the news of which he is full, that his
enemies are to die that day at Pomfret. Yet this very
journey of Hastings is his journey to the block ; the same
cruel fate which had descended upon his opponents, from
the same agent and by the same unscrupulous doom, is dealt
out to Hastings in his turn. In this treacherous casting off *Bucking-*
of Hastings when he is no longer useful, Buckingham has *ham.*
been a prime agent. Buckingham amused himself with the iii. ii, from
false security of Hastings, adding to Hastings's innocent 114.
expression of his intention to stay dinner at the Tower the
aside

> And supper too, although thou know'st it not ;

while in the details of the judicial murder he plays second to
Richard. By precisely similar treachery he is himself cast

off when he hesitates to go further with Richard's villainous
schemes ; and in precisely similar manner the treachery is
flavoured with contempt.

> *Buck.* I am thus bold to put your grace in mind
>   Of what you promised me.
> *K. Rich.*   Well, but what 's o'clock ?
> *Buck.* Upon the stroke of ten.
> *K. Rich.*   Well, let it strike.
> *Buck.* Why let it strike ?
> *K. Rich.* Because that, like a Jack, thou keep'st the stroke
>   Betwixt thy begging and my meditation.
>   I am not in the giving vein to-day.
> *Buck.* Why, then resolve me whether you will or no.
> *K. Rich.* Tut, tut,
>   Thou troublest me ; I am not in the vein.
>   [*Exeunt all but Buckingham.*
> *Buck.* Is it even so ? rewards he my true service
>   With such deep contempt ? made I him king for this ?
>   O, let me think on Hastings, and be gone
>   To Brecknock, while my fearful head is on !

*The four
nemeses
formed into
a system by
Nemesis as
a link.*

These four Nemesis Actions, it will be observed, are not
separate trains of incident going on side by side, they are
linked together into a system, the law of which is seen to be
that those who triumph in one nemesis become the victims
of the next ; so that the whole suggests a 'chain of destruction,' like that binding together the orders of the brute
creation which live by preying upon one another. When
Clarence perished it was the King who dealt the doom and
the Queen's party who triumphed : the wheel of Nemesis goes
round and the King's death follows the death of his victim,
the Queen's kindred are naked to the vengeance of their
enemies, and Hastings is left to exult. Again the wheel of
Nemesis revolves, and Hastings at the moment of his highest
exultation is hurled to destruction, while Buckingham stands
by to point the moral with a gibe. Once more the wheel
goes round, and Buckingham hears similar gibes addressed
to himself and points the same moral in his own person.
Thus the portion of the drama we have so far considered

yields us a pattern within a pattern, a series of Nemesis *Chap. v.* Actions woven into a complete underplot by a connecting-link which is also Nemesis.

Following out the same general idea we may proceed to *The 'En-* notice how the dramatic pattern is surrounded by a fringe or *veloping Action' a* border. The picture of life presented in a play will have the *Nemesis.* more reality if it be connected with a life wider than its own. There is no social sphere, however private, but is to some extent affected by a wider life outside it, this by one wider still, until the great world is reached the story of which is History. The immediate interest may be in a single family, but it will be a great war which, perhaps, takes away some member of this family to die in battle, or some great commercial crisis which brings mutation of fortune to the obscure home. The artists of fiction are solicitous thus to suggest connections between lesser and greater; it is the natural tendency of the mind to pass from the known to the unknown, and if the artist can derive the movements in his little world from the great world outside, he appears to have given his fiction a basis of admitted truth to rest on. This device of enclosing the incidents of the actual story in a framework of great events—technically, the 'Enveloping Action' —is one which is common in Shakespeare; it is enough to instance such a case as *A Midsummer Night's Dream*, in which play a fairy story has a measure of historic reality given to it by its connection with the marriage of personages so famous as Theseus and Hippolyta. In the present case, the main incidents and personages belong to public life; nevertheless the effect in question is still secured, and the contest of factions with which the play is occupied is represented as making up only a few incidents in the great feud of Lancaster and York. This Enveloping Action of the whole play, the War of the Roses, is marked with special clearness: two personages are introduced for the sole purpose of giving it prominence. The Duchess of York is by her years and **ii.** ii. 80.

CHAP. V. position the representative of the whole house; the factions
———   who in the play successively triumph and fall are all descended from herself; she says:

> Alas, I am the mother of these moans!
> Their woes are parcell'd, mine are general.

i. iii, from   And probabilities are forced to bring in Queen Margaret,
111 ; and   the head and sole rallying-point of the ruined Lancastrians:
iv. iv. 1–
125.   when the two aged women are confronted the whole civil
war is epitomised.   It is hardly necessary to point out that
this Enveloping Action is itself a Nemesis Action.   All the
rising and falling, the suffering and retaliation that we
actually see going on between the different sections of the
Yorkist house, constitute a detail in a wider retribution: the
esp. ii. ii ;   presence of the Duchess gives to the incidents a unity, Queen
iv.i;iv.iv.   Margaret's function is to point out that this unity of woe is
ii. iii; and   only the nemesis falling on the house of York for their
iv. iv.   wrongs to the house of Lancaster.   Thus the pattern made
up of so many reiterations of Nemesis is enclosed in a
border which itself repeats the same figure.

The En-   The effect is carried further.   Generally the Enveloping
veloping   Action is a sort of curtain by which our view of a drama is
Nemesis
carried on   bounded; in the present case the curtain is at one point
into indefi-   lifted, and we get a glimpse into the world beyond.   Queen
niteness.   Margaret has surprised the Yorkist courtiers, and her prophetic denunciations are still ringing, in which she points to
the calamities her foes have begun to suffer as retribution for
the woes of which her fallen greatness is the representative
i. iii. 174–   —when Gloster suddenly turns the tables upon her:
194.

> The curse my noble father laid on thee,
> When thou didst crown his warlike brows with paper
> And with thy scorns drew'st rivers from his eyes,
> And then, to dry them, gavest the duke a clout
> Steep'd in the faultless blood of pretty Rutland,—
> His curses, then from bitterness of soul
> Denounced against thee, are all fall'n upon thee;
> And God, not we, hath plagu'd thy bloody deed.

And the new key-note struck by Gloster is taken up in CHAP. V.
chorus by the rest, who find relief from the crushing effect of
Margaret's curses by pressing the charge home upon her.
This is only a detail, but it is enough to carry the effect of
the Enveloping Action a degree further back in time : the
events of the play are nemesis on York for wrongs done to
Lancaster, but now, it seems, these old wrongs against
Lancaster were retribution for yet older crimes Lancaster had
committed against York. As in architecture the vista is
contrived so as to carry the general design of the building
into indefiniteness, so here, while the grand nemesis, of
which Margaret's presence is the representative, shuts in the
play like a veil, the momentary lifting of the veil opens up a
vista of nemeses receding further and further back into
history.

Once more. All that we have seen suggests it as a sort *The one*
of law to the feud of York and Lancaster that each is *attempt to*
reverse the
destined to wreak vengeance on the other, and then itself *nemesis*
suffer in turn. But at one notable point of the play an *confirms it.*
i. ii.
attempt is made to evade the hereditary nemesis by the
marriage of Richard and Lady Anne. Anne, daughter to
Warwick—the grand deserter to the Lancastrians and martyr
to their cause—widow to the murdered heir of the house
and chief mourner to its murdered head, is surely the
greatest sufferer of the Lancastrians at the hands of the
Yorkists. Richard is certainly the chief avenger of York
upon Lancaster. When the chief source of vengeance and
the chief sufferer are united in the closest of all bonds, the
attempt to evade Nemesis becomes ideal. Yet what is the
consequence? This attempt of Lady Anne to evade the
hereditary curse proves the very channel by which the curse
descends upon herself. We see her once more : she is then iv. i. 66–
on her way to the Tower, and we hear her tell the strange 87.
story of her wooing, and wish the crown were ' red hot steel
to sear her to the brain '; never, she says, since her union

CHAP. V.   with Richard has she enjoyed the golden dew of sleep ; she is
————   but waiting for the destruction, by which, no doubt, Richard
will shortly rid himself of her.

*To counter-   An objection may, however, here present itself, that con-
act the
effect of re-*   tinual repetition of an idea like Nemesis, tends to weaken its
petition the artistic effect, until it comes to be taken for granted.   No
*nemeses are
specially*   doubt it is a law of taste that force may be dissipated by
empha-   repetition if carried beyond a certain point.   But it is to be
sised :   noted, on the other hand, what pains Shakespeare has taken
to counteract the tendency in the present instance.   The
force of a nemesis may depend upon a fitness that addresses
itself to the spectator's reflection, or it may be measured by
the degree to which the nemesis is brought into prominence
in the incidents themselves.   In the incidents of the present
by recog-   play special means are adopted to make the recognition of
nition,   the successive nemeses as they arise emphatic.   In the first
place the nemesis is in each case pointed out at the moment
of its fulfilment.   In the case of Clarence his story of crime
i. iv, from   and retribution is reflected in his dream before it is brought
18.   to a conclusion in reality ; and wherein the bitterness of this
review consists, we see when he turns to his sympathising
jailor and says :

i. iv. 66.   O Brackenbury, I have done those things,
Which now bear evidence against my soul,
For Edward's sake : and see how he requites me !

The words have already been quoted in which the King recognises how God's justice has overtaken him for his part in
Clarence's death, and those in which the children of Clarence
taunt the Queen with her having herself to bear the bereavement she has made them suffer.   As the Queen's kindred are
being led to their death, one of them exclaims :

iii. iii. 15.   Now Margaret's curse is fall'n upon our heads
For standing by when Richard stabb'd her son.

Hastings, when his doom has wakened him from his infatuation, recollects a priest he had met on his way to the

Tower, with whom he had stopped to talk about the dis- CHAP. V.
comfiture of his enemies :

> O, now I want the priest that spake to me! iii. iv. 89.

Buckingham on his way to the scaffold apostrophises the
souls of his victims :

> If that your moody discontented souls v. i. 7.
> Do through the clouds behold this present hour,
> Even for revenge mock my destruction.

And such individual notes of recognition are collected into a
sort of chorus when Margaret appears the second time to iv. iv. 1, 35.
point out the fulfilment of her curses, and sits down beside
the old Duchess and her daughter-in-law to join in the
'society of sorrow' and 'cloy her' with beholding the revenge for which she has hungered.

Again, the nemeses have a further emphasis given to *by pro-*
them by prophecy. As Queen Margaret's second appear- *phecy,*
ance is to mark the fulfilment of a general retribution, so her i. iii, from
first appearance denounced it beforehand in the form of 195.
curses. And the effect is carried on in individual prophecies : the Queen's friends as they suffer foresee that the
turn of the opposite party will come :

> You live that shall cry woe for this hereafter ; iii. iii. 7.

and Hastings prophesies Buckingham's doom :

> They smile at me that shortly shall be dead. iii. iv. 109.

It is as if the atmosphere cleared for each sufferer with the
approach of death, and they then saw clearly the righteous
plan on which the universe is constructed, and which had
been hidden from them by the dust of life.

But there is a third means, more powerful than either re- *and especi-*
cognition or prophecy, which Shakespeare has employed to *ally by*
make his Nemesis Actions emphatic. The danger of an effect *irony.*
becoming tame by repetition he has met by giving to each
train of nemesis a flash of irony at some point of its course.
In the case of Lady Anne we have already seen how the
exact channel Nemesis chooses by which to descend upon

CHAP. V.   her is the attempt she made to avert it.   She had bitterly
cursed her husband's murderer :

iv. i. 75.
> And be thy wife—if any be so mad—
> As miserable by the life of thee
> As thou hast made me by my dear lord's death !

In spite of this she had yielded to Richard's mysterious
power, and so, as she feels, proved the *subject of her own
heart's curse.*   Again, it was noticed in the preceding study
how the Queen, less hard than the rest in that wicked court,
or perhaps softened by the spectacle of her dying husband,
essayed to reverse, when too late, what had been done
against Clarence ; Gloster skilfully turned this compunction
ii. i. 134.   of conscience into a ground of suspicion on which he traded
to bring all the Queen's friends to the block, and thus a
moment's relenting was made into a means of destruction.
In Clarence's struggle for life, as one after another the
i. iv. 187,   threads of hope snap, as the appeal to law is met by the
199, 200,   King's command, the appeal to heavenly law by the re-
206.   minder of his own sin, he comes to rest for his last and surest
i. iv. 232.   hope upon his powerful brother Gloster—and the very murderers catch the irony of the scene :

> *Clar.* If you be hired for meed, go back again,
>   And I will send you to my brother Gloster,
>   Who shall reward you better for my life
>   Than Edward will for tidings of my death.
> *Sec. Murd.* You are deceived, your brother Gloster hates you.
> *Clar.* O, no, he loves me, and he holds me dear :
>   Go you to him from me.
> *Both.*   Ay, so we will.
> *Clar.* Tell him, when that our princely father York
>   Bless'd his three sons with his victorious arm,
>   And charg'd us from his soul to love each other,
>   He little thought of this divided friendship :
>   Bid Gloster think of this, and he will weep.
> *First Murd.* Ay, millstones ; as he lesson'd us to weep.
> *Clar.* O, do not slander him, for he is kind.
> *First Murd.*   Right,
>   As snow in harvest. Thou deceivest thyself :
>   'Tis he that sent us hither now to slaughter thee.

> *Clar.*   It cannot be; for when I parted with him,
> He hugg'd me in his arms, and swore, with sobs,
> That he would labour my delivery.
> *Sec. Murd.*   Why, so he doth, now he delivers thee
> From this world's thraldom to the joys of heaven.

In the King's case a special incident is introduced into the
scene to point the irony.   Before Edward can well realise
the terrible announcement of Clarence's death, the decorum
of the royal chamber is interrupted by Derby, who bursts
in, anxious not to lose the portion of the king's life that yet
remains, in order to beg a pardon for his follower.   The
King feels the shock of contrast: ii. i. 95.

> Have I a tongue to doom my brother's death,
> And shall the same give pardon to a slave?

The prerogative of mercy that exists in so extreme a case as
the murder of a ' righteous gentleman,' and is so passionately
sought by Derby for a servant, is denied to the King himself
for the deliverance of his innocent brother.   The nemesis
on Hastings is saturated with irony; he has the simplest
reliance on Richard and on ' his servant Catesby,' who has
come to him as the agent of Richard's treachery; and the
very words of the scene have a double significance that all
see but Hastings himself. iii. ii, from 41.

> *Hast.*   I tell thee Catesby,—
> *Cate.*   What, my lord?
> *Hast.*   Ere a fortnight make me elder
> I'll send some packing that yet think not on it.
> *Cate.*   'Tis a vile thing to die, my gracious lord,
> When men are unprepared, and look not for it.
> *Hast.*   O monstrous, monstrous! and so falls it out
> With Rivers, Vaughan, Grey: and so 'twill do
> With some men else, who think themselves as safe
> As thou and I.

As the scenes with Margaret constituted a general summary
of the individual prophecies and recognitions, so the Reconciliation Scene around the King's dying bed may be said to
gather into a sort of summary the irony distributed through ii. i.

the play; for the effect of the incident is that the different
parties pray for their own destruction. In this scene Buckingham has taken the lead and struck the most solemn notes
in his pledge of amity; when Buckingham comes to die, his
bitterest thought seems to be that the day of his death is All

Souls' Day.

> *This is the day* that, in King Edward's time,
> I wish'd might fall on me, when I was found
> False to his children or his wife's allies;
> This is the day wherein I wish'd to fall
> By the false faith of him I trusted most; . . . .
> That high All-Seer that I dallied with
> Hath turn'd my feigned prayer on my head
> And given in earnest what I begg'd in jest.

By devices, then, such as these; by the sudden revelation of
a remedy when it is just too late to use it; by the sudden
memory of clear warnings blindly missed; by the spectacle
of a leaning for hope upon that which is known to be ground
for despair; by attempts to retreat or turn aside proving
short cuts to destruction; above all by the sufferer's perception
that he himself has had a chief share in bringing about his
doom:—by such irony the monotony of Nemesis is relieved,
and fatality becomes flavoured with mockery.

*This multi-
plication of
Nemesis
a dramatic
background
for the
villainy of
Richard.* Dramatic design, like design which appeals more directly
to the eye, has its perspective: to miss even by a little the
point of view from which it is to be contemplated is enough
to throw the whole into distortion. So readers who are not
careful to watch the harmony between Character and Plot
have often found in the present play nothing but wearisome
repetition. Or, as there is only a step between the sublime
and the ridiculous, this masterpiece of Shakespearean plot
has suggested to them only the idea of Melodrama,—that
curious product of dramatic feeling without dramatic inven-
tiveness, with its world in which poetic justice has become
prosaic, in which conspiracy is never so superhumanly secret
but there comes a still more superhuman detection, and how-

ever successful villainy may be for a moment the spectator
confidently relies on its being eventually disposed of by a
summary ' off with his head.'   The point of view thus missed
in the present play is that this network of Nemesis is all
needed to give dramatic reality to the colossal villainy of the
principal figure.   When isolated, the character of Richard is
unrealisable from its offence against an innate sense of retribution.   Accordingly Shakespeare projects it into a world
of which, in whatever direction we look, retribution is the sole
visible pattern ; in which, as we are carried along by the
movement of the play, the unvarying reiteration of Nemesis
has the effect of *giving rhythm to fate.*

What the action of the play has yielded so far to our in-   *The motive*
vestigation has been independent of the central personage :   *force of the*
whole play
we have now to connect Richard himself with the plot.   *is another*
Although the various Nemesis Actions have been carried on   *nemesis :*
the Life
by their own motion and by the force of retribution as a   *and Death*
principle of moral government, yet there is not one of them   *of Richard.*
which reaches its goal without at some point of its course
receiving an impetus from contact with Richard.   Richard
is thus the source of movement to the whole drama, commu-
nicating his own energy through all parts.   It is only fitting
that the motive force to this system of nemeses should be
itself a grand Nemesis Action, the *Life and Death*, or crime
and retribution, *of Richard III.*   The hero's rise has been
sufficiently treated in the preceding study ; it remains to trace
his fall.

This fall of Richard is constructed on Shakespeare's   *The fall of*
favourite plan ; its force is measured, not by suddenness and   *Richard :*
not a shock
violence, but by protraction and the perception of distinct   *but a suc-*
stages—the crescendo in music as distinguished from the   *cession of*
stages.
fortissimo.   Such a fall is not a mere passage through the air
—one shock and then all is over—but a slipping down the
face of the precipice, with desperate clingings and consciously increasing impetus : its effect is the one inexhaust-

ible emotion of suspense. If we examine the point at which
the fall begins we are reminded that the nemesis on Richard
Not a is different in its type from the others in the play.   These
nemesis of
equality but are (like that on Shylock) of the *equality* type, of which the
of sureness. motto is measure for measure : and, with his usual exactness,
Shakespeare gives us a turning-point in the precise centre
iii. iii. 15. of the play, where, as the Queen's kindred are being borne
to their death, we get the first recognition that the general
retribution denounced by Margaret has begun to work.   But
the turning-point of Richard's fate is reserved till long past
the centre of the play ; his is the nemesis of *sureness*, in
which the blow is delayed that it may accumulate force.
Not that this turning-point is reserved to the very end ; the
The turn- change of fortune appears just when Richard has *com-*
ing-point :
irony of its *mitted himself* to his final crime in the usurpation—the
delay. murder of the children—the crime from which his most
iv. ii. from unscrupulous accomplice has drawn back.   The effect of
46.
this arrangement is to make the numerous crimes which
follow appear to come by necessity ; he is 'so far in blood
that sin will pluck on sin ' ; he is forced to go on heaping up
his villainies with Nemesis full in his view.   This turning-
point appears in the simple announcement that ' Dorset has
fled to Richmond.'   There is an instantaneous change in
Richard to an attitude of defence, which is maintained to the
end.   His first instinct is action : but as soon as we have
heard the rapid scheme of measures—most of them crimes—
by which he prepares to meet his dangers, then he can give
from 98. himself up to meditation ; and we now begin to catch the
significance of what has been announced.   The name of
Richmond has been just heard for the first time in this play.
But as Richard meditates we learn how Henry VI prophesied that Richmond should be a king while he was but a
peevish boy.   Again, Richard recollects how lately, while
viewing a castle in the west, the mayor, who showed him
over it, mispronounced its name as ' Richmond '—and he had

started, for a bard of Ireland had told him he should not
live long after he had seen Richmond. Thus the irony that
has given point to all the other retributions in the play is
not wanting in the chief retribution of all : Shakespeare
compensates for so long keeping the grand nemesis out
of sight by thus representing Richard as gradually realising
that *the finger of Nemesis has been pointing at him all his life
and he has never seen it !*

From this point fate never ceases to tantalise and mock *Tantalis-*
Richard. He engages in his measures of defence, and with *ing mock-*
their villainy his spirits begin to recover : *ery in Rich-*
ard's fate.

> The sons of Edward sleep in Abraham's bosom, **iv.** iii. 38.
> And Anne my wife hath bid the world good night ;

young Elizabeth is to be his next victim, and

> To her I go, a jolly thriving wooer.

Suddenly the Nemesis appears again with the news that comp. 49.
Ely, the shrewd bishop he dreads most of all men, is with **iv.** iii. 45.
Richmond, and that Buckingham has raised an army.
Again, his defence is completing, and the wooing of Elizabeth—his masterpiece, since it is the second of its kind—has
been brought to an issue that deserves his surprised exultation :

> Relenting fool, and shallow, changing woman ! **iv.** iv. 431.

Suddenly the Nemesis again interrupts him, and this time is
nearer : a puissant navy has actually appeared on the west.
And now his equanimity begins at last to be disturbed. He *His equa-*
storms at Catesby for not starting, forgetting that he has *nimity af-*
fected.
given him no message to take. More than this, a little **iv.** iv. 444.
further on *Richard changes his mind!* Through the rest of 540.
the long scene destiny is openly playing with him, giving
him just enough hope to keep the sense of despair warm.
Messenger follows messenger in hot haste : Richmond is on
the seas—Courtenay has risen in Devonshire—the Guild-
fords are up in Kent.—But Buckingham's army is dis-

CHAP. V. persed.—But Yorkshire has risen.—But, a gleam of hope, the Breton navy is dispersed—a triumph, Buckingham is taken.—Then, finally, Richmond has landed! The suspense is telling upon Richard. In this scene he strikes a messenger before he has time to learn that he brings good tidings.

v. iii. 2, 5, When we next see him he wears a false gaiety and scolds
8, &c.
his followers into cheerfulness; but with the gaiety go sudden fits of depression:

> Here will I lie to-night;
> But where to-morrow?

v. iii, from A little later he becomes nervous, and we have the minute
47.
attention to details of the man who feels that his all depends upon one cast; he will not sup, but calls for ink and paper to plan the morrow's fight, he examines carefully as to his beaver and his armour, selects White Surrey to ride, and at last calls for wine and *confesses* a change in himself:

> I have not that alacrity of spirit,
> Nor cheer of mind, that I was wont to have.

Climax of Then comes night, and with it the full tide of Nemesis.
Richard's
fate: signi- By the device of the apparitions the long accumulation of
ficance of crimes in Richard's rise are made to have each its due re-
the appari-
tions. presentation in his fall. It matters not that they are only
v. iii, from apparitions. Nemesis itself is the ghost of sin: its sting lies
118.
not in the physical force of the blow, but in the close *con-nection* between a sin and its retribution. So Richard's victims rise from the dead only to secure that the weight of each several crime shall lie heavy on his soul in the morrow's doom. This point moreover must not be missed—that the

Signifi- climax of his fate comes to Richard in his *sleep*. The
cance of
Richard's supreme conception of resistance to Deity is reached when
sleep. God is opposed by God's greatest gift, the freedom of the will. God, so it is reasoned, is omnipotent, but God has made man omnipotent in setting no bounds to his will; and God's omnipotence to punish may be met by man's omni-potence to endure. Such is the ancient conception of Pro-

metheus, and such are the reasonings Milton has imagined CHAP. V.
for his Satan: to whom, though heaven be lost,

> All is not lost, the unconquerable will . . .
> And courage never to submit or yield.

But when that strange bundle of greatness and littleness
which makes up man attempts to oppose with such weapons
the Almighty, how is he to provide for those states in which
the will is no longer the governing force in his nature ; for
the sickness, in which the mind may have to share the
feebleness of the body, or for the daily suspension of will in
sleep ?   Richard can to the last preserve his will from faltering.   But, like all the rest of mankind, he must some time
sleep : that which is the refuge of the honest man, when he
may relax the tension of daily care, sleep, is to Richard his
point of weakness, when the safeguard of invincible will can
protect him no longer.   It is, then, this weak moment which
a mocking fate chooses for hurling upon Richard the whole
avalanche of his doom ; as he starts into the frenzy of his
half-waking soliloquy we see him, as it were, tearing off
layer after layer of artificial reasonings with which the will-
struggles of a lifetime have covered his soul against the touch
of natural remorse.   With full waking his will is as strong
as ever : but meanwhile his physical nature has been shattered to its depths, and it is only the wreck of Richard that
goes to meet his death on Bosworth field.

There is no need to dwell on the further stages of the *Remaining*
fall : to the last the tantalising mockery continues.   Richard's *stages of the fall.*
spirits rise with the ordering of the battle, and there comes *v.* iii. 303.
the mysterious scroll to tell him he is bought and sold.   His
spirits rise again as the fight commences, and news comes of *v.* iii. 342.
Stanley's long-feared desertion.   Five times in the battle he
has slain his foe, and five times it proves a false Richmond. *v.* iv. 11.
Thus slowly the cup is drained to its last dregs and Richard
dies.   The play opened with the picture of peace, the peace *i,* i, from 1.
which led Richard's turbid soul, no longer finding scope in

CHAP. V. physical warfare, to turn to the moral war of villainy ; from
          that point through all the crowded incidents has raged the
          tumultuous battle between Will and Nemesis; with Richard's
          death it ceases, and the play may return to its keynote :

v. v. 40.   Now civil wounds are stopp'd, peace lives again.

VI.

How Nemesis and Destiny are inter-woven in Macbeth.

A further Study in Plot.

CHAP. VI.

THE present study, like the last, is a study in Plot. The last illustrated Shakespeare's grandeur of conception, how a single principle is held firm amidst the intricacies of history, and reiterated in every detail. The present purpose is to give an example of Shakespeare's *subtlety*, and to exhibit the incidents of a play bound together not by one, but by three, distinct threads of connection—or, if a technical term may be permitted, three Forms of Dramatic Action—all working harmoniously together into a design equally involved and symmetrical. One of these forms is Nemesis; the other two are borrowed from the ancient Drama: it thus becomes necessary to digress for a moment, in order to notice certain differences between the ancient and modern Drama, and between the ancient and modern thought of which the Drama is the expression.

Macbeth as a study of subtlety in Plot.

Its three-fold action.

In the ancient Classical Drama the main moral idea under-lying its action is the idea of Destiny. The ancient world recognised Deity, but their deities were not supreme in the universe; Zeus had gained his position by a revolution, and in his turn was to be overthrown by revolution; there was thus, in ancient conception, behind Deity a yet higher force to which Deity itself was subject. The supreme force of the universe has by a school of modern thought been de-fined as a stream of tendency in things not ourselves making

In the passage from ancient to modern, Destiny changes into Providence.

for righteousness: if we attempt to adapt this formula to the ideas of antiquity the difficulty will be in finding anything to substitute for the word 'righteousness.' Sometimes the sum of forces in the universe did seem, in the conception of the ancients, to make for righteousness, and Justice became the highest law. At other times the world seemed to them governed by a supernatural Jealousy, and human prosperity was struck down for no reason except that it was prosperity. In such philosophy as that of Lucretius, again, the tendency of all things was towards Destruction; while in the handling of legends such as that of Hippolytus there is a suggestion of a dark interest to ancient thought in conceiving Evil itself as an irresistible force. It appears, then, that the ancient mind had caught the idea of *force* in the universe, without adding to it the further idea of a motive by which that force was guided: *blind* fate was the governing power over all other powers. With this simple conception of force as ruling the world, modern thought has united as a motive righteousness or law: the transition from ancient to modern thought may be fairly described by saying that Destiny has become changed into Providence as the supreme force of the uni-

The change reflected in ancient and modern Nemesis. verse. The change may be well illustrated by comparing the ancient and modern conception of Nemesis. To ancient thought Nemesis was simply one phase of Destiny; the story of Polycrates has been quoted in a former study to illustrate how Nemesis appeared to the Greek mind as capricious a deity as Fortune, a force that might at any time, heedless of desert, check whatever happiness was high enough to attract its attention. But in modern ideas Nemesis and justice are strictly associated: Nemesis may be defined as the artistic side of justice.

So far as Nemesis then is concerned, it has, in modern thought, passed altogether out of the domain of Destiny and been absorbed into the domain of law: it is thus fitted to be one of the regular forms into which human history may be

represented as falling, in harmony with our modern moral CHAP. VI.
conceptions. But even as regards Destiny itself, while the
notion as a whole is out of harmony with the modern notion
of law and Providence as ruling forces of the world, yet
certain minor phases of Destiny as conceived by antiquity
have survived into modern times and been found not irre- *Nemesis*
concilable with moral law. Two of these minor phases of *and Des-*
tiny in-
Destiny are, it will be shown, illustrated in *Macbeth*: and *terwoven*
we may thus take as a general description of its plot, the *in the plot*
of Macbeth.
interweaving of Destiny with Nemesis.

That the career of Macbeth is an example of Nemesis *The whole*
needs only to be stated. As in the case of *Richard III*, we *plot a*
Nemesis
have the rise and fall of a leading personage; the rise is a *Action.*
crime of which the fall is the retribution. Nemesis has just
been defined as the artistic aspect of justice; we have in
previous studies seen different artistic elements in different
types of Nemesis. Sometimes, as with Richard III, the
retribution becomes artistic through its sureness; its long
delay renders the effect of the blow more striking when it
does come. More commonly the artistic element in Nemesis *of the type*
consists in the perfect equality between the sin and its retri- *of equality.*
bution; and of the latter type the Nemesis in the play of
Macbeth is perhaps the most conspicuous illustration. The
rise and fall of Macbeth, to borrow the illustration of
Gervinus, constitute a perfect arch, with a turning-point in
the centre. Macbeth's series of successes is unbroken till it
ends in the murder of Banquo; his series of failures is unbroken from its commencement in the escape of Fleance.
Success thus constituting the first half and failure the second
half of the play, the transition from the one to the other is
the expedition against Banquo and Fleance, in which success
and failure are mingled: and this expedition, the keystone to
the arch, is found to occupy the exact middle of the middle **iii.** iii.
Act.

But this is not all: not only is the play as a whole an

CHAP. VI. example of nemesis, but if its two halves be taken sepa-

The rise of Macbeth a separate Nemesis action.

rately they will be found to constitute each a nemesis complete in itself.   To begin with the first half, that which is
occupied with the rise of Macbeth.   If the plan of the play
extended no further than to make the hero's fall the retribution upon his rise, it might be expected that the turning-
point of the action would be reached upon Macbeth's
elevation to the throne.   As a fact, however, Macbeth's rise
does not stop here; he still goes on to win one more success
in his attempt upon the life of Banquo.   What the purpose of
this prolonged flow of fortune is will be seen when it is considered that this final success of the hero is in reality the
source of his ruin.   In Macbeth's progress to the attainment
of the crown, while of course it was impossible that crimes so
violent as his should not incur suspicion, yet circumstances
had strangely combined to soothe these suspicions to sleep.
But—so Shakespeare manipulates the story—when Macbeth,
seated on the throne, goes on to the attempt against Banquo,
this additional crime not only brings its own punishment, but
has the further effect of unmasking the crimes that have gone
before.   This important point in the plot is brought out to us
in a scene, specially introduced for the purpose, in which
Lennox and another lord represent the opinion of the
court.

iii. vi. 1.   *Lennox.* My former speeches have but hit your thoughts,
                     Which can interpret further: only, I say,
                     Things have been strangely borne.   The gracious Duncan
                     Was pitied of Macbeth: marry, he was dead:
                     And the right-valiant Banquo walk'd too late;
                     Whom, you may say, if't please you, Fleance kill'd,
                     For Fleance fled: men must not walk too late.
                     Who cannot want the thought how monstrous
                     It was for Malcolm and for Donalbain
                     To kill their gracious father? damned fact!
                     How it did grieve Macbeth! did he not straight
                     In pious rage the two delinquents tear,
                     That were the slaves of drink and thralls of sleep?

Was not that nobly done? Ay, and wisely too;
For 'twould have anger'd any heart alive
To hear the men deny 't. So that, I say,
He has borne all things well: and I do think
That had he Duncan's sons under his key—
As, an 't please heaven, he shall not—they should find
What 'twere to kill a father; so should Fleance.

Under the bitter irony of this speech we can see clearly
enough that Macbeth has been exposed by his *series* of
suspicious acts; he has 'done all things well'; and in
particular by peculiar resemblances between this last incident
of Banquo and Fleance and the previous incident of Duncan
and his son. It appears then that Macbeth's last successful
crime proves the means by which retribution overtakes all his
other crimes; the latter half of the play is needed to develop
the steps of the retribution, but, in substance, Macbeth's fall
is latent in the final step of his rise. Thus the first half of
the play, that which traces the rise of Macbeth, is a complete
Nemesis Action—a career of sins in which the last sin secures
the punishment of all.

The same reasoning applies to the latter half of the play: *The fall of Macbeth a separate Nemesis Action.*
the fall of Macbeth not only serves as the retribution for his
rise, but further contains in itself a crime and its nemesis
complete. What Banquo is to the first half of the play
Macduff is to the latter half; the two balance one another as,
in the play of *Julius Cæsar*, Cæsar himself is balanced by
Antony; and Macduff comes into prominence upon Banquo's
death as Antony upon the fall of Cæsar. Now Macduff, when
he finally slays Macbeth, is avenging not only Scotland, but
also his own wrongs; and the tyrant's crime against Macduff,
with its retribution, just gives unity to the second half of the
play, in the way in which the first half was made complete by
the association between Macbeth and Banquo, from their joint
encounter with the Witches on to the murder of Banquo as *iii. i. 57-*
a consequence of the Witches' prediction. Accordingly we *72.*
find that no sooner has Macbeth, by the appearance of the

CHAP. VI. Ghost at the banquet, realised the turn of fate, than his first
—— thoughts are of Macduff:

iii. iv. 128. *Macbeth.* How say'st thou, that Macduff denies his person
At our great bidding?
Lady M. Did you send to him, sir?
Macbeth. I hear it by the way; but I will send.

When the Apparitions bid Macbeth 'beware Macduff,' he answers,

iv. i. 74. Thou hast harp'd my fear aright!

iv. i, from On the vanishing of the Apparition Scene, the first thing that
139. happens is the arrival of news that Macduff has fled to
England, and is out of his enemy's power; then Macbeth's
bloody thoughts devise a still more cruel purpose of vengeance
to be taken on the fugitive's family.

> Time, thou anticipatest my dread exploits:
> The flighty purpose never is o'ertook
> Unless the deed go with it . . . .
> The castle of Macduff I will surprise;
> Seize upon Fife; give to the edge o' the sword
> His wife, his babes, and all unfortunate souls
> That trace him in his line.

iv. ii, iii. In succeeding scenes we have this diabolical massacre carried
out, and see the effect which the news of it has in rousing
v. vii. 15. Macduff to his revenge; until in the final scene of all he feels
that if Macbeth is slain and by no stroke of his, his wife and
children's ghosts will for ever haunt him. Thus Macduff's
function in the play is to be the agent not only of the grand
nemesis which constitutes the whole plot, but also of a
nemesis upon a private wrong which occupies the latter half
of the play. And, putting our results together, we find that
a Nemesis Action is the description alike of the whole plot
and of the rise and fall which are its two halves.

The Oracu- With Nemesis is associated in the play of *Macbeth* Destiny
lar as one in two distinct phases. The first of these is *the Oracular.* In
phase of ancient thought, as Destiny was the supreme governor of the
Destiny: universe, so oracles were the revelation of Destiny; and thus
its partial
revelation.

the term 'the Oracles of God' is appropriately applied to CHAP. VI.
the Bible as the Christian revelation. With the advent of ——
Christianity the oracles became dumb. But the triumph of
Christianity was for centuries incomplete; heathen deities
were not extirpated, but subordinated to the supernatural
personages of the new religion; and the old oracles declined *A minor*
into oracular beings such as witches and wizards, and *form of the*
Oracular
oracular superstitions, such as magic mirrors, dreams, appa- *in modern*
ritions—all means of dimly revealing hidden destiny. Shake- *oracular*
beings.
speare is never wiser than the age he is pourtraying; and
accordingly he has freely introduced witches and apparitions
into the machinery of *Macbeth*, though in the principles that
govern the action of this, as of all his other plays, he is true
to the modern notions of Providence and moral law. An *The Oracu-*
lar Action:
oracle and its fulfilment make up a series of events eminently *Destiny*
fitted to constitute a dramatic interest; and no form of *working*
ancient Drama and Story is more common than this of the *from*
mystery to
'Oracular Action.' Its interest may be formulated as Destiny *clearness:*
working from mystery to clearness. At the commencement
of an oracular story the fated future is revealed indeed, but
in a dress of mystery, as when the Athenians are bidden to
defend themselves with only wooden walls; but as the story
of Themistocles develops itself, the drift of events is throwing
more and more light on to the hidden meaning of the oracle,
until by the naval victory over the Persians the oracle is at
once clear and fulfilled.

The Oracular Action is so important an element in plot,
that it may be worth while to prolong the consideration of it
by noting the three principal varieties into which it falls, all
of which are illustrated in the play of *Macbeth*. In each case
the interest consists in tracing the working of Destiny out of
mystery into clearness: the distinction between the varieties
depends upon the agency by which Destiny works, and the (1) *by the*
agency of
relation of this agency to the original oracle. In the first *blind obedi-*
variety Destiny is fulfilled by the agency of blind obedience. *ence;*

The Spartans, unfortunate in their war with the Messenians, enquire of an oracle, and receive the strange response that they must apply for a general to the Athenians, their hereditary enemies. But they resolve to obey the voice of Destiny, though to all appearance they obey at their peril; and the Athenians mock them by selecting the most unfit subject they can find—a man whose bodily infirmities had excluded him from the military exercises altogether. Yet in the end the faith of the Spartans is rewarded. It had been no lack of generalship that had caused their former defeats, but discord and faction in their ranks; now Tyrtæus turned out to be a lyric poet, whose songs roused the spirit of the Spartans and united them as one man, and when united, their native military talent led them to victory. Thus in its fulfilment the hidden meaning of the oracle breaks out into clearness: and blind obedience to the oracle is the agency by which it has been fulfilled.

(2) by the agency of free will; In the second variety the oracle is fulfilled by the agency of indifference and free will: it is neither obeyed nor disobeyed, but ignored. One of the best illustrations is to be found in the plot of Sir Walter Scott's novel, *The Betrothed.* Its heroine, more rational than her age, resists the family tradition that would condemn her to sleep in the haunted chamber; overborne, however, by age and authority, she consents, and the lady of the bloody finger appears to pronounce her doom:

> Widow'd wife, and wedded maid;
> Betrothed, Betrayer, and Betrayed.

This seems a mysterious destiny for a simple and virtuous girl. The faithful attendant Rose declares in a burst of devotion that betrayed her mistress may be, but betrayer never; the heroine herself braces her will to dismiss the foreboding from her thoughts, and resolves that she will not be influenced by it on the one side or on the other. Yet it all comes about. Gratitude compels her to give her hand to the elderly

Constable, who on the very day of betrothal is summoned Chap. VI.
away to the Crusade, from which, as it appears, he is never to
return, leaving his spouse at once a widowed wife and a
wedded maid. In the troubles of that long absence, by a
perfectly natural series of events, gratitude again leads the
heroine to admit to her castle her real deliverer and lover in
order to save his life, and in protecting him amidst strange
circumstances of suspicion to bid defiance to all comers.
Finally the castle is besieged by the royal armies, and the
heroine has to hear herself proclaimed a traitor by the herald
of England; from this perplexity a deliverance is found only
when her best friend saves her by betraying the castle to the
king. So every detail in the unnatural doom has been in the
most natural manner fulfilled : and the woman by whose
action it has been fulfilled has been all the while maintaining
the freedom of her will and persistently ignoring the oracle.

But the supreme interest of the Oracular Action is reached (3) *by the*
when the oracle is fulfilled by an agency that has all the *agency of*
opposing
while set itself to oppose and frustrate it. A simple illustra- *will.*
tion of this is seen in the Eastern potentate who, in opposition
to a prophecy that his son should be killed by a lion, forbad
the son to hunt, but heaped upon him every other indulgence.
In particular he built him a pleasure-house, hung with
pictures of hunting and of wild beasts, on which all that art
could do was lavished to compensate for the loss of the for-
bidden sport. One day the son, chafing at his absence from
the manly exercise in which his comrades were at that
moment engaged, wandered through his pleasure-house, until,
stopping at a magnificent picture of a lion at bay, he began
to apostrophise it as the source of his disgrace, and waxing
still more angry, drove his fist through the picture. A nail,
hidden behind the canvas, entered his hand; the wound
festered, and he died. So the measures taken to frustrate the
destiny proved the means of fulfilling it. But in this third
variety of the Oracular Action the classical illustration is the

CHAP. VI. story of Œdipus : told fully, it presents three examples woven
———   together. Laius of Thebes learns from an oracle that the son
about to be born to him is destined to be his murderer ;
accordingly he refuses to rear the child, and it is cast out to
perish. A herdsman rescues the infant, and afterwards disposes of it surreptitiously to the childless wife of Polybus,
king of Corinth, keeping the secret of its birth. In due
time this Œdipus seeks advice of the oracle as to his future
career, and receives the startling response that he is destined
to slay his own father. Resolved to frustrate so terrible a
fate, he will not return to Corinth, but, as it happens, *takes
the road to Thebes*, where he falls in accidentally with Laius,
and, in ignorance of his person, quarrels with him and slays
him. Now if Laius had not resisted the oracle by casting
out the infant, it would have grown up like other sons, and
every probability would have been against his committing
so terrible a crime as parricide. Again, if the herdsman had
not, by sending the child out of the country, sought to bar him
against a chance of the dreadful fate prophesied for him,
he would have known the person of Laius and spared him.
Once more, if Œdipus had not, in opposition to the oracle,
avoided his supposed home, Corinth, he would never have
gone to Thebes and fallen in with his real father. Three
different persons acting separately seek to frustrate a declared
destiny, and their action unites in fulfilling it.

The plot of *Macbeth*, both as a whole and in its separate
parts, is constructed upon this form of the Oracular Action,
in combination with the form of Nemesis. The play deals
with the rise and fall of Macbeth : the rise, and the fall, and
again the two taken together, present each of them an

The rise of example of an Oracular Action. ˊ Firstly, the former half of
Macbeth an the play, the rise of Macbeth, taken by itself, consists in an
Oracular
Action,   oracle and its fulfilment—the Witches' promise of the crown
and the gradual steps by which the crown is attained.
Amongst the three varieties of the Oracular Action we have

just distinguished, the present example wavers between the
first and the second. After his first excitement has passed
away, Macbeth resolves that he will have nothing to do with
the temptation that lurked in the Witches' words ; in his
disjointed meditation we hear him saying :

> If chance will have me king, why chance may crown me   i. iii. 143.
> Without my stir ;

and again :

> Come what come may,   i. iii. 146.
> Time and the hour runs through the roughest day ;

in which last speech the very rhyming may, according to
Shakespeare's subtle usage, be pointed to as marking a mind
made up. So far then we appear to be following an Oracular
Action of the second type, that of indifference and ignoring.
But in the very next scene the proclamation of a Prince of
Cumberland—that is, of an heir-apparent like our Prince of
Wales—takes away Macbeth's ' chance ' :

> *Macb.* [*Aside*]. The prince of Cumberland! that is a step   i. iv. 48.
> On which I must fall down, or else o'erleap,
> For in my way it lies.

He instantly commits himself to the evil suggestion, and thus
changes the type of action to the first variety, that in which
the oracle is fulfilled by the agency of obedience.

Similarly Macbeth's fall, taken by itself, constitutes an
Oracular Action, consisting as it does of the ironical promises
given by the Apparitions which the Witches raise for Macbeth
on his visit to them, and the course of events by which these
promises are fulfilled. Its type is a highly interesting
example of the first variety, that of blind obedience. The
responses of the Apparitions lay down impossible conditions,
and as long as these conditions are unfulfilled Macbeth is to
be secure ; he will fall only when one not born of woman
shall be his adversary, only when Birnam Wood shall come
to Dunsinane. Macbeth trusts blindly to these promises ;
further he obeys them, so far as a man can be said to obey

an oracle which enjoins no command : he obeys in the sense of relying on them, and making that reliance his ground of action. But this reliance of Macbeth on the ironical promises is an agency in fulfilling them in their real mean-

iv. i. 144–156.
ing. In his reckless confidence he strikes out right and left, and amongst others injures one to whom the description 'not born of woman' applies. In his reliance on the Apparitions he proceeds, when threatened by the English, to *shut himself up in Dunsinane Castle* ; but for this fact the English army would not have approached Dunsinane Castle by the route of Birnam Wood, and the incident of the boughs would never have taken place. Thus Macbeth's fate was made to depend upon impossibilities : by his action in reliance on these impossibilities he is all the while giving them occasion to become possible. In this way an ironical oracle comes to be fulfilled by the agency of blind obedience.

The whole plot an Oracular Action of the third type.
Thirdly, the rise and fall of Macbeth are so linked together as to constitute the whole plot another example of the Oracular Action. The original oracle given by the Witches on the blasted heath was a double oracle : besides the promise of the thaneships and the crown there was another revelation

i. iii. 48–50, 62–66.
of destiny, that Banquo was to be lesser than Macbeth and yet greater, that he was to get kings though to be none. In this latter half of the oracle is found the link which binds together the rise and fall of Macbeth. When the first half of the Witches' promise has been fulfilled in his elevation to the throne, Macbeth sets himself to prevent the fulfilment of the second half by his attempt upon Banquo and Fleance. Now we have already seen how this attempt has the effect of drawing attention, not only to itself, but also to Macbeth's other crimes, and proves indeed the foundation of his ruin. Had Macbeth been content with the attainment of the crown, all might yet have been well : the addition of just one more precaution renders all the rest vain. It appears, then, that that

which binds together the rise and the fall, that which makes CHAP. VI.
the fall the retribution upon the rise, is the expedition against ——
the Banquo family; and the object of this crime is to
frustrate the second part of the Witches' oracle. So the
original oracle becomes the motive force to the whole play,
setting in motion alike the rise and fall of the action. The
figure of the whole plot we have taken as a regular arch; its
movement might be compared to that terrible incident of
mining life known as 'overwinding,' in which the steam engine
pulls the heavy cage from the bottom to the top of the shaft,
but, instead of stopping then, winds on till the cage is carried
over the pulley and dashed down again to the bottom. So
the force of the Witches' prediction is not exhausted when it
has tempted Macbeth on to the throne, but carries him on to
resist its further clauses, and in resisting to bring about the
fall by which they are fulfilled. Not only then are the rise
and the fall of Macbeth taken separately oracular, but the whole
plot, compounded of the two taken together, constitutes
another Oracular Action; and the last is of that type in which
Destiny is fulfilled by the agency of a will that has been
opposing it.

A second phase of Destiny enters into the plot of *Macbeth*: *Irony a*
this is Irony. Etymologically the word means no more than *phase of*
saying. Pressing the idea of saying as distinguished from *Destiny.* *malignant*
meaning we get at the ordinary signification, ambiguous
speech; from which the word widens in its usage to include
double-dealing in general, such as the 'irony of Socrates,'
his habit of assuming the part of a simple enquirer in order
to entangle the pretentious sophists in their own wisdom.
The particular extension of meaning with which we are
immediately concerned is that by which irony comes to be
applied to a double-dealing in Destiny itself; the link between
this and the original sense being no doubt the ambiguous
wording of oracular responses which has become proverbial.
In ancient conception Destiny wavered between justice and

malignity; a leading phase of malignant destiny was this Irony or double-dealing; Irony was the laughter or mockery of Fate. It is illustrated in the angry measures of Œdipus for penetrating the mystery that surrounds the murder of Laius in order to punish the crime, impunity for which has brought the plague upon his city: when at last it is made clear that Œdipus himself has been unknowingly the culprit, there arises an irresistible sensation that Destiny has been all the while playing with the king, and using his zeal as a means for working his destruction. In modern thought the supreme force of the universe cannot possibly be represented

A modified Irony: Justice in a mocking humour. as malignant. But mockery, though it may not be enthroned in opposition to justice, may yet, without violating modern ideas, be made to appear in the *mode of operation* by which justice is brought about; here mockery is no longer malignant, but simply an index of overpowering force, just as we smile at the helpless stubbornness of a little child, whereas a man's opposition makes us angry. For such a reconciliation of mockery with righteousness we have authority in the imagery of Scripture.

> Why do the heathen rage?
>   And the people imagine a vain thing?
> The kings of the earth set themselves
>   And the rulers take counsel together
> Against the Lord
>   And against His Anointed:
> Saying, Let us break their bonds,
>   And cast away their cords from us.
>
> He that sitteth in the heavens shall laugh:
> The Lord shall have them in derision.
>
> Then shall He speak unto them in His wrath;
>   And vex them in His sore displeasure.

There could not be a more perfect type of Irony, in that form of it which harmonises with justice, than this picture in three touches, of the busy security of the wicked, of justice pausing to mock their idle efforts, and then with a

burst of wrath and displeasure annihilating their projects at a CHAP. VI.
stroke.

In modern thought, then, Irony is Justice in a mocking
humour. The mockery that suddenly becomes apparent in
the mysterious operations of Providence, and is a measure of
their overpowering force, is clearly capable of giving a highly
dramatic interest to a train of events, and so is fitted to be
a form of dramatic action. The operation of Destiny as *Irony in*
exhibited in the plot of *Macbeth* is throughout tinctured with *the plot of Macbeth:*
irony: the element of mockery appearing always in this, that *obstacles*
apparent checks to Destiny turn out the very means Destiny *converted into step-*
chooses by which to fulfil itself. Irony of this kind is *ping-stones.*
regularly attached to what I have called the third variety of
the Oracular Action, that in which the oracle is fulfilled by the
agency of attempts to oppose it; but in the play under
consideration the destiny, whether manifesting itself in that
type of the Oracular Action or not, is never dissociated
from the attitude of mockery to resistance which converts
obstacles into stepping-stones. It remains to show how
the rise of Macbeth, the fall of Macbeth, and again the
rise and the fall taken together, are all of them Irony
Actions.

The basis of Macbeth's rise is the Witches' promise of the *The rise of*
crown. Scarcely has it been given when an obstacle starts *Macbeth an Irony*
up to its fulfilment in the proclamation of Malcolm as heir- *Action.*
apparent. I have already pointed out that it is this very
proclamation which puts an end to Macbeth's wavering, and
leads him to undertake the treasonable enterprise which only
in the previous scene he had resolved he would have nothing
to do with. Later in the history a second obstacle appears: ii. iii. 141.
the king is slain, but his two sons, this heir-apparent and
his brother, escape from Macbeth's clutches and place two
lives between him and the fulfilment of his destiny. But, as
events turn out, it is this very flight of the princes that, by
diverting suspicion to them for a moment, causes Macbeth to

CHAP. VI. be named as Duncan's successor. A conversation in the play
————   itself is devoted to making this point clear.

ii. iv. 22.   *Ross.*   Is 't known who did this more than bloody deed?
                 Macduff.   Those that Macbeth hath slain.
                 Ross.   Alas, the day!
                 What good could they pretend?
                 Macduff.   They were suborn'd:
                 Malcolm and Donalbain, the king's two sons,
                 Are stol'n away and fled; which puts upon them
                 Suspicion of the deed.
                 Ross.   'Gainst nature still!
                 Thriftless ambition, that will ravin up
                 Thine own life's means!   Then 'tis most like
                 The sovereignty will fall upon Macbeth.
                 Macduff.   He is already named, and gone to Scone
                 To be invested.

The fall an   Twice, then, in the course of the rise Destiny allows
Irony   obstacles to appear only for the sake of using them as an
Action.   unexpected means of fulfilment.   The same mockery marks
               the fall of the action.   The security against a fall promised
               by the Apparitions to Macbeth had just one drawback—
iv. i. 71.   'beware Macduff'; and we have already had occasion to
               notice Macbeth's attempt to secure himself against this
iv. ii, &c.   drawback in the completest manner by extirpating the
               dangerous thane and his family to the last scion of his stock,
               and also how this cruel purpose succeeded against all but
               Macduff himself.   Now it is to be noted that this attempt
               against the fulfilment of the destined retribution proves the
               very source of the fulfilment, without which it would never
               have come about.   For at one point of the story Macduff,
               the only man who, according to the decrees of Fate, can
               harm Macbeth, resolves to abandon his vengeance against
               him.   In his over-cautious policy Macduff was unwilling to
               move without the concurrence of Malcolm the rightful heir.
iv. iii.   In one of the most singular scenes in all Shakespeare
               Macduff is represented as urging Malcolm to assert his
               rights, while Malcolm (in reality driven by the general panic

to suspect even Macduff) discourages his attempts, and CHAP. VI.
affects to be a monster of iniquity, surpassing the tyrant of
Scotland himself. At last he succeeds in convincing Macduff iv. iii, from
of his villainies, and in a burst of despair the fate-appointed 100.
avenger renounces vengeance.

> *Macduff.*   Fit to govern?
>   No, not to live . . . . Fare thee well!
>   These evils thou repeat'st upon thyself
>   Have banish'd me from Scotland. O my breast,
>   Thy hope ends here!

Malcolm, it is true, then drops the pretence of villainy, but
he does not succeed in reassuring his companion.

> *Macduff.* Such welcome and unwelcome things at once iv. iii. 138.
>   'Tis hard to reconcile.

At this moment enters Ross with the news of Macbeth's
expedition against Fife, and tells how all Macduff's household, 'wife, children, servants, all,' have been cut off 'at
one swoop': before the agony of a bereavement like this
hesitation flies away for ever.

> Gentle heavens, iv. iii. 231.
>   Cut short all intermission; front to front
>   Bring thou this fiend of Scotland and myself;
>   Within my sword's length set him: if he 'scape,
>   Heaven forgive him too!

The action taken by Macbeth with a view to prevent Macduff's being the instrument of retribution, is brought by a
mocking Fate to impel Macduff to his task at the precise
moment he had resolved to abandon it.

Finally, if the rise and the fall be contemplated together *The plot as*
as constituting one action, this also will be found animated *a whole an Irony*
by the same spirit of irony. The original promise of the *Action.*
Witches, as well as the later promise of the Apparition, had
its drawback in the destiny that Banquo was to be lesser i. iii. 62–
than Macbeth and yet greater, to get kings though to be 66.
none; and to secure against this drawback is Macbeth's

purpose in his plot against Banquo and Fleance, by which the rival family would be extirpated. The plot only *half succeeds*, and by its half-success contributes to the exactness with which the destiny is fulfilled. Had Macbeth's attempt fully succeeded, Banquo would neither have got kings nor been one; had no such attempt at all been made, then, for anything we see to the contrary in the play, Banquo would have preceded his sons on the throne, and so again the oracle would not have been fulfilled which made Banquo lesser than Macbeth. But by the mixture of success and failure in Macbeth's plot Banquo is slain before he can attain the crown, and Fleance lives to give a royal house to Scotland. Once more, then, mockery appears a characteristic of the Destiny that finds in human resistance just the one peculiar device needed for effecting the peculiar distribution of fortune it has promised.

Summary.   Such is the subtlety with which Shakespeare has constructed this plot of *Macbeth*, and interwoven in it Nemesis and Destiny. To outward appearance it is connected with the rise and fall of a sinner : the analysis that searches for inner principles of construction traces through its incidents three forms of action working harmoniously together, by which the rise and fall of Macbeth are so linked as to exhibit at once a crime with its Nemesis, an Oracle with its fulfilment, and the Irony which works by the agency of that which resists it. Again the separate halves of the play, the rise and the fall of the hero, are found to present each the same triple pattern as the whole. Once more, with the career of Macbeth are associated the careers of Banquo and Macduff, and these also reflect the threefold spirit. Macbeth's rise involves Banquo's fall : this fall is the subject of oracular prediction, it is the starting-point of nemesis on Macbeth, and it has an element of irony in the fact that Banquo *all but* escaped. With Macbeth's fall is bound up Macduff's rise ; this also had been predicted in oracles, it is an agency

in the main nemesis, and Macduff's fate has the irony that
he *all but* perished at the outset of his mission.   Through all
the separate interests of this elaborate plot, the three forms
of action—Nemesis, the Oracular, Irony—are seen perfectly
harmonised and perfectly complete.   And over all this is
thrown the supernatural interest of the Witches, who are
agents of nemesis working by the means of ironical oracles.

MACBETH, LORD AND LADY.

A Study in Character-Contrast.

CHAP. VII. $\quad$ CONTRASTS of character form one of the simplest
elements of dramatic interest. Such contrasts are often
obvious; at other times they take definitiveness only when
looked at from a particular point of view. The contrast of
character which it is the object of the present study to sketch
rests upon a certain distinction which is one of the funda-

The anti- mental ideas in the analysis of human nature—the distinction
thesis of the between the outer life of action and the inner life of our
outer and
inner life. own experience. The recognition of the two is as old as
the *Book of Proverbs*, which contrasts the man that ruleth
his spirit with the man that taketh a city. The heathen
oracle, again, opened out to an age which seemed to have
exhausted knowledge a new world for investigation in the
simple command, Know thyself. The Stoics, who so de-
spised the busy vanity of state cares, yet delighted to call
their ideal man a king; and their particular tenet is univer-
salised by Milton when he says:

> Therein stands the office of a king,
> His honour, virtue, merit, and chief praise,
> That for the public all this weight he bears:
> Yet he who reigns within himself, and rules
> Passions, desires, and fears, is more a king.

And the modern humourist finds the idea indispensable for
his pourtrayal of character and experience. 'Sir,' says one of
Thackeray's personages, 'a distinct universe walks about

under your hat and under mine ... You and I are but a pair Chap. VII.
of infinite isolations with some fellow-islands more or less
near to us.' And elsewhere the same writer says that 'each
creature born has a little kingdom of thought of his own,
which it is a sin in us to invade.'

This antithesis of the practical and inner life is so accepted a commonplace of the pulpit and of the essayist on
morals and culture that it may seem tedious to expound it.
But for the very reason that it belongs to all these spheres,
and that these spheres overlap, the two sides of the antithesis are not kept clearly distinct, nor are the terms
uniformly used in the same sense. For the present purpose
the exact distinction is between the outer world, the world of
practical action, the sphere of making and doing, in which
we mingle with our fellow men, join in their enterprises, and
influence them to our ideas, in which we investigate nature
and society, or seek to build up a fabric of power: and, on
the other hand, the inner intellectual life, in which our
powers as by a mirror are turned inwards upon ourselves,
finding a field for enterprise in self-discipline and the contest
with inherited notions and passions, exploring the depths of
our consciousness and our mysterious relations with the
unseen, until the thinker becomes familiar with strange situations of the mind and at ease in the presence of its problems.
The antithesis is thus not at all the same as that between
worldly and religious, for the inner life may be cultivated
for evil: self-anatomy, as Shelley says,

> Shall teach the will
> Dangerous secrets: for it tempts our powers,
> Knowing what must be thought and may be done,
> Into the depth of darkest purposes.

Still less is it the antithesis between intellectual and commonplace; the highest intellectual powers find employment in
practical life. The various mental and moral qualities belong to both spheres, but have a different meaning for each.

Practical experience is a totally different thing from what the religious thinker means by his 'experience.' The discipline given by the world often consists in the dulling of those powers which self-discipline seeks to develope. Knowledge of affairs, with its rapid and instinctive grasp, is often possessed in the highest degree by the man who is least of all men versed in the other knowledge, which could explain and analyse the processes by which it operated. And every observer is struck by the different forms which courage takes in the two spheres, courage in action, and courage where nothing can be done and men have only to endure and wait. Macaulay in a well-known passage contrasts the active and passive courage as one of the distinctions between the West and the East.

> An European warrior, who rushes on a battery of cannon with a loud hurrah, will sometimes shriek under the surgeon's knife, and fall into an agony of despair at the sentence of death. But the Bengalee, who would see his country overrun, his house laid in ashes, his children murdered or dishonoured, without having the spirit to strike one blow, has yet been known to endure torture with the firmness of Mucius, and to mount the scaffold with the steady step and even pulse of Algernon Sidney.

The two lives are complete, each with its own field, its own qualities, culture, and fruit.

The anti-thesis an element in Character-Interpreta-tion. It is obvious that relation to these two lives will have a very great effect in determining individual character. In the same man the two sides of experience may be most un-equally developed; an intellectual giant is often a child in the affairs of the world, and a moral hero may be found in the person of some bedridden cripple. On the other hand, to some the inner life is hardly known: familiar perhaps with every other branch of knowledge they go down to their graves strangers to themselves.

> All things without, which round about we see,
>   We seek to know and how therewith to do;
> But that whereby we reason, live, and be
>   Within ourselves, we strangers are thereto.

We seek to know the moving of each sphere,
  And the strange cause of the ebbs and flows of Nile:
But of that clock within our breasts we bear,
  The subtle motions we forget the while.

We, that acquaint ourselves with every zone,
  And pass both tropics, and behold each pole,
When we come home, are to ourselves unknown,
  And unacquainted still with our own soul.

The antithesis then between the outer and inner life will be among the ideas which lie at the root of Character-Interpretation.

When the idea is applied to an age like that of Macbeth, the antithesis between the two lives almost coincides with the distinction of the sexes: amid the simple conditions of life belonging to such an age the natural tendency would be for genius in men to find scope in the outer and practical world, while genius in women would be restricted to the inner life. And this is the idea I am endeavouring to work out in the present study :—that the key to Shakespeare's portraiture of Macbeth and Lady Macbeth will be found in regarding the two as illustrations of the outer and inner life. Both possess force in the highest degree, but the two have been moulded by the exercise of this force in different spheres; their characters are in the play brought into sharp contrast by their common enterprise, and the contrast of practical and intellectual mind is seen maintained through the successive stages of their descent to ruin. *In a simple age it coincides with the distinction of the sexes.* *The antithesis the key to the characters of Macbeth and Lady Macbeth.*

Thus Macbeth is essentially the practical man, the man of action, of the highest experience, power, and energy in military and political command, accustomed to the closest connection between willing and doing. He is one who in another age would have worked out the problem of free trade, or unified Germany, or engineered the Suez Canal. On the other hand, he has concerned himself little with things transcendental; he is poorly disciplined in thought and goodness; prepared for any emergency in which there is anything *Macbeth as the practical man.*

to be *done*, yet a mental crisis or a moral problem afflicts him with the shock of an unfamiliar situation. This is by no means a generally accepted view : amongst a large number of readers the traditional conception of Macbeth lingers as a noble disposition dragged down by his con-

His no-bility conventional. nection with the coarser nature of his wife. According to the view here suggested the nobility of Macbeth is of the flimsiest and most tawdry kind. The lofty tone he is found at times assuming means no more than virtuous education and surroundings. When the purely practical nature is examined in reference to the qualities which belong to the intellectual life, the result is not a blank but ordinariness : the practical nature will reflect current thought and goodness as they appear from the outside. So Macbeth's is the morality of inherited notions, retained just because he has no disposition to examine them ; he has all the practical man's distrust of wandering from the beaten track of opinion, which gives the working politician his prejudice against doctrinaires, and has raised up stout defenders of the Church amongst men whose lives were little influenced by her teaching. And the traditionary morality is more than merely retained. When the seed fell into stony ground forthwith it sprang up *because* it had no deepness of earth : the very shallowness of a man's character may lend emphasis to his high professions, just as, on the other hand, earnestness in its first stage often takes the form of hesitation. So Macbeth's practical genius takes in strongly what it takes in at all, and gives it out vigorously. But that the nobility has gone beyond the stage of passive recognition, that it has become absorbed into his inner nature, there is not a trace ; on the contrary, it is impossible to follow Macbeth's history far without abundant evidence that real love of goodness for its own sake, founded on intelligent choice or deep affection, has failed to root a single fibre in his nature.

First, we have the opportunity of studying Macbeth's

character in the analysis given of it in the play itself by the
one person who not only saw Macbeth in his public life, but
knew also the side of him hidden from the world.

> *Lady Macbeth.*   I fear thy nature ;
> It is too full o' the milk of human kindness
> To catch the nearest way.

I believe that this phrase, the ' milk of human kindness,'
divorced from its context and become the most familiar of
all commonplaces, has done more than anything else towards giving a false twist to the general conception of
Macbeth's character. The words *kind, kindness* are amongst
the most difficult words in Shakespeare. The wide original
signification of the root, *natural, nature,* still retained in the
noun *kind,* has been lost in the adjective, which has been
narrowed by modern usage to one sort of naturalness, tender-heartedness ; though in a derivative form the original
sense is still familiar to modern ears in the expression ' the
kindly fruits of the earth.' In Elizabethan English, however,
the root signification still remained in all usages of *kind* and
its derivatives. In Schmidt's analysis of the adjective, two
of its four significations agree with the modern use, the
other two are ' keeping to nature, natural,' and ' not degenerate and corrupt, but such as a thing or person ought to
be.' Shakespeare delights to play upon the two senses of
this family of words : tears of joy are described as a ' kind *Much Ado,*
overflow of kindness'; the Fool says of Regan that she will *i. i. 26.*
use Lear ' kindly,' i. e. according to her nature ; ' the worm *Lr. i. v. 15.*
will do his kind,' i. e. bite. How far the word can wander *Ant. and*
from its modern sense is seen in a phrase of the present *Cleop. v. ii.*
264.
play, ' at your kind'st leisure,' where it is simply equivalent *ii. i. 24.*
to ' convenient.' Still more will the wider signification of
the word obtain, when it is associated with the word *human* ;
' humankind' is still an expression for human nature, and
the sense of the passage we are considering would be more
obvious if the whole phrase were printed as one word, not

CHAP. VII. 'human kindness,' but 'humankind-ness':—that shrinking from what is not natural, which is a marked feature of the practical nature. The other part of the clause, *milk* of humankind-ness, no doubt suggests absence of hardness : but it equally connotes natural, inherited, traditional feelings, imbibed at the mother's breast. The whole expression of Lady Macbeth, then, I take to attribute to her husband an instinctive tendency to shrink from whatever is in any way unnatural. That this is the true sense further appears, not only from the facts—for nothing in the play suggests that

i. ii. 54. Macbeth, 'Bellona's bridegroom,' was distinguished by kindness in the modern sense—but from the context. The form of Lady Macbeth's speech makes the phrase under discussion a summing up of the rest of her analysis, or rather a general text which she proceeds to expand into details. Not one of these details has any connection with tender-heartedness : on the other hand, if put together the details do amount to the sense for which I am contending, that Macbeth's character is a type of commonplace morality, the shallow unthinking and unfeeling man's lifelong hesitation between God and Mammon.

> Thou would'st be great ;
> Art not without ambition, but without
> The illness should attend it : what thou would'st highly
> That would'st thou holily ; would'st not play false,
> And yet would'st wrongly win : thou'ldst have, great Glamis,
> That which cries 'Thus thou must do, if thou have it,
> And that which *rather thou dost fear to do*
> *Than wishest should be undone.'*

If the delicate balancing of previous clauses had left any doubt as to the meaning, the last two lines remove it, and assert distinctly that Macbeth has no objection to the evil itself, but only a fear of evil measures which must be associated to a practical mind with failure and disgrace. It is striking that at the very moment Lady Macbeth is so medi-

i. iv. 48–53. tating, her husband is giving a practical confirmation of her

description in its details as well as its general purport. He
had resolved to take no steps himself towards the fulfilment
of the Witches' prophecy, but to leave all to chance ; then
the proclamation of Malcolm, removing all apparent chance
of succession, led him to change his mind and entertain the
scheme of treason and murder : the words with which he
surrenders himself seems like an echo of his wife's analysis.

i. iii. 143,
146.

> Stars, hide your fires ;
> Let not light see my black and deep desires:
> The eye wink at the hand ; *yet let that be*
> *Which the eye fears, when it is done, to see.*

But we are not left to descriptions of Macbeth by others.
We have him self-displayed ; and that in a situation so
framed that if there were in him the faintest sympathy with
goodness it must here be brought into prominence. Macbeth has torn himself away from the banquet, and, his mind
full of the desperate danger of the treason he is meditating,
he ponders over the various motives that forbid its execution.
A strong nobility would even amid incentives *to* crime feel
the attraction of virtue and have to struggle against it ; but
surely the weakest nobility, when facing motives *against* sin,
would be roused to some degree of virtuous passion. Yet,
if Macbeth's famous soliloquy be searched through and
through, not a single thought will be found to suggest that
he is regarding the deep considerations of sin and retribution in any other light than that of immediate practical
consequences. First, there is the thought of the sureness of
retribution even in this world. It may be true that hope of
heaven and fear of hell are not the highest of moral incentives, but at least they are a degree higher than the thought
of worldly prosperity and failure ; Macbeth however is willing
to take his chance of the next world if only he can be
guaranteed against penalties in this life.

*Macbeth's
soliloquy :
of an em-
inently
practical
character.*
i. vii. 1–28.

> If it were done when 'tis done, then 'twere well
> It were done quickly: if the assassination

> Could trammel up the consequence, and catch
> With his surcease success; that but this blow
> Might be the be-all and the end-all here.
> But here, upon this bank and shoal of time,
> We'ld jump the life to come. But in these cases
> We still have judgement here; that we but teach
> Bloody instructions, which, being taught, return
> To plague the inventor: this even-handed justice
> Commends the ingredients of our poisoned chalice
> To our own lips.

So far he has reached no higher consideration, in reference to treason and murder, than the fear that he may be suggesting to others to use against himself the weapon he is intending for Duncan. Then his thoughts turn to the motives against crime which belong to the softer side of our nature.

> He's here in double trust,
> First, as I am his kinsman and his subject,
> Strong both against the deed; then, as his host,
> Who should against his murderer shut the door,
> Not bear the knife myself. Besides, this Duncan
> Hath borne his faculties so meek, hath been
> So clear in his great office, that his virtues
> Will plead like angels, trumpet-tongued, against
> The deep damnation of his taking-off;
> And pity—

At all events it is clear this is no case of a man blinded for the moment to the emotions which resist crime; and as we hear him passing in review kinship, loyalty, hospitality, pity, we listen for the burst of remorse with which he will hurl from him the treachery he had been fostering. But, on the contrary, his thoughts are still practical, and the climax to which this survey of motives is to lead up is no more than the effect they will have on others: pity

> Shall blow the horrid deed in every eye,
> That tears shall drown the wind.

And then he seems to regret that he cannot find more incentives to his villainy.

> I have no spur
> To prick the sides of my intent, but only
> Vaulting ambition, which o'erleaps itself
> And falls on the other.

So Macbeth's searching self-examination on topics of sin and retribution, amid circumstances specially calculated to rouse compunction, results in thoughts not more noble than these— that murder is a game which two parties can play at, that heartlessness has the effect of drawing general attention, that ambition is apt to defeat its own object.

Again: that Macbeth's union of superficial nobility with real moral worthlessness is connected with the purely practical bent of his mind will be the more evident the wider the survey which is taken of his character and actions. It may be observed that Macbeth's spirits always rise with evil deeds: however he may have wavered in the contemplation of crime, its execution strings him up to the loftiest tone. This is especially clear in the Dagger Scene, and in the scene in which he darkly hints to his wife the murder of Banquo, which is in a brief space to be in actual perpetration. As he feels the moment of crime draw near, his whole figure seems to dilate, the language rises, and the imagery begins to flow. Like a poet invoking his muse, Macbeth calls on seeing night to scarf up the tender eye of pitiful day. He has an eye to dramatic surroundings for his dark deeds.

Macbeth rises with external deeds and sinks with internal conflicts.

ii. i, from 31; and iii. ii, from 39.

> Now, o'er the one half-world
> Nature seems dead, and wicked dreams abuse
> The curtain'd sleep; witchcraft celebrates
> Pale Hecate's offerings, and wither'd murder,
> Alarum'd by his sentinel, the wolf,
> Whose howl's his watch, thus with his stealthy pace,
> With Tarquin's ravishing strides, towards his design
> Moves like a ghost. Thou sure and firm-set earth,
> Hear not my steps, which way they walk, for fear
> The very stones prate of my whereabout,
> *And take the present horror from the time,*
> *Which now suits with it.*

The man who had an hour or two before been driven from

Chap. VII. the table of his guests by the mere thought of a crime moves to the deed itself with the exalted language of a Hebrew prophet. On the other hand, in his spiritual struggles there is a simpleness that sometimes suggests childishness. His ii. ii. 31. trouble is that he could not say 'Amen' when the sleepers cried 'God bless us'; his conscience seems a voice outside ii. ii. 35–46. him; finally, the hardened warrior dare not return to the darkness and face the victim he had so exultingly done to death.

Macbeth, then, is the embodiment of one side of the antithesis with which we started; his is pre-eminently the practical nature, moulded in a world of action, but uninfluenced by the cultivation of the inner life. Yet he is not perfect as a man of action : for the practical cannot reach its per-*Two flaws in Macbeth as an embodiment of the practical : his superstition ;* fection without the assistance of the inner life. There are two flaws in Macbeth's completeness. For one, his lack of training in thought has left him without protection against the superstition of his age. He is a passive prey to supernatural imaginings. He himself tells us he is a man whose v. v. 10. senses would cool to hear a night-shriek, and his fell of hair rouse at a dismal treatise. And we see throughout the play how he never for an instant doubts the reality of the supernatural appearances : a feature the more striking from its e. g. iii. iv. 60 ; i. iii. 107, 122. iii. i. 6. contrast with the scepticism of Lady Macbeth, and the hesitating doubt of Banquo. Again : no active career can be without its periods when action is impossible, and it is in *and his helplessness under suspense.* such periods that the training given by the intellectual life makes itself felt, with its self-control and passive courage. All this Macbeth lacks : in suspense he has no power of compare i. iii. 137, and iii. ii. 16. self-restraint. When we come to trace him through the stages of the action we shall find that one of these two flaws springing out of Macbeth's lack of the inner life, his superstition and his helplessness in suspense, is at every turn the source of his betrayal.

In the case of Lady Macbeth, the old-fashioned view of

her as a second Clytæmnestra has long been steadily giving
way before a conception higher at least on the intellectual
side. The exact key to her character is given by regarding
her as the antithesis of her husband, and an embodiment of
the inner life and its intellectual culture so markedly wanting
in him. She has had the feminine lot of being shut out
from active life, and her genius and energy have been turned
inwards; her soul—like her 'little hand'—is not hardened
for the working-day world, but is quick, delicate, sensitive.
She has the keenest insight into the characters of those
around her. She is accustomed to moral loneliness and
at home in mental struggles. She has even solved for
herself some of their problems. In the very crisis of Duncan's murder she gives utterance to the sentiment:

> the sleeping and the dead
> Are but as pictures.

When we remember that she must have started with the
superstitions of her age such an expression, simple enough
in modern lips, opens up to us a whole drama of personal
history: we can picture the trembling curiosity, the struggle
between will and quivering nerves, the triumph chequered
with awe, the resurrection of doubts, the swayings between
natural repulsion and intellectual thirst, the growing courage
and the reiterated victories settling down into calm principle. Accordingly, Lady Macbeth has won the grand
prize of the inner life: in the kingdom of her personal
experience her WILL is unquestioned king. It may seem
strange to some readers that Lady Macbeth should be held
up as the type of the inner life, so associated is that phrase
to modern ears with the life fostered by religion. But the
two things must not be confused—religion and the sphere in
which religion is exercised. 'The kingdom of God is within
you,' was the proclamation of Christ, but the world within
may be subjugated to other kings than God. Mental discipline and perfect self-control, like that of Lady Macbeth,

CHAP. VII. would hold their sway over evil passions, but they would also be true to her when she chose to contend against goodness, and even against the deepest instincts of her *A struggle* feminine nature. This was ignored in the old conception of *against not* the character, and a struggle *against* the softer side of her *the softer* nature was mistaken for its total absence. But her in- *qualities.* tellectual culture must have quickened her finer sensibilities at the same time that it built up a will strong enough to hold them down; nor is the subjugation so perfect but that a sympathetic insight can throughout trace a keen delicacy of nature striving to assert itself. In particular, i. v. 41. when she calls upon the spirits that tend on mortal thoughts to unsex and fill her from crown to toe with direst cruelty, she is thrilling all over with feminine repugnance to the bloody enterprise, which nevertheless her royal will insists upon her undertaking. Lady Macbeth's career in the play is one long mental civil war; and the strain ends, as such a strain could only end, in madness.

The Cha- Such is the general conception of Lord and Lady Macbeth *racter-Con-* from the point of view of the antithesis between the outer *trast traced* *through the* and inner life. We have now to turn from character to action, *action.* and trace the contrasted pair through the stages of their common career.

Situation The two opposing natures have been united in a happy *at the open-* marriage, the happier because a link between characters so *ing of the* *play.* forceful and so antithetic, if it held at all, must be a source of compare interest: the dark tragedy of this unhappy pair is softened by i. v. 55–60; i. vii. 38; the tenderness of demeanour which appears on both sides. iii. ii. 27, Another source of marriage happiness is added: there is not 29, 36, 45; iii. iv. 141. a trace of self-seeking in Lady Macbeth. Throughout the play she is never found meditating upon what she is to gain by the crown; wife-like, she has no sphere but the career of *The origin-* her husband. In a picture of human characters, great in *al impulse* *to evil came* their scale, overwhelmed in moral ruin, the question of *from Mac-* absorbing interest is the commencement of the descent, and *beth.*

the source from which the impulse to evil has come. This, CHAP. VII. in the present case, Shakespeare has carefully hidden from us : before the play opens the essential surrender of spirit has taken place, and all that we are allowed to see is its realisation in life and fact. If, however, we use the slight material afforded us for speculation on this point, it would appear that the original choice for evil has for both been made by Macbeth. In the partnership of man and wife it is generally safe to assume that the initiative of action has come from the husband, if nothing appears to the contrary. In the present case we are not left to assumptions, Lady Macbeth distinctly speaks of her husband as first breaking i. vii. 48. to her the enterprise of treacherous ambition.

> What beast was 't, then,
> Which made you break this enterprise to me ?
> . . . . Nor time nor place
> Did then adhere, and yet you would make both.

The reference can only be to a period before the commencement of the play ; and the general drift of the passage suggests that it was no mere choice, made by Macbeth with deliberation during which he would be open to conviction, but an impulse of uncontrollable passion that it would have been vain for his wife to resist, supposing that she had had the desire to resist it—so uncontrollable, indeed, that it appears to Lady Macbeth stronger than the strongest of i. vii. 54. feminine passions, a mother's love.

> I have given suck, and know
> How tender 'tis to love the babe that milks me :
> I would, while it was smiling in my face,
> Have pluck'd my nipple from his boneless gums,
> And dash'd the brains out, had I so sworn as you
> Have done to this.

The only sense in which Lady Macbeth can be pronounced the ruin of her husband is that her firm nature holds him in the path to which he has committed them both, and will not

CHAP. VII. allow his fatal faltering to lose both the virtue he has re-
nounced and the price for which he has bartered it.   Denied
by her feminine position, the possibility—even if she had
had the desire—of directing the common lot for good, she
has recognised before we make her acquaintance that this
lot has been cast for evil, and she is too well-trained in self-
knowledge to attempt the self-deception her husband tries to
keep up.   And to this evil lot she applies her full force.   Her

i. vii. 54.   children have died, and this natural outlet for passion is
wanting; the whole of her energy is brought to bear upon
her husband's ambition, and she is waiting only an occasion for concentrating her powers upon some definite
project.

*Four
stages in
the action.*   With such mutual relations between the hero and the
heroine the play opens: we are to watch the contrasted
characters through the successive stages of the Temptation,
the Deed, the Concealment, the Nemesis.

*The Tempt-
ation.*   The Temptation accosts the two personages when separated from one another, and we thus have the better
opportunity of watching the different forms it assumes in
adapting itself to the different characters.   The expedition,
which has separated Macbeth from his wife, is one which
must have led him to brood over his schemes of ambition.
Certainly it exhibits to him an example of treason and shows
him the weakness of his sovereign.   Probably he sees events
shaping in a direction that suggests opportunity; he may
have known that the king must pass in the direction of his
castle, or in some other way may have anticipated a royal
visit; at all events the king's intimation of this visit in the
play itself—

i. iv. 42.   From hence to Inverness,
                     And bind us further to you,—

does not look like a first mention of it.   To a mind so pre-
i. iii. 38-   pared the supernatural solicitation brings a shock of tempta-
78.   tion ; and as the Witches in their greeting reach the promise,

' Thou shalt be KING hereafter,' Macbeth gives a start that CHAP. VII.
astonishes Banquo :

> Good sir, why do you start ; and seem to fear
> Things that do sound so fair ?

To Banquo this prediction of the Witches seems no more
than curious ; for it must be remembered that Macbeth's
position in the kingdom was not such as to exclude hope of
succession to the crown, though the hope was a remote one.
But Macbeth's start tells a tale of his inner thoughts at the
time. This alone should be sufficient to vindicate Shakespeare from the charge sometimes brought against him of
turning a great character from virtue to vice by demoniac
agency; his is the higher conception that a soul which has
commenced the surrender to evil will find in the powers of
darkness agencies ready to expedite its descent, it matters
not what form these agencies assume. Macbeth has been
for years playing with the idea of treason, while never
bracing himself up to the point of acting it : suddenly the
thought he fancied so safe within his bosom appears outside
him in tangible form, gleaming at him in the malignant
glances of recognition the Witches are casting at him. To a
mind utterly undefended by culture against superstitious
terror this objective presentation of his own thought proves
a Rubicon of temptation which he never attempts to recross.
On Lady Macbeth the supernatural incident makes not the i. v. 1–55.
slightest impression of any kind ; we see her reading her
husband's excited account of the interview with the most
deliberate calmness, weighing its suggestions only with reference to the question how it can be used upon her husband.
To her temptation comes with the suggestion of *opportunity*.
The messenger enters during her quiet meditation :

> *Mess.* The king comes here to-night.
> *Lady M.*   Thou 'rt mad to say it !

The shock that passes over her is like the shock of chemical
change. In an instant her whole nature is strung up to

CHAP. VII. a single end; the long-expected occasion for the concen-
———   tration of a whole life's energy upon a decisive stroke is
            come.   So rapidly does her imagination move that she sees
            the deed before her as already done, and, as she casts her
            eyes upwards, the very ravens over her head seem to be
            croaking the fatal entrance of Duncan under her battle-
            ments.

*The meet-   The stage of Temptation cannot be considered complete
ing after-* without taking in that important section of the play which
wards.   intervenes between the meeting of the two personages after
i. v, from their separate temptations and the accomplishment of the
55; i. vii. treason.   This is essentially a period of suspense, and ac-
            cordingly exhibits Macbeth at his weakest.   As he enters
            his castle his tell-tale face is as a book where men may
            read strange matters; and his utter powerlessness of self-
            control throws upon his wife's firm will the strongest of all
            strains, that of infusing her own tenacity into a vacillating
            ally.   I have already dealt with the point at which Macbeth's
            suspense becomes intolerable, and he leaves the supper-table ;
            and I have drawn attention to the eminently practical nature
            of his thoughts even at this crisis.   The scene which follows,
            when his wife labours to hold him to the enterprise he has
            undertaken, illustrates perhaps better than any other incident
            in the play how truly this practical bent is the key to Mac-
            beth's whole character.   At first he takes high ground, and
            rests his hesitation on considerations of gratitude.   Lady
            Macbeth appeals to consistency, to their mutual love, and,
            her anger beginning to rise at this wavering of will in a
            critical moment, she taunts her husband with cowardice.
            Then it is that Macbeth, irritated in his turn, speaks the
            noble words that have done so much to gain him a place in
            the army of martyrs to wifely temptations.

> Prithee, peace:
> I dare do all that may become a man ;
> Who dares do more is none.

But it is difficult to share Macbeth's self-deception long. At CHAP. VII.
his wife's reminder how he had been the one to first moot
the undertaking, and swear to it in spite of overwhelming obstacles, already the noble attitude looks more like the sour
grapes morality of the man who begins to feel indignation
against sin at the precise moment when the sin becomes
dangerous. And the whole truth comes sneaking out at
Macbeth's next rejoinder: ' If we should fail? ' Here is
the critical point of the scene. At its beginning Macbeth is i. vii, from
for abandoning the treason, at its end he prepares for his 61.
task of murder with animation: where does the change
come? *The practical man is nerved by having the practical
details supplied to him.* Lady Macbeth sketches a feasible
scheme: how that the King will be wearied, his chamberlains
can by means of the banquet be easily drugged, their confusion on waking can be interpreted as guilt—before she has
half done her husband interrupts her with a burst of enthusiasm, and completes her scheme for her. The man who
had thought it was manliness that made him shrink from
murder henceforward never hesitates till he has plunged his
dagger in his sovereign's bosom.

In the perpetration of the Deed itself we have the woman *The Deed.*
passing from weakness to strength, the man from strength to ii. i. 31 to
weakness. To Lady Macbeth this actual contact with a deed ii. ii.
of blood is the severest point of the strain, the part most
abhorrent to her more delicate nature. For a single moment
she feels herself on the verge of the madness which eventually
comes upon her:

> These deeds must not be thought   ii. ii. 33.
> After these ways; so, it will make us mad!

And at the beginning of the scene she has been obliged to
have recourse to stimulants in order to brace her failing
nerves:

> That which hath made them drunk hath made me bold.   ii. ii. 1.

Chap. VII. And in part the attempt to bring her delicate nature to the repugnant deed does fail. It is clear that, knowing how little her husband could be depended upon, she had intended to have a hand in the murder itself:

i. vii. 69;
compare
i. v. 68.

> What cannot *you and I* perform upon
> The unguarded Duncan?

But the will which was strong enough to hold down conscience gave way for a moment before an instinct of feminine tenderness:

ii. ii. 13.

> Had he not resembled
> My father as he slept, I had done 't.

The superiority, however, of the intellectual mind is seen in this, that it can nerve itself from its own agitation, it can draw strength out of the weakness surrounding it, or out of the necessities of the situation: *must* is the most powerful of spells to a trained will. And so it is that Lady Macbeth rises to the occasion when her husband fails. At first Macbeth in the perpetration of the murder appears in his proper sphere of action, and we have already noticed how the Dagger Soliloquy shows no shrinking, but rather excitement on the side of exultation. The change in him comes with a moment of suspense, caused by the momentary waking of the grooms:

ii. ii. 24. 'I stood and heard them.' With this, no longer sustained by action, he utterly breaks down under the unfamiliar terrors of a fight with his conscience. His prayer sticks in his throat; his thoughts seem so vivid that his wife can hardly tell whether he did not take them for a real voice outside him.

> Who was it that thus cried? Why, worthy thane,
> You do unbend your noble strength, to think
> So brainsickly of things.

In his agitation he forgets the plan of action, brings away the daggers instead of leaving them with the grooms, and finally dares not return to finish what he has left uncompleted. And accordingly his wife has to make another demand upon her overwrought nature: with one hysterical jest,

> If he do bleed,
> I 'll *gild* the faces of the grooms withal,
> For it must seem their *guilt*,

her nature rallies, and the strength derived from the inner life fills up a gap in action where the mere strength of action had failed.

The Concealment of the murder forms a stage of the action which falls into two different parts: the single effort which faces the first shock of discovery, and the very different strain required to meet the slowly gathering evidence of guilt. In the Scene of the Discovery Macbeth is perfectly at home : energetic action is needed, and he is dealing with men.   His acted innocence appears to me better than his wife's ; Lady Macbeth goes near to suggesting a personal interest in the crime by her over-anxiety to disclaim it.

The first Shock of Conceal-ment. ii. iii, from 68.

> *Macduff.*   O Banquo, Banquo,
>   Our royal master 's murder'd !
> *Lady M.*   Woe, alas !
>   What, in our house ?
> *Banquo.*   Too cruel anywhere.

Yet in this scene, as everywhere else, the weak points in Macbeth's character betray him : for one moment he is left to himself, and that moment's suspense ruins the whole episode.   In the most natural manner in the world Macbeth had, on hearing the announcement, rushed with Lennox to the scene of the murder.   Lennox quitted the chamber of blood first, and for an instant Macbeth was alone, facing the grooms still heavy with their drugged sleep, and knowing that in another moment they would be aroused and telling their tale : the sense of crisis proves too much for him, and under an ungovernable impulse he stabs them.   He thus wrecks the whole scheme.   How perfectly Lady Macbeth's plan would have served if it had been left to itself is shown by Lennox's account of what he had seen, and how the grooms

> stared, and were distracted ; no man's life
> Was to be trusted with them.

CHAP. VII. Nothing, it is true, can be finer than the way in which Mac-
        beth seeks to cover his mistake and announces what he has
        done.   But in spite of his brilliant outburst,

> Who can be wise, amazed, temperate and furious,
> Loyal and neutral, in a moment?

and his vivid word-picture of his supposed sensations, his
efforts are in vain, and at the end of his speech we feel that
there has arisen in the company of nobles the indescribable
effect known as 'a sensation,' and we listen for some one to
speak some word that shall be irrevocable.   The crisis is
ii. iii. 124. acute, but Lady Macbeth comes to the rescue *and faints !*
It matters little whether we suppose the fainting assumed,
or that she yields to the agitation she has been fighting
against so long.   The important point is that she chooses
this exact moment for giving way : she holds out to the end
of her husband's speech, then falls with a cry for help ; there
is at once a diversion, and she is carried out.   But the crisis
ii. iii. 132. has passed, and a moment's consideration has suggested to
the nobles the wisdom of adjourning for a fitter occasion the
enquiry into the murder they all suspect : before that occasion
ii. iv. 24–   arrives the flight of the king's sons has diverted suspicion into
32.   an entirely new channel.   Lady Macbeth's fainting saved her
husband.

The long   To convey dramatically the continuous strain of keeping
Strain of   up appearances in face of steadily accumulating suspicion is
Conceal-
ment. iii. more difficult than to depict a single crisis.   Shakespeare
i. ii.   manages it in the present case chiefly by presenting Macbeth
to us on the eve of an important council, at which the whole
truth is likely to come out.

iii. i. 30.   We hear, our bloody cousins are bestowed
                In England and in Ireland, not confessing
                Their cruel parricide, filling their hearers
                With strange invention : but of that to-morrow.

It is enough to note here that Macbeth takes the step—the
fatal step, as was pointed out in the last study—of contriving

Banquo's murder simply because he cannot face the suspense
of waiting for the morrow, and hearing the defence of the ——
innocent princes made in presence of Banquo, who knows
the inducement he had to such a deed. That he feels the
danger of the crime, which nevertheless he cannot hold himself back from committing, is clear from the fact that he will
not submit it to the calmer judgment of his wife. The con- iii. ii. 45.
trast of the two characters appears here as everywhere. Lady
Macbeth can *wait* for an opportunity of freeing themselves
from Banquo :

> *Macb.* Thou know'st that Banquo, and his Fleance, lives.   iii. ii. 37.
> *Lady M.* But in them nature's copy's not eterne.

To Macbeth the one thing impossible is to wait ; and once
more his powerlessness to control suspense is his ruin.

We have reviewed the contrasted characters under Tempta-   *The first*
tion, in the Deed of sin itself, and in the struggle for Conceal-   *Shock of*
ment : it remains to watch them face to face with their *Nemesis.*
Nemesis. In the present play Shakespeare has combined the   iii. iv.
nemesis which takes the form of a sudden shock with the yet
severer nemesis of a hopeless resistance through the stages of
a protracted fall. The first Shock of Nemesis comes in the
Banquet Scene. Macbeth has surrendered himself to the
supernatural, and from the supernatural his retribution comes.
This is not the place to draw out the terrible force of this
famous scene ; for its bearing on the contrast of character
under delineation it is to be remarked that Macbeth faces his
ghostly visitation with unflinching courage, yet without a
shadow of doubt as to the reality of what nevertheless no one
sees but himself. Lady Macbeth is equally true to her
character, and fights on to the last in the now hopeless
contest—her double task of keeping up appearances for herself and for her husband. Her keen tact in dealing with
Macbeth is to be noted. At first she rallies him angrily, and
seeks to shame him into self-command ; a moment shows

CHAP. VII. that he is too far gone to be reached by such motives. In-
——　　stantly she changes her tactics, and, employing a device so
often effective with patients of disordered brain, she endeavours to recall him to his senses by assuming an ordinary
tone of voice ; hitherto she has whispered, now, in the hearing of all, she makes the practical remark :

iii. iv. 83.　　　　　　　　　　My worthy lord,
　　　　　　　　Your noble friends do lack you.

The device proves successful, his nerves respond to the tone
of everyday life, and recovering himself he uses all his skill
of deportment to efface the strangeness of the episode, until
the reappearance of his victim plunges the scene in confusion
past recovery. In the moment of crisis Lady Macbeth had
used roughness to rouse her husband ; when the courtiers
iii. iv, from are gone she is all tenderness. She utters not a word of re-
122.　　proach : perhaps she is herself exhausted by the strain she has
gone through ; more probably the womanly solicitude for the
physical sufferer thinks only how to procure for her husband
' the season of all natures, sleep.'

The full　　At last the end comes. The final stage, like the first is
Nemesis.　brought to the two personages separately. Lady Macbeth
has faced every crisis by sheer force of nerve ; the nemesis
v. i.　　comes upon her fitly in madness, the brain giving way under
the strain of contest which her will has forced upon it. In
the delirium of her last appearance before us we can trace
three distinct tones of thought working into one another as if
in some weird harmony. There is first the mere reproduction
of the horrible scenes she has passed through.

　　One : two : why then 'tis time to do 't. . . . Yet who would have
thought the old man to have had so much blood in him. . . . The thane
of Fife had a wife : where is she now ?

Again there is an inner thought contending with the first, the
struggle to keep her husband from betraying himself by his
irresolution.

　　No more o' that, my lord, no more o' that : you mar all with this

starting. . . . Wash your hands, put on your night-gown; look not so CHAP. VII.
pale. . . . Fie! a soldier and afear'd?

And there is an inmost thought of all; the uprising of her
feminine nature against the foulness of the violent deed.

Out, damn'd spot! . . . Here's the smell of blood still: all the per-
fumes of Arabia will not sweeten this little hand—

and the 'sorely charged heart' vents itself in a sigh which
the attendants shudder to hear. On Macbeth Nemesis heaps
itself in double form. The purely practical man, without
resources in himself, finds nemesis in an old age that receives
no honour from others.

My way of life v. iii. 22.
Is fall'n into the sear, the yellow leaf;
And that which should accompany old age,
As honour, love, obedience, troops of friends,
I must not look to have, but, in their stead,
Curses, not loud, but deep.

Again, as the drunkard finds his refuge in drink, so the
victim of superstition longs for deeper draughts of the supernatural. Macbeth seeks the Witches, forces himself to hear iv. i.
the worst, and suffers nemesis in anticipation in viewing
future generations which are to see his foes on his throne. iv. i. 110–
Finally from the supernatural comes the climax of retribution ¹³⁵·
when Macbeth is seen resting in unquestioning reliance on an from iv. i.
ironical oracle: till the shock of revelation comes, the pledge ⁸⁰·
of his safety is converted into the sign of his doom, and the ᵥ. ᵥ, from
brave Macbeth, hero of a hundred battles, throws down his ₃₃; v. viii,
sword and refuses to fight. from 13.
v. viii. 22.

VIII.

Ch. VIII.
——
Character-Grouping.

EVERY lover of art feels that the different fine arts form not a crowd but a family; the more familiar the mind becomes with them the more it delights to trace in them the application of common ideas to different media of expression. We are reminded of this essential unity by the way in which the arts borrow their terms from one another. 'Colour' is applied to music, 'tone' to painting; we speak of costume as 'loud,' of melody as 'bright,' of orchestration as 'massive'; 'fragrance' was applied by Schumann to Liszt's playing. Two classes of oratorical style have been distinguished as 'statuesque' and 'picturesque'; while the application of a musical term, 'harmony,' and a term of sculpture, 'relief,' to all the arts alike is so common that the transference is scarcely felt. Such usages are not the devices of a straitened vocabulary, but are significant of a single *Art* which is felt to underlie the special *arts*. So the more Drama is brought by criticism into the family of the fine arts the more it will be seen to present the common features. We have already had to notice repeatedly how the idea of pattern or design is the key to dramatic plot. We are in the present study to see how contrast of character, such as was traced in the last study between Lord and Lady Macbeth, when applied to a larger number of personages, produces an effect on the mind analogous to that of *grouping* in pictures and statuary: the different personages not only present points of contrast with

one another, but their varieties suddenly fall into a unity of
effect if looked at from some one point of view. An example
of such Character-Grouping is seen in the play of *Julius
Cæsar*, where the four leading figures, all on the grandest
scale, have the elements of their characters thrown into
relief by comparison with one another, and the contrast
stands out boldly when the four are reviewed in relation
to one single idea.

Ch. VIII.
————
*The
grouping
in Julius
Cæsar rests
on the anti-
thesis of the
practical
and inner
life.*

This idea is the same as that which lay at the root of the
Character-Contrast in *Macbeth*—the antithesis of the practical
and inner life. It is, however, applied in a totally different
sphere. Instead of a simple age in which the lives coincide
with the sexes we are carried to the other extreme of civilisation, the final age of Roman liberty, and all four personages
are merged in the busy world of political life. Naturally, then,
the contrast of the two lives takes in this play a different
form. In the play of *Macbeth* the inner life was seen in the
force of will which could hold down alike bad and good
impulses; while the outer life was made interesting by its
confinement to the training given by action, and an exhibition of it devoid of the thoughtfulness and self-control for
which the life of activity has to draw upon the inner life.
But there is another aspect in which the two may be regarded. The idea of the inner life is reflected in the word
'individuality,' or that which a man has not in common with
others. The cultivation of the inner life implies not merely
cultivation of our own individuality, but to it also belongs
sympathy with the individuality of others; whereas in the
sphere of practical life men fall into classes, and each
person has his place as a member of these classes. Thus
benevolence may take the form of enquiring into individual wants and troubles and meeting these by personal
assistance; but a man has an equal claim to be called
benevolent who applies himself to such sciences as political
economy, studies the springs which regulate human society,

*This takes
the form of
individual
sympathies
v. public
policy.*

and by influencing these in the right direction confers benefits upon whole classes at a time. Charity and political science are the two forms benevolence assumes correspondent to the inner life of individual sympathies and the outer life of public action. Or, if we consider the contrast from the side of rights as distinguished from duties, the supreme form in which the rights of individuals may be summed up is justice; the corresponding claim which public life makes upon us is (in the highest sense of the term) policy: wherever these two, justice and policy, seem to clash, the outer and inner life are brought into conflict. It is in this form that the conflict is raised in the play of *Julius Cæsar*. To get it in its full force, the dramatist goes to the world of antiquity, for one of the leading distinctions between ancient and modern society is that the modern world gives the fullest play to the individual, while in ancient systems the individual was treated as existing solely for the state. 'Liberty' has been a watchword in both ages; but while we mean by liberty the least amount of interference with personal activity, the liberty for which ancient patriots contended was freedom of the government from external or internal control, and the ideal republic of Plato was so contrived as to reduce individual liberty to a minimum. And this subordination of private to public was most fully carried out in Rome. 'The common weal,' says Merivale, 'was after all the grand object of the heroes of Roman story. Few of the renowned heroes of old had attained their eminence as public benefactors without steeling their hearts against the purest instincts of nature. The deeds of a Brutus or a Manlius, of a Sulla or a Cæsar, would have been branded as crimes in private citizens: it was the public character of the actors that stamped them with immortal glory in the eyes of their countrymen.' Accordingly, the opposition of outer and inner life is brought before us most keenly when, in Roman life, a public policy, the cause of republican freedom, seems

to be bound up with the supreme crime against justice and Сн. VIII.
the rights of the individual, assassination.

Brutus is the central figure of the group: in his character *Brutus's*
the two sides are so balanced that the antithesis disappears. *character*
so evenly
This evenness of development in his nature is the thought of *developed*
those who in the play gather around his corpse; giving *that the*
antithesis
prominence to the quality in Brutus hidden from the casual *disappears.*
observer they say:

> His life was gentle; and the elements   **v. v. 73.**
> So mix'd in him that Nature might stand up
> And say to all the world ' This was a man!'

Of another it would be said that he was a poet, a philosopher; of Brutus the only true description was that he was a
man! It is in very few characters that force and softness
are each carried to such perfection. The strong side of *Force of his*
Brutus's character is that which has given to the whole play *character.*
its characteristic tone. It is seen in the way in which he
appreciates the issue at stake. Weak men sin by hiding from
themselves what it is they do; Brutus is fully alive to the
foulness of conspiracy at the moment in which he is con-
spiring.

> O conspiracy,   **ii. i. 77.**
> Shamest thou to show thy dangerous brow by night,
> When evils are most free? O, then by day
> Where wilt thou find a cavern dark enough
> To mask thy monstrous visage?

His high tone he carries into the darkest scenes of the play.
The use of criminal means has usually an intoxicating effect
upon the moral sense, and suggests to those once committed
to it that it is useless to haggle over the amount of the crime
until the end be obtained. Brutus resists this intoxication,
setting his face against the proposal to include Antony in **ii. i. 162.**
Cæsar's fate, and resolving that not one life shall be unneces-
sarily sacrificed. He scorns the refuge of suicide; and with
warmth adjures his comrades not to stain—

Ch. VIII.

ii. i. 114.

> The even virtue of our enterprise,
> Nor the insuppressive mettle of our spirits,
> To think that or our cause or our performance
> Did need an oath ; when every drop of blood
> That every Roman bears, and nobly bears,
> Is guilty of a several bastardy,
> If he do break the smallest particle
> Of any promise that hath pass'd from him.

The scale of Brutus's character is again brought out by his relations with other personages of the play. Casca, with all his cynical depreciation of others, has to bear unqualified testimony to Brutus's greatness :

i. iii. 157.

> O, he sits high in all the people's hearts;
> And that which would appear offence in us,
> His countenance, like richest alchemy,
> Will change to virtue and to worthiness.

ii. i, fin.

We see Ligarius coming from a sick-bed to join in he knows not what : ' it sufficeth that Brutus leads me on.' And the hero's own thought, when at the point of death he pauses to take a moment's survey of his whole life, is of the unfailing

v. v. 34.

power with which he has swayed the hearts of all around him :

> My heart doth joy that yet in all my life
> I found no man but he was true to me.

Above all, contact with Cassius throws into relief the great-

i. ii.

ness of Brutus. At the opening of the play it is Cassius that we associate with the idea of force ; but his is the ruling mind only while Brutus is hesitating ; as soon as Brutus has thrown in his lot with the conspirators, Cassius himself is swept along with the current of Brutus's irresistible influence.

Cf. ii. i.
162–190 ;
iii. i. 140–
146, 231–
243; iv.
iii. 196–
225, &c.

iii. i. 19.

In the councils every point is decided—and, so far as success is concerned, wrongly decided—against Cassius's better judgment. In the sensational moment when Popilius Lena enters the Senate-house and is seen to whisper Cæsar, Cassius's presence of mind fails him, and he prepares in despair for suicide ; Brutus retains calmness enough to *watch faces* :

> Cassius, be constant :
> Popilius Lena speaks not of our purposes ;
> For, look, he smiles, and Cæsar doth not change.

In the Quarrel Scene Cassius has lost all pretensions to iv. iii.
dignity of action in the impatience sprung from a ruined
cause ; Brutus maintains principle in despair.   Finally, at the
close of the scene, when it is discovered that under all the
hardness of this contest for principle Brutus has been hiding iv. iii, from
a heart broken by the loss of Portia, Cassius is forced to give ¹⁴⁵.
way and acknowledge Brutus's superiority to himself even in
his own ideal of impassiveness :

> I have as much of this in art as you,   iv. iii. 194.
> But yet my nature could not bear it so.

The force in Brutus's character is obvious : it is rather its *Its softness.*
softer side that some readers find difficulty in seeing.   But this
difficulty is in reality a testimony to Shakespeare's skill, for
Brutus is a Stoic, and what gentleness we see in him appears
in spite of himself.   It may be seen in his culture of art,
music, and philosophy, which have such an effect in softening
the manners.   Nor is this in the case of the Roman Brutus
a mere conventional culture : these tastes are among his
strongest passions.   When all is confusion around him on the
eve of the fatal battle he cannot restrain his longing for the iv. iii.
refreshing tones of his page's lyre ; and, the music over, he
takes up his philosophical treatise at the page he had turned
down.   Again Brutus's considerateness for his dependants is iv. iii. 242
in strong contrast with the harshness of Roman masters.
On the same eve of the battle he insists that the men who
watch in his tent shall lie down instead of standing as discipline would require.   An exquisite little episode brings out iv. iii, from
Brutus's sweetness of demeanour in dealing with his youthful ²⁵².
page ; this rises to womanly tenderness at the end when,
noticing how the boy, wearied out and fallen asleep, is lying
in a position to injure his instrument, he rises and disengages
it without waking him.

Bru. Look, Lucius, here's the book I sought for so;
I put it in the pocket of my gown.
Luc. I was sure your lordship did not give it me.
Bru. Bear with me, good boy; I am much forgetful.
Can'st thou hold up thy heavy eyes awhile,
And touch thy instrument a strain or two?
Luc. Ay, my lord, an't please you.
Bru.   It does, my boy:
I trouble thee too much, but thou art willing.
Luc. It is my duty, sir.
Bru. I should not urge thy duty past thy might;
I know young bloods look for a time of rest.
Luc. I have slept my lord, already.
Bru. It was well done; and thou shalt sleep again;
I will not hold thee long: if I do live
I will be good to thee.   [*Music and a song.*
This is a sleepy tune. O murderous slumber,
Lay'st thou thy leaden mace upon my boy,
That plays thee music? Gentle knave, good night;
I will not do thee so much wrong to wake thee.—
If thou dost nod, thou break'st thy instrument;
I'll take it from thee; and, good boy, good night.

ii. i, from   Brutus's relations with Portia bear the same testimony.
233.   Portia is a woman with as high a spirit as Lady Macbeth,
and she can inflict a wound on herself to prove her courage
and her right to share her husband's secrets.   But she lacks
the physical nerve of Lady Macbeth; her agitation on the
ii. iv.   morning of the assassination threatens to betray the conspirators, and when these have to flee from Rome the
suspense is too much for her and she commits suicide.
Brutus knew his wife better than she knew herself, and was
right in seeking to withhold the fatal confidence; yet he
allowed himself to be persuaded: no man would be so
swayed by a tender woman unless he had a tender spirit of
his own.   In all these ways we may trace an extreme of
This is   gentleness in Brutus.   But it is of the essence of his character
concealed   that this softer side is concealed behind an imperturbability
under stoic
imper-   of outward demeanour that belongs to his stoic religion:
turbability. this struggle between inward and outward is the main feature

for the actor to bring out. It is a master stroke of Shakespeare that he utilises the euphuistic prose of his age to
express impassiveness in Brutus's oration. The greatest
man of the world has just been assassinated; the mob are
swaying with fluctuating passions; the subtlest orator of his
day is at hand to turn those passions into the channel of
vengeance for his friend: Brutus called on amid such surroundings to speak for the conspirators still maintains the
artificial style of carefully balanced sentences, such as
emotionless rhetoric builds up in the quiet of a study.

> As Cæsar loved me, I weep for him; as he was fortunate, I rejoice
> at it; as he was valiant, I honour him : but, as he was ambitious, I slew
> him. There is tears for his love; joy for his fortune; honour for his
> valour; and death for his ambition.

Brutus's nature then is developed on all its sides; in his *The anti-*
character the antithesis of the outer and inner life disappears. *thesis re-*
appears for
It reappears, however, in the action; for Brutus is compelled *Brutus in*
to balance a weighty issue, with public policy on the one *the action.*
side, and on the other, not only justice to individual claims, *ii. i. 10-85.*
but further the claims of friendship, which is one of the
fairest flowers of the inner life. And the balance dips to
the wrong side. If the question were of using the weapon
of assassination against a criminal too high for the ordinary
law to reach, this would be a moral problem which, however doubtful to modern thought, would have been readily
decided by a Stoic. But the question which presented
itself to Brutus was distinctly not this. Shakespeare has *ii. i. 18-34.*
been careful to represent Brutus as admitting to himself
that Cæsar has done no wrong: he slays him *for what he
might do.*

> The abuse of greatness is, when it disjoins
> Remorse from power: and, *to speak truth of Cæsar,*
> *I have not known when his affections sway'd*
> *More than his reason.* But 'tis a common proof,
> That lowliness is young ambition's ladder,
> Whereto the climber-upward turns his face;

> But when he once attains the upmost round,
> He then unto the ladder turns his back,
> Looks in the clouds, scorning the base degrees
> By which he did ascend. So Cæsar may.
> Then, lest he may, prevent. And *since the quarrel*
> *Will bear no colour for the thing he is,*
> Fashion it thus; that what he is, augmented,
> Would run to these and these extremities :
> And therefore think him as a serpent's egg
> Which hatch'd, would, as his kind, grow mischievous,
> And kill him in the shell.

It is true that Shakespeare, with his usual ' dramatic hedging,' softens down this immoral bias in a great hero by representing him as both a Roman, of the nation which beyond all other nations exalted the state over the individual, and a Brutus, representative of the house which had risen to greatness by leading violence against tyranny.   But, Brutus's own conscience being judge, the man against whom he moves is guiltless ; and so the conscious sacrifice of justice and friendship to policy is a fatal error which is source sufficient for the whole tragedy of which Brutus is the hero.

compare i. ii. 159.

Cæsar: discrepancies in his character to be reconciled.

The character of Cæsar is one of the most difficult in Shakespeare.   Under the influence of some of his speeches we find ourselves in the presence of one of the master spirits of mankind; other scenes in which he plays a leading part breathe nothing but the feeblest vacillation and weakness. It is the business of Character-Interpretation to harmonise this contradiction ; it is not interpretation at all to ignore one side of it and be content with describing Cæsar as vacillating. The force and strength of his character is seen in the impression he makes upon forceful and strong men.   The attitude of Brutus to Cæsar seems throughout to be that of looking up ; and notably at one point the thought of Cæsar's greatness seems to cast a lurid gleam over the assassination plot itself, and Brutus feels that the grandeur of the victim gives a dignity to the crime :

ii. i. 173.

> Let 's carve him as a dish fit for the gods.

The strength and force of Antony again no one will ques- CH. VIII.
tion ; and Antony, at the moment when he is alone with the ——
corpse of Cæsar and can have no motive for hypocrisy,
apostrophises it in the words—

> Thou art the ruins of the noblest man iii. i. 256.
> That ever lived in the tide of times.

And we see enough of Cæsar in the play to bear out the
opinions of Brutus and Antony. Those who accept vacillation as sufficient description of Cæsar's character must explain his strong speeches as vaunting and self-assertion. But
surely it must be possible for dramatic language to distinguish
between the true and the assumed force ; and equally surely
there is a genuine ring in the speeches in which Cæsar's
heroic spirit, shut out from the natural sphere of action in
which it has been so often proved, leaps restlessly at every
opportunity into pregnant words. We may thus feel certain
of his lofty physical courage.

> Cowards die many times before their deaths ; ii. ii. 32.
> The valiant never taste of death but once.
> Of all the wonders that I yet have heard,
> It seems to me most strange that men should fear . . .
> .   .   .   .
> Danger knows full well ii. ii. 44.
> That Cæsar is more dangerous than he :
> We are two lions litter'd in one day,
> And I the elder and more terrible.

A man must have felt the thrill of courage in search of its
food, danger, before his self-assertion finds language of this
kind in which to express itself. In another scene we have
the perfect *fortiter in re* and *suaviter in modo* of the trained
statesman exhibited in the courtesy with which Cæsar receives ii. ii, from
the conspirators, combined with his perfect readiness to ' tell 57.
graybeards the truth.' Nor could imperial firmness be more iii. i. 35.
ideally painted than in the way in which Cæsar ' prevents '
Cimber's intercession.   Be not fond,
>   To think that Cæsar bears such rebel blood

That will be thaw'd from the true quality
With that which melteth fools; I mean, sweet words,
Low-crooked court'sies, and base spaniel-fawning.
Thy brother by decree is banished:
If thou dost bend and pray and fawn for him,
I spurn thee like a cur out of my way.
Know, Cæsar doth not wrong, nor without cause
Will he be satisfied.

Commonplace authority loudly proclaims that it will never relent: the true imperial spirit feels it a preliminary condition to see first that it never does wrong.

Reconcili-
ation:
Cæsar the
highest
type of the
practical;

It is the antithesis of the outer and inner life that explains this contradiction in Cæsar's character. Like Macbeth, he is the embodiment of one side and one side only of the antithesis; he is the complete type of the practical—though in special qualities he is as unlike Macbeth as his age is unlike Macbeth's age. Accordingly Cæsar appears before us perfect up to the point where his own personality comes in. The military and political spheres, in which he has been such a colossal figure, call forth practical powers, and do not involve introspection and meditation on foundation principles of thought.

Theirs not to reason why:
Theirs but to do.

The tasks of the soldier and the statesman are imposed upon them by external authority and necessities, and the faculties exercised are those which shape means to ends. But at last Cæsar comes to a crisis that does involve his personality; he attempts a task imposed on him by his own ambition. He plays in a game of which the prize is the world and the stake himself, and to estimate chances in such a game tests *but lacking* self-knowledge and self-command to its depths. How want-*in the inner* ing Cæsar is in the cultivation of the inner life is brought out *life.* by his contrast with Cassius. The incidents of the flood and *i. ii. 100–* the fever, retained by the memory of Cassius, illustrate this. *128.* The first of these was no mere swimming-match; the flood in the Tiber was such as to reduce to nothing the difference

between one swimmer and another. It was a trial of nerve :
and as long as action was possible Cæsar was not only as
brave as Cassius, but was the one attracted by the danger. i. ii. 102.
Then some chance wave or cross current renders his chance
of life hopeless, and no buffeting with lusty sinews is of any
avail; that is the point at which the *passive* courage born of
the inner life comes in, and gives strength to submit to the
inevitable in calmness. This Cæsar lacks, and he calls for
rescue : Cassius would have felt the water close over him and
have sunk to the bottom and died rather than accept aid from
his rival. In like manner the sick bed is a region in which
the highest physical and intellectual activity is helpless; the
trained self-control of a Stoic may have a sphere for exercise
even here ; but the god Cæsar shakes, and cries for drink
like a sick girl. It is interesting to note how the two types *The con-*
of mind, when brought into personal contact, jar upon one *ception*
brought out
another's self-consciousness. The intellectual man, judging *by personal*
the man of action by the test of mutual intercourse, sees *contact*
with
nothing to explain the other's greatness, and wonders what *Cassius.*
people find in him that they so admire him and submit to his
influence. On the other hand, the man of achievement is
uneasily conscious of a sort of superiority in one whose intellectual aims and habits he finds it so difficult to follow—yet
superiority it is not, for what has he *done ?* Shakespeare has
illustrated this in the play by contriving to bring Cæsar and
his suite across the 'public place' in which Cassius is dis- i. ii. 182–
coursing to Brutus. Cassius feels the usual irritation at 214.
being utterly unable to find in his old acquaintance any
special qualities to explain his elevation.

> Now, in the names of all the gods at once,   i. ii. 148.
> Upon what meat doth this our Cæsar feed,
> That he is grown so great ?

Similarly Cæsar, as he casts a passing glance at Cassius, becomes at once uneasy. ' He thinks too much,' is the ex-
clamation of the man of action :

> He loves no plays,
> As thou dost, Antony; he hears no music.

The practical man, accustomed to divide mankind into a few simple types, is always uncomfortable at finding a man he cannot classify. Finally there is a climax to the jealousy that exists between the two lives: Cæsar complains that Cassius ' *looks quite through the deeds of men.*'

A change in Cæsar and a change in Rome itself. comp. **i.** i, *and* **iii.** iii; **i.** ii. 151, 164; **i.** iii. 82, 105; **iii.** i. 66–70; **v.** v. 69–72, &c.

There is another circumstance to be taken into account in explaining the weakness of Cæsar. A change has come over the spirit of Roman political life itself—such seems to be Shakespeare's conception : Cæsar on his return has found Rome no longer the Rome he had known. Before he left for Gaul, Rome had been the ideal sphere for public life, the arena in which principles alone were allowed to combat, and from which the banishment of personal aims and passions was the first condition of virtue. In his absence Rome has gradually degenerated ; the mob has become the ruling force, and introduced an element of uncertainty into political life ; politics has passed from science into gambling. A new order of public men has arisen, of which Cassius and Antony are the types ; personal aims, personal temptations, and personal risks are now inextricably interwoven with public action. This is a changed order of things to which the mind of Cæsar, cast in a higher mould, lacks the power to adapt itself. His vacillation is the vacillation of unfamiliarity with the new political conditions. He refuses the crown 'each time gentler than the other,' showing want of decisive reading in dealing with the fickle mob; and on his return from the Capitol he is too untrained in hypocrisy to conceal the angry spot upon his face ; he has tried to use the new weapons which he does not understand, and has failed. It is a subtle touch of Shakespeare's to the same effect that Cæsar is represented as having himself undergone a change *of late* :

i. ii. 230.

i. ii. 183.

ii. i. 195.

> For he is superstitious grown of late,
> Quite from the main opinion he held once
> Of fantasy, of dreams and ceremonies.

To come back to a world of which you have mastered the Cн. VIII.
machinery, and to find that it is no longer governed by
machinery at all, that causes no longer produce their effects—
this, if anything, might well drive a strong intellect to superstition. And herein consists the pathos of Cæsar's situation.
The deepest tragedy of the play is not the assassination of
Cæsar, it is rather seen in such a speech as this of Decius:

> If he be so resolved, ii. i. 202.
> I can o'ersway him ; for he loves to hear
> That unicorns may be betray'd with trees,
> And bears with glasses, elephants with holes,
> Lions with toils and men with flatterers ;
> But when I tell him, he hates flatterers,
> He says he does, being then most flattered.

Assassination is a less piteous thing than to see the giant
intellect by its very strength unable to contend against the
low cunning of a fifth-rate intriguer.

Such, then, appears to be Shakespeare's conception of
Julius Cæsar. He is the consummate type of the practical:
emphatically the public man, complete in all the greatness
that belongs to action. On the other hand, the knowledge
of self produced by self-contemplation is wanting, and
so when he comes to consider the relation of his individual
self to the state he vacillates with the vacillation of a strong
man moving amongst men of whose greater intellectual
subtlety he is dimly conscious : no unnatural conception for a
Cæsar who has been founding empires abroad while his
fellows have been sharpening their wits in the party contests
of a decaying state.

The remaining members of the group are Cassius and *Cassius:*
Antony. In Cassius thought and action have been equally *his whole*
character
developed, and he has the qualities belonging to both *developed*
and sub-
the outer and the inner life. But the side which in Brutus *jected to a*
barely preponderated, absolutely tyrannises in Cassius ; his *master-*
passion
public life has given him a grand passion to which the whole *that is dis-*
of his nature becomes subservient. Inheriting a 'rash *interested.*

CH. VIII. humour' from his mother, he was specially prepared for im-
iv. iii. 120. patience of political anomalies; republican independence has
become to him an ideal dearer than life.

i. ii. 95.   I had as lief not be as live to be
                       In awe of such a thing as I myself.

i. ii, iii; ii. He has thus become a professional politician. Politics is to
i; iii. i. him a game, and men are counters to be used; Cassius finds
177, &c.
i. ii. 312– satisfaction in discovering that even Brutus's 'honourable
319. metal may be wrought from that it is disposed.' He has the
politician's low view of human nature; while Brutus talks of
principles Cassius interposes appeals to interest: he says to
Antony,

iii. i. 177.   Your voice shall be as strong as any man's
                       In the disposing of new dignities.

His party spirit is, as usual, unscrupulous; he seeks to
work upon his friend's unsuspecting nobility by concocted
i. ii. 319. letters thrown in at his windows; and in the Quarrel Scene
loses patience at Brutus's scruples.

iv. iii. 7,   I'll not endure it: you forget yourself,
29, &c.   To hedge me in; I am a soldier, I,
                       Older in practice, abler than yourself
                       To make conditions.

At the same time he has a party politician's tact; his advice
throughout the play is proved by the event to have been
right, and he does himself no more than justice when he says
iii. i. 145. his misgiving 'still falls shrewdly to the purpose.' Antony
Antony: also has all the powers that belong both to the intellectual
his whole and practical life; so far as these powers are concerned, he
character
developed has them developed to a higher degree than even Brutus and
and sub- Cassius. His distinguishing mark lies in the use to which
jected to these powers are put; like Cassius, he has concentrated his
selfish
passion. whole nature in one aim, but this aim is not a disinterested
object of public good, it is unmitigated self-seeking. Antony
has greatness enough to appreciate the greatness of Cæsar;
hence in the first half of the play he has effaced himself,

choosing to rise to power as the useful tool of Cæsar. Here, CH. VIII.
indeed, he is famed as a devotee of the softer studies, but
it is not till his patron has fallen that his irresistible strength esp. i. ii, from 190 ;
is put forth. There seems to be but one element in Antony comp. ii. i.
that is not selfish : his attachment to Cæsar is genuine, and 165.
its force is measured in the violent imagery of the vow with iii. i, from
which, when alone for a moment with the corpse, he promises 254: comp. 194-213.
vengeance till all pity is ' choked with custom of fell deeds.'
And yet this perhaps is after all the best illustration of his
callousness to higher feelings ; for the one tender emotion of
his heart is used by him as the convenient weapon with which
to fight his enemies and raise himself to power.

Such, then, is the Grouping of Characters in the play of *The Group-*
Julius Cæsar. To catch it they must be contemplated in the *ing as a whole sur-*
light of the antithesis between the outer and inner life. In *veyed.*
Brutus the antithesis disappears amid the perfect balancing
of his character, to reappear in the action, when Brutus has
to choose between his cause and his friend. In Cæsar the
practical life only is developed, and he fails as soon as action
involves the inner life. Cassius has the powers of both outer
and inner life perfect, and they are fused into one master-
passion, morbid but unselfish. Antony has carried to an even
greater perfection the culture of both lives, and all his powers
are concentrated in one purpose, which is purely selfish. In
the action in which this group of personages is involved the
determining fact is the change that has come over the spirit
of Roman life, and introduced into its public policy the
element of personal aggrandisement and personal risk. The
new spirit works upon Brutus : the chance of winning
political liberty by the assassination of one individual just
overbalances his moral judgment, and he falls. Yet in his fall
he is glorious : the one false judgment of his life brings him,
what is more to him than victory, the chance of maintaining
the calmness of principle amid the ruins of a falling cause,
and showing how a Stoic can fail and die. The new spirit

Ch. VIII. affects Cæsar and tempts him into a personal enterprise in
——— which success demands a meanness that he lacks, and he
is betrayed to his fall. Yet in his fall he is glorious: the
assassins' daggers purge him from the stain of his momentary
personal ambition, and the sequel shows that the Roman
world was not worthy of a ruler such as Cæsar. The spirit
of the age affects Cassius, and fans his passion to work itself
out to his own destruction, and he falls. Yet in his fall he is
glorious : we forgive him the lowered tone of his political
action when we see by the spirit of the new rulers how
desperate was the chance for which he played, and how
Cassius and his loved cause of republican freedom expire
together. The spirit of the age which has wrought upon the
rest is controlled and used by Antony, and he rises on their
ruins. Yet in his rise he is less glorious than they in their
fall : he does all for self ; he may claim therefore the prize
of success, but in goodness he has no share beyond that
he is permitted to be the passive instrument of punishing
evil.

IX.

How the Play of Julius Cæsar works
to a Climax at the Centre.

A Study in Passion and Movement.

THE preceding chapters have been confined to two of the main elements in dramatic effect, Character and Plot : the third remains to be illustrated. Amongst other devices of public amusement the experiment has been tried of arranging a game of chess to be played by living pieces on a monster board; if we suppose that in the midst of such a game the real combative instincts of the living pieces should be suddenly aroused, that the knight should in grim earnest plunge his spear into his nearest opponent, and that missiles should actually be discharged from the castles, then the shock produced in the feelings of the bystanders by such a change would serve to bring out with emphasis the distinction between Plot and the third element of dramatic effect, Passion. Plot is an interest of a purely intellectual kind, it traces laws, principles, order, and design in the incidents of life. Passion, on the other hand, depends on the human character of the personages involved; it consists in the effects produced on the spectator's emotional nature as his sympathy follows the characters through the incidents of the plot; it is War as distinguished from *Kriegspiel*. Effects of such Passion are numerous and various : the present study is concerned with its *Movement*. This Movement comprehends a class of dramatic effects differing in one obvious

CHAP. IX. particular from the effects considered so far. Character-
―――――   Interpretation and Plot are both analytical in their nature ;
           the play has to be taken to pieces and details selected from
           various parts have to be put together to give the idea of a
           complete character, or to make up some single thread of
Passion design. Movement, on the contrary, follows the actual order
connected
with the of the events as they take place in the play itself. The
movement emotional effects produced by such events as they succeed
of a drama. one another will not be uniform and monotonous ; the skill
           of the dramatist will lie in concentrating effect at some points
           and relieving it at others ; and to watch such play of passion
           through the progress of the action will be a leading dramatic
           interest. Now we have already had occasion to notice the
           prominence which Shakespeare in his dramatic construction
           gives to the central point of a play ; symmetry more than
           sensation is the effect which has an attraction for his genius,
           and the finale to which the action is to lead is not more im-
           portant to him than the balancing of the whole drama about
           a turning-point in the middle. Accordingly it is not surprising
           to find that in the Passion-Movement of his dramas a similar
           plan of construction is often followed ; that all other varia-
           tions are subordinated to one great Climax of Passion at the
The   centre. To repeat an illustration already applied to·Plot : the
regular
arch-form movement of the passion seems to follow the form of a
applicable regular arch, commencing in calmness, rising through
to Passion-
Movement. emotional strain to a summit of agitation at the centre, then
           through the rest of the play declining into a calmness of a
           different kind. It is the purpose of this and the next studies
           to illustrate this kind of movement in two very different
           plays. *Julius Cæsar* has the simplest of plots ; our attention
           is engaged with a train of emotion which is made to rise
           gradually to a climax at the centre, and then equally
           gradually to decline. *Lear*, on the contrary, is amongst the
           most intricate of Shakespeare's plays ; nevertheless the
           dramatist contrives to keep the same simple form of emotional

effect, and its complex passions unite in producing a concen- CHAP. IX.
tration of emotional agitation in a few central scenes.

The passion in the play of *Julius Cæsar* gathers around *In Julius*
the conspirators, and follows them through the mutations of *Cæsar the*
their fortunes. If however we are to catch the different parts *movement*
of the action in their proper proportions we must remember *justifica-*
the character of these conspirators, and especially of their *tion of the*
leaders Brutus and Cassius. These are actuated in what *conspira-*
tors to the
they do not by personal motives but by devotion to the *audience :*
public good and the idea of republican liberty ; accordingly
in following their career we must not look too exclusively at
their personal success and failure. The exact key to the
movement of the drama will be given by fixing attention
upon the *justification of the conspirators' cause* in the minds of
the audience ; and it is this which is found to rise gradually *this rises to*
to its height in the centre of the play, and from that point to *the centre*
decline to the end. I have pointed out in the preceding *clines from*
study how the issue at stake in *Julius Cæsar* amounts to a *the centre.*
conflict between the outer and inner life, between devotion
to a public enterprise and such sympathy with the claims of
individual humanity as is specially fostered by the cultivation
of the inner nature. The issue is reflected in words of
Brutus already quoted :

> The abuse of greatness is, when it disjoins   **ii. i. 18.**
> Remorse from power.

Brutus applies this as a test to Cæsar's action, and is forced
to acquit him : but is not Brutus here laying down the very
principle of which his own error in the play is the violation ?
The assassin's dagger puts Brutus and the conspirators in
the position of power ; while ' remorse '—the word in Shakespearean English means human sympathy—is the due of
their victim Cæsar, whose rights to justice as a man, and to
more than justice as the friend of Brutus, the conspirators
have the responsibility of balancing against the claims of a
political cause. These claims of justice and humanity are

deliberately ignored by the stoicism of Brutus, while the rest of the conspirators are blinded to them by the mists of political enthusiasm ; this outraged human sympathy asserts itself after Cæsar's death in a monstrous form in the passions of the mob, which are guided by the skill of Antony to the destruction of the assassins. Of course both the original violation of the balance between the two lives and the subsequent reaction are equally corrupt. The stoicism of Brutus, with its suppression of the inner sympathies, arrives practically at the principle—destined in the future history of the world to be the basis of a yet greater crime—that it is expedient that one man should die rather than that a whole people should perish. On the other hand, Antony trades upon the fickle violence of the populace, and uses it as much for personal ends as for vengeance. This demoralisation of both the sides of character is the result of their divorce. Such is the essence of this play if its action be looked at as a whole ; but it belongs to the movement of dramatic passion that we see the action only in its separate parts at different times. Through the first half of the play, while the justification of the conspirators' cause is rising, the other side of the question is carefully hidden from us ; from the point of the assassination the suppressed element starts into prominence, and sweeps our sympathies along with it to its triumph at the conclusion of the play.

First stage: the conspiracy forming. Passion indistinguishable from mere interest. i. i, ii.

In following the movement of the drama the action seems to divide itself into stages. In the first of these stages, which comprehends the first two scenes, the conspiracy is only forming ; the sympathy with which the spectator follows the details is entirely free from emotional agitation ; passion so far is indistinguishable from mere interest. The opening scene strikes appropriately the key-note of the whole action.

Starting-point: signs of reaction in the

In it we see the tribunes of the people—officers whose whole *raison d'être* is to be the mouthpiece of the commonalty—restraining their own clients from the noisy honours they are dis-

posed to pay to Cæsar. To the justification in our eyes of a CHAP. IX
conspiracy against Cæsar, there could not be a better starting-
point than this hint that the popular worship of Cæsar, *popular worship of*
which has made him what he is, is itself reaching its *Cæsar.*
reaction-point. Such a suggestion moreover makes the i. i.
whole play one complete *wave* of popular fickleness from
crest to crest.

The second is the scene upon which the dramatist mainly *The Rise*
relies for the *crescendo* in the justification of the con- *begins. The cause seen*
spirators. It is a long scene, elaborately contrived so as to *at its best,*
keep the conspirators and their cause before us at their very *the victim at his*
best, and the victim at his very worst. Cassius is the life *worst.*
and spirit of this scene, as he is of the whole republican i. ii.
movement. Cassius is excellent soil for republican principles. The 'rash humour' his mother gave him would pre-
dispose him to impatience of those social inequalities and conventional distinctions against which republicanism sets itself.
Again he is a hard-thinking man, to whom the perfect
realisation of an ideal theory would be as palpable an aim as
the more practical purposes of other men. He is a Roman
moreover, at once proud of his nation as the greatest in the
world, and aware that this national greatness had been
through all history bound up with the maintenance of a
republican constitution. His republicanism gives to Cassius
the dignity that is always given to a character by a grand
passion, whether for a cause, a woman, or an idea—the
unification of a whole life in a single aim, by which the
separate strings of a man's nature are, as it were, tuned into
harmony. In the present scene Cassius is expounding the
cause which is his life-object. Nor is this all. Cassius was
politician enough to adapt himself to his hearers, and could
hold up the lower motives to those who would be influenced
by them; but in the present case it is the 'honourable metal'
of a Brutus that he has to work upon, and his exposition
of republicanism must be adapted to the highest possible

CHAP. IX. standard.   Accordingly, in the language of the scene we find
the idea of human equality expressed in its most ideal form.
Without it Cassius thinks life not worth living.

i. ii. 95.

> I had as lief not be as live to be
> In awe of such a thing as I myself.
> I was born free as Cæsar; so were you;
> We both have fed as well, and we can both
> Endure the winter's cold as well as he.

The examples follow of the flood and fever incidents, which
show how the majesty of Cæsar vanished before the violence
of natural forces and the prostration of disease.

115.

>   And this man
> Is now become a god, and Cassius is
> A wretched creature and must bend his body,
> If Cæsar carelessly but nod on him.

In the eye of the state, individuals are so many members of
a class, in precisely the way that their names are so many
examples of the proper noun.

142.

> Brutus and Cæsar: what should be in that ' Cæsar ' ?
> Why should that name be sounded more than yours?
> Write them together, yours is as fair a name;
> Sound them, it doth become the mouth as well;
> Weigh them, it is as heavy; conjure with them,
> Brutus will start a spirit as soon as Cæsar.
> Now, in the names of all the gods at once,
> Upon what meat doth this our Cæsar feed,
> That he is grown so great?

And this exposition of the conspirators' cause in its highest
form is at the same time thrown into yet higher relief by a
background to the scene, in which the victim is presented at
his worst.   All through the conversation between Brutus and
Cassius, the shouting of the mob reminds of the scene which
from 182. is at the moment going on in the Capitol, while the conversation is interrupted for a time by the returning procession of
Cæsar.   In this action behind the scenes which thus mingles
with the main incident Cæsar is committing the one fault of
his life: this is the fault of ' treason,' which can be justified

only by being successful and so becoming 'revolution,'
whereas Cæsar is failing, and deserving to fail from the
vacillating hesitation with which he sins. Moreover, unfavourable as such incidents would be in themselves to our
sympathy with Cæsar, yet it is not the actual facts that we
are permitted to see, but they are further distorted by
the medium through which they reach us—the cynicism of
Casca which belittles and disparages all he relates.

> *Bru.* Tell us the manner of it, gentle Casca.   **i. ii. 235.**
>
> *Casca.* I can as well be hanged as tell the manner of it : it was mere
> foolery ; I did not mark it. I saw Mark Antony offer him a crown ;—
> yet 'twas not a crown neither, 'twas one of these coronets :—and, as I
> told you, he put it by once : but, for all that, to my thinking, he would
> fain have had it. Then he offered it to him again ; then he put it by
> again : but, to my thinking, he was very loath to lay his fingers off it.
> And then he offer'd it the third time ; he put it the third time by : and
> still as he refused it, the rabblement hooted and clapped their chapped
> hands and threw up their sweaty night-caps and uttered such a deal of
> stinking breath because Cæsar had refused the crown that it had almost
> choked Cæsar ; for he swounded and fell down at it : and, for mine own
> part, I durst not laugh, for fear of opening my lips and receiving the
> bad air. . . . When he came to himself again, he said, If he had done or
> said anything amiss, he desired their worships to think it was his
> infirmity. Three or four wenches, where I stood, cried, 'Alas, good
> soul !' and forgave him with all their hearts ; but there 's no heed to be
> taken of them ; if Cæsar had stabbed their mothers they would have
> done no less.

At the end of the scene Brutus is won, and we pass *Second*
immediately into the second stage of the action : the con- *stage : the*
spiracy is now formed and developing, and the emotional *conspiracy*
formed and
strain begins. The adhesion of Brutus has given us con- *developing.*
fidence that the conspiracy will be effective, and we have *Passion-*
Strain be-
only to *wait* for the issue. This mere notion of *waiting* is *gins.*
itself enough to introduce an element of agitation into the *i. iii–ii. ii.*
passion sufficient to mark off this stage of the action from *Suspense*
one element
the preceding. How powerful suspense is for this purpose we *in the*
have expressed in the words of the play itself : *strain of*
passion.

> Between the acting of a dreadful thing   **ii. i. 63.**
> And the first motion, all the interim is

> Like a phantasma, or a hideous dream :
> The Genius and the mortal instruments
> Are then in council ; and the state of man,
> Like to a little kingdom, suffers then
> The nature of an insurrection.

*The back-
ground of
tempest
and super-
natural
portents a
device for
increasing
the strain.*

But besides the suspense there is a special device for securing the agitation proper to this stage of the passion : throughout there is maintained a Dramatic Background of night, storm, and supernatural portents.

The conception of nature as exhibiting sympathy with sudden turns in human affairs is one of the most fundamental instincts of poetry. To cite notable instances : it is this which accompanies with storm and whirlwind the climax to the *Book of Job*, and which leads Milton to make the whole universe sensible of Adam's transgression :

> Earth trembl'd from her entrails, as again
> In pangs, and Nature gave a second groan ;
> Sky lowr'd, and muttering thunder, some sad drops
> Wept at completing of the mortal sin
> Original.

So too the other end of the world's history has its appropriate accompaniments : 'the sun shall be darkened and the moon shall not give her light, and the stars shall be falling from heaven.' There is a *vagueness* of terror inseparable from these outbursts of nature, so mysterious in their causes and aims. They are actually the most mighty of forces—for human artillery is feeble beside the earthquake—yet they are invisible : the wind works its havoc without the keenest eye being able to perceive it, and the lightning is never seen till it has struck. Again, there is something weird in the feeling that the most frightful powers in the material universe are all *soft things*. The empty air becomes the irresistible wind ; the fluid and yielding water wear down the hard and massive rock and determines the shape of the earth ; impalpable fire that is blown about in every direction can be roused till it devours the solidest constructions of human skill; while the most powerful agencies of all, electricity and CHAP. IX.; atomic force, are imperceptible to any of the senses and are known only by their results. This uncanny terror attaching to the union between force and softness is the inspiration of one of Homer's most unique episodes, in which the bewildered Achilles, struggling with the river-god, finds the strength and skill of the finished warrior vain against the ever-rising water, and bitterly feels the violation of the natural order—

> That strong might fall by strong, where now weak water's luxury
> Must make my death blush.

To the terrible in nature are added portents of the super- i. iii; ii. natural, sudden violations of the uniformity of nature, the ii. &c principle upon which all science is founded. The solitary bird of night has been seen in the crowded Capitol; fire has played around a human hand without destroying it; lions, forgetting their fierceness, have mingled with men; clouds drop fire instead of rain; graves are giving up their dead; the chance shapes of clouds take distinctness to suggest tumult on the earth. Such phenomena of nature and the supernatural, agitating from their appeal at once to fear and mystery, and associated by the fancy with the terrible in human events, have made a deep impression upon primitive thought; and the impression has descended by generations of inherited tradition until, whatever may be the attitude of the intellect to the phenomena themselves, their associations in the emotional nature are of agitation. They thus become appropriate as a Dramatic Background to an agitated passion in the scenes themselves, calling out the emotional effect by a vague sympathy, much as a musical note may set in vibration a distant string that is in unison with it.

This device then is used by Shakespeare in the second stage of the present play. We see the warning terrors through the eyes of men of the time, and their force is

·CHAP. IX. measured by the fact that they shake the cynical Casca into
eloquence.

i. iii. 3.

> Are not you moved, when all the sway of earth
> Shakes like a thing unfirm? O Cicero,
> I have seen tempests, when the scolding winds
> Have rived the knotty oaks, and I have seen
> The ambitious ocean swell and rage and foam,
> To be exalted with the threatening clouds:
> But never till to-night, never till now,
> Did I go through a tempest dropping fire.
> Either there is a civil strife in heaven,
> Or else the world, too saucy with the gods,
> Incenses them to send destruction.

And the idea thus started at the commencement is kept
before our minds throughout this stage of the drama by
compare
ii. i. 44,
101, 198,
221, 263;
ii. ii. perpetual allusions, however slight, to the sky and external
nature. Brutus reads the secret missives by the light of
exhalations whizzing through the air; when some of the
conspirators step aside, to occupy a few moments while the
rest are conferring apart, it is to the sky their thoughts
naturally seem to turn, and they with difficulty can make out
the East from the West; the discussion of the conspirators
includes the effect on Cæsar of the night's prodigies. Later
Portia remonstrates against her husband's exposure to the
raw and dank morning, to the rheumy and unpurged air;
even when daylight has fully returned, the conversation is of
Calpurnia's dream and the terrible prodigies.

i. iii.
ii. i. 1–85.
ii. i. 86–
228.
ii. i, from
233.
ii. ii. Against this background are displayed, first single figures
of Cassius and other conspirators; then Brutus alone in calm
deliberation: then the whole band of conspirators, their wild
excitement side by side with Brutus's immovable moderation.
Then the Conspiracy Scene fades in the early morning light
into a display of Brutus in his softer relations; and with
complete return of day changes to the house of Cæsar on
the fatal morning. Cæsar also is displayed in contact with
the supernatural, as represented by Calpurnia's terrors and
repeated messages of omens that forbid his venturing upon

public action for that day. Cæsar faces all this with his CHAP. IX.
usual loftiness of mind; yet the scene is so contrived that, as
far as immediate effect is concerned, this very loftiness is *Cæsar still*
made to tell against him. The unflinching courage that *disadvan-*
overrides and interprets otherwise the prodigies and warnings *tage;*
seems presumption to us who know the reality of the danger.
It is the same with his yielding to the humour of his wife. ii. ii. 8–56.
Why should he not? his is not the conscious weakness that
must be firm to show that it is not afraid. Yet when, upon
Decius's explaining away the dream and satisfying Calpurnia's fears, Cæsar's own attraction to danger leads him to
persevere in his first intention, this change of purpose seems
to us, who have heard Decius's boast that he can o'ersway ii. i. 202.
Cæsar with flattery, a confirmation of Cæsar's weakness. So
in accordance with the purpose that reigns through the first
half of the play the victim is made to appear at his worst:
the *passing* effect of the scene is to suggest weakness in
Cæsar, while it is in fact furnishing elements which, upon
reflection, go to build up a character of strength. On the *and the*
other hand, throughout this stage the justification of the *justifica-*
tion of the
conspirators' cause gains by their confidence and their high *conspira-*
tone; in particular by the way in which they interpret to *tors still*
rising.
their own advantage the supernatural element. Cassius feels i. iii. 42–
the wildness of the night as in perfect harmony with his own 79.
spirit.

> For my part, I have walk'd about the streets,   i. iii. 46.
> Submitting me unto the perilous night,
> And, thus unbraced, Casca, as you see,
> Have bared my bosom to the thunder-stone;
> And when the cross blue lightning seem'd to open
> The breast of heaven, I did present myself
> Even in the aim and very flash of it.

And it needs only a word from him to communicate his
confidence to his comrades.

> *Cassius.* Now could I, Casca, name to thee a man   i. iii. 72.
> Most like this dreadful night,
> That thunders, lightens, opens graves, and roars

> As doth the lion in the Capitol,
> A man no mightier than thyself or me
> In personal action, yet prodigious grown
> And fearful, as these strange eruptions are—
> *Casca.* 'Tis Cæsar that you mean; is it not, Cassius?

Third stage. The Crisis: the passion-strain rises to a Climax.
ii. iii–iii. i. 121.

The third stage of the action brings us to the climax of the passion; the strain upon our emotions now rises to a height of agitation. The exact commencement of the crisis seems to be marked by the soothsayer's words at the opening of Act III. Cæsar observes on entering the Capitol the soothsayer who had warned him to beware of this very day.

> *Cæsar.* The ides of March are come.
> *Sooth.* Ay, Cæsar; but not gone.

Such words seem to measure out a narrow area of time in which the crisis is to work itself out. There is however no distinct break between different stages of a dramatic move-

Devices for working up the agitation.

Artemidorus;
ii. iii and iii. i. 3.

ment like that in the present play; and two short incidents have preceded this scene which have served as emotional devices to bring about a distinct advance in the intensification of the strain. In the first, Artemidorus appeared reading a letter of warning which he purposed to present to Cæsar on his way to the fatal spot. In the Capitol Scene he presents it, while the ready Decius hastens to interpose another petition to take off Cæsar's attention. Artemidorus conjures Cæsar to read his first for 'it touches him nearer'; but the imperial chivalry of Cæsar forbids:

> What touches us ourself shall be last served.

Portia;
ii. iv.

The momentary hope of rescue is dashed. In the second incident Portia has been displayed completely unnerved by the weight of a secret to the anxiety of which she is not equal; she sends messengers to the Capitol and recalls them as she recollects that she dare give them no message; her agitation has communicated itself to us, besides suggesting the fear that it may betray to others what she is anxious to conceal. Our sympathy has thus been tossed

from side to side, although in its general direction it still
moves on the side of the conspirators. In the crisis itself
the agitation becomes painful as the entrance of Popilius
Lena and his secret communication to Cæsar cause a panic
that threatens to wreck the whole plot on the verge of its
success. Brutus's nerve sustains even this trial, and the way
for the accomplishment of the deed is again clear. Emotional
devices like these have carried the passion up to a climax of
agitation; and the conspirators now advance to present
their pretended suit and achieve the bloody deed. To the
last the double effect of Cæsar's demeanour continues.
Considered in itself, his unrelenting firmness of principle
exhibits the highest model of a ruler ; yet to us, who know
the purpose lurking behind the hypocritical intercession of
the conspirators, Cæsar's self-confidence resembles the infatuation that goes before Nemesis. He scorns the fickle
politicians before him as mere wandering sparks of heavenly
fire, while he is left alone as a pole-star of true-fixed and
resting quality:—and in answer to his presumptuous boast
that he can never be moved come the blows of the assassins
which strike him down ; while there is a flash of irony as he
is seen to have fallen beside the statue of Pompey, and the
marble seems to gleam in cold triumph over the rival at last
lying bleeding at its feet. The assassination is accomplished,
the cause of the conspirators is won: pity notwithstanding
we are swept along with the current of their enthusiasm ;
and the justification that has been steadily rising from the
commencement reaches its climax as, their adversaries dis-
persing in terror, the conspirators dip their hands in their
victim's blood, and make their triumphant appeal to the
whole world and all time.

Cassius. Stoop, then, and wash. How many ages hence
    Shall this our lofty scene be acted over
    In states unborn and accents yet unknown !
Brutus. How many times shall Cæsar bleed in sport,

> That now on Pompey's basis lies along,
> No worthier than the dust!
> *Cassius.*   So oft as that shall be,
> So often shall the knot of us be call'd
> The men that gave their country LIBERTY!

Catas-
trophe, and   *Enter a servant:* this simple stage-direction is the
commence- 'catastrophe,' the turning-round of the whole action; the
ment of the arch has reached its apex and the Reaction has begun. So
Reaction.
iii. i, from instantaneous is the change, that though it is only the servant
122. of Antony who speaks, yet the first words of his message
ring with the peculiar tone of subtly-poised sentences
which are inseparably associated with Antony's eloquence;
it is like the first announcement of that which is to be a final
theme in music, and from this point this tone dominates the
scene to the very end.

125.   Thus he bade me say:
> Brutus is noble, wise, valiant, and honest,
> Cæsar was mighty, bold, royal, and loving,
> Say I love Brutus, and I honour him;
> Say I fear'd Cæsar, honour'd him, and lov'd him.
> If Brutus will vouchsafe that Antony
> May safely come to him, and be resolv'd
> How Cæsar hath deserved to lie in death,
> Mark Antony shall not love Cæsar dead
> So well as Brutus living.

In the whole Shakespearean Drama there is nowhere such a
swift swinging round of a dramatic action as is here marked
by this sudden up-springing of the suppressed individuality
ii. i. 165. in Antony's character, hitherto so colourless that he has
been spared by the conspirators as a mere limb of Cæsar.
The tone of exultant triumph in the conspirators has in an
iii. i. 144. instant given place to Cassius's 'misgiving' as Brutus grants
Antony an audience; and when Antony enters, Brutus's first
from 164. words to him fall into the form of apology. The quick
subtlety of Antony's intellect has grasped the whole situation, and with irresistible force he slowly feels his way
towards using the conspirators' aid for crushing themselves

and avenging their victim. The bewilderment of the con- CHAP. IX.
spirators in the presence of this unlooked-for force is seen
in Cassius's unavailing attempt to bring Antony to the point, iii. i. 211;
as to what compact he will make with them. Antony, on compare 177.
the contrary, reads his men with such nicety that he can
indulge himself in sailing close to the wind, and grasps
fervently the hands of the assassins while he pours out a from 184.
flood of bitter grief over the corpse. It is not hypocrisy,
nor a trick to gain time, this conciliation of his enemies.
Steeped in the political spirit of the age, Antony knows, as
no other man, the mob which governs Rome, and is conscious of the mighty engine he possesses in his oratory to
sway that mob in what direction he pleases; when his bold
plan has succeeded, and his adversaries have consented to
meet him in contest of oratory, then ironical conciliation
becomes the natural relief to his pent-up passion.

> Friends am I with you all and love you all,   220.
> *Upon this hope, that you shall give me reasons*
> Why and wherein Cæsar was dangerous.

It is as he feels the sense of innate oratorical power and of
the opportunity his enemies have given to that power, that
he exaggerates his temporary amity with the men he is
about to crush : it is the executioner arranging his victim
comfortably on the rack before he proceeds to apply the
levers. Already the passion of the drama has fallen under
the guidance of Antony. The view of Cæsar as an innocent victim is now allowed full play upon our sympathies
when Antony, left alone with the corpse, can drop the from 254.
artificial mask and give vent to his love and vengeance.
The success of the conspiracy had begun to decline as we 231-243.
marked Brutus's ill-timed generosity to Antony in granting
him the funeral oration ; it crumbles away through the cold iii. ii, from
unnatural euphuism of Brutus's speech in its defence ; it is 13.
hurried to its ruin when Antony at last exercises his spell iii. ii, from
upon the Roman people and upon the reader. The speech 78.

CHAP. IX. of Antony, with its mastery of every phase of feeling, is a
——— perfect sonata upon the instrument of the human emotions.

iii. ii. 78. Its opening theme is sympathy with bereavement, against
which are working as if in conflict anticipations of future

95, 109, themes, doubt and compunction.   A distinct change of
&c. movement comes with the first introduction of what is to be

133. the final subject, the mention of the will.   But when this new
movement has worked up from curiosity to impatience, there

177. is a diversion : the mention of the victory over the Nervii
turns the emotions in the direction of historic pride, which

178. harmonises well with the opposite emotions roused as the
orator fingers hole after hole in Cæsar's mantle made by the
daggers of his false friends, and so leads up to a sudden

200. shock when he uncovers the body itself and displays the
popular idol and its bloody defacement.   Then the finale

243. begins : the forgotten theme of the will is again started, and
from a burst of gratitude the passion quickens and inten-

The mob sifies to rage, to fury, to mutiny.   The mob is won to the
won to the *Reaction.* Reaction ; and the curtain that falls upon the third Act rises
iii. iii. for a moment to display the populace tearing a man to
pieces simply because he bears the same name as one of the
conspirators.

Last stage. The final stage of the action works out the development
Develop- *ment of an* of an inevitable fate.   The emotional strain now ceases,
inevitable and, as in the first stage, the passion is of the calmer order,
fate: pas- *sion-strain* the calmness in this case of pity balanced by a sense of
ceases. justice.   From the opening of the fourth Act the decline in
the justification of the conspirators is intimated by the logic
of events.   The first scene exhibits to us the triumvirate that
now governs Rome, and shows that in this triumvirate

Acts iv, v. Antony is supreme : with the man who is the embodiment
iv. i. of the Reaction thus appearing at the head of the world,
the fall of the conspirators is seen to be inevitable.   The
decline of our sympathy with them continues in the following

iv. ii. 3. scenes.   The Quarrel Scene shows how low the tone of

Cassius has fallen since he has dealt with assassination as a CHAP. IX.
political weapon; and even Brutus's moderation has hardened into unpleasing harshness. There is at this point iv. iii. 148,
plenty of relief to such unpleasing effects: there is the &c.
exhibition of the tender side of Brutus's character as shown iv. iii, from 239.
in his relations with his page, and the display of friendship iv. iii.
maintained between Brutus and Cassius amid falling fortunes.
But such incidents as these have a different effect upon us
from that which they would have had at an earlier period;
the justification of the conspirators has so far declined that
now attractive touches in them serve only to increase the
pathos of a fate which, however, our sympathy no longer
seeks to resist. We get a supernatural foreshadowing of the
end in the appearance to Brutus of Cæsar's Ghost, and the iv. iii. 275.
omen Cassius sees of the eagles that had consorted his army v. i. 80.
to Philippi giving place to ravens, crows, and kites on the
morning of battle: this lends the authority of the invisible
world to our sense that the conspirators' cause is doomed.
And judicial blindness overtakes them as Brutus's authority iv. iii. 196
in council overweighs in point after point the shrewder −230.
advice of Cassius. Through the scenes of the fifth Act we
see the republican leaders fighting on without hope. The *Justifica-*
last remnant of justification for their cause ceases as the *tion entire-ly vanishes*
conspirators themselves seem to acknowledge their error and *as the con-*
fate. Cassius as he feels his death-blow recognises the very *spirators recognise*
weapon with which he had committed the crime: *Cæsar's victory.*

> Cæsar, thou art revenged,
> Even with the sword that kill'd thee. v. iii. 45.

And at last even the firm spirit of Brutus yields:

> O Julius Cæsar, thou art mighty yet! v. v. 94.
> Thy spirit walks abroad, and turns our swords
> In our own proper entrails.

X

How Climax meets Climax in the Centre of Lear.

A Study in more complex Passion and Movement.

IN *Julius Cæsar* we have seen how, in the case of a very simple play, a few simple devices are sufficient to produce a regular rise and fall in the passion. We now turn to a highly elaborate plot and trace how, notwithstanding the elaborateness, a similar concentration of the passion in the centre of the play can be secured. *King Lear* is one of the most complex of Shakespeare's tragedies; its plot is made up of a number of separate actions, with their combinations accurately carried out, the whole impressing us with a sense of artistic involution similar to that of an elaborate musical fugue. Here, however, we are concerned only indirectly with the plot of the play: we need review it no further than may suffice to show what distinct interests enter into it, and enable us to observe how the separate trains of passion work toward a common climax at the centre.

Starting from the notion of pattern as a fundamental idea we have seen how Plot presents trains of events in human life taking form and shape as a crime and its nemesis, an oracle and its fulfilment, the rise and fall of an individual, or even as simply a story. The particular form of action under-

lying the main plot of *King Lear* is different from any we have yet noticed. It may be described as a *Problem Action*. A mathematician in his problem assumes some unusual com-

bination of forces to have come about, and then proceeds to Chap. X.
trace its consequences: so the Drama often deals with
problems in history and life, setting up, before the com- *dramatic action.*
mencement of the play or early in the action, some peculiar
arrangement of moral relations, and then throughout the
rest of the action developing the consequences of these to the
personages involved. Thus the opening scene of *King Lear*
is occupied in bringing before us a pregnant and suggestive
state of affairs : imperiousness is represented as overthrowing
conscience and setting up an unnatural distribution of power.
A human problem has thus been enunciated which the re- *The prob-*
mainder of the play has to work out to its natural solution. *lem stated.*

Imperiousness seems to be the term appropriate to Lear's
conduct in the first scene. This is no case of dotage dividing
an inheritance according to public declarations of affection. The division had already been made according to
the best advice : in the case of two of the daughters ' equali- *i. i. 3, &c.*
ties had been so weighed that curiosity in neither could
make choice of either's moiety'; and if the portion of the
youngest and best loved of the three was the richest, this
is a partiality natural enough to absolute power. The
opening scene of the play is simply the court ceremony in
which the formal transfer is to be made. Lear is already *38.*
handing to his daughters the carefully drawn maps which
mark the boundaries of the provinces, when he suddenly *49.*
pauses, and, with the yearning of age and authority for tes-
timonies of devotion, calls upon his daughters for declarations
of affection, the easiest of returns for the substantial gifts he
is giving them, and which Goneril and Regan pour forth
with glib eloquence. Then Lear turns to Cordelia, and, *84.*
thinking delightedly of the special prize he has marked out
for the pet of his old age, asks her :

> What can you say to draw
> A third more opulent than your sisters?

But Cordelia has been revolted by the fulsome flattery of the

Chap. X. sisters whose hypocrisy she knows so well, and she bluntly
refuses to be drawn into any declaration of affection at all.
Cordelia might well have found some other method of
separating herself from her false sisters, without thus flouting
her father before his whole court in a moment of tenderness
to herself; or, if carried away by the indignation of the
moment, a sign of submission would have won her a ready
pardon. But Cordelia, sweet and strong as her character is
compare
i. i. 131. in great things, has yet inherited a touch of her father's
temper, and the moment's sullenness is protracted into ob-
stinacy. Cordelia then has committed an offence of manner ;
Lear's passion vents itself in a sentence proper only to a
moral crime : now the punishment of a minute offence with
wholly disproportionate severity simply because it is an
offence against personal will is an exact description of imperiousness.

As Lear stands for imperiousness, so conscience is represented by Kent, who, with the voice of authority derived
from lifelong intimacy and service, interposes to check the
King's passion in its headlong course.

141–190.   *Kent.*   Royal Lear,
         Whom I have ever honour'd as my king,
         Loved as my father, as my master follow'd,
         As my great patron thought on in my prayers,—
     Lear. The bow is bent and drawn, make from the shaft.
     Kent. Let it fall rather, though the fork invade
         The region of my heart : be Kent unmannerly
         When Lear is mad. What wilt thou do, old man ?
         Think'st thou that duty shall have dread to speak,
         When power to flattery bows ? To plainness honour's bound,
         When majesty stoops to folly. Reverse thy doom . . .
     Lear. Kent, on thy life, no more.
     Kent. My life I never held but as a pawn
         To wage against thy enemies, nor fear to lose it,
         Thy safety being the motive . . .
     Lear.   O, vassal ! miscreant !
                                  [*Laying his hand on his sword.*

     Albany.   }
     Cornwall. } Dear sir, forbear.

Kent. Do:
> Kill thy physician, and the fee bestow
> Upon thy foul disease. Revoke thy doom ;
> Or, whilst I can vent clamour from my throat,
> I'll tell thee thou dost evil.

In the banishment of this Kent, then, the resistance of Lear's conscience is overcome, and his imperious passion has full swing in transferring Cordelia's kingdom to her treacherous sisters.

The opening scene has put before us, not in words but figured in action, a problem in human affairs : the violation of moral equity has set up an unnatural arrangement of power—power taken from the good and lodged in the hands of the bad. Here is, so to speak, a piece of moral unstable equilibrium, and the rebound from it is to furnish the remainder of the action. The very structure of the plot corresponds with the simple structure of a scientific proposition. The latter consists of two unequal parts : a few lines are sufficient to enunciate the problem, while a whole treatise may be required for its solution. So in *King Lear* a single scene brings about the unnatural state of affairs, the consequences of which it takes the rest of the play to trace. The 'catastrophe,' or turning-point of the play at which the ultimate issues are decided, appears in the present case, not close to the end of the play, nor (as in *Julius Cæsar*) in the centre, but close to the commencement : at the end of the opening scene Lear's act of folly has in reality determined the issue of the whole action ; the scenes which follow are only working out a determined issue to its full realisation.

We have seen the problem itself, the overthrow of conscience by imperiousness and the transfer of power from the good to the bad : what is the solution of it as presented by the incidents of the play ? The consequences flowing from what Lear has done make up three distinct tragedies, which go on working side by side, and all of which are essential to the full solution of the problem. First, there is the nemesis

The solution of the problem in a triple tragedy.

CHAP. X. upon Lear himself—the double retribution of receiving nothing
but evil from those he has unrighteously rewarded, and
(1) *Tragedy of Lear.* nothing but good from her whom, he bitterly feels, he has
cruelly wronged. But the punishment of the wrong-doer is
(2) *Tragedy of Cordelia and Kent.* only one element in the consequences of wrong ; the innocent also are involved, and we get a second tragedy in the
sufferings of the faithful Kent and the loving Cordelia, who,
through Kent as her representative, watches over her father's
safety, until at the end she appears in person to follow up her
devotion to the death. When, however, the incidents making
up the sufferings of Lear, of Kent, and of Cordelia are taken
out of the main plot, there is still a considerable section left—
(3) *Tragedy of Goneril and Regan.* that which is occupied with the mutual intrigues of Goneril
and Regan, intrigues ending in their common ruin. This
constitutes a third tragedy which, it will be seen, is as necessary to the solution of our problem as the other two. To
place power in the hands of the bad is an injury not only to
others, but also to the bad themselves, as giving fuel to the
fire of their wickedness : so in the tragedy of Goneril and
Regan we see evil passions placed in improper authority
using this authority to work out their own destruction.

An under-plot on the same basis as the main plot.   To this main plot is added an underplot equally elaborate.
As in *The Merchant of Venice*, the stories borrowed from two
distinct sources are worked into a common design ; and the
interweaving in the case of the present play is perhaps
Shakespeare's greatest triumph of constructive skill. The
two stories are made to rest upon the same fundamental idea—
compare
i. i, fin. that of undutifulness to old age : what Lear's daughters
actually do is that which is insinuated by Edmund as his
false charge against his brother.

i. ii. 76, &c.   I have heard him oft maintain it to be fit, that, sons at perfect age,
and fathers declining, the father should be as ward to the son, and the
son manage his revenue.

So obvious is this fundamental connection between the main
and the underplot, that our attention is called to it by a

personage in the play itself: 'he childed as I father'd,' is

Edgar's pithy summary of it when he is brought into contact

with Lear. But in this double tragedy, drawn from the

two families of Lear and of Gloucester, the chief bond

between its two sides consists in the sharp contrast which

extends to every detail of the two stories. In the main plot

we have a daughter, who has received nothing but harm from

her father, who has unjustly had her position torn from her

and given to undeserving sisters : nevertheless she sacrifices

herself to save the father who did the injury from the sisters

who profited by it. In the underplot we have a son, who has

received nothing but good from his father, who has, contrary

to justice, been advanced by him to the position of an elder

brother whom he has slandered : nevertheless, he is seeking

the destruction of the father who did him the unjust kindness,

when he falls by the hand of the brother who was wronged

by it. Thus as the main and underplot go on working side

by side, they are at every turn by their antithesis throwing up

one another's effect; the contrast is like the reversing of the

original subject in a musical fugue. Again, as the main

plot consisted in the initiation of a problem and its solution,

so the underplot consists in the development of an intrigue

and its consequences. The tragedy of the Gloucester family

will, if stated from the point of view of the father, correspond

in its parts with the tragedy in the family of Lear.

It must be remembered, however, that the position of the

father is different in the two cases ; Gloucester is not, as Lear,

the agent of the crime, but only a deceived instrument in the

hands of the villain Edmund, who is the real agent; if the

proper allowance be made for this difference, it will be seen

that the three tragedies which make up the consequences of

Lear's error have their analogies in the three tragedies which

flow from the intrigue of Edmund. First, we have the

nemesis on Gloucester, and this, in analogy with the nemesis

on Lear, consists in receiving nothing but evil from the son

CHAP. X.

iii. vi. 117.
*The main
and under-
plot parallel
and con-
trasted
through-
out.*

*The under-
plot an
Intrigue
Action :*

*involving
a triple
tragedy
parallel
with that
of the main
plot.*

CHAP. X.

(1) *Tragedy of Gloucester.*

(2) *Tragedy of Edgar.*

(3) *Tragedy of Edmund.*

he has so hastily advanced, and nothing but good from the other son whom, he comes gradually to feel, he has unintentionally wronged. In the next place we have the sufferings of the innocent Edgar. Then, as we before saw a third tragedy in the way in which the power conferred upon Goneril and Regan is used to work out their destruction, so in the underplot we find that the position which Edmund has gained involves him in intrigues, which by the development of the play are made to result in a nemesis upon his original intrigue. And it is a nemesis of exquisite exactness : for he meets his death in the very moment of his success, at the hands of the brother he has maligned and robbed, while the father he has deceived and sought to destroy is the means by which the avenger has been brought to the scene.

Complexity of plot not incon . ... ent with simplicity of movement.

We have gone far enough into the construction of the plot to perceive its complexity and the principal elements into which that complexity can be analysed. Two separate systems, each consisting of an initial action and three resulting tragedies, eight actions in all, are woven together by common personages and incidents, by parallelism of spirit, and by movement to a common climax ; not to speak of lesser Link Actions which assist in drawing the different stories closer together. As with plot generally, these separate elements are fully manifest only to the eye of analysis ; in following the course of the drama itself, they make themselves felt only in a continued sense of involution and harmonious symmetry. It is with passion, not with plot, that the present study is concerned ; and the train of passion which the common movement of these various actions calls out in the sympathy of the reader is as simple as the plot itself is intricate. In the case both of the main plot and the underplot the emotional effect rises in intensity ; moreover at this central height of intensity the two merge in a common Climax. The construction of the play resembles, if such a comparison may be allowed, the patent gas-apparatus,

which secures a high illuminating power by the simple CHAP. X.
device of several ordinary burners inclined to one another at
such an angle that the apexes of their flames meet in a point.
So the present play contains a Centrepiece of some three *from* ii. iv.
scenes, marked off (at least at the commencement) decisively, 290 to iii.
in which the main and underplot unite in a common Climax, interrup-
with special devices to increase its effect; the diverse interests iii, iii. v.
to which our sympathy was called out at the commencement, *The differ-*
and which analysis can keep distinct to the end, are *focussed*, *ent trains*
so far as passion is concerned, in this Centrepiece, in which *focussed in*
human emotion is carried to the highest pitch of tragic *a central*
agitation that the world of art has yet exhibited.

The emotional effect of the main plot rises to a climax in *The pas-*
the madness of Lear. This, as the highest form of human *sions of the*
agitation, is obviously a climax to the story of Lear himself. *gather to a*
It is equally a climax to the story of Kent and Cordelia, who *common*
suffer solely through their devoted watching over Lear, and *the madness*
to whom the bitterest point in their sufferings is that they feel *of Lear.*
over again all that their fallen master has to endure. Finally,
in the madness of Lear the third of the three tragedies, the
Goneril and Regan action, appears throughout in the background as the cause of all that is happening. If we keep our
eye upon this madness of Lear the movement of the play
assumes the form we have so often had to notice—the
regular arch. The first half of the arch, or rise in emotional
strain, we get in symptoms of mental disturbance preparing
us for actual madness which is to come. It is important to
note the difference between passion and madness: passion is
a disease of the mind, madness is a disease extending to the
mysterious linking of mind and body. At the commencement Lear is dominated by the passion of imperiousness, an
imperiousness born of his absolute power as king and father;
he has never learned from discipline restraint of his passion,
but has been accustomed to fling himself upon obstacles and
see them give way before him. Now the tragical situation is

Chap. X. prepared for him of meeting with obstacles which will not give way, but from which his passion rebounds upon himself with a physical shock. As thus opposition follows opposition, we see *waves* of physical, that is of hysterical, passion, sweeping over Lear, until, as it were, a tenth wave lands him in the full disease of madness.

i. iv.   The first case occurs in his interview with Goneril after that which is the first check he has received in his new life, the insolence shown to his retinue. Goneril enters his presence with a frown. The wont had been that Lear frowned and all cowered before him: and now he waits for his daughter to remember herself with a rising passion ill concealed under the forced calmness with which he enquires, 'Are you our daughter?' 'Doth any here know me?' But Goneril, on the contrary, calmly assumes the position of reprover, and details her unfounded charges of insolence against her father's sober followers, until at last he hears himself desired

> By her, that else will take the thing she begs,

to disquantity his train.   Then Lear breaks out:

> Darkness and devils!
> Saddle my horses; call my train together.
> Degenerate bastard! I'll not trouble thee:
> Yet have I left a daughter.

In a moment the thought of Cordelia's 'most small fault' and how it had been visited upon her occurs to condense into a single pang the whole sense of his folly; and here it is that the first of these waves of physical passion comes over Lear, its physical character marked by the physical action which accompanies it:

i. iv. 292.   O Lear, Lear, Lear!
> Beat at this gate, that let thy folly in,   [*Striking his head.*
> And thy dear judgement out.

i. v.   It lasts but for a moment: but it is a wave, and it will return. Accordingly in the next scene we see Lear on his journey from one daughter to the other. He is brooding over the scene he is leaving behind, and he cannot disguise a CHAP. X. shade of anxiety, in his awakened judgment, that some such scene may be reserved for him in the goal to which he is journeying. He is half listening, moreover, to the Fool, who harps on the same thought, that the King is suffering what he might have expected, that the other daughter will be like the first :—until there comes another of these sudden outbursts of passion, in which Lear for a moment half foresees the end to which he is being carried.

> O, let me not be mad, not mad, sweet heaven ! i. v. 49.
> Keep me in temper : I would not be mad !

Imperiousness is especially attached to outward signs of reverence : it is reserved for Lear when he arrives at Regan's ii. iv. 4. palace to find the messenger he has sent on to announce him suffering the indignity of the stocks. At first he will not believe that this has been done by order of his daughter and son.

> *Kent.* It is both he and she ; 13.
> Your son and daughter.
> *Lear.* No.
> *Kent.* Yes.
> *Lear.* No, I say.
> *Kent.* I say, yea.
> *Lear.* No, no, they would not.
> *Kent.* Yes, they have.
> *Lear.* By Jupiter, I swear, no.
> *Kent.* By Juno, I swear, ay.
> *Lear.* They durst not do 't ;
> They could not, would not do 't ; 'tis worse than murder,
> To do upon respect such violent outrage.

But he has to listen to a circumstantial account of the insult, and, further, reminded by the Fool that

> Fathers that wear rags
> Do make their children blind,

he comes at last to realise it all,—and then there sweeps over him a third and more violent wave of hysterical agitation.

> O, how this mother swells up toward my heart ! 56.
> Hysterica passio, down, thou climbing sorrow,
> Thy element's below !

He has mastered the passion by a strong effort : but it is a wave, and it will return. He has mastered himself in order to confront the culprits face to face : his altered position is brought home to him when they refuse to receive him. And the refusal is made the worse by the well-meant attempt of Gloucester to palliate it, in which he unfortunately speaks of the ' fiery quality ' of the duke.

> *Lear.* Vengeance ! plague ! death ! confusion !
> Fiery ? what quality ?

Nothing is harder than to endure what one is in the habit of inflicting on others; it was Lear's own ' fiery quality ' by which he had been accustomed to scorch all opposition out of his way; now he has to hear another man's ' fiery quality ' quoted to him. But this outburst is only momentary; the very extremity of the case seems to calm Lear, and he begins himself to frame excuses for the duke, how sickness and infirmity neglect the ' office ' to which health is bound—until his eye lights again upon his messenger sitting in the stocks, and the recollection of this deliberate affront brings back again the wave of passion.

122.   O me, my heart, my rising heart ! but, down !

Lear had a strange confidence in his daughter Regan. As we see the two women in the play, Regan appears the more cold-blooded ; nothing in Goneril is more cruel than Regan's

204.   I pray you, Father, being weak, seem so ;

or her meeting Lear's ' I gave you all ' with the rejoinder,

253.   And in good time you gave it.

But there was something in Regan's personal appearance that belied her real character; her father says to her in this scene :

173.   Her eyes are fierce, but thine
                Do comfort and not burn.

Judas betrayed with a kiss, and Regan persecutes her father CHAP. X.
in tears. But Regan has scarcely entered her father's presence ———
when the trumpet announces the arrival of Goneril, and Lear 185.
has to see the Regan in whom he is trusting take Goneril's 197.
hand before his eyes in token that she is making common
cause with her. When following this the words ' indiscretion,'
' dotage,' reach his ear there is a momentary swelling of the
physical passion within :

> O sides, you are too tough ;   200.
> Will you yet hold ?

He has mastered it for the last time : for now his whole
world seems to be closing in around him ; he has committed
his all to the two daughters standing before him, and they from 233.
unite to beat him down, from fifty knights to twenty-five,
from twenty-five to ten, to five, until the soft-eyed Regan
asks, ' What need one ? '   A sense of crushing oppression
stifles his anger, and Lear begins to answer with the same
calmness with which the question had been asked :

> O, reason not the need : our basest beggars
> Are in the poorest thing superfluous :
> Allow not nature more than nature needs,
> Man's life 's as cheap as beast's : thou art a lady ;
> If only to go warm were gorgeous,
> Why, nature needs not what thou gorgeous wear'st,
> Which scarcely keeps thee warm. But, for true need,—

He breaks off at finding himself actually pleading : and the
blinding tears come as he recognises that the kingly passion
in which he had found support at every cross has now
deserted him in his extremity.   He appeals to heaven against
the injustice.

> You heavens, give me that patience, patience I need !
> You see me here, you gods, a poor old man,
> As full of grief as age ; wretched in both !
> If it be you that stir these daughters' hearts
> Against their father, fool me not so much

> To bear it tamely; touch me with noble anger,
> And let not women's weapons, water-drops,
> Stain my man's cheeks!

The prayer is answered; the passion returns in full flood, and at last brings Lear face to face with the madness which has threatened from a distance.

> No, you unnatural hags,
> I will have such revenges on you both,
> That all the world shall—I will do such things,—
> What they are, yet I know not; but they shall be
> The terrors of the earth. You think I'll weep;
> No, I'll not weep:
> I have full cause of weeping; but this heart
> Shall break into a hundred thousand flaws,
> Or ere I'll weep. O fool, I SHALL go mad!

ii. iv. 290.
The storm marks off the Centre-piece of the play.

As Lear with these words rushes out into the night, we hear the first sound of the storm—the storm which here, as in *Julius Cæsar*, will be recognised as the dramatic background to the tempest of human emotions; it is the signal that we have now entered upon the mysterious Centrepiece of the play, in which the gathering passions of the whole drama are to be allowed to vent themselves without check or bound. And it is no ordinary storm: it is a night of bleak winds sorely ruffling, of cataracts and hurricanoes, of curled waters swelling above the main, of thought-executing-fires, and oak-cleaving thunderbolts; a night

iii. i. 12, &c.

> wherein the cub-drawn bear would couch,
> The lion and the belly-pinched wolf
> Keep their fur dry.

And all of it is needed to harmonise with the whirlwind of human passions which finds relief only in outscorning its fury. The purpose of the storm is not confined to this of marking the emotional climax: it is one of the agencies which assist in carrying it to its height. Experts in mental disease have noted amongst the causes which convert mere mental excitement into actual madness two leading ones, external physical shocks and imitation. Skakespeare has made use of both in

the central scenes of this play. For the first, Lear is exposed CHAP. X.
without shelter to the pelting of the pitiless storm, and he iii. i. 3;
waxes wilder with its wildness. Again when all this is at its iii. ii, &c.
height he is suddenly brought into contact with a half-naked iii. iv, from
Tom o'Bedlam. This gives the final shock. So far he had 39.
not gone beyond ungovernable rage ; he had not lost self-
consciousness, and could say, 'My wits begin to turn';
but the sight of Edgar completely unhinges his mind, and iii. iv. 66.
hallucinations set in ; a moment after he has seen him the
spirit of imitation begins to work, and Lear commences to
strip off his clothes. Thus perfect is the regular arch of
effect which is connected with Lear's madness. We have its
gradual rise in the waves of hysterical passion which ebbed
after they had flowed, until, at the point separating the
Centrepiece from the rest of the play, Lear's ' O fool I *shall*
go mad' seems to mark a change from which he never goes
back. Through these central scenes exposure to the storm is
fanning his passion more and more irretrievably into mad-
ness ; at the exact centre of all, imitation of Edgar comes to iii. iii. 39.
make the insanity acute. After the Centrepiece Lear dis- *Decline*
appears for a time, and when we next see him agitation has *after the Centrepiece*
declined into what is more pathetic : the acute mania has *from vio-*
given place to the pitiful spectacle of a shattered intellect ; *lent mad-*
there is no longer sharp suffering, but the whole mind is *shattered*
wrecked, gleams of coherence coming at intervals to mark *intellect.*
what a fall there has been; the strain upon our emotions iv. vi. 81.
sinks into the calm of hopelessness. compare
iv. vi. 178;

> He hates him much v. iii. 314.
> That would upon the rack of this tough world
> Stretch him out longer.

But who is this madman with whom Lear meets at the *The pas-*
turning-point of the play? It is Edgar, the victim of the *sions of the underplot*
underplot, whose life has been sought by his brother and *gather to a*
father until he can find no way of saving himself but the *common*
disguise of feigned madness. This feigned madness of *the madness of Edgar.*

Edgar, as it appears in the central scenes, serves as emotional climax to the underplot, just as the madness of Lear is the emotional climax of the main plot. Edgar's madness is obviously the climax to the tragedy of his own sufferings, but it is also a central point to the movement of the other two tragedies which with that of Edgar make up the underplot. One of these is the nemesis upon Gloucester, and this, we have seen, is double, that he receives good from the son he has wronged and evil from the son he has favoured. The

iii. iv. 170. turning-point of such a nemesis is reached in the Hovel Scene, where Gloucester says :

> I'll tell thee, friend,
> I am almost mad myself : I had a son,
> Now outlaw'd from my blood ; he sought my life,
> But lately, very late : I loved him, friend :
> No father his son dearer : truth to tell thee,
> This grief hath crazed my wits !

He says this in the presence of the very Edgar, disguised under the form of the wretched idiot he hardly marks. Edgar now learns how his father has been deceived ; in his heart he is re-united to him, and from this point of re-union springs the devotion he lavishes upon his father in the

compare
iii. iii. 15. affliction that presently falls upon him. On the other hand, that which brings Gloucester to this Hovel Scene, the attempt

iii. iii. 22 ; to save the King, is betrayed by Edmund, who becomes
iii. vii. thereby the cause of the vengeance which puts out his father's eyes. Thus from this meeting of the mad Edgar with the mad Lear there springs at once the final stroke in the misery Gloucester suffers from the son he has favoured, and the beginning of the forgiving love he is to experience from the son he has wronged : that meeting then is certainly the central climax to the double nemesis which makes up the Gloucester action. The remaining tragedy of the underplot embraces the series of incidents by the combination of which the success of Edmund's intrigue becomes gradually converted into the nemesis which punishes it. Now the

squalid wretchedness of a Bedlamite, together with the
painful strain of supporting the assumed character amidst
the conflicting emotions which the unexpected meeting of
the Hovel Scene has aroused, represent the highest point to
which the misery resulting from the intrigue can rise. At
the same time the use Edgar makes of this madness after
hearing Gloucester's confession is to fasten himself in attend- iv. i, &c.
ance upon his afflicted father, and proves in the sequel the
means by which he is brought to be the instrument of the
vengeance that overtakes Edmund. The central climax of
a tragedy like this of intrigue and nemesis cannot be more
clearly marked than in the incident in which are combined
the summit of the injury and the foundation of the retribution. Thus all three tragedies which together make up
the resultant of the intrigue constituting the underplot reach
their climax of agitation in the scene in which Lear and
Edgar meet.

It appears, then, that the Centrepiece of the play is occupied *The Centre-*
with the contact of two madnesses, the madness of Lear and *piece a*
duet, or
the madness of Edgar; that of Lear gathering up into a *by the ad-*
climax trains of passion from all the three tragedies of the *dition of*
the Fool.
main plot, and that of Edgar holding a similar position to the *a trio of*
three tragedies of the underplot. Further, these madnesses *madness.*
do not merely go on side by side; as they meet they
mutually affect one another, and throw up each other's
intensity. By the mere sight of the Bedlamite, Lear, already
tottering upon the verge of insanity, is driven really and
incurably mad; while in the case of Edgar, the meeting with
Lear, and through Lear with Gloucester, converts the burden
of feigning idiocy from a cruel stroke of unjust fate into a
hardship voluntarily undergone for the sake of ministering to
a father now forgiven and pitied. And so far as the general
effect of the play is concerned this central Climax presents a
terrible *duet of madness,* the wild ravings and mutual inter-
workings of two distinct strains of insanity, each answering

CHAP. X. and outbidding the other. The distinctness is the greater as
the two are different in kind. In Lear we have the madness
of passion, exaggeration of ordinary emotions; Edgar's is
the madness of idiocy, as idiocy was in early ages when the
cruel neglect of society added physical hardship to mental
affliction. In Edgar's frenzy we trace rapid irrelevance
with gleams of unexpected relevance, just sufficient to partly
answer a question and go off again into wandering; a sense
of ill-treatment and of being an outcast; remorse and
thoughts as to close connection of sin and retribution; visions
of fiends as in bodily presence; cold, hunger : these alter-
nating with mere gibberish, and all perhaps within the
compass of a few lines.

iii. iv. 51.   Who gives anything to poor Tom ? whom the foul fiend hath led
through fire and through flame, and through ford and whirlipool, o'er
bog and quagmire; that hath laid knives under his pillow, and halters
in his pew ; set ratsbane by his porridge ; made him proud of heart, to
ride on a bay trotting-horse over four-inched bridges, to course his own
shadow for a traitor. Bless thy five wits ! Tom's a-cold,—O, do de,
do de, do de. Bless thee from whirlwinds, star-blasting, and taking !
Do poor Tom some charity, whom the foul fiend vexes : there could
I have him now,—and there,—and there again, and there.

But this is not all. When examined more closely this
Centrepiece exhibits not a duet but a *trio of madness*; with
the other two there mingles a third form of what may be
called madness, the professional madness of the court fool.
Institution This court fool or jester is an institution of considerable
of the court interest. It seems to rest upon three mediæval and ancient
fool. notions. The first is the barbarism of enjoying personal
defects, illustrated in the large number of Roman names
derived from bodily infirmities, Varus the bandy-legged, Bal-
bus the stammerer, and the like ; this led our ancestors to
find fun in the incoherence of natural idiocy, and finally
made the imitation of it a profession. A second notion
underlying the institution of a jester is the connection to the
ancient mind between madness and inspiration; the same

Greek word *entheos* stands for both, and to this day the idiot of a Scotch village is believed in some way to see further than sane folk. A third idea to be kept in mind is the mediæval conception of wit. With us wit is weighed by its intrinsic worth; the old idea, appearing repeatedly in Shakespeare's scenes, was that wit was a mental game, a sort of battledore and shuttlecock, in which the jokes themselves might be indifferent since the point of the game lay in keeping it up as smartly and as long as possible. The fool, whose title and motley dress suggested the absence of ordinary sense or propriety, combines in his office all three notions: from the last he was bound to keep up the fire of badinage, even though it were with witless nonsense; from the second he was expected at times to give utterance to deep truths; and in virtue of the first he had license to make hard hits under protection of the 'folly' which all were supposed to enjoy.

> He that a fool doth very wisely hit,
> Doth very foolishly, although he smart,
> Not to seem senseless of the bob.

The institution, if it has died out as a personal office attached to kings or nobles, has perhaps been preserved by the nation as a whole in a form analogous to other modern institutions: the all-embracing newspaper has absorbed this element of life, and Mr. Punch is the national jester. His figure and face are an improvement on the old motley habit; his fixed number of pages have to be filled, if not always with wit, yet with passable padding: no one dare other than enjoy the compliment of his notice, under penalty of showing that 'the cap has fitted'; and certainly Mr. Punch finds ways of conveying to statesmen criticisms to which the proprieties of parliament would be impervious. The institution of the court fool is eagerly utilised by Shakespeare, and is the source of some of his finest effects: he treats it as a sort of chronic Comedy, the function of which may be described as that of trans-

The institution adapted to modern times in Punch.

lating deep truths of human nature into the language of
laughter.

In applying, then, this general view of the court fool to the
present case we must avoid two opposite errors. We must
not pass over all his utterances as unmeaning folly, nor, on
the other hand, must we insist upon seeing a meaning in
everything that he says: what truth he speaks must be expected to make its appearance amidst a cloud of nonsense.
The func- Making this proviso we may lay down that the function of
tion of the the Fool in *King Lear* is to keep vividly before the minds of
Fool in
Lear is to the audience (as well as of his master) the idea at the root
keep before
us the of the main plot—that unstable moral equilibrium, that un-
original natural distribution of power which Lear has set up, and of
problem:
which the whole tragedy is the rebound. In the first scene
v. in which he appears before us he is, amid all his nonsense,
harping upon the idea that Lear has committed the folly of
trusting to the gratitude of the ungrateful, and is reaping the
inevitable consequences. As he enters he hands his cox-
comb, the symbol of folly, to the King, and to Kent for
taking the King's part. His first jingling song,

> Have more than thou showest,
> Speak less than thou knowest,
> Lend less than thou owest, &c.,

is an expansion of the maxim, Trust nobody. And however
irrelevant he becomes, he can in a moment get back to this
root idea. They tell him his song is nothing:

Fool. Then 'tis like the breath of an unfee'd lawyer; you gave me
nothing for 't. Can you make no use of nothing, nuncle?
Lear. Why, no, boy; nothing can be made out of nothing.
Fool [*to Kent*]. Prithee, tell him, so much the rent of his land comes
to: he will not believe a fool.

i. i. 92. 'Nothing will come of nothing' had been the words Lear
had used to Cordelia; now he is bidden to see how they
have become the exact description of his own fortune. No
wonder Lear exclaims, ' A bitter fool!'

Fool. Dost thou know the difference, my boy, between a bitter fool CHAP. X.
and a sweet one?

Lear. No, lad; teach me.

Fool.
> That lord that counsell'd thee
> To give away thy land,
> Come place him here by me,
> Do thou for him stand:
> The sweet and bitter fool
> Will presently appear;
> The one in motley here,
> The other found out there.

Lear. Dost thou call me fool, boy?

Fool. All thy other titles thou hast given away; that thou wast
born with.

Again and again he turns to other topics and comes suddenly
back to the main thought.

Fool. Prithee, nuncle, keep a schoolmaster that can teach thy fool i. iv. 195.
to lie: I would fain learn to lie.

Lear. An you lie, sirrah, we'll have you whipped.

Fool. I marvel what kin thou and thy daughters are: they'll have
me whipped for speaking true, thou'lt have me whipped for lying;
and sometimes I am whipped for holding my peace. I had rather be
any kind o' thing than a fool: and yet I would not be thee, nuncle;
thou hast pared thy wit o' both sides, and left nothing i' the middle:
here comes one o' the parings.

It is Goneril who enters, and who proceeds to state her case i. iv. 207.
in the tone of injury, detailing how the order of her household state has been outraged, but ignoring the source from
which she has received the power to keep up state at all:
what she has omitted the Fool supplies in parable, as if continuing her sentence—

> For, you trow, nuncle,
> The hedge-sparrow fed the cuckoo so long,
> That it's had it head bit off by it young,

and then instantly involves himself in a cloud of irrelevance,

> So, out went the candle, and we were left darkling.

In the scene which follows, the Fool is performing a variation i. v.
on the same theme: the sudden removal from one sister

CHAP. X.   to the other is no real escape from the original foolish
————   situation.

i. v. 8.   *Fool.* If a man's brains were in 's heels, were 't not in danger of
kibes?
  Lear. Ay, boy.
  Fool. Then, I prithee, be merry; thy wit shall ne'er go slip-shod.

To say that Lear is in no danger of suffering from brains in
his heels is another way of saying that his flight is folly. He
goes on to insist that the other daughter will treat her father
'kindly,' that 'she's as like this as a crab's like an apple.'
His laying down that the reason why the nose is in the
middle of the face is to keep the eyes on either side of the
nose, and that the reason why the seven stars are no more
than seven is 'a pretty reason—because they are not eight,'
suggests (if it be not pressing it too far) that we must not
look for depth where there is only shallowness—the mistake
Lear has made in trusting to the gratitude of his daughters.
And the general thought of Lear's original folly he brings
out, true to the fool's office, from the most unlikely beginnings.

i. v. 26.   *Fool.* Canst tell how an oyster makes his shell?
  Lear. No.

'Nor I neither,' answers the Fool, with a clown's impudence;
'but,' he adds, 'I can tell why a snail has a house.'

  Lear. Why?
  Fool. Why, to put his head in; not to give it away to his daughters.

ii. iv. 1–   All through the scene in front of the stocks the Fool is harp-
128.   ing on the folly of expecting gratitude from such as Goneril
and Regan.   It is fathers who bear bags that see their children
kind; the wise man lets go his hold on a great wheel running
down hill, but lets himself be drawn after by the great wheel
that goes up the hill; he himself, the Fool hints, is a fool for
staying with Lear; to cry out at Goneril and Regan's behaviour is as unreasonable as for the cook to be impatient
with the eels for wriggling; to have trusted the two

daughters with power at all was like the folly of the man that, Chap. X.
' in pure kindness to his horse, buttered his hay.'

The one idea, then, stationary amidst all the Fool's gyrations
of folly is the idea of Lear's original sin of passion, from the
consequences of which he can never escape; only the idea is *but in an*
put, not rationally, but translated into an emotional form *emotional*
form as
which makes it fit to mingle with the agitation of the central *adapted to*
the agita-
scenes. The emotional form consists partly in the irrelevance *tion of the*
amid which the idea is brought out, producing continual *Centre-*
shocks of surprise. But more than this an emotional form is *piece.*
given to the utterances of the Fool by his very position with
reference to Lear. There is a pathos that mingles with his iii. i. 16;
humour, where the Fool, a tender and delicate youth, is found iii. ii. 10,
25, 68; iii.
the only attendant who clings to Lear amid the rigour of the iv. 80, 150.
storm, labouring with visibly decreasing vigour to out-jest
his master's heart-struck injuries, and to keep up holiday
abandon amidst surrounding realities. Throughout he is i. iv. 107;
Lear's best friend, and epithets of endearment are continually iii. ii. 68,
72, &c.
passing between them: he has been Cordelia's friend (as
Touchstone was the friend of Rosalind), and pined for Cor- i. iv. 79.
delia after her banishment. Nevertheless he is the only one
who can deliver hard thrusts at Lear, and bring home to him,
under protection of his double relation to wisdom and folly,
Lear's original error and sin. So faithful and so severe, the
Fool becomes an outward conscience to his master : he keeps
before Lear the unnatural act from which the whole tragedy
springs, but he converts the thought of it into the emotion of
self-reproach.

Our total result then is this. The intricate drama of *King* Summary.
Lear has a general movement which centres the passion of
the play in a single Climax. Throughout a Centrepiece of a
few scenes, against a background of storm and tempest is
thrown up a tempest of human passion—a madness trio, or
mutual play of three sorts of madness, the real madness of
passion in Lear, the feigned madness of idiocy in Edgar, and

CHAP. X. the professional madness of the court fool. When the
elements of this madness trio are analysed, the first is found
to gather up into itself the passion of the three tragedies
which form the main plot; the second is a similar climax to
the passion of the three tragedies which make up the underplot; the third is an expression, in the form of passion, of the
original problem out of which the whole action has sprung.
Thus intricacy of plot has been found not inconsistent with
simplicity of movement, and from the various parts of the
drama the complex trains of passion have been brought to a
focus in the centre.

XI.

'OTHELLO' AS A PICTURE OF JEALOUSY
AND INTRIGUE.

A Study in Character
and Plot.

IN no play of Shakespeare is the organic connection be-tween Character and Plot so simply and so emphatically marked as in the play of *Othello*. Viewed from the side of Character, its personages fall into a magnificent piece of Grouping around the passion of Suspicious Jealousy[1]. When we turn to analyse the Plot, this is found to be a network of Intrigue—the mode of action in which Jealousy most naturally finds vent; and the intrigues, however elaborate, are by the movement of the plot drawn to a simple culmination which remains for all literature the typical climax of tragic jealousy.

The leading personages in *Othello* are, in character, variations of a single passion, suspicious jealousy, and their position in the play is exactly determined by their relation

---

[1] It is important to remember that in Shakespearean English the word 'jealousy' comes nearer in meaning to 'suspicion' than in modern usage. Compare *Oth*. **iii**. iii. 198: 'not jealous nor secure;' or *Henry V*, **ii**. ii. 126:

> O, how hast thou with jealousy infected
> The sweetness of affiance!

Compare Scotch usage: 'They *jaloused* the opening of our letters at Fairport.' (*Antiquary*, chapter xxiv.)

CHAP. XI. to this passion.　Othello himself represents jealousy in a
—— trusting nature:

> one not easily jealous, but, being wrought,
> Perplex'd in the extreme.

Iago sees truly that his leader's 'unbookish jealousy' must
construe things wrong; how unbookish it is would be sufficiently proved by the wearisome iteration with which he
applies the epithet 'honest' to Iago.　On the contrary,
Iago's is the jealousy of a nature that believes in nothing;

ii. i. in his soliloquies he lets it appear that he suspects both
304, 316; Othello and Cassio to have tampered with his wife, and this
&c. obviously baseless jealousy is largely the motive of Iago's
action, as the jealousy of other persons is mainly the instrument with which he works.　Both his subordinate agents hold
their place in the play by the same thread of connection.　In
Roderigo we have the ordinary jealousy of a love intrigue
utilised by the skill of Iago; and where the virtue of
Desdemona makes Iago's scheme too transparent in its

ii. i. 215. weakness, it is only by working on Roderigo's jealousy of
Cassio that the plotter is able to retain his tool.　Bianca
strikes a yet lower key—the jealousy of a vulgar liaison.
Her connection is with only a single phase of the action,
the misunderstanding in the matter of the handkerchief.　For
this link in the plot it is merely necessary for her to appear
at two points: at the first it is jealousy that brings her to look
for Cassio, and reproach him for long absence—when he
gives her the handkerchief; and it is jealousy that brings her
again to fling it back at him in the sight of the concealed
Othello.　Finally, Cassio and Desdemona are prominent in
the play by the *utter* absence of the passion.　This appears

ii. iii. 12– negatively in Cassio; for example, when Iago, inviting him
33. to the drinking-bout, insinuates that Desdemona even is
susceptible, Cassio in sheer simplicity misunderstands all he
says.　In Desdemona the absence of jealousy and suspicion
amounts to a phenomenon, and when we come to trace the

story we shall see how it is her simplicity which is for ever
betraying her. Such are the varieties of form, positive and
negative, which jealousy assumes in these various personages,
and they thus blend themselves into a character-group round
this passion as the central point of view.

What Jealousy is to the Character of this play Intrigue is *Plot*
to its Plot. Shakespeare's plots are, almost without exception, *founded on Intrigue.*
distinguished by their complexity : the fulness of life he has
drawn within the field of his drama can have design given
to it only by a plan of system within system. He keeps
going side by side several different stories, or interests, or
technically, 'actions,' and the triumph of his plot-handling is
the exquisite symmetry between these different drifts of events,
and the way in which they move on to a common consummation. The analysis of such plot falls into two divisions :
Economy views the play as a whole, and the relation of its
various parts to one another ; Movement traces the development of the total effect through the successive scenes, from
imperfect to complete. Whether we review the Economy or
the Movement one idea is found to animate the present
play. Its plot presents a number of separate intrigues or
other ' actions,' gradually by the course of the play merged
in one, which rushes on to a tragic consummation of Jealousy,
and a reaction of Nemesis on the Intriguer.

I distinguish in the play eight of these ' actions,' or
separate trains of incident.

The first, and slightest, is the illicit liaison between Bianca *Economy*
and Cassio. It appears in no more than four incidents of the *of the Plot.*
story ; twice Bianca appears to reproach her lover ; once the *Three*
tie between the two is made a subject of conversation between *actions : Bianca,*
Cassio and Iago, in order that the by-play of this conversa- iii. iv. 169 ;
tion may be seen by and deceive the concealed Othello ; and iv. i. 152,
82–219 ;
yet again accident brings Bianca to the spot where her lover v. i. 73.
has just fallen wounded. Yet slight as this liaison is,—a
mere matter of course for an Italian gentleman of that corrupt

CHAP. XI. age,—Shakespeare must needs give it a touch of individuality. He has reversed the usual relations of mistress and lover; the pretty Bianca, who no doubt has been cruel to many adorers in her time, has now to feel the slights of the still more handsome Cassio; she is the one genuinely in love, and it is Cassio who *se laisse aimer*. Moreover, it is a tragic action; for though the two know no evil in the bond which has united them, yet it comes to an end with the arrest of Bianca on the false suspicion of murdering her lover, and as she is borne off in custody she has to hear from the wife of Iago the plain language which conveys the honest matron's opinion of loose life.

Roderigo,   The second action is Roderigo's pursuit of Desdemona. No name can be given to it worthier than 'pursuit.' Roderigo is merely a Venetian youth without parts or character, a typical man about town, one who is no fool, as he thinks, yet has just wit enough to be used by Iago for his own purposes. He has in due course fallen head over heels in love with the great beauty of Venice. It is hardly necessary to remark that the passion is all on one side. There is nothing to show that Desdemona so much as knows of Roderigo's existence; certain it is that she never once speaks to him,

i. i. 95.   nor he to her, in the whole play. Roderigo had indeed got as far as Desdemona's father, but only to be warned off the premises as one not fit to pay addresses to Brabantio's daughter. It is true that the shock of Desdemona's elopement with Othello, announced to her father by Roderigo, throws him for a time into the arms of Brabantio, but only on the principle that misfortune makes strange bedfellows; and we must understand it only as a measure of Brabantio's disgust at Othello, that he turns to Roderigo with the words,

i. i. 176.   'O, would you had had her!' The whole of this action is simply a piece of amorous hunting. Yet it has a tragic dignity given to it, for it costs poor Roderigo his life.

Third in order I place that which is the main action of

the whole play,—the love of Othello and Desdemona. Not
only does this remain as one of the world's most tragic
stories—

> O, the pity of it! the pity of it!

but it further stands out as one of the great fundamental
types of love. It is the love that attracts contraries into the
closest of bonds. Desdemona is above all things the 'gentle'
Desdemona—

> A maiden never bold;
> Of spirit so still and quiet, that her motion
> Blush'd at herself.

She is essentially domestic:

> So opposite to marriage that she shunn'd
> The wealthy curled darlings of our nation.

Yet she is drawn to the 'thick-lipped,' 'sooty' Moor, who is
in Venetian eyes the type of ugliness, the battered soldier
whose only charms are his scars from disastrous chances and
moving accidents by flood and field, and the 'rude speech'
which tells of them.

> For since these arms of mine had seven years' pith,
> Till now some nine moons wasted, they have used
> Their dearest action in the tented field,
> And little of this great world can I speak,
> More than pertains to feats of broil and battle.

True, he is the great warrior of his age, whose genius
haughty Venice is glad to purchase. And the quiet life
drinks in the story of the life of action, until the opposites run
together with a shock, and Desdemona is the one to speak i. iii. 164.
the first word of wooing. Yet, opposites though they be,
they have one heritage in common, which plays a great part
in their characters and their fate. Their common quality is
utter simplicity. Like Siegfried, who had learned everything
but how to fear, so Othello with all his knocking about the
world has never learned how to suspect. Desdemona thinks

that the sun where Othello was born had drawn from him all
such humours as jealousy; and must not we think so too
when we find him throughout the play treating Iago as his
type of honesty? And a like absence of suspiciousness
betrays Desdemona into acts that look equivocal. If we
knew nothing of the plot, we should feel a note of danger in
her enthusiastic sympathy:

> My lord shall never rest;
> I 'll watch him tame, and talk him out of patience;
> His bed shall seem a school, his board a shrift;
> I 'll intermingle everything he does
> With Cassio's suit.

When language has been used to her that there is no misunderstanding, she asks her attendant:

> Dost thou in conscience think,—tell me, Emilia,—
> That there be women do abuse their husbands
> In such gross kind?

It is like seething a kid in its own mother's milk when Iago
trades upon this simple unsuspiciousness in order to rouse a
fiend of jealousy. Yet it is only too easily intelligible. To
such simplicity of nature human character appears only
simple; men must be classified as sheep or goats; there is
good and evil only, without fine shadings or neutral colours,
without compromises or allowances. Let Desdemona once
appear guilty, and all the whiteness of her soul is the white
hypocrisy that makes the black all the blacker. So the true
love of Othello and Desdemona ends in murder and suicide:
though even these are scarcely more terrible than for such a
love to end in jealousy.

All these three actions are trains of affairs moving on side
by side when the play opens. We now come to four actions
which are conscious intrigues, all carried on by the master-
Four In- plotter Iago. The first is Iago's intrigue against Roderigo,
trigues of which is as simple as intrigue can be; it is merely the
Iago. sharper's planning to get all the money he can out of his

dupe and then get rid of him. When Desdemona is married
beyond the possibility of undoing, Iago tells the disappointed
suitor, 'I could never better stead thee than now.'

> Put money in thy purse; follow thou the wars; defeat thy favour
> with an usurped beard; I say, put money in thy purse. It cannot be
> that Desdemona should long continue her love to the Moor,—put
> money in thy purse,—nor he his to her: it was a violent commence-
> ment, and thou shalt see an answerable sequestration :—put but money
> in thy purse. These Moors are changeable in their wills :—fill thy
> purse with money:—the food that to him now is as luscious as locusts,
> shall be to him shortly as bitter as coloquintida. She must change for
> youth : when she is sated . . . she must have change, she must : there-
> fore put money in thy purse.

So Roderigo cheers up and goes to sell his land, while Iago
soliloquises :

> Thus do I ever make my fool my purse.

When the orange has been sucked dry it is naturally thrown
away, and so in the fifth act Iago soliloquises :

> Live Roderigo,
> He calls me to a restitution large
> Of gold and jewels that I bobbed from him,
> As gifts to Desdemona ;
> It must not be.

Accordingly, when other means have failed, he seizes a
favourable opportunity for stabbing Roderigo. The whole
affair is quite simple.

Against Cassio Iago has, not one, but two, distinct intrigues, animated by two separate motives. Iago's first
grudge is that all the interest he had made among the great
ones of Venice had been insufficient to gain him the post of
Othello's lieutenant, which had instead fallen to a foreigner.

> And what was he?
> Forsooth, a great arithmetician,
> One Michael Cassio, a Florentine,
> A fellow almost damned in a fair wife ;

> That never set a squadron in the field,
> Nor the division of a battle knows
> More than a spinster; unless the bookish theoric,
> Wherein the toged consuls can propose
> As masterly as he: mere prattle, without practice,
> Is all his soldiership. But he, sir, had the election:
> And I, of whom his eyes had seen the proof
> At Rhodes, at Cyprus and on other grounds
> Christian and heathen, must be be-leed and calmed
> By debitor and creditor: this counter-caster,
> He, in good time, must his lieutenant be,
> And I—God bless the mark!—his Moorship's ancient.

Disappointed rivalry, pressure of debts, the combined prejudices of practical man against doctrinaire and of Venetian against Florentine, make up a formidable motive for action in a nature such as Iago's. Accordingly he has studied the new-comer until he has found the weak side by which he may **ii. iii. 34–53.** be betrayed. This weak side, it is worth noting, is not the moral vice of intemperance so much as the physical weakness of stomach which makes a small dose of alcohol produce upon Cassio the effect that excess produces on other men. Cassio drinks most unwillingly, and in circumstances which made refusal almost impossible ; but the poison acts on him instantly, and he is betrayed into unmilitary conduct which Iago adroitly magnifies into a brawl. So his purpose is gained, and a little past the middle of the play Iago hears the **iii. iii. 478.** welcome words, ' Now art thou my lieutenant.' But it is only after this point that we are allowed to see a wider and more fundamental antagonism between Cassio and the villain of our play. Iago in the fifth act mutters :

> If Cassio do remain,
> He hath a daily beauty in his life
> That makes me ugly . . .

It is the primitive feud of light and darkness, reinforced by a **ii. i. 316.** suspicion—for Iago turns his foul suspicions in all impossible directions—that Cassio has played him false with Emilia, that brings Iago to the conclusion that Cassio must die.

The same antagonism of light and darkness makes Iago CHAP. XI.
hate the Moor, and there is the same additional motive of
suspicions, grounded on nothing but his own foul thoughts,
that by Othello also he has been wronged in his wedded
life.

> *Emilia.* The Moor's abused by some most villainous knave.
> . . . . Some such squire he was
> That turned your wit the seamy side without,
> And made you to suspect me with the Moor.

Iago has said of this in soliloquy :—

> I know not if 't be true ;
> But I, for mere suspicion in that kind,
> Will do as if for surety.

By the end of the next act the feeling has grown the stronger
by brooding :—

> —the thought whereof
> Doth, like a poisonous mineral, gnaw my inwards ;
> And nothing can or shall content my soul
> Till I am even'd with him, wife for wife,
> Or, failing so, yet that I put the Moor
> At least into a jealousy so strong
> That judgment cannot cure.

Here again are fine materials for an intrigue, and this
constitutes one of the main actions in our plot.

We have now before us three trains of circumstances
moving on independently at the opening of the play, and four
evil intrigues added to them by the villainy of Iago : in all
seven 'actions,' each an intelligible whole, which can be
traced separately through the details of the story in the way
in which an historian distinguishes movements and tendencies
underlying the complex events of human life. It may assist
clearness to recapitulate and number these actions :—

1. Bianca's liaison with Cassio.
2. Roderigo's pursuit of Desdemona.
3. The love of Othello and Desdemona.

4. Iago's intrigue against Roderigo.

     5. Iago's intrigue to gain Cassio's place.

     6. Iago's intrigue to get rid of Cassio altogether.

     7. Iago's intrigue to destroy the happiness of Othello and
        Desdemona.

But the dramatic interest of Economy finds its highest
satisfaction in watching these separate actions become united ;
in seeing how, by a series of dramatic devices, one after
another they are drawn together, and merged in one common
movement to a goal of tragic ruin.

Economic   The first of these devices is that Iago, having it as a fixed
devices
linking the purpose to arouse jealousy in the guileless Othello, hits at
actions last upon Cassio as the one to be made the object of these
together. suspicions.   We are allowed to see this idea gradually dawn
upon Iago.

i. iii. 398.   Cassio's a proper man : let me see now :
                       .   .   .   .   .   .   How, how ?—Let 's see :—
                       After some time, to abuse Othello's ear
                       That he is too familiar with his wife.
                       He hath a person and a smooth dispose
                       To be suspected, framed to make women false.

When Iago proceeds to act upon this notion he gains the
economic advantage of making his evil machinations against
Othello serve as the instrument of his evil purpose to ruin
Cassio ; in other words, Nos. 6 and 7 of our actions are
now merged in one.

In carrying out this double scheme of ruining Cassio and
Othello at once, by making the one the object of the other's
jealousy, accident suggests to Iago a further device, which
produces further amalgamation of our different actions.
Cassio's ruin has already been so far compassed that he has
been cast from office, and is seeking restoration ; the
ii. iii. 250. momentary appearance of Desdemona on the scene suggests
to Iago that Cassio should be led to use Desdemona's
intervention in his behalf.   It will be easy to misinterpret

her warmhearted intervention as dictated by more than good- CHAP. XI.
nature. By this simple device the whole force of the love
between Desdemona and her lord is utilised to help forward
the evil intrigue against Cassio, which we have seen to be at
the same time an intrigue against Othello's happiness. Thus
now No. 3 of our actions is united with Nos. 6 and 7 in one
common drift.

Two more devices serve to draw in Roderigo's pursuit of
Desdemona, and make this part of the general attack upon
Cassio. Cassio is made the object of Roderigo's jealousy,
but—that there may not be too much sameness in the devices
of this drama—the suggestion this time is, not that Cassio
loves Desdemona, which to Roderigo would seem a matter
of course, but that Desdemona loves Cassio.   ii. i, from
                                                  220.

> *Iago.* . . . Desdemona is directly in love with him.
> *Rod.* With him! why, 'tis not possible.
> *Iago.* Lay thy finger thus, and let thy soul be instructed. Mark me
> with what violence she first loved the Moor, but for bragging and
> telling her fantastical lies : and will she love him still for prating? let
> not thy discreet heart think it. Her eye must be fed ; and what delight
> shall she have to look on the devil!

He proceeds to dilate on Cassio's advantages of person :

> The knave is handsome, young, and hath all those requisites in him
> that folly and green minds look after : a pestilent complete knave; and
> the woman hath found him already.
> *Rod.* I cannot believe that in her; she's full of most blessed con-
> dition.
> *Iago.* Blessed fig's end!

Roderigo is soon sufficiently indoctrinated with this suspicion
to make him bear his part in the comedy which is to present
Cassio as a brawler, and hurl him from his office. But when
this is accomplished the jealous suspicions still live, and a
second bit of ingenuity on Iago's part utilises them to assist
his deeper scheme against Cassio. A commission has arrived
from Venice : affairs in Cyprus no longer need Othello, the iv. ii, from
                                                             225.

Senate consider Cassio sufficient for this government while the great general goes forward to the war in Mauretania. Iago adroitly suggests to the love-sick Roderigo that Othello will take Desdemona away with him, and that there is only one way of preventing this :—

> . . . unless his abode be lingered here by some accident : wherein none can be so determinate as the removing of Cassio.
> *Rod.* How do you mean, removing of him ?
> *Iago.* Why, by making him uncapable of Othello's place; knocking out his brains.
> *Rod.* And that you would have me to do ?

Roderigo this time needs a good deal of persuading ; but when he does give consent we have the whole force of his passion for Desdemona working into Iago's intrigues against Cassio. That is to say, No. 2 of our scheme of actions is now seen to co-operate with Nos. 5 and 6.

But this No. 6 (the attempt to make Cassio a victim of Othello's jealousy) has already been seen to have amalgamated with two other actions, Nos. 3 and 7. We have thus five of our separate trains of incidents—Nos. 2, 3, 5, 6, 7 —now merged in one, and assisting each other's course. But further : the same devices which succeeded in drawing in Roderigo as a force against Cassio have at the same time been assisting another purpose in the play—Iago's scheme of getting money out of his dupe Roderigo ; for Iago sees

v. i. 15. clearly that, once Roderigo despairs of success, all his own pecuniary chances are gone, and indeed he may be called upon to make restitution. So the action we have numbered as No. 4 is now seen to be working in the same direction as the other five. There remains only one more—the affair of

iii. iv; iv. i. Bianca and Cassio. Every reader will remember how this paltry bit of low life crosses the main tragedy at just the point where it can serve as an unintended link in a terrible chain of events. Desdemona's handkerchief, dropped, given to Bianca to be altered, brought back by her in a moment of

suspicion, is made by the contrivance of the plotter to seem CHAP. XI.
like a final proof of Desdemona's abandoned passions. This
handkerchief device has drawn in action No. 1 into the drift
of the rest; and all the actions of our scheme, from 1 to 7,
are now blended in a single stream of movement.

Every reader who has in the smallest degree developed
interest in plot must appreciate this triumph of dramatic
economy, by which so many separate trains of action are, by
a touch here and there of a great contriver, made to coalesce
with one another and unite their forces, so that the author
can reduce in amount the demand he has to make upon evil
contrivance, and can show himself thrifty in making each
device produce the maximum of results. But if the reader *The*
does not appreciate it, there is one in the play who does, *Economic effect sug-*
and that is the arch-villain himself: for what is it but a *gested in*
rhapsody on dramatic economy which Iago gives us when, *the play itself.*
after hitting upon the idea of utilising Desdemona to plead
for Cassio, he reflects that the very counsel he has given with
a view to his dark purposes is the counsel which an honest
adviser would have given to Cassio for his own sake?

> And what's he then that says I play the villain?   ii. iii. 342.
> When this advice is free I give, and honest,
> Probal to thinking, and indeed the course
> To win the Moor again? For 'tis most easy
> The inclining Desdemona to subdue
> In any honest suit: she's framed as fruitful
> As the free elements. And then for her
> To win the Moor—were't to renounce his baptism,
> All seals and symbols of redeemed sin,
> His soul is so enfetter'd to her love,
> That she may make, unmake, do what she list,
> Even as her appetite shall play the god
> With his weak function. How am I then a villain
> To counsel Cassio to this parallel course,
> Directly to his good? Divinity of hell!
> When devils will the blackest sins put on,
> They do suggest at first with heavenly shows,
> As I do now: for whiles this honest fool

Plies.Desdemona to repair his fortunes
And she for him pleads strongly to the Moor,
I 'll pour this pestilence into his ear,
That she repeals him for her body's lust;
And by how much she strives to do him good,
She shall undo her credit with the Moor.
So will I turn her virtue into pitch,
And out of her own goodness make the net
That shall enmesh them all.

No one will suppose that Iago has any other interest in reducing the amount of evil in the world beyond this economic interest of watching one device produce two effects, and leaving the hostile forces of goodness to work his ends without his troubling to draw upon his own resources of evil.

Reaction: Nemesis upon Iago.

We have counted seven actions, and seen them unite in a tragic catastrophe. The scheme of the play includes an eighth action, or rather, reaction; the recoil of this catastrophe upon Iago himself. What is the source of this nemesis upon Iago? In part it arises from accident: his final intrigue against Cassio is only partially successful, Cassio being wounded, but not killed. But Cassio comes only to complete the retribution upon the villain of the play, which has begun before his arrival, and in another and un-

v. ii, from 139.

suspected quarter. It is Iago's own wife Emilia whose quick woman's wit is the first to pierce the web of intrigue, and stimulated by sight of her murdered mistress she gives her suspicions vent, though at the point of her husband's sword. The principle underlying this nemesis is one of the profoundest of Shakespeare's moral ideas—that evil not only corrupts the heart, but equally undermines the judgment. To Iago is applicable the biting sentence of *Junius :* 'Virtue and simplicity have so long been synonymous that the reverse of the proposition has grown into credit, and every villain fancies himself a man of ability.' It is because he knows himself unfettered by scruples that Iago feels himself infallible,

and considers honest men fools ; he never sees how his foul CHAP. XI.
thoughts have blinded his perceptive powers, and made him
blunder where simple men would have gone straight.   True,
he brings infinite acuteness to bear upon the details of his
intrigues ; but he never perceives, what the reader sees at a
glance, that the whole ground of his action in these intrigues
—his suspicions that Emilia has been tampered with by
Cassio and Othello—is a stupid mistake, which no one with
any wholesome knowledge of human nature would make.
And the same want of insight into honest human nature,
which made him set up his atrocious schemes, is the cause
now of their failure.   He thought he had foreseen everything :
it never occurred to him that his wife might betray him *with
nothing to gain by such betrayal*, simply from affection and
horror.

> I care not for thy sword ; I'll make thee known,
> Though I lost twenty lives.—Help! help, ho! help!
> The Moor hath kill'd my mistress!

In vain Iago seeks to stop her mouth ; a few words put all
the suspicious circumstances together, until in rage and spite
Iago stabs Emilia, though the blow seals his own ruin.
This detail is a fresh touch in the perfection of the nemesis
upon Iago : in a sense different from what he intended he is
now 'evened' with Othello, 'wife for wife.'   The nemesis
draws items of equal retribution from all the intrigues of
Iago.   It was on account of Emilia that he played the villain,
and it is Emilia who betrays him.   He had made a tool of
Roderigo, and the contents of the dead Roderigo's pockets v. ii. 308.
furnish the final links of evidence against him.   His main
purpose was to oust Cassio both from office and life : Cassio
lives to succeed Othello as Governor, and make his first v. ii. 367.
official act the superintendence of Iago's torturing.

   I turn to the other side of plot interest—Movement: the *Movement*
life and development of the play through the succession of *of the play.*

CHAP. XI. scenes, as distinguished from the dissection of its component parts when it is considered as a whole. In this drama the movement is as simple as the economic analysis is complex. Hardly in any other play have we so direct a motive force as Iago is here; and the stages into which the development of the whole falls are both few and clear; moreover, the successive soliloquies of Iago are the author's own index to the gathering *Its turn-* fulness of the development. We may note the usual turning-*ing-points.* points in the general action. In the middle of the middle act comes the central turning-point, with the words :

iii. iii. 90.

> Excellent wretch! Perdition catch my soul,
> But I do love thee! and when I love thee not,
> Chaos is come again.

The tide of Othello's love has reached its height, and from here the ebb begins. And of course it is in the fifth act that we get the outer change, or 'catastrophe,' where the tragic consummation gives place to the reaction upon Iago.

Stage of   The first act is not so much the commencement of the *Prepara-* movement as a preparation for it. It is devoted to bringing *tion.* out the situation of the various parties at the opening of the story. This is just what a classical dramatist, tied by the unities, would merely assume, and bring it out by incidental reference. Shakespeare, on the contrary, often puts his most vivid dramatic setting into the preparatory phase of his action (witness the first acts of *Lear* and *Henry V.*); and here the marriage of Othello and Desdemona is made known with passionate emphasis. Moreover, the casting-off of his daughter by Brabantio, and her resolution to accompany her husband to the war, serve to isolate our hero and heroine from their previous surroundings; they have no world now but their mutual love, and when that is invaded it means ruin. The motive force of the action, again, appears in this act only in an embryonic stage; Iago exhibits his animus against Othello and Cassio, and begins to feel about for plots and instruments; the final words of his soliloquy

mark well the embryonic character of his purposes at CHAP. XI.
present :

> I have 't. It is engendered. Hell and night
> Must bring this monstrous birth to the world's light.

Nevertheless, this act of preparation culminates in a note of warning which points to the coming development, when Brabantio, made quick-sighted by sorrow, cries to his unwelcome son-in-law :

> Look to her, Moor, if thou hast eyes to see :
> She has deceived her father, and may thee.

The second act presents the plot in transition stage. One *Stage of* hundred and eighty lines of it are given to a dramatic *Transition.* interval, made by the transference of the parties from Venice to Cyprus. Desdemona is here separated from her husband, and the interest of plot yields to other effects : the spectacular effect of the storm (which wrecks the enemy's fleet and leaves Othello free when he arrives for home affairs), the pageant of arrival, and the thrust and parry of wit when Iago is seen in the unwonted character of a lady's man. We get back to ii. i. 168. business in the soliloquy in which Iago mocks Cassio's courtly bearing to Desdemona :

> 'Tis so, indeed : if such tricks as these strip you out of your lieutenantry, it had been better you had not kiss'd your three fingers so oft. . . . Very good ; well kissed ! an excellent courtesy ! 'tis so, indeed.

Now the separate intrigues become apparent, and are being loosely drawn together. Even in the first scene Iago has made Roderigo jealous, and suggested that he should pick a quarrel with the touchy Cassio ; but his purposes are still only forming, and his last words in the scene are :

> 'Tis here, but yet confused :
> Knavery's plain face is never seen till used.

Then comes Othello's proclamation of a festival, and with it ii. ii.

CHAP. XI. Iago's idea of making Cassio drunk; the action has now
made progress, and the lesser intrigue against Cassio is successful. But the moment of its success is the great moment
of advance in the movement, when the scene, already busy
ii. iii. 249. enough, culminates in an emotional shock. Othello, with
gentle, regretful firmness, has just spoken the memorable
words of dismissal:

> Cassio, I love thee:
> But never more be officer of mine—

when we have the stage-direction : '*Re-enter* DESDEMONA,
attended.' Othello is in an instant transformed :

> Look, if my gentle love be not raised up!
> I'll make thee an example.

By this unexpected appearance of Desdemona not only has
the love of Othello become a force that tells against Cassio,
but the master-thought is flashed into Iago's mind of utilising
Desdemona's intervention,—the device which more than any
other carries forward the plot. He at once suggests this
to Cassio, and, as soon as he is alone, bursts into the
exultation already quoted. His scheme he now feels complete; and in concluding this second act he speaks not of
planning, but of acting.

The plot   In the third and fourth acts the plot is working. We may
working.   note four stages. The first is the famous Suggestion Scene.
iii. iii.   Iago's skill in this is a skill that soars above analysis. It is
easy to note the indirectness and affected unwillingness of
his hints; how he dares to sail close to the wind, admitting
145.   his own tendency to over-suspiciousness, and even, when
Othello begins to boil over, warning him against jealousy :

> —the green-eyed monster which doth mock
> The meat it feeds on.

Or how he covers the weakness of his actual case against
193.   Desdemona until Othello is frantic with suspense, and would

sooner hear evil than hear nothing ; how he recalls Brabantio's CHAP. XI.
warning, and makes Othello's sure ground of trust— 206, 229.
Desdemona's strange preference for himself—a suggestion
of rank will and intemperate nature.   When the suffering
Othello turns upon Iago—

> If thou dost slander her and torture me,
> Never pray more; abandon all remorse—

Iago flings up office and everything, thus utilising Othello's 375.
outburst in order to speak from the standpoint of injured
friendship.   Finally, when the whole is complete, and Othello
breaks into an oath of vengeance, the astute plotter allows 462.
himself to be swept away by the tempest he has raised, and
kneeling down includes himself in Othello's vow.

In the second stage, the intermingling of the various ii. iv.
intrigues produces a fine piece of dramatic irony.   Desdemona
is questioned as to the handkerchief, and seeking to evade
the question—for she knows not what has become of it—
she hits upon an unhappy ' happy thought,' which leads her
on to pour oil on fire :

Des.	This is a trick to put me from my suit :
	Pray you, let Cassio be received again.
Oth.	Fetch me the handkerchief : my mind misgives.
Des.	Come, come ;
	You'll never meet a more sufficient man.
Oth.	The handkerchief !
Des.	I pray, talk me of Cassio.
Oth.	The handkerchief !
Des.	A man that all his time
	Hath founded his good fortunes on your love,
	Shared dangers with you,—
Oth.	The handkerchief !
Des.	In sooth, you are to blame.
Oth.	Away !

In the third stage ocular evidence is furnished to Othello, iv. i.
when Iago in his presence draws gestures of amused contempt
by his talk of Bianca, and Othello applies them all to

CHAP. XI. Desdemona; and further, by an accident that not even Iago
could have contrived, Bianca comes at the moment and flings
down the very handkerchief itself at the feet of Cassio. The
arrival of the Commission installing Cassio in Othello's place
draws from the still unsuspicious Desdemona a cry of joy,
and brings the blow on her cheek that shocks all the court,
making the overt act from which there can be no turning
iv. ii. back. Accordingly the fourth stage merely displays a
jealousy strong enough to transmute impediments into stimulants; reading Aemilia's honest indignation as a procuress's
brazen-facedness, and interpreting Desdemona's innocent
The beauty as making the deeper sin. Then comes the tragic
Climax and consummation, the achievement of the minor intrigues
Reaction. serving as relief scenes between the long-drawn agonies of
the main tragedy. The final scene of the fourth act has been
a dramatic foreshadowing of the end, in the sad song of
death that will haunt Desdemona as she prepares for bed on
v. ii. the fatal night. The Murder Scene freezes us with its awful
calmness: Othello's belief in his wife's guilt is deep enough
to give his act the deliberateness of Justice.

> If you bethink yourself of any crime
> Unreconciled as yet to heaven and grace,
> Solicit for it straight . . .
> I would not kill thy unprepared spirit.

Desdemona's protestations of innocence are met with—

> Sweet soul, take heed,
> Take heed of perjury; thou art on thy death-bed.

And this is just the note of the tragic discord which is
carried into the equally tragic resolution, when Emilia and
the rest have poured in, and explanation is dawning.

> O, I were damned beneath all depth in hell,
> But that I did proceed upon just grounds
> To this extremity.

Othello has pronounced his own doom in these words, and

when Emilia has sealed her tidings with her blood, Othello CHAP. XI.
feels this more than any of those who look on horror-struck:

> This look of thine will hurl my soul from heaven,
> And fiends will snatch at it.

The movement has been carried from first preparation to tragic consummation; but there is still the reaction as a final stage wherein we may recover ourselves in artistic sense of satisfaction. Nemesis is satisfied over Iago, caught helplessly in toils of his own over-astute blundering. And there is time for Othello to die calmly on his own sword, amid his enemies' recognition of his 'great heart,' and having survived his shock of discovery long enough to do justice even to himself.

v. ii. 342.

> Speak
> Of one that loved not wisely but too well;
> Of one not easily jealous, but being wrought
> Perplex'd in the extreme; of one whose hand,
> Like the base Indian, threw a pearl away
> Richer than all his tribe.

XII.

How The Tempest is a
Drama of Enchantment.

*A Study in Dramatic
Colouring.*

Ch. XII.

*The super-
natural a
difficulty
in art.
Three
modes of
treatment.*

SHAKESPEARE'S play, *The Tempest*, is, on the face of it, a story of Enchantment. But this Enchantment, like all other forms of the supernatural and to a greater degree than most of them, constitutes one of the standard difficulties in dramatic art. A foundation task of the artist is to give creative reality to his story. But we realise through our memories, our sympathies, our experience: now Enchantment is a thing wholly outside our experience, it has no associations of memory interweaved with it, nor has it ever appealed to our sympathies in real life. The artist who dramatises a supernatural story is perpetually facing the practical difficulty— how to bridge over the gulf between his supernatural matter and the experience of his hearers or readers. There are three modes of treatment open to a dramatist by which he may meet such a difficulty. First, he may *derationalise*, or remove as far as possible from commonplace experience, the general surroundings amidst which the supernatural is to appear. Again, he may *rationalise* the supernatural element itself, that is, give it as many points of contact as possible with thought and experience. Yet again, he may give further support to the supernatural element by uniting with it as much as possible of what is nearest akin to it in the world of reality. All three modes of treatment are combined in Shakespeare's handling of Enchantment in the present play.

To begin with, Shakespeare has prepared a suitable background for his drama of enchantment by removing its scene *(1) Dera-*
to a distance from busy town life, and loading it with sug- *tionalisa-*
gestions of pure external nature—the accepted haunt of the *tion.*
supernatural : while associations of artificial civilisation are *Back-*
rigidly excluded. The scene is a desert island, impressing *ground of*
itself at first as uninhabitable, and almost inaccessible, the *Nature.*
secret of a few sailors, and of ocean currents that convey men *A desert*
to it ' by accident most strange,' ' by providence divine,' ' by *island,*
bountiful fortune.' It is guarded by a belt of fierce storms *ii. i. 35–52*
and i. ii.
that have given a name to the play; and by a further barrier *passim.*
of forbidding cliffs that o'er their wave-worn basis bow, huge
enough to contain deep nooks in which a king's ship may lie
hid. Yet the island is of wondrous charm when the boundary
is once passed : it is of a ' subtle, tender, and delicate temperance'; 'the air breathes most sweetly'; the grass looks *loaded with*
' lush and lusty'; 'there is everything advantageous to life.' *details of*
out-door
All the elements of life on the island belong to outdoor *nature.*
nature. For dwellings we find a cell weatherfended by a line-
grove; the very prisons are the prisons of nature—the rift of
a cloven pine, the knotty entrails of an oak. Labour on the
island is to fetch in wood for firing, or make dams for fish;
education is learning how to name the bigger light, and how
the less, that burn by day and night; for food there are fresh-
brook muscles, wither'd roots, and husks of acorns. By
accident some artificial wealth has found its way to the
island—store of glistering apparel—but it is used only as stale *iv. i. 187.*
to catch thieves : when, however, the islanders boast of their
treasures it is the treasures of nature :

> I prithee, let me bring thee where crabs grow;
> And I with my long nails will dig thee pig-nuts;
> Show thee a jay's nest, and instruct thee how
> To snare the nimble marmoset; I 'll bring thee
> To clustering filberts, and sometimes I 'll get thee
> Young scamels from the rock.

Ch. XII.

ii. ii. 1, 18;
iv. i. 180;
iii. iii. 3.

v. i. 33.

ii. i. 143.

If there are drawbacks to the beauty of the landscape they are bushless and shrubless deserts, or the over-luxurance of nature, the toothed briers, sharp furzes, pricking goss and thorns of the tropical jungle. It is just such scenery that tradition has linked with fairy life, and in the island we hear songs and conversations which fill into the scene its invisible inhabitants. Its hills, brooks, standing lakes and groves have each its band of elves; the long reaches of yellow sands are a playground for the fairies, who now chase the ebbing Neptune, and now fly him when he comes back, or take hands and foot it featly here and there, while the wild waves hush themselves to be spectators[1] of that dance, sweet sprites hum the music, and cheerful farmyard sounds of barking dogs and crowing cocks come in *pat* for the chorus. Remoteness from ordinary busy life is just the impression the island makes on the courtiers who behold it. It sets Gonzalo thinking of a golden age when civilisation should not be known: no traffic nor name of magistrate, no riches, poverty, or service, no use of metal, corn, or wine, or oil, no treason nor need for weapons, but nature should pour forth of its own kind all foison, all abundance, to feed the innocent people. And, while suggestions of nature are scattered broadcast through every scene, they are

Masque of nature-wealth.

gathered to a climax in the Masque of the fourth act, which has for its function to pour forth a prodigal accumulation of nature-wealth. In form it is a meeting of mythical deities; but the language presents them as embodiments of the different elements of landscape. Ceres is addressed as the owner of

> Rich leas
> Of wheat, rye, barley, vetches, oats, and pease;
> Thy turfy mountains, where live nibbling sheep,
> And flat meads thatch'd with stover, them to keep;

---

[1] i. ii. 379. I take the punctuation of the Leopold edition which makes 'the wild waves whist' parenthetical.

> Thy banks with pioned and twilled brims,
> Which spongy April at thy hest betrims,
> To make cold nymphs chaste crowns ; and thy broom-groves
> Whose shadow the dismissed bachelor loves,
> Being lass-lorn; thy pole-clipt vineyard;
> And thy sea-marge, sterile and rocky-hard,
> Where thou thyself dost air.

To her is added Iris, of the rainbow hue, diffusing honey-drops on the flowers, and crowning with her blue bow the bosky acres and the unshrubb'd down—a rich scarf for the proud earth. These unite with Juno, Queen of Heaven—the sky in its softer moods—to invoke marriage blessings on the wedded couple : but these are seen to be blessings of nature.

> Earth's increase, foison plenty,
> Barns and garners never empty,
> Vines with clustering bunches growing,
> Plants with goodly burthen bowing ;
> Spring come to you at the farthest
> In the very end of harvest !

That water as a feature of scenery may not be omitted, an invocation follows to the

> Nymphs, call'd Naiads, of the windring brooks,
> With your sedg'd crowns and ever-harmless looks ;

these mingle with the ' sun-burnt sicklemen of August weary ' in a dance of harvest home, and so complete the Masque as a symphony of all joys of landscape, lulling us to pastoral repose with its flow of sleepy verse.

The effect is carried on from still life to the inhabitants of the island. If ever a ' child of nature ' has been painted it is Miranda. Brought up from infancy on the island without ever seeing one of her sex, she has been formed by nature alone ; analysis can discover in her only the elementary features of female character, unconditioned by social forms or by individuality ; she might almost be called a desert island of humanity. The most distinctive note of Miranda is a simplicity that acts like a charm, and, in the wooing scenes,

Miranda, a child of nature.

i. ii ; iii. i, &c.

needs the best acting to distinguish it from forwardness; it becomes a child-like *naïveté* of admiration when she first has the chance of seeing 'how beauteous mankind is.' Yet there is in her plenty of womanly strength : capacity for the most vivid appreciation of nature in the storm, and the 'very virtue of compassion' for those suffering in it; she exhibits an equally quick and intelligent play of emotion as she follows her father's story, and still more at the end of the scene, where she is distracted between two tendernesses. For beauty, Miranda is almost a definition of ideal—'created of every creature's best.' And her creed seems to be a simple faith in beauty : even the 'brave vessel' she doubts not contains 'noble creatures in her,' and this instinctive confidence that a fair outside must mean fairness within leaps forth to defend Ferdinand when, in the glory of his youthful beauty, he stands accused of treachery.

> There 's nothing ill can dwell in such a temple :
> If the ill spirit have so fair a house,
> Good things will strive to dwell with 't.

Caliban a natural savage.

At the opposite pole from Miranda, yet equally with her linked to the idea of nature, stands Caliban, the natural savage, or wild man of the woods : we shall see later on that this does not exhaust the description of Caliban, but this is undoubtedly one aspect of him. And in connection with this Shakespeare has thrown in an effect of a very special kind, one which, when we consider the date of the play, seems almost a flash of prophecy. The name 'Caliban'

i. ii. 321.

is an anagram for 'cannibal'; and in a single dialogue between Caliban and Prospero we have painted, in successive clauses, the whole history of the relations between savage races and civilisation, wherever at least that civilisation has not been reinforced by the elevating power of religion. First, we have the wrongs of the savage, and his dispossession by the white man :

> This island's mine, by Sycorax my mother,
> Which thou takest from me.

Next, we see the early and pleasant relations between the
two; the white man pets the savage almost like an animal,— Ch. XII.

> When thou camest first,
> Thou strokedst me and madest much of me, wouldst give me
> Water with berries in't—

There is an interchange of good offices, education on the
one side, on the other reverence and gifts of natural riches:

> [Thou wouldest] teach me how
> To name the bigger light, and how the less,
> That burn by day and night: and then I lov'd thee
> And show'd thee all the qualities o' the isle,
> The fresh springs, brine-pits, barren place and fertile.

But soon there appears a moral gulf between the two that
forbids equal intercourse:

> Thy vile race,
> Though thou didst learn, had that in't which good natures
> Could not abide to be with.

There is nothing for it but the forced domination of the
white man:

> Therefore wast thou
> Deservedly confined into this rock,
> Who hadst deserved more than a prison.

So that the gift of civilisation is turned into a curse:

> You taught me language; and my profit on't
> Is, I know how to curse!

And a later scene completes the analogy, and exhibits ii. ii.
civilisation introducing one undeniably new gift into savage
life—the gift of intoxicating drink! In this way Caliban
presents the aborigines of nature crushed beneath the advance of artificial life. Yet the impartial dramatist finds an
attractiveness even for him. Beside Caliban, the dregs of
natural life, he places the drunken sailors, the dregs of
civilisation: and as Caliban kneels to Stephano we feel that
the savage is the nobler of the two, for he has not exhausted
his faculty of reverence.

So far we have been occupied with the remote nature that (2) *The En-*
chantment

CH. XII.　is proper as a dramatic background for enchantment. But
rational-　a great mass of details is occupied in presenting the enchant-
ised.　ment itself; and so fully is it displayed that it is *rationalised,*
this thing of the supernatural seeming here to fall into laws
Laws of　of its own, and take consistency as a system. Enchantment,
Enchant-
ment. Ar-　in one of its aspects, is felt as the arbitrary suspension of the
bitrary　link between cause and effect. On the one hand a train of
causation.
causes is in full array, yet the effects refuse to follow: the
voyagers plunge from the burning ship into the boiling
ocean, yet
i. ii. 217.　　　　　　　　　　not a hair perish'd:

> On their sustaining garments not a blemish,
> But fresher than before.

On the other hand, beside these effectless causes we see
i. ii. 466.　causeless effects: the warrior in his full strength drawing
his sword to strike, yet 'charm'd from moving,' his 'spirits,
The casual　as in a dream, all bound up.' Again, we see the casual
permeated
by design.　becoming permeated by design. The distracted scrambling
of the shipwrecked courtiers on shore, each saving himself
i. ii. 219–　as he can, we see as the 'disposing' by Ariel of actors, each
237.　to take his proper part in a drama of which he is unconscious.
Still more is this aspect of enchantment illustrated in the
expulsion of Prospero from Milan.

i. ii. 144.　　　　　　　　They hurried us aboard a bark,

> Bore us some leagues to sea; where they prepared
> A rotten carcass of a boat, not rigg'd,
> Nor tackle, sail, nor mast; the very rats
> Instinctively had quit it: there they hoist us,
> To cry to the sea that roar'd to us, to sigh
> To the winds, whose pity, sighing back again,
> Did us but loving wrong.

What is the outcome of this multiplication of possibilities
of destruction? The exposed victims are found drifting to
the exact spot, to which years after their persecutors will
i. ii. 178.　drift at the precise moment of Prospero's power:—a contrived
accumulation of chances eventuates in design. Yet, again,

a third aspect of enchantment is seen in the partial breaking Сн. XII.
down of the barrier between mind and matter; in the island
The barrier
thought and the external world can at times act upon one *between*
another without any medium of communication. When *mind and*
matter
Ferdinand is musing alone on his father's loss, a voice from *breaking*
the unseen suddenly answers him, and sets his doubts at *down.*
rest; so, when the revellers cannot recall the tune of their i. ii. 396.
catch, it is played for them on an invisible pipe and tabor. iii. ii. 133.
Very noticeable under this head is the conclusion of the
Masque. In the midst of the spectacle which Prospero has
called up for his children his mind happens to revert to the
forgotten conspiracy:—the unspoken thought is enough for
the spirit-actors, and 'to a strange, hollow and confused
noise, they heavily vanish.' Of enchantment like this, the
consequences on those who suffer it are just what we might
expect. For this linking of cause and effect, this 'law of
uniformity,' is the foundation upon which the edifice of
reason is built; it is to the scientific thinker what his creed
is to the man of religion. And the helpless despair of the
religionist, whose creed has been shattered, is the only
parallel for the hopeless bewilderment of wanderers in the
island when their confidence in natural order has broken
down: they suffer 'ecstasy,' the 'subtilties of the isle' will
not 'let them believe things certain'; their 'brains are use- v. i. 60, 80,
less, boil'd within their skull'; the 'tide' of understanding 124.
has ebb'd, and left the shore of reason foul and muddy.

In handling enchantment one point of art will be to mark *Passage*
the process of passing from the real to the supernatural. *from the*
real to the
The usage of some artists makes this passage a very gradual *super-*
one; notably Goethe, in his *Walpurgis Night*, takes us by *natural.*
numerous and almost imperceptible stages from a scene of
spring evening into the very heart of magic. Shakespeare's
play recognises only a single transition stage between reality
and enchantment—music, strangely linked with dreamy
slumber.

> The isle is full of noises,
> Sounds and sweet airs, that give delight and hurt not.
> Sometimes a thousand twangling instruments
> Will hum about mine ears, and sometime voices
> That, if I then had waked after long sleep,
> Will make me sleep again: and then, in dreaming,
> The clouds methought would open and show riches
> Ready to drop upon me, that, when I waked,
> I cried to dream again.

The sleepy atmosphere seems a fixed quality of the climate, dulling the critical faculty that might question the visionary appearances. The music, however, that breaks out from time to time is always an immediate herald of some supernatural effect: it is through this gate alone [1] that we pass out into the world of enchantment.

Agencies of the supernatural.
ii. ii. 3;
iii. iii; iv.
i. 256.

Agents from the spirit world are the instrument with which the magician works his will; and his power of inflicting harm on his enemies becomes enhanced when the very instrument of punishment can add its own quota of malice.

> For every trifle are they set upon me;
> Sometime like apes that mow and chatter at me,
> And after bite me; then like hedgehogs which
> Lie tumbling in my barefoot way, and mount
> Their pricks at my footfall; sometime am I
> All wound with adders who with cloven tongues
> Do hiss me into madness.

The spirits may be invisible, and thus distance from the enchanter is no protection:

> His spirits hear me,
> And yet I needs must curse.

Or they can take shapes, passing in monstrosity travellers' tales of mountaineers dew-lapp'd like bulls, or men whose heads do grow beneath their shoulders; and they can increase the uncanniness by the inexplicable uncertainty of

---

[1] It is not directly mentioned in the case of the spirits that chase the drunken sailors; but I presume 'a noise of hunters' includes a blast of horns. [iv. i. 256.]

their behaviour, inviting to a supernatural banquet with Ch. XII.
gentle actions of salutation, and again with mops and mows
dancing out with it ere the courtiers have had time to
partake. Sometimes in the form of hounds they 'hunt'
their victim, lengthening his torture by the chance they give
him of flight ; while, as a climax of torture, there is always
held in reserve the horror of transformation.

> [We shall] all be turn'd to barnacles, or to apes
> With foreheads villanous low.

But the most important point in connection with this use of
spirit agency is the wide command it suggests of the powers
of nature. As modern science sees law pervading all things,
so ancient magic placed every department of nature under
different orders of spirits, and to have learnt the art of
controlling spirits is to be able to play upon the whole
gamut of nature-forces. Such is the 'rough magic' which
Prospero boasts.

> By [your] aid, v. i. 40.
> Weak masters though ye be, I have bedimm'd
> The noontide sun, call'd forth the mutinous winds,
> And 'twixt the green sea and the azured vault
> Set roaring war : to the dread rattling thunder
> Have I given fire, and rifted Jove's stout oak
> With his own bolt; the strong-based promontory
> Have I made shake, and by the spurs pluck'd up
> The pine and cedar : graves at my command
> Have waked their sleepers, oped and let 'em forth
> By my so potent art.

There is yet an aspect of enchantment to be noted, one *Enchant-*
which in *The Tempest* is so developed as to become a leading *ment as*
interest of the play. It is a function of magic to humanise *human-*
ised
the external universe, and we have just seen personality *nature.*
given to some of the minor forces of nature in the spirits
employed by Prospero. But the grand division of nature
has always been that into the 'four elements' of Earth,
Air, Fire, Water ; and poetic imagination has loved to endow
these with human tempers and sympathies, and an occasional

appearance of human will.   To a certain degree language
itself retains traces of such humanising of the elements, as
when we talk of a gust of passion, raging fire, greedy ocean,
an earthy disposition, a fiery temper; enchantment can
complete the process, and give us fully developed Elemental
Elemental Beings—Sylphs of Air, Naiads of Water, Salamanders of
Beings. Fire, Gnomes of Earth.   The employment of these Elemental
Beings is one of the common-places of magic.   But Shakespeare in using it has stamped it with his own originality.
He has not given us the orthodox four orders of spirits,
nor has he, like Sir Walter Scott in his *Monastery*, framed
a being compounded of all four elements.   But, in giving
us *two* Elemental Beings he has been able to suggest a
deep analogy between human nature and the four elements
—how these have their division into upward-tending and
downward-tending, just as man has his higher and his lower
nature.   Shakespeare has made Ariel an Elemental Being
of the higher order, identified with the upward-tending
elements of Air and Fire, and with the higher nature of
man; and he has made Caliban an Elemental Being of the
lower order, identified with the downward-tending elements
of Earth and Water, and the lower nature of man.

Ariel up-   The identification is too detailed to be fanciful.   The very
ward-tend-
ing, identi- name of Ariel is borrowed from air, and he is directly
fied with addressed: 'Thou, which art but air.'   The identification
air and
fire. with fire is not less complete : when describing the lightning
v. i. 21; i. Ariel does not say that he *set* the ship a-fire, but that the
ii. 189-304. ship was 'all a-fire *with me* :'

> Now in the waist, the deck, in every cabin,
> *I* flamed amazement : sometime *I* 'ld divide,
> And burn in many places.

We can see in him just the qualities of air and fire.   He is
invisible, but, like the lightning, can take shape as he acts.
Like air and fire he can penetrate everywhere, treading the
ooze of the salt deep, running upon the sharp wings of the

north, doing business in the veins of earth when it is
baked with frost. His natural speech is music, or waves of
air. His ideas are the ideas associated with the atmosphere
—liberty and omnipresence: to be 'free as mountain winds,'
to fly on the bat's back merrily, couch in the cowslip's
bell, live under the blossom that hangs on the bough.
Like the atmosphere he *reflects* human emotions without
feeling them.

> *Ariel.* If you now beheld them, your affections **v. i. 17.**
>   Would become tender.
> *Prospero.*   Dost thou think so, spirit?
> *Ariel.* Mine would, sir, were I human.

The analogy extends to character. Even a character can
be found for the atmosphere: in place of our motive and
passion it substitutes *caprice*—'the wind bloweth where it
listeth.' So Ariel is 'moody,' or full of moods: and one **i. ii. 244.**
of the most difficult incidents of the play—the quarrel **i. ii. 237–**
between Prospero and Ariel—takes coherency, if we see in **304.**
it Prospero governing this incarnation of caprice *by out-
capricing him*; there is an absence of moral seriousness
throughout, and a curious irony, by which Prospero, under
the guise of invective, is bringing out Ariel's brave endur-
ance and delicate refinement, and in the form of threats
gives his rebellious subject more than he had asked for.
Finally, a single passage is sufficient to connect Ariel with **i. ii. 270.**
the upward tendencies of human nature. We hear the
reason of his cruel sufferings at the hands of Sycorax.

> For thou wast a spirit too delicate
> To act her earthy and abhorr'd commands,
> Refusing her grand hests, she did confine thee,
> By help of her more potent ministers,
> And in her most unmitigable rage,
> Into a cloven pine.

Nothing could more clearly paint the instincts of light
oppressed by the power of darkness until the deliverer
comes.

Ch. XII.

*Caliban
downward-
tending,
identified
with earth
and water.* Over against Ariel, an Elemental Being of the higher order, is set an Elemental being of the lower order, Caliban. Caliban approaches near enough to humanity to stand, as we have seen, for the natural savage ; but his origin—from the Devil and the Island Witch [1]—forbids us to rank him as human. And marks are not wanting of his identification with the downward-weighing elements of earth and water.

i. ii. 314. He is directly addressed by Prospero as, ' Thou Earth, thou'; and terms like 'monster,' 'moon-calf,' 'disproportioned shape,' so constantly applied to him, just express the uncouthness traditionally associated with the Earth-Gnome. The connection with the element of water is not so clear. Yet what else can be the significance of Shakespeare's perpetually attaching the idea *fish* to his personal appearance?

ii. ii. Wherever he is seen for the first time—by Trinculo, and in the last scene of all by the whole body of courtiers— the sight of him provokes exclamations of 'fish,' and doubts whether he is fish or man; epithets, 'fish-monster,' 'deboshed fish,' are showered upon him, and prolonged joking on the same idea is maintained while he is in presence [2]. When Trinculo calls him 'half a fish and half a monster,' the identification with Elemental Beings of both Water and Earth is complete. And he is only too evidently identified with the lower side of human nature. How animal he is the words describing his birth will sufficiently suggest :

i. ii. 282.
> — the son that she did *litter* here,
> A freckled *whelp*, hag-born.

i. ii. 349. He not only indulges the lowest passions, but gloats over them. And he is incapable of rising above them :

---

[1] This is distinctly said in i. ii. 319. Perhaps this is the ' one thing which she did' for which the sailors would not take her life (i. ii. 266).

[2] No such expressions are used by Stephano on his first introduction to Caliban in ii. ii. But it must be remembered that what he sees is not Caliban, but Caliban and Trinculo mixed together under the same gaberdine: hence he talks of a four-leg'd monster.

> Abhorred slave,
> Which any print of goodness wilt not take,
> Being capable of all ill.

It is true that we do not in the play itself see Caliban performing superhuman feats such as distinguish Ariel. But it must be remembered that Ariel exercises these powers only in the service of Prospero; and the corresponding source from which Caliban would derive his wonder-working strength—his mother Sycorax—is dead before the play opens. This Sycorax introduces into the drama Witchcraft, as a dark counterpart to the enchantment of Prospero that works for good. Like Prospero, she has been conveyed by force to the island, and she has ruled it by her charms before he arrives. She uses as her instruments malignant things of nature—wicked dew brushed with black raven's feather from unwholesome fen; her charms are toads, beetles, bats—creatures that hate the light; her son's curse is the infections that the sun sucks up from bog and fen and flat. She has an ugliness which is deformity alike of body and mind—

i. ii. 279.

Witch-craft : dark enchant-ment.

i. ii. 258, 270, &c.

i. ii. 321, 340; ii. ii. 1, &c.

> —with age and envy grown into a hoop;

and—if the reading be correct—the epithet, '*blue-eyed* hag,' may suggest that worst ugliness which comes of corrupted beauty. This addition of Sycorax as a foil to Prospero completes the balance of good and evil, of light and dark; and a moral tinge is cast over the purely imaginative matter of the play, especially suitable in a drama which has to connect enchantment with the providential government of the world.

i. ii. 269.

Two of the modes of treatment by which an artist seeks to reduce the strain made upon our imaginative faculty by the introduction of a supernatural element into fiction have now been illustrated. But when a suitable background has been prepared for Enchantment, and when all that is possible has been done to give a rational aspect to that which is

(3) Addition of Reality akin to Enchant-ment.

outside reason, it still remains to give increased reality to the story by exhibiting the supernatural element as intimately associated with phases of common life that already possess a hold upon our sympathies.   Where then are to be found elements of common life that have kinship with enchantment?   May not one of them be seen in what is described *Love at first sight.* by the phrase, 'love at first sight,' which, as if miraculously, *Story of* transforms the lovers to one another's eyes by the mere *Ferdinand* shock of their first meeting?   Ordinary parlance suggests as *and Miranda.* much when it describes such lovers as 'smitten' with one another,—touched with an enchanter's wand, causing them to see in each other visions of perfection not perceptible to ordinary beholders.   At all events, this is the idea which **i.** ii. 375; gives unity to the Story of Ferdinand and Miranda; it is not **iii.** i; **iv.** merely one of the hundred love stories of the Elizabethan **i;** **v.** i. 172. drama, but it is an ideal study of 'love at first sight,' complete in all its stages.   First we have the lovers prepared for their meeting.   Miranda awakes out of a charmed sleep to behold Ferdinand for the first time:

> *Prospero.*   The fringed curtains of thine eye advance
> And say what thou seest yond.
> *Miranda.*   What is't? a spirit?

So Ferdinand is drawn to the spot by supernatural music, until he sees—
> Most sure, the goddess
> On whom these airs attend.

The mutual shock follows.   'At the first sight they have changed eyes,' says the delighted Prospero, and Ferdinand confesses:

> The very instant that I saw you, did
> My heart fly to your service; there resides,
> To make me slave to it.

Accident favours the immediate betrayal of their feelings:

> *Miranda.*   This
> Is the third man that e'er I saw, the first
> That e'er sighed I for . . . .

Ferdinand forgets his own danger to exclaim :

> O, if a virgin,
> And your affection not gone forth, I 'll make you
> The queen of Naples.

Trouble follows to bind them closer and closer together, and
Miranda steals away to the log-house to cast the gleam of
her sympathy and pretty fancies over Ferdinand's ignoble
service, until it is 'fresh morning with him when she is by at
night.' Finally the cloud of trouble rolls away, and the
incidents of the Masque and the game of chess give us
glimpses into the pure intercourse of a lovers' paradise.

Similarly, the comic side of common life contains a
counterpart to enchantment in intoxication, that fills its
victim with delusions alike of heart and of head. And it is
this which gives unity to the Underplot of the Butler and
Jester ; the bottle saved from the wreck dominates it throughout. Moreover, while intoxication might be presented in
many different aspects—as loathsome, as wicked, as grotesque, as dangerous—here its transforming power is dwelt
upon. Caliban is transformed into a worshipper, with the
drunken butler for his god. Stephano pours wine down the
throat of the supposed dead moon-calf, and, by a fine stroke
of detail, Shakespeare makes Caliban, at this first taste of
alcohol, break from prose into blank verse, which he maintains through the scene :

*Intoxica-
tion a comic
counterpart
to En-
chantment.
Comic
Under-
plot.*

ii. ii; iii
ii; iv. i.
165 ; v. i.
256.

> These be fine things, an if they be not sprites ;
> That 's a brave god, and bears celestial liquor.

Another pull at the bottle, and the apotheosis of Stephano is
far advanced :

Caliban. Hast thou not dropp'd from heaven ?
Stephano. Out o' the moon, I do assure thee : I was the man i' the
moon when time was.
Caliban. I have seen thee in her, and I do adore thee.

Another draught and he is kissing his god's foot, and
devoting himself to his service ; a few more, and he is

dancing on the threshold of a new dispensation. So Stephano is transformed into a king, and disposes the spoils of the clothes-line; Trinculo into an expectant viceroy; all three into an expeditionary force on the point of achieving a conquest :

> So full of valour that they smote the air
> For breathing in their faces, beat the ground
> For kissing of their feet.

With drunken infirmity of purpose they pursue their project, and are diverted by easy lures of Ariel into the paths of destruction; drunk they appear at the close under their punishment; and the last stroke in the comic underplot is the awakening of Caliban out of his enchantment :

> What a thrice-double ass
> Was I, to take this drunkard for a god.

It is such treatment as this which Shakespeare has applied to *The Tempest* that entitles it to be called a Drama of Enchantment. The term does not merely mean a story of ordinary life in which superhuman beings are allowed to interpose : the world of this play is penetrated through and through by the supernatural ; from the supernatural it takes *Dramatic* its tone and colour. The very scene, insulated like a magic *Colouring.* circle, is excluded from the commonplace, and is confined to that remoteness of nature in which distance from the real presents itself as nearness to the unseen. On the enchanted island there is nothing to break the spell by a suggestion of every-day experience, and the atmosphere is electrical with enchantment; while the inhabitants, untouched by social influences, are formed equally by nature and magic. As the story moves before us, the laws of nature—the basis of our sense of reality—appear suspended, and it is the unnatural which presents itself as a thing of law. When at last personages of familiar experience are introduced they fall wholly under the mysterious influence, and their realism— their tender loving and brutal carousing—only serves to

remind us how much of real life is permeated by Enchant- CH. XII.
ment. It only remains to add how a single passage goes
beyond the field of the story, and flashes the dominant
colour of the play upon human life as a whole, hinting in
powerful language that real life is the greatest enchantment
of all. The Masque of Spirits has vanished into air,—into
thin air :

> And, like the baseless fabric of this vision, iv. i. 150.
> The cloud-capp'd towers, the gorgeous palaces,
> The solemn temples, the great globe itself,
> Yea, all which it inherit, shall dissolve,
> And, like this insubstantial pageant faded,
> Leave not a rack behind !

XIII.

How the Enchantment of The Tempest presents Personal Providence.

A Study in Central Ideas.

THE criticism that addresses itself to the function of inter-preting literature was early attracted to the discovery of Central Ideas in plays and poems. The treatment, how-ever, has not always been favourably received. For one thing, critics were found not to agree in their results : and, when different suggestions were put forward, each as a com-plete explanation of the same work, the suspicion naturally would arise that the interpreters had put into the plays the ideas which they professed to bring out of them. Moreover, a hasty use of terms led to the confusion between a ' central idea ' and a mere lesson, or reflection, derivable (with fifty others) from the course of a story, in the way in which an accomplished preacher will draw the whole gospel out of half a clause. Thus the theory of Central Ideas has been discredited : yet surely the presumption is in its favour. The existence of some harmony binding together all varieties of detail into a unity is a fundamental conception of art : the only further question is whether, for any particular play, this unity can be formulated in words. In contending, as I am in the present work, for a strictly inductive treatment of literature, I would point out that the question of Central Ideas is, at all events, one that admits of definite treatment.

A central idea, to be worthy of the name, must be based, not upon the authority of the expounder, nor even on the beauty of the idea itself, but entirely upon the degree in which it associates itself with the details of which the play is made up—a matter which admits of accurate examination. It is, in fact, a scientific hypothesis, and the details are the phenomena which the hypothesis has to explain; none of these details must be outside the proposed unity, all of them must have a function in connection with it, and the degree to which any phase of the whole is developed must be in proportion to the closeness or remoteness of its bearing upon the central idea.

From this definition it is clear that an approach to such a central idea for *The Tempest* may be found in the Enchantment described in the preceding study, which connects itself with all parts of the play. In analysing such connection it is well to draw a distinction between direct and indirect bearing. The greater part of a work of art may be expected to connect itself directly with its central idea. But there may be some portions, the bearing of which on the central idea itself may not seem clear; but these upon examination will be found to have the closest connection with some other notion, which notion is in its turn closely related to the central idea, throwing it out by contrast, or importing some kindred conception, without which the central idea would be deficient in intelligibility or interest. So, in the play under consideration, the great mass of details has been seen to be occupied in presenting Enchantment. Another set of details, numerous and scattered through every scene, group themselves around the idea of remote nature needed as a suitable background for the Enchantment. Once more, the underplot—that is, the Story of Ferdinand and Miranda, and the Story of Caliban with the Sailors—was seen to have a bearing, though an indirect bearing, upon the same fundamental notion, the function of

Ch. XIII. this underplot being, not to depict Enchantment, but to introduce some elements of real life closely akin to Enchantment. It is surely no weakening of the theory of Central Ideas, but the reverse, that the underplot should appear, not to repeat the central idea itself, but to display its counterpart in a different medium. Such treatment is just what we should expect from the analogy of the other arts : thus to relieve imagination with ordinary experience, to throw up enchantment by a contrast of real life, seems as natural as to set off vivid colouring by neutral tints, or to use a *scherzo* for separating an *adagio* from a march. Putting all these considerations together we may see that, not only is the play full in a general sense of Enchantment, but further that the distribution of its parts corresponds with their bearing on this fundamental notion.

But Enchantment would seem the central idea of the play only if we confined our attention to the matter of which it is made up : when we proceed to take in the drift of the action and movement we see that the unity of the whole may be formulated in a more compact manner thus:—the

Central idea for The Tempest : Enchantment presenting Personal Providence. presentation of Enchantment as an engine of Personal Providence. A double bond weaves the parts of this play into a whole : its action is occupied equally in throwing up a picture of Enchantment, and in working out ideas of Providence, while every single detail has an active function in elaborating one or both of these.

Providence as a dramatic motive. Providence is a leading motive in fiction; indeed, every dramatist is not only a creator, but also the providence that moulds events in the sphere of his creation. This is partly· recognised in the common phrase, Poetic Justice : but the term is not wide enough to cover the practice of artists in their moral government of the world of fiction. Poetic Justice has a great function to perform in making retribution artistic, or, where the term retribution will not apply, in tracing an artistic harmony between character and fate.

But great part of life, whether in reality or fiction, lies outside the sphere of justice ; nay, it often impresses our sympathies, and thus becomes matter for art-treatment, by its
very opposition to our conception of justice. What else is
implied in the fundamental conception of tragedy ? Tragedy,
of course, includes retribution, but it becomes most dis-
tinctively tragic where retribution is not: where not only
Lear pays the penalty of his errors, but the innocent
Cordelia suffers with him, where honest Othello endures
more agony than Iago is capable of, where rescue comes too
late to save Antigone from her martyrdom. Were this
not so there would be a gulf between nature and art : the
negation of Poetic Justice has been one of the inspirations of
poetry in every age.

> How oft is it that the lamp of the wicked is put out ?
>   That their calamity cometh upon them ?
>   That God distributeth sorrows in his anger ?
> That they are as stubble before the wind,
>   And as chaff that the storm carrieth away ? . . . .
> One dieth in his full strength,
> Being wholly at ease and quiet :
> His breasts are full of milk,
> And the marrow of his bones is moistened.
>   And another dieth in bitterness of soul,
>   And never tasteth of good.
>   They lie down alike in the dust,
>   And the worm covereth them.

What the lyric poet describes and meditates upon, the dramatist pourtrays in action ; and thus no term less wide than
' Providence ' will convey his handling of moral government.
Any principle which the course of the universe suggests to
thinkers has a right to be reflected in fiction, with the emphasis of artistic setting. Now the dramatist will show combinations of evil overthrown in a moment by the irony of
fate ; now, exhibiting the best effort met by overpowering
external antagonism, or overthrown by the smallest of flaws
within itself, he will appeal to our sense of pathos. What-

ever other impressions underlie the spectacle of human issues will be added; and, if these principles seem mutually contradictory, it is the business of philosophy to systematise, poetry may choose to stop short at pourtraying.

In The Tempest: Personal Providence. When these general considerations are applied to *The Tempest* we shall find a peculiarity that separates this from all other plays of Shakespeare. The course of human events leaves upon thinkers two impressions, different but not inconsistent. All spectators behold the chaos of chance giving place to order, and see the emergence of moral laws. But some thinkers go further, and trace in what happens the guidance of a Personal Providence, never losing touch of the issues of life, though hiding himself till he appears in striking displays of his will. So Shakespeare's dramas as a whole make up a world in which moral law is for ever being displayed. But in this one play of *The Tempest* something more has been done. The whole course of circumstances is controlled by Prospero, who is for the purpose endowed with the power of enchantment. Now enchantment is, within its sphere, omnipotence : thus within the field of the play Prospero has been made the Providence which irresistibly controls the issues of events. Of course the mere *v. i. 201–13.* sense of an overruling providence, such as Gonzalo expresses, may be paralleled from many other plays, as simply the opinion of an individual personage. But in *The Tempest* it is the dramatic machinery itself that unveils to us the governing power of its universe in the magically-endowed Prospero. If then we review the successive incidents of this play as they unfold themselves, we shall be seeing, under Shakespeare's guidance, the different aspects of Personal Providence.

Opening Scene a prologue. The opening scene is of the nature of a prologue : in the incident of the storm and shipwreck, with its tossings to and fro of sharp rough dialogue, we are passing from the outer world into the magic region within which Prospero reigns

omnipotent. With the majestic blank verse of the second Сн. XIII.
scene we find ourselves upon the island, and are met by
i. ii.
an unexpected effect : a note of trouble opens Prospero's *Sorrows*
triumph, and he commences his glory of playing Providence *of Pro-*
vidence.
by having to console the being he loves best in the world,
who is heartstruck at the ravages of the storm. So he who
would sway the moral government of the universe must be
prepared to bear upon his soul the weight of all the troubles
and sufferings of the innocent inherent to the very machinery
of government, all the questionings and heart-searchings of
the reverent while the designs of Providence are dark. As
Prospero speaks his words of consolation another aspect of a *Providence*
under re-
Personal Providence is called up : *straint.*

> The direful spectacle of the wreck, which touch'd   i. ii. 26.
> The very virtue of compassion in thee,
> I have with such provision in mine art
> So safely order'd, that there is no soul—
> No, not so much perdition as an hair
> Betid to any creature in the vessel.

A judgment is abroad that is to strike princes and revolu-
tionise kingdoms, yet is under restraint that it touch not the
simplest individual who crosses its path.

The greater part of this long second scene is outside the *Movement*
scenic unity of the play. It will be noted that in this one *suspended*
incidents
play Shakespeare has followed the classic unities of time and *outside*
place ; not traversing the long period of time, and touching *the scenic*
unity.
the variety of locality usual to a romantic drama, but con- i. ii. 32–
fining the action to a single island and a single day,—an 374.
arrangement peculiarly harmonious with the central idea,
as if marking off the charmed circle within which alone the
enchanter's power prevails. But it usually is found in plays
of the classic type that a few incidents of the story, prevented
by their distance of time and place from being acted, are
introduced into the play by means of narrative. So in the
present case, when the keynote of the action has been struck
by the brief dialogue between Prospero and Miranda, the

Ch. XIII.

Prospero's
Story :
genesis of
his provi-
dential
position.
33–186.

action stands still for more than three hundred lines, and the interval is used to give us back-glances into the past. First Prospero tells his daughter the story of his life; and it is worth noting how he lays his magic mantle aside, as if to mark the suspension of the enchantment, which is the unity of the play. This story of Prospero is no part of his playing Providence, but gives the genesis of the situation which makes him a Providence for the island. We see the price he has had to pay for his magic power: a life devoted to study, the surrender of the world and its prizes, tragic suffering for himself and his child on the open sea, twelve years of solitary toil in the island to master his art, amid privations and constant watchfulness, where a moment's inattention would leave him to be torn to pieces by the spirits he has raised. With all this strange accidents must concur, such as the preservation of the rotten boat; and there is the waiting of a whole lifetime for a single moment of opportunity :

> By my prescience
> I find my zenith doth depend upon
> A most auspicious star, whose influence
> If now I court not, but omit, my fortunes
> Will ever after droop.

Dramatic
Prepara-
tion.

The action still remains stationary while the dialogues with Ariel and with Caliban continue to review the past. These illustrate the dramatic effect of 'preparation': just as the musician will let us hear at the beginning of his piece a hint of the theme which is to dominate the close, so dramatists prepare for their main effects by introducing them in a modified form at an earlier stage. Prospero in the sequel is to control the fate of his human friends and enemies : these early sections survey his providential sway over the world of spirits during his long years in the island. Mercy and judgment, the two chief works of providence, have been exercised on Ariel and on Caliban. Ariel so bright and loving, suffering cruel tortures such as made wolves howl,

Ariel's
Story :
Mercy.
187–304.

and penetrated the breasts of ever-angry bears, all because CH. XIII.
his delicacy shrank from the earthy abominations of the
hideous witch—to have delivered such a sufferer when
Sycorax was dead, and there was none but Prospero to undo
the charm, this is the very luxury of mercy. And the luxury
of punishment is a phrase hardly out of place when used in
connection with Caliban. A creature humanised from his *Caliban's*
brutality by the assiduous care of Prospero, and brought by *Story: Judgment.*
him within his family circle, who has repaid such benefits 321–374.
with attempted foulness, which he still chuckles to think of,
and for which the only repentance he shows is bitter dis-
appointment at his unsuccess—in dealing with him there is a
sense of satisfaction in the possession of irresistible torture :

> Shrug'st thou, malice ?
> If thou neglect'st or dost unwillingly
> What I command, I'll rack thee with old cramps,
> Fill all thy bones with aches, make thee roar
> That beasts shall tremble at thy din.
> *Cal.*   No, pray thee.
> [*Aside*] I must obey: his art is of such power,
> It would control my dam's god, Setebos,
> And make a vassal of him.

The suspended action begins to move forward again as *Movement*
Ferdinand is drawn by Ariel's music into the scene. The *resumed: Episode of*
episode of Ferdinand and Miranda has an independent *Ferdinand*
interest of its own in its bearing upon the central idea. It *and Mi-randa.*
must be remembered that providence, as a dramatic motive, i. ii. 375.
must always be *artistic* shaping of events: it may be so by
giving artistic setting to some moral interest, or it may
consist in the exercise of purely artistic handling on the
control of events. Now it is one of the instincts of the
imagination to work out the welfare of the attractive, and
poetic providence could not have a more congenial task than
in moving the course of incidents so as to draw together two
lovers so rich in gifts of youth and beauty as Ferdinand and
Miranda. Yet here also a moral touch is added when we

CH. XIII.   see how Prospero's unlimited power uses trouble in order to procure the happiness of the lovers and make it greater. The progress of the episode, as it mingles with the other scenes, is suggestive on the subject of Personal Providence at every stage. Prospero's aside,

i. ii. 450.

> This swift business
> I must uneasy make, lest too light winning
> Make the prize light,

may be taken as the unfolding, before the event, of a providential purpose such as in real life, after the event, is sometimes seen to explain some phase of dark experience. Suggestive again is the harshness under which Prospero is veiling his schemes of happiness, and which has the effect of displaying Miranda in the full beauty of her soul as she seeks

iii. i.   to mediate between father and lover. And very suggestive is the stolen visit of Miranda to the log-house, with ' Prospero above '—to use the stage-phrase—watching the two lovers carry forward his plans, while they fancy they are escaping his notice, and Miranda feels compunction for disobedience.

iv. i ; v.   Then the whole trouble is seen by Ferdinand as no more
172.   than a trial of his love, which has strangely stood the test ; and the episode at last merges itself in the main plot, and becomes the chief link in the universal restoration that crowns it.

Main Story : darker providential mysteries. ii. i.   With the second act and the arrival of the courtiers the main story is in full progress. The elaborate scene which stands first in that act is devoted to one of the darker and more terrible mysteries of providential government. The idea of Personal Providence must not be limited to that which a Christian would understand by the term. The ancient fatalistic systems of thought would recognise an occasional personality in the governing power of the universe—a malice in circumstances that enticed a sinner on in his sin till his punishment should be ripe. Nor is the notion entirely without sanction in Biblical thought, as where a lying spirit is put in the mouths of the evil king's prophets.

A similar conception animates the incident now ensuing : Ch. XIII.
Providence seems there to contrive for the irreclaimable
evil-doers a malicious vengeance, that operates by encourage-
ment to fresh crime. Antonio and Sebastian are villains for *Intrigue of*
whom no sympathy can be evoked. Yet when they reach *Antonio and Sebas-*
the sphere of Prospero's power they alone appear unaffected *tian.*
by his enchantment ; and when, at a strain of music from *ii. i. 191.*
Ariel, all the rest of the party drop off in deep and overpowering slumber, they are left unvisited by the quality of the
climate, staring at one another as they stand alone among
the sleeping courtiers with mutual consciousness of the
treason in their hearts. Then Antonio, as the bolder of the
two, begins bit by bit to read into hard definite speech the
hideous suggestiveness of the situation from which his companion shrinks, and a providential concurrence of circumstances is made to stand out, pointing to a deed of murder
—the rightful heir that morning drowned, the king and his
faithful followers bound in leaden slumber, the next of kin in
regions distant ten leagues beyond man's life. One by one
Sebastian's scruples give way, and with a burst of enthusiasm
he embraces the project. All is ready—no, one thing has
been forgotten, and they ' talk apart,' as if shrinking from
their victims while they complete the plot for their death. It
is just at this last moment, when they are stopping to put a
final touch of perfection to their scheme, that the turn in
events comes. The death-like stillness is broken by the
distant sighing of the wind ; it seems to come nearer, playing
with the white hairs of the sleeping Gonzalo and fanning his
aged cheek ; it sounds more human in its sighing, it takes to
itself articulate words and becomes the voice of Ariel :

> While you here do snoring lie,
> Open-eyed conspiracy
>   His time doth take.
> If of life you keep a care,
> Shake off slumber, and beware :
>   Awake, awake !

CH. XIII. The sound has died away again into silence; the conspirators return on tiptoe intoxicated with the excitemént of
murder; they draw their swords together.

> *Antonio.* Then let us both be sudden.
> *Gonzalo.*   Now, good angels
>   Preserve the King!

In an instant Gonzalo has awoke and roused his fellows,
and all stand facing the intending traitors. A mocking fate
has led them on to fully stain their souls with purpose of
crime, while the crowning deed and prize has been snatched
from them.

Comic matter and Providence.
ii. ii;
iii. ii;
iv. i. 165;
v. i. 256.

The next scene opens the comic business, which continues
to mingle with and relieve the other incidents. These relief
incidents are bound into a whole, not only by their development of the enchantment of intoxication, but equally by their
bearing on poetic justice. Even sin has a comic side, and
the resources of dramatic providence are sufficient to visit it
with comic nemesis; but for all the comedy the spectacle
none the less brings out one deep principle of moral government—how much force for the punishment of evil is latent
in the evil itself. In the present case Ariel, as the instrument
of retribution, has no need to draw upon his stores of supernatural might: he makes his victims furnish the force for
their punishment, he himself only giving a touch of impulse
to their passions, or twisting their purposes in a different
direction. After the first scene has displayed the transforming power of alcohol upon Caliban, the second scene opens
with a situation in which already are visible elements of
discord. Stephano, possessed of the bottle, is the man in
power, and Caliban's eyes are 'set in his head' with hero-
worship. Trinculo has no bottle, and Caliban has no worship
for him; a spirit of depreciatory criticism is thus pitted
against the hero-worship, and all that Ariel need do when he
encounters the party is to draw the spirit of quarrel to a head.
A few words he casts on the air from his shroud of in-

visibility are mistaken for words of Trinculo, and the comrades are plunged in civil war. They are united again by
the project against Prospero, and inflamed with a martial
spirit already referred to in the words of the play:

> So full of valour that they smote the air
> For breathing in their faces; beat the ground
> For kissing of their feet.

This drunken valour Ariel harnesses to his purpose, and
makes it pull them to their confusion:

> I beat my tabor;
> At which, like unback'd colts, they prick'd their ears,
> Advanced their eyelids, lifted up their noses
> As they smelt music: so I charm'd their ears
> That calf-like they my lowing followed through
> Tooth'd briers, sharp furzes, pricking goss and thorns,
> Which enter'd their frail shins; at last I left them
> I' the filthy-mantled pool beyond your cell,
> There dancing up to the chins.

Once more, their martial guise much bedraggled, they are
led on by the indomitable will of Caliban to the very
threshold of Prospero's cell. But even here the magician
will not summon force to his protection ; he simply appeals
from one form of covetousness to another, and, bidding Ariel
strew glistening baubles in their path, waits to see ambition
diverted from its object by cupidity. Only when he has
by such means sufficiently defended himself, and the conspirators are engrossed in the division of their spoil, does
Prospero, as an extra effect, throw in the external vengeance
of cramps and dry convulsions to complete his discipline on
creatures whose souls can be reached only through their
bodies. The whole suggests an idea equally artistic and *Provi-*
moral—a sense of economy in the governing power of the *dential Economy.*
universe : the ends of justice are secured with the least
expenditure of supernatural force, a few touches of direction
being sufficient to exhibit evil working out its own destruction.

The matter reviewed brings us to the last scene of the third act. This is the climax, the magician's nemesis upon his human persecutors. Judgment is one of the great works of Providence, and judgment translated into the language of art is nemesis : its force lies not in the weight of the blow struck, but in the artistic links that connect the retribution with the sin. Enchantment serves to make the present nemesis ideal : no external force [1] appears from first to last, yet all the resources of artistic retribution are lavished upon it. There is preparation of the victims for the great shock. The antithesis to a sense of a Personal Providence is the confidence in the uniformity of the order of nature ; this confidence is sapped by the 'quality of the isle,' with its suggestions of mysteries all around, and still more on the threshold of the Nemesis Scene by the incident of the supernatural banquet, where moreover the 'gentle actions of salutation' of the spirit-attendants assist in giving a personal reference to what follows. The courtiers have just overcome their shrinking from the supernatural, and braced themselves to partake, when the sudden reversal takes place : the banquet changes into the horror of a harpy, and from the harpy's ruffled feathers looks forth the infant face of Ariel to speak the doom.

> You are three men of sin, whom Destiny,
> That hath to instrument this lower world
> And what is in 't, the never-surfeited sea
> Hath caused to belch up you ; and on this island
> Where man doth not inhabit, you 'mongst men,
> Being most unfit to live. I have made you mad ;
> And even with such-like valour men hang and drown
> Their proper selves.   [*They draw their swords.*
>   You fools ! I and my fellows
> Are ministers of Fate : the elements,
> Of whom your swords are temper'd, may as well
> Wound the loud winds, or with bemock'd-at stabs

[1] The word 'pinch'd' in **v.** i. 74 I understand in the light of ' inward pinches' (three lines lower) and the general context to be metaphorical.

Kill the still-closing waters, as diminish
One dowle that's in my plume : my fellow-ministers
Are like invulnerable. If you could hurt,
Your swords are now too massy for your strengths,
And will not be uplifted. But remember—
For that's my business to you—that you
From Milan did supplant good Prospero ;
Exposed unto the sea, which hath requit it,
Him and his innocent child : for which foul deed
The powers, delaying, not forgetting, have
Incensed the seas and shores, yea, all the creatures,
Against your peace. Thee of thy son, Alonso,
They have bereft ; and do pronounce by me :
Lingering perdition, worse than any death
Can be at once, shall step by step attend
You and your ways ; whose wraths to guard you from—
Which here, in this most desolate isle, else falls
Upon your head—is nothing but heart-sorrow
And a clear life ensuing.

It is only a speech ; yet, set in its framework of enchantment
what sting of retribution does it omit ? The guilty ones feel
their power of physical resistance mysteriously paralysed,
and that in face of the strongest stimulus of external
mockery ; they are reminded of the loneliness of the island
from which all help of man is far ; what sense of safety there
is in the steady course of nature has already been snatched
from them. In its place a terrible Destiny has emerged, of
which the whole world is the instrument : its voice speaks
in the voice of Ariel, and fellow-ministers are waiting all
around to become visible. Their whole past stands out
before them as no more than the story of one foul deed
and its avenging ; the very sea, which they had made the
innocent accomplice of their crime, has bided his time to
requite them, and the shores, yea, every creature, are incensed against them. For their present, they hear hurled
at them the word 'mad,' the very sound of which has power
to work that which it signifies, and they are told of the self-
slaughter to which madness prompts. Their future looms

Cʜ. XIII. before them as lingering perdition stretching beyond death, and they know its first stroke has already been accomplished in the drowning of the king's son. All space and time seems to have resolved itself into a trap of fate for them ; and there is but one small avenue of escape hinted at in 'heart-sorrow and a clear life ensuing.'

The nemesis has fallen : and what is its effect on those who suffer it ? Here Shakespeare is faithful to that wide conception of dramatic providence, which makes it reproduce all the impressions that the world of reality leaves upon thinkers, not alone those that are pleasing, but also those which disturb. Shakespeare is not satisfied with the easy morality which converts all its villains before the fall of the curtain. In the play, as in actual fact, men are seen divided into two classes : those in whom evil is only accidental, to be purged out of them by the discipline of experience, and those in whom the evil seems to be a part of their nature, and all the working of events upon them serves only to drive it deeper in. Alonso is by his doom driven to ecstasies of remorse : why ? because he has before had a heart that could feel compunction.

iii. iii. 95.

O, it is monstrous, monstrous !
Methought the billows spoke and told me of it ;
The winds did sing it to me, and the thunder,
That deep and dreadful organ-pipe, pronounced
The name of Prosper : it did bass my trespass.

But, on the other hand, the hard hearts of Antonio and Sebastian are carried forward in blind resistance :

iii. iii. 102.

Sebastian.   But one fiend at a time,
I 'll fight their legions o'er.
    Antonio.   I 'll be thy second.

Mystery of the dividing-line amongst mankind. From first to last there is no note of softening in them. The play is reflecting a view of the course of the universe, which has troubled so many thinkers—the conception of a terrible dividing-line amongst mankind, on one side of which is purification making purer and purer, on the other side evil

becoming hardened and more hard; and there is nothing CH. XIII.
in Shakespeare's treatment to suggest that this double process stops short of the climax, ' He that is righteous let him
be righteous still, and he that is filthy let him be filthy
still.'

This nemesis has presented itself as a climax; and yet *The higher*
there is in reserve a higher climax still, when judgment re- *Climax of*
Mercy.
solves itself into mercy. By a graceful stroke of art, the **v**. i. 1–33,
intercession of Ariel is made the occasion for accomplishing and from
58.
a purpose which has long before formed itself in Prospero's
breast[1]. Like day stealing upon night, sound understanding
is allowed to replace the distraction of the guilty sinners, and
it is a triumph of enchantment to cancel the wrongs of a
whole life in a moment of time. So the action has scope for
gratifying that which is one of the most passionate instincts
of the imagination—the longing for an ultimate universal *Universal*
restoration, however distant, from which none shall be ex- *restoration.*
cluded. If it be asked how this is reconcilable with what has
just been said about the dividing-line, I can only answer that
Shakespeare has been content to let these two aspects of
providential government stand side by side in his play un-
reconciled, precisely as philosophic meditation on the course
of the universe suggests the two thoughts without giving any
clue as to their harmony. In *The Tempest* the universal
restoration is unbroken by exception: not the impenitent
Antonio and Sebastian are excluded, nor the brutalised
Stephano and Trinculo; Alonso is restored to his kingdom,
Ferdinand and Miranda, already restored to one another, are
given to the bereaved father; Ariel is restored to liberty, and
Caliban to his island: Gonzalo adds:

> All of us to ourselves
> When no man was his own.

Nay, the restoration extends to things inanimate, and the

---

[1] This seems clear from **v**. i. 29; the whole speech, **v**. i. 21–30, seems
a justification of a plan previously formed, not a change of purpose.

CH. XIII.

Mystery of Evil producing Good.

ship, which in the opening scene we beheld sunk in the stormy sea, reappears in the sequel in all her gallant trim, her master capering to behold her. There is more than restoration, and Gonzalo in his musing on the strange experience catches a glimpse of one of the deepest providential mysteries—evil itself proved to be the outer husk of a higher good :

> Was Milan thrust from Milan that his issue
> Should become KINGS of Naples ?

The Climax extended to the Personal Providence himself :

The universal restoration makes a grand final chord, on which this drama of Providence may conclude. But must there not of necessity be in it one note of discord ? A goal of happiness is found for all the rest, but what of the magician himself? Though dukedoms and kingdoms are in disposal, yet for one who wields the empire of enchantment can any prize be found without making the end an anti-climax for him ? If we examine the way in which, as an actual fact, Shakespeare has treated this point, we shall find dimly suggested in it a moral idea worthy even a ruler of the universe.

iv. i. fin. and v. i. init.

There comes a point at which Prospero's project passes beyond the reach of failure :

> At this hour
> Lie at my mercy all mine enemies . . . .
> My charms crack not, my spirits obey, and time
> Goes upright with his carriage.

v. i. 33.

He pauses to take survey of the unbroken completeness of his power, that has every department of nature under its control, that marshals all the elements to his will, that is obeyed beyond the grave itself. And to what does such a survey lead him ? He realises the extent of his dominion only to lay it down.

> This rough magic
> I here abjure . . . . . I 'll break my staff,
> Bury it certain fathoms in the earth,
> And deeper than did ever plummet sound
> I 'll drown my book.

self-renunciation.

The human mind has conceived no higher moral notion than

self-renunciation; and where the power is nearest to omni- potence the renunciation comes nearest to divine. Such a climax is reserved for the Providence of the enchanted island, who, while he feels the fulness of his sway, empties himself, and descends to simple human station. So the last note in the play is the human note of parting. Ariel, however regretted, must be dismissed to the elements; Miranda must follow the course of nature in quitting her father and cleaving to her husband; and for Prospero himself there is in full view the greatest parting of all :

> Thence retire me to my Milan, where
> Every third thought shall be my grave.

I have thus endeavoured to justify my choice of a central *Summary.* idea for *The Tempest*, showing how all the matter of the play falls into place in such a scheme ; due regard being had to the general principle, that the central idea must not be expected to connect itself with every single detail directly, but that it will attract round it other kindred notions, each in its turn a centre for a group of details. *The Tempest* bears the closest examination as a dramatic study of Providence ; the fact that we are kept in contact with Prospero's meditations on his schemes of control makes this Providence take a personal form, while the engine by which he works his will is Enchantment. The personages of the play find their *raison d'être* as agents or victims of Providential Enchantment ; their characters interpret themselves and show development, they fall into contrasts and groupings according to their bearing on this fundamental purpose. The incidents, situations and effects of the play are those of Enchantment; its movement is the unfolding of a supernatural scheme of providential government. If we consider the poem from the side of plot we see the dramatist here (and in scarcely any other case) going to the Classical Drama for his mode of treatment, because its narrow unities are more in keeping with the confined circle of a magician's power ; while the

CH. XIII. relation between the main and the underplots is precisely the same as that between the central idea itself and the kindred ideas required to give it reality by associating it with commonplace experience. One remark only is yet necessary to make the analysis of the play complete; and it is a remark of *Mechanical* general application. In every romantic drama there must of *Personages,* necessity be a large number of *mechanical personages,* intro-
especially
Gonzalo, duced not for their own sake but to assist the presentation of others: yet, in proportion to the space they cover in the field of view, Shakespeare will endow them with some dramatic interest. Their function is not unlike that of the Chorus in Ancient Tragedy, except that they are distributed amongst the scenes of the drama instead of being kept as a body of external commentators. Such personages are in *The Tempest* to be found in the crowd of courtiers led by Gonzalo, and the crowd of sailors led by the boatswain. Their part is mainly to illuminate and reflect the various situations that arise: outside the movement of the play themselves they furnish a *point d'appui* on which that movement rests. Thus the busy opening scene has spice given to it by the clashing between the wit of Gonzalo and the rough tongue of the
ii. i. boatswain. In the island it is the forced talk of Gonzalo that brings out the marvel of the deliverance from the sea, and the character of the enchanted island; then his passages of irritable wit with Antonio and Sebastian help to paint the character of the two by suggestion of the antipathy between them and honesty. Gonzalo takes the lead in helping us to
iii. iii. 27, realise the incident of the supernatural banquet, and the
104, &c. condition of the guilty after the blow has fallen; while, during
v. i, from the long-drawn finale, Gonzalo follows exactly the function
120. of chorus-leader, and reads into meaning every stage of the universal restoration; when its last note is complete the boat-
also touched swain and he resume their passage of arms. Yet these
by the Cen- mechanical personages are not entirely outside the central
tral Idea. idea; the sailors have their loss and recovery of the ship,

and Gonzalo has connection enough with the original crime CH. XIII.
to feel his heart stirred by the final issue. Moreover, his
personal character is one well fitted to be a stationary point
in a moving drama of Providence. He is pre-eminently a
man of an even temperament; good, but easy; like an
ancient chorus, little elevated or depressed by the storms of
circumstance. He has not been heroic to resist evil, though
finessing to reduce by his practical compassion the suffering it i. ii. 161.
entailed. But the changes of fortune do little to shake him;
he does not forget his humour amid shipwreck, he maintains i. i ; ii. i.
laborious cheerfulness when depression is all around; treason
scorns him as merely a 'spirit of persuasion,' yet will do ii. i. 235,
murder rather than face his 'upbraidings.' He has elected 286.
to be a spectator of life, so much as may be, and not an
actor; and he is valuable in the spectacle of Providence from
the eye he has to its fine dramatic effects, while as to the
action his place is that of one who stands at an equal distance
from the prizes of life and from its crimes.

XIV.

How 'Love's Labour's Lost' presents Simple Humour in conflict with Various Affectations and Conventionalities.

A further Study in Central Ideas.

THE title of this chapter contains the word 'humour.' The word is as varied and interesting as the thing it describes. Starting from a material signification, 'moisture,' it became early appropriated by the various forms of moisture within the human body—the blood, the phlegm, the bile. In this connection it encountered the theory of mediaeval physiology, which made the particular tempers and dispositions of men dependant upon the preponderance of one or other of these juices of the body: if a man was 'phlegmatic' in disposition, it was because he had too much phlegm in him, bright (arterial) blood would make him 'sanguine,' and dark (venous) blood 'melancholy' (or black-juiced). It was then an easy transition for men's 'humours' to mean the bent of their individual characters, and a 'humourist' was a painter of character. But these individualities of character in men are a leading source of the ludicrous: as the north-country proverb puts it, 'there's nought so queer as folk.' Hence the word 'humour' widens, to include the whole range of the ludicrous. But again, such a wide range must invite fresh specialisation, and a specialisation has taken place which I know not how to describe, unless by calling humour the *human interest in the ludicrous*, distinguished in the clearest manner from wit, with its cold intellectual brightness. In this final sense of humour the ludicrous can appear in happy combination with every passion of the human heart, the tragic and pathetic not excepted, and the humour of Dickens and Thackeray is often more nearly allied to tears than to laughter.

Shakespeare illustrates every phase and variety of humour : a complete analysis of Shakespeare's humour would make a system of psychology. I have here to deal with only a single one among its countless varieties, and one which is intelligible enough. Humour is a complete solvent to every form of *Humour* affectation. It is a more subtle foe to unnaturalness than *as the* *solvent of* satire itself, because satire is on the face of it hostile : *Affectation.* humour may be keenly alive to the ludicrous even in that with which it is in sympathy. Satire is the wind in the fable, and may be met by resistance : humour is the sunshine which succeeds by getting the traveller himself on its side. Humour is thus the great vindicator of the natural ; it is an exquisite perception of the normal in human affairs ; it is common sense etherealised ; the readiness with which it is roused by every unreasonable excess constitutes it a sort of comic nemesis. The special interest which dominates the *This the* play *Love's Labour's Lost* is the bringing of humour into *Central* *Idea of* contact with its antipathetic, with some train of unnatural *the play.* circumstances, or the various artificial conventionalities of its age : these are, by the mere contact, exposed and shattered.

The unnaturalness to be exposed consists, first, in a forced *Main* and unnatural social regimen, to which the king and his *Affectation* *attacked:* friends have bound themselves by oath : *the Celibacy* *scheme.* *i. i.*

> To live and study here three years,
> . . . not to see a woman in that term, . . .
> And one day in a week to touch no food
> And but one meal on every day beside, . . .
> And then to sleep but three hours in the night,
> And not be seen to wink of all the day.

CH. XIV. This artificial life prescribed by authority produces time-serving and hypocritical imitation amongst lesser personages, and we have an underplot of Don Armado, who, having discovered a man violating the royal edict by being found in company with a woman within the precincts of the court, shows his zeal by sending the man to the king for punishment, while of the woman (who is a beauty) he undertakes *Lesser Affectations exposed: Euphuism,* i. i, ii. the custody himself. There are further various conventionalities of the age, introduced for incidental effects. One is the euphuism of this Armado. He addresses the king in his letter :

> Great deputy, the welkin's vicegerent and sole dominator of Navarre, my soul's earth's god, and body's fostering patron.

The circumstances under which he discovered the guilty pair, were that—

> besieged with sable-coloured melancholy, I did commend the black-oppressing humour to the most wholesome physic of thy health-giving air.

When he has had time to make acquaintance with the pretty peasant girl who is his captive, he affects the very ground, which is base, where her shoe, which is baser, guided by her foot, which is basest, has trod. For a second conventionality, word-play and pedantry have their representative in Holo-*Pedantry,* fernes. In his extempore epitaph on the deer, he 'something affects the letter, for it argues facility' :

iv. ii. 58.
> The preyful princess pierced and prick'd a pretty pleasing pricket ;
>   Some say a sore ; but not a sore, till now made sore with shooting.
> The dogs did yell : put L to sore, then sorel jumps from thicket ;
>   Or pricket sore, or else sorel ; the people fall a-hooting.
> If sore be sore, then L to sore makes fifty sores one sorel.
> Of one sore I an hundred make by adding but one more L.

iv. ii. &c.; v. i. 18. This effect is doubled by the addition of the curate, Sir Nathaniel, who follows Holofernes at an admiring distance, and takes out his tablets to note down his expression 'peregrinate,' as applied to Don Armado. This last is an illus-

tration of another affectation attacked, the striving after CH. XIV.
unusual and at that time new words. Armado employs
Novelty in
Costard to carry a letter, and gives him something for *Words.*
'remuneration':

> *Costard.* Now will I look to his remuneration. Remuneration!
> O, that's the Latin word for three farthings: three farthings—remunera-
> tion.—'What's the price of this inkle?'—'One penny.'—'No, I'll give
> you a remuneration': why, it carries it. . . . I will never buy and sell
> out of this word.

Biron comes up and accosts him, and sends him on a similar
errand: 'There's thy guerdon: go.'

> *Costard.* Gardon, O sweet gardon! better than remuneration, a iii. i. 136–
> 'levenpence farthing better: most sweet gardon! I will do it, sir, in 174.
> print. Gardon! Remuneration!

It is quite in accordance with humour, as distinguished *Humor-*
from satire, that it should to some extent sympathise with *ous attack*
not incon-
what it is laughing at; and no one can rise from a perusal *sistent with*
of *Love's Labour's Lost* without feeling that the dramatist is *sympathy.*
himself, in moderation, a euphuist at heart. Biron is represented as the antagonist of excess in the king's circle; yet
Biron when soliloquising, and therefore under no control from
his fellows, is found to indulge in sustained hairsplitting. iv. iii. 1.

> The king he is hunting the deer; I am coursing myself: they have
> pitched a toil; I am toiling in a pitch,—pitch that defiles: defile! a
> foul word. Well, set thee down, sorrow! for so they say the fool said,
> and so say I, and I the fool: well proved, wit! By the Lord, this love
> is as mad as Ajax: it kills sheep; it kills me, I a sheep: well
> proved again o' my side!

Even when the play at its close turns serious, the euphuistic
strain has still a place, and a formidable exhibition of this
elaborate style is offered by Biron as 'plain words.' v. ii. 763.

> Honest plain words best pierce the ear of grief;
> And by these badges understand the king.
> For your fair sakes we have neglected time,
> Play'd foul play with our oaths: your beauty, ladies,

> Hath much deform'd us, fashioning our humours
> Even to the opposed end of our intents:
> And what in us hath seem'd ridiculous,—
> As love is full of unbefitting strains,
> All wanton as a child, skipping and vain,
> Form'd by the eye, and therefore, like the eye,
> Full of strange shapes, of habits and of forms,
> Varying in subjects as the eye doth roll
> To every varied object in his glance :
> Which parti-coated presence of loose love
> Put on by us, if, in your heavenly eyes,
> Have misbecomed our oaths and gravities,
> Those heavenly eyes, that look into these faults,
> Suggested us to make. Therefore, ladies,
> Our love being yours, the error that love makes
> Is likewise yours : we to ourselves prove false,
> By being once false for ever to be true
> To those that make us both,—fair ladies, you:
> And even that falsehood, in itself a sin,
> Thus purifies itself and turns to grace.

Word-play as a dramatic weapon.
iv. i.

It would seem that euphuism was recognised by the poet as a dramatic weapon with specific uses; and throughout the play, where a pause takes place in the action, the interest is maintained by verbal subtleties. Thus, the plot brings the Princess and her suite, under pretext of a shooting match, to a certain spot in order that a letter intended for another quarter may accidentally come into their hands: the brief interval before the messenger falls in with them is occupied less with the shooting than with a battle of puns. Again, in the scene which presents the first formal interview between the court of Navarre and their exalted visitors, as soon as the king has withdrawn, the relief to the strain of courtesy is admirably conveyed by an outburst of verbal subtleties. One more example fills up an interval in the fifth act.

ii. i, from 180.

v. ii. 15.

> *Katherine.* And so she died : had she been light, like you,
> Of such a merry, nimble, stirring spirit,
> She might ha' been a grandam ere she died :
> And so may you; for a light heart lives long.
> *Rosaline.* What's your dark meaning, mouse, of this light word?

Katherine.	A light condition in a beauty dark.
Rosaline.	We need more light to find your meaning out.
Katherine.	You'll mar the light by taking it in snuff;
	Therefore I'll darkly end the argument.
Rosaline.	Look, what you do, you do it still i' the dark.
Katherine.	So do not you, for you are a light wench.
Rosaline.	Indeed I weigh not you, and therefore light.
Katherine.	You weigh me not? O, that's you care not for me.
Rosaline.	Great reason; for 'past cure is still past care.'
Princess.	Well bandied both; a set of wit well play'd.

The last line is specially interesting; it clearly puts Shakespeare's conception of word-play as mental fencing, in which the mind finds a channel for redundant energy, and delights in exercise for exercise sake.

With such unnaturalness and such affectations the plot is *The repre-* contriving constantly to bring humour into contact. The *sentatives of humour* main source of the humour is found in an accidental circum- *in the play.* stance, which disconcerts the king's elaborate scheme: the arrival of a French princess with a train of ladies, on a lengthy embassy. The king does go so far as to keep these fair ambassadors outside the court; but to avoid visiting them is impossible, and thus the play settles down into a contest between the force of natural attraction and artificial resolution. The French ladies, and particularly their agent Boyet, *i. i, from* stand for the triumphant humour; they are exhibited as *133.* giving full play to their natural feelings; they have a rich flow of spirits, and perhaps they are all the better representatives of humour from the fact that their wit is indifferent, needing youth and good spirits to carry it through. They exhibit, moreover, the special note of humour,—that it can be turned on themselves; and with all their mockings the princess makes no attempt to conceal from herself that she is in love.

We are wise girls to mock our lovers so.   *v. ii. 58.*

These representatives of humour, then, are kept by the plot in a position of advantage throughout, and by sheer force of

fun they are able to disconcert the celibates at every turn;
humour thus coming to be a sort of poetic justice, which visits
the different characters in exact proportion to their artificiality and offence against the natural.

The Hu-
morous
and the
Artificial
in conflict.

There was a double unnaturalness in the scheme of the
celibates, and the comic nemesis upon it is double.   In the
first place, it was an unnatural state of things as regarded
their relations to one another, and they needed a mutual
oath to support their resolution; accordingly, they attempt
to conceal their lapses from one another, but are betrayed.

iv. iii.

In a superbly comic scene the four come one after another to
a sequestered spot in the park, seeking a secret place where
they may indulge in a recitation of the love-sonnet which
each has composed to his mistress, believing himself to be
the only offender; and each in turn hides as he sees his
comrade coming on the same errand, hoping to surprise
his fellow in an act of perjury, while he conceals his own.
The last to arrive is so surprised by the third, when suddenly
the second leaps out of ambush to confront the third, and
then the first in his turn comes down upon the second.
Nor has he enjoyed his triumph over the three long, when
the arrival of an intercepted letter reduces him to the level of
his companions.   Again, the celibate scheme of life was a
violation of nature in reference to the ladies; and consequently there is a further nemesis of ridicule when the men
break through their vow, after having urged it to their
visitors by such overt means as keeping them outside the
palace.

Compare
ii. i. from
91 and **v.**
ii. from
395.

> *Princess.* None are so surely caught, when they are catch'd,
>   As wit turn'd fool . . .
> *Rosaline.* The blood of youth burns not with such excess
>   As gravity's revolt to wantonness.

The celibates can recover their position only by entering
into the humour of the circumstances which have turned
against them.   In the scene of their betrayal to one another,

after a spirited attempt to brazen it out, they yield to the CH. XIV.
force of the situation, calling on Biron to give them reasons
for the course they have resolved on, to cheat the devil after
iv. iii. 221–
282 ; 283–
the sin has been committed ; this he does in a mock pompous end.
oration, after which they lay these glozings by, and set about
wooing these girls of France. But they are not yet completely
purged of their sin against humour, and resolve to cover
their approach with an elaborate masque—another of the
conventionalities of the age to be pilloried. This purpose v. ii. from
unfortunately is overheard, and communicated to the ladies, 80.
who determine to disconcert it, solemnly turning their backs
at the supreme moment of the compliment, and afterwards,
in the more miscellaneous conversation, arranging to exchange masks, so that each courtier pours his adoration into
the ear of the wrong mistress. The celibates fully recover
their equality with their visitors only when they enter into
the humour of their persecutors, and—hardest test of all—
join in abuse of their spoiled pageants. Then the action
reaches its climax in a prolonged cascade of humorous v. ii, from
fireworks.   512.

    In this nemesis of humour upon affectation, the different *Fate of*
personages fare exactly according to the sense of humour *personages*
determined
they possess. Of the celibates Biron has most sense of *by sense of*
humour, especially seen in his ready appreciation of the *humour.*
arch-persecutor Boyet, and accordingly he always has the v. ii. 315,
advantage over his fellows : he alone objects to the scheme 395, 472 ;
i. i. 47; iv.
at the outset, he is the last to be exposed in the discovery iii. 200.
scene, and the first to enter into the spirit of the finale.
The king is a constant contrast. Of the lesser personages v. ii. 335,
the dramatist keeps our sympathy with those that are the &c.
most natural, and have most sense of fun. Moth, the bright
page of Armado, is always natural, always seen to advantage, i. ii. &c.
and even proves not unequal to the exigencies of the reception scene, where he is the speaker of the conventional
compliment :

CH. XIV.
_____

v. ii. 158.

Moth. All hail, the richest beauties on the earth. . . .
         A holy parcel of the fairest dames
                              [*The Ladies turn their backs to him.*
         That ever turn'd their—backs—to mortal views !
Biron. [*Aside to Moth*]. Their eyes, villain, their eyes.

E. g. iii. i.
71–174; v.
i. 158, &c.

Costard and Dull are natural by the side of Armado and
Holofernes. Costard's humorous termination to his presentation of Pompey in the pageant—

    If your ladyship would say, 'Thanks, Pompey,' I had done—

v. ii.

secures him an easy dismissal ; whereas Holofernes' pedantry
is drowned in a shower of puns and wit-thrusts, and
Armado not only fares hard as Hector, but by an accidental word of his gives opportunity to the simple Costard
to bring out the whole scandal of Jaquenetta his captive.
So the triumph of comic justice has become complete, and
in affectation thus melting away at the touch of humour the
play has found its motive and inspiration.

*The Cen-
tral Idea
underlies
the Struc-
ture of
the play.*

So far I have discussed only in a general way the matter
of which this drama is composed. If we now proceed to
analyse it with due attention to the disposition and proportion
of its parts, which are the basis of plot, we shall find that the
structure of the play, no less than its general spirit, rests upon
the conflict between humorous and artificial.

Main plot.

Love's Labour's Lost has a very regular plot, of the type
'Complication and Resolution.' Its Main Action may be
stated as a series of humorous situations, produced by the
incidence of the Complication—the Princess's visit, with
all the forces of social attraction it brings—upon the unnatural mode of life set up at the beginning of the play.
As already intimated, it falls into a double action, corresponding to the double unnaturalness of the celibates'
scheme. Their plan of life implied an artificial bond
amongst themselves, needing a mutual oath to support their
resolution : when this artificial barrier against love has broken

down, they attempt each to deceive the rest, but are all
betrayed to one another. Agreed among themselves to give
way they still, as against their visitors, seek to cover their
yielding by the disguise of their approach, but the betrayal
of their purpose involves them in a second humorous exposure,
where Biron leads the way in complete surrender to simplicity
and nature.

> *Biron.* Can any face of brass hold longer out?   **v. ii. 395.**
>   Here stand I: lady, dart thy skill at me;
>   Bruise me with scorn, confound me with a flout;
>   Thrust thy sharp wit quite through my ignorance;
>   Cut me to pieces with thy keen conceit;
>   And I will wish thee never more to dance,
>   Nor never more in Russian habit wait.
>   O, never will I trust to speeches penn'd,
>   Nor to the motion of a schoolboy's tongue,
>   Nor never come in vizard to my friend,
>   Nor woo in rhyme, like a blind harper's song!
>   Taffeta phrases, silken terms precise,
>   Three-piled hyperboles, spruce affectation,
>   Figures pedantical; these summer flies
>   Have blown me full of maggot ostentation:
>   I do forswear them; and I here protest,
>   By this white glove,—how white the hand, God knows!—
>   Henceforth my wooing mind shall be express'd
>   In russet yeas and honest kersey noes:
>   And, to begin, wench,—so God help me, la!—
>   My love to thee is sound, sans crack or flaw.
> *Rosaline.* Sans *sans*, I pray you.

We thus seem to see two successive waves of pretentious *Underplot.*
artificiality break in humour; and this makes the main action
of the play. There is further an Underplot, analogous in
spirit and in form to this main action. It rests upon two
groups of inferior personages, embodying two conventionalities of the period placed in conflict with influences making
for naturalness and humour. The centre of the first group
is Don Armado, who never speaks but in the conventional
language of euphuism, and whose life is as showy and

deceitful as his talk. He is kept in continual contact with Moth and his genuine sparkle of youthful vivacity.

Armado. I will hereupon confess I am in love : and as it is base for a soldier to love, so am I in love with a base wench. If drawing my sword against the humour of affection would deliver me from the reprobate thought of it, I would take Desire prisoner, and ransom him to any French courtier for a new-devised courtesy. I think scorn to sigh : methinks I should outswear Cupid. Comfort me, boy : what great men have been in love ?

Moth. Hercules, master.

Armado. Most sweet Hercules ! More authority, dear boy, name more ; and, sweet my child, let them be men of good repute and carriage.

Moth. Samson, master : he was a man of good carriage, great carriage, for he carried the town-gates on his back like a porter ; and he was in love.

Armado. O well-knit Samson ! strong-jointed Samson ! I do excel thee in my rapier as much as thou didst me in carrying gates. I am in love too. Who was Samson's love, my dear Moth ?

Moth. A woman, master.

Armado. Of what complexion ?

Moth. Of all the four, or the three, or the two, or one of the four.

Armado. Tell me precisely of what complexion.

Moth. Of the sea-water green, sir.

Armado. Is that one of the four complexions ?

Moth. As I have read, sir ; and the best of them too.

Armado. Green indeed is the colour of lovers ; but to have a love of that colour, methinks Samson had small reason for it. He surely affected her for her wit.

Moth. It was so, sir ; for she had a green wit.

Armado. My love is most immaculate white and red.

Moth. Most maculate thoughts, master, are masked under such colours.

Armado. Define, define, well-educated infant.

Moth. My father's wit and my mother's tongue, assist me !

Armado. Sweet invocation of a child ; most pretty and pathetical !

Moth.   If she be made of white and red,
        Her faults will ne'er be known,
    For blushing cheeks by faults are bred,
        And fears by pale white shown :
    Then if she fear, or be to blame,
        By this you shall not know,
    For still her cheeks possess the same
        Which native she doth owe.

Nor is Moth the only foil to Armado: even when he encounters the rough common sense of Costard, or the simple
human nature of the pretty Jaquenetta, the pompous knight
regularly, in the reader's eyes, gets the worse, though the
wit of such contests is too thin to be adequately brought
out by quotations unsupported by the actors' by-play. i. ii. 138.

Armado. I do betray myself with blushing. Maid!
Jaquenetta. Man?
Armado. I will visit thee at the lodge.
Jaquenetta. That's hereby [1].
Armado. I know where it is situate.
Jaquenetta. Lord, how wise you are!
Armado. I will tell thee wonders.
Jaquenetta. With that face?
Armado. I love thee.
Jaquenetta. So I heard you say.
Armado. And so, farewell.
Jaquenetta. Fair weather after you!
Dull. Come, Jaquenetta, away!   [*Exeunt Dull and Jaquenetta.*
Armado. Villain, thou shalt fast for thy offences ere thou be
pardoned.
Costard. Well, sir, I hope, when I do it, I shall do it on a full
stomach.
Armado. Thou shalt be heavily punished.
Costard. I am more bound to you than your fellows, for they are but
lightly rewarded.
Armado. Take away this villain.

The second group gathers around the pedantry of Holofernes, which is set off by a double foil: an admiring rival in
Sir Nathaniel the curate, and a foil of a different kind in
goodman Dull, whose density is continually contrasting with
the other's learning, and at the same time spoiling the intended effect.

Holofernes. The deer was, as you know, sanguis, in blood; ripe as iv. ii. 2.
the pomewater, who now hangeth like a jewel in the ear of caelo, the
sky, the welkin, the heaven; and anon falleth like a crab on the face of
terra, the soil, the land, the earth.
Nathaniel. Truly, Master Holofernes, the epithets are sweetly varied,

[1] A phrase for 'That's as it may turn out.'

like a scholar at the least: but, sir, I assure ye, it was a buck of the first head.

Holofernes. Sir Nathaniel, haud credo.

Dull. 'Twas not a haud credo; 'twas a pricket.

Holofernes. Most barbarous intimation! yet a kind of insinuation, as it were, in via, in way, of explication; facere, as it were, replication, or rather, ostentare, to show, as it were, his inclination, after his undressed, unpolished, uneducated, unpruned, untrained, or rather, unlettered, or ratherest, unconfirmed fashion, to insert again my haud credo for a deer.

Dull. I said the deer was not a haud credo; 'twas a pricket.

Holofernes. Twice-sod simplicity, bis coctus!

O thou monster of Ignorance, how deformed dost thou look!

Nathaniel. Sir, he hath never fed of the dainties that are bred in a book;

he hath not eat paper, as it were; he hath not drunk ink: his intellect is not replenished; he is only an animal, only sensible in the duller parts:

And such barren plants are set before us that we thankful should be,
Which we of taste and feeling are, for those parts that do fructify
  in us more than he.
For as it would ill become me to be vain, indiscreet, or a fool,
So were there a patch set on learning, to see him in a school:
But omne bene, say I; being of an old father's mind,
Many can brook the weather that love not the wind.

Dull. You two are book-men: can you tell me by your wit
What was a month old at Cain's birth, that's not five weeks old
  as yet?

Holofernes. Dictynna, goodman Dull; Dictynna, goodman Dull.

Dull. What is Dictynna?

Nathaniel. A title to Phœbe, to Luna, to the moon.

Holofernes. The moon was a month old when Adam was no more,
And raught not to five weeks when he came to five-score.

The allusion holds in the exchange.

Dull. 'Tis true indeed; the collusion holds in the exchange.

Holofernes. God comfort thy capacity! I say, the allusion holds in the exchange.

Dull. And I say, the pollusion holds in the exchange; for the moon is never but a month old: and I say beside that, 'twas a pricket that the princess killed.

Out of these two character groups rise two Sub-Actions, which are drawn into the general movement of the play. The first is the intrigue of Armado with Jaquenetta. This

gives support to the earlier of the two phases in the main Ch. XIV.
action: there is a blunder in the delivery of the love-letters, ———
the effect of which extends to the King and his fellow-
conspirators, and completes their mutual betrayal. By the
same mistake Armado's intrigue is itself betrayed, and this iv. iii. 189;
sub-action in the end reaches a position of equilibrium when i. 57.
the pretentious impostor descends to naturalness, sees the
day of wrong through the little hole of discretion, and vows
to hold the plough three years for love of his base peasant v. ii. 732,
girl. Again, the stationary interest of the pedantic display 893.
takes movement to support the later phase of the main action,
Holofernes being charged with the pageant under cover v. i. 119; ii.
of which, with all its Classic Worthies, the lovers are to
approach their mistresses: but the turn in the main action
overthrows the sub-action also, and the pageant-manager,
in his hour of importance, finds employers, audience, and
half his actors uniting to overwhelm the performance in
chaff.

One more remark has to be made before the statement *Enveloping*
of the plot is complete. The main body of the play—plot *Action.*
and underplot—is surrounded by a wider Enveloping Action,
slightly sketched: the comic interchange of personal per-
plexities and reconciliations is framed in a sober interest
of high politics—the illness and death of the French king,
that just appears at the beginning and end. It is in accordance with Shakespeare's usual handling of plot thus to
enclose action within action, like the sphere within sphere of
the Ptolemaic astronomy, as Holofernes would no doubt have
remarked. If I may continue in the spirit of Holofernes,
I would point out that in this case the outer Enveloping
Action is like the *primum mobile* of that astronomic system,
and imparts motion to all the interior actions. For it is
the embassy necessitated by the king's failing health which
brings the French ladies into the play, and sets up the
conflict of humour and convention. When this conflict has

worked itself out to its natural resolution, the enveloping
action appears a second time to effect a further resolution.
In the height of the mirth over the discomfited pageant
the sudden announcement is made of the King's death. In
an instant the play becomes serious. But the lovers take
advantage of the seriousness to press their suits in earnest.
The ladies take advantage of the period of mourning to fix
conditions. The King of Navarre is bidden to immure
himself in some forlorn and naked hermitage, remote from
the pleasures of the world, for twelve months : if his love
stands this test he may challenge his princess, who will
have been a solitary mourner all the time, and she vows
to be his. Similar terms are made with Navarre's companions, and Biron in particular is to exercise his jesting
humour in a hospital, to see

> If sickly ears,
> Deaf'd with the clamours of their own dear groans,
> Will hear your idle scorns—

if not, to reform : but in either case Rosaline will have him.
The plot has thus provided for a dramatic nemesis : the
self-inflicted unnatural regimen of the celibates, at the beginning of the play, is balanced by the *forced* unnatural
regimen imposed on them as a preliminary condition when
they desire to marry : and this stipulation of celibacy seems to
follow naturally from the King of France's death. The
dramatist who feels equally all attractions, will not build
up his light structure of humour and passing affectation
without giving us a glimpse of some foundation for it in the
sober political world.

Thus the whole play of *Love's Labour's Lost* appears permeated with these clashings between humorous and artificial;
whether we look at the personages and their fate in the story,
or survey the subject-matter, or watch the succession of
comic effects, or technically analyse the structure of the
drama, we find that every kind of interest refers back to the

same source. The conflict, then, of humour with affectation CH. XIV.
and conventionality is, in the fullest sense of the word, the
Central Idea of this play. And the following chapter will
show that the same idea largely colours another play which is
too many-sided in its interest to be referred to any single
motive.

How 'As You Like It' presents Varied Forms of Humour in conflict with a Single Conventionality.

A Study of more Complex Dramatic Colouring.

*L*OVE'S *Labour's Lost* is an early play. But in another drama, more complex in its general character, Shakespeare has again introduced the impact of humour upon affectation as a dominant motive. Between the two there is the difference we should expect. The earlier play we have seen resolve as a whole into the central idea, which gives significance to its every part; in *As You Like It* the conflict of humour with convention is only one motive amongst several. Moreover, the idea itself, which is common to the two plays, takes different form in each. In *Love's Labour's Lost* the humour is one and the same throughout, the artificialities with which it is in conflict are many. In *As You Like It*, on the other hand, there are three distinct types of humour: while, for the artificial element, we have that one great conventionality of poetry beside which all others may be called secondary.

Three types of humour in As You Like It.

Healthy Humour of Rosalind.

I distinguish the *healthy* humour of Rosalind, the *professional* humour of Touchstone, and the *morbid* humour of Jaques. The fun, that plays like sunlit ripples about Rosalind and her friends, Celia and Orlando, there is no need to discuss; every reader drinks it in eagerly, and no

one, I imagine, will object to the description of it as
'healthy.' I do not doubt that, as an individual, Touchstone is worthy to be added to this set: but the office he
holds gives a different tone to his humour. In connection
with another play it has been pointed out that the jester
occupied, in the age of court officials, the same position
which in this age of newspapers is held by *Punch:* both
are national institutions for flashing a comic light on every
passing topic. As a professional Fool, Touchstone has
privileges: he may attack everything, and every sufferer
must applaud his own castigation. But equally he has ii. vii. 50.
professional duties: he must use his folly as a stalking-horse
under which to present wisdom, or, in other words, he must v. iv. 111.
from time to time hint deep truths as well as keep up a
continuous stream of vapid nonsense. The absence of
spontaneity is the note which distinguishes this professional
folly from natural wit such as Rosalind's. In the course of
this play Touchstone has to draw fun on demand from such
diverse topics as courtiers' oaths, travellers' complaints, the
course of Time, the irregularities of Fortune, shepherd life,
court life, music, versification, and his own intended wife—
'a poor virgin, sir, an ill-favoured thing, sir, but mine own.'
And, to fill up a moment of waiting, he is called upon to
exercise his professional function at length, and extemporises
a whole system of scientific quarrelling, through its degrees
of Retort Courteous, Quip Modest, Reply Churlish, Reproof
Valiant, Countercheck Quarrelsome, Lie with Circumstance, v. iv, from
up to the unpardonable Lie Direct. 70.

Of Jaques humour is a prominent feature, no less than of
Touchstone and Rosalind: but to determine this third type of
humour is much more difficult. The whole character of Jaques
is one not easy to define, and one which leaves the most
strangely opposite impressions upon different readers. He
is a general favourite with audiences in the theatre. Actors,
so far as I have observed, seem to form an exalted opinion

of him; and it must be difficult for them to do otherwise when they have to speak in his character the most famous of quotations that compares all the world to a stage. On the other hand, Jaques is certainly not a favourite with the personages in the story : he is least liked by the best of them, and the poet himself takes pains to except him from the happy ending which crowns the careers of the rest. The epithet 'philosophical' has stuck to Jaques, and there is good reason for it. We find him everywhere showing, not only seriousness of bent, but also that deep eye to the lessons of life underlying the outward appearances of things which is traditionally associated with wisdom. Yet in the scenes of the play his seriousness is not treated with much respect, and his wisdom by no means gives him the victory when he has to encounter much more unpretentious personages. Interpretation must find some view of him which will be consistent with all this; and we get a hint as to the direction in which we are to look for such a view in the play itself, where the Duke, in answer to Jaques' longing for the Fool's licence of universal satire, says that by such satire he would do—

ii. vii. 64.

> Most mischievous foul sin, in chiding sin :
> For thou thyself hast been a libertine,
> As sensual as the brutish sting itself ;
> And all the embossed sores and headed evils,
> That thou with license of free foot hast caught,
> Wouldst thou disgorge into the general world.

The hypothesis which will make the whole character clear, so far as it can be summed up in a single phrase, might be expressed as the *morbid humour of melancholy*.

Humour is the flower of healthy mental growth; it is mental exertion not for a practical purpose but for its own sake, arbitrary and delighting in its own arbitrariness; it is turned on everything good or bad, great or trivial (for to humour all things are humorous), drawing from everything its sparkling surprises and for ever catching unexpected novelties

of aspect; it is an insight into the singularities that lie just
below the surface of things, estimated more by their number
and the quickness with which they present themselves than by
weight and lasting worth; it is further in its sharpest strokes
the outcome of the genial good-will which is the normal condition of a well-balanced mind. There is, however, a special
Elizabethan view of humour, which emphasised one single
element of it,—it was an *arbitrary* assumption of some
mental attitude: 'tis my humour' is excuse sufficient for any
perverse and unnatural mental condition that Ben Jonson's
personages choose to indulge in. Amongst humours in this
second sense one of the commonest is ' melancholy'; it was,
we find, a specially English affectation, and so much a thing
of fashion that in Ben Jonson's *Every Man in his Humour*
Stephen practises it before his looking-glass, and in asides
asks his mentors whether he is melancholy enough. Yet
this fashion rests on a weakness of human nature that is
universal. At all times discontent has been affected as a
sign of superiority; a chronic turned-up nose is to the
superficial a suggestion of select taste. Every one is familiar
with one form of such discontent,—the depreciation of home
which travelling almost always produces in a shallow mind,
and which is in the play itself alluded to as a·characteristic
of Jaques.

Farewell, Monsieur Traveller; look you lisp and wear strange suits, **iv**. i. 33.
disable all the benefits of your own country, be out of love with your
nativity, and almost chide God for making you that countenance you
are, or I will scarce think you have swam in a gondola.

Jaques has adopted this Elizabethan humour of melancholy.
But more than this, his humour is totally opposed to all that
is healthy, and has become morbid; natural emotions have
been worn out by his course of dissipation, and discontent
supplies their place; with the corruption of his soul his
humour, so to speak, has gone bad, and while he retains all
the analytic power and insight into unexpected singularities,

yet his humour is no longer spontaneous but laboured, no longer genial, but flavoured with malevolence and self-exaltation.

Its morbid character traced in detail.
Examined in detail, Jaques' character exhibits the paradox and perversity of view which belongs to humour, but these are gloomy instead of bright, and suggest laborious search, and not involuntary mind-play. He is ' compact of jars '; he can suck melancholy out of a song as a weasel sucks eggs; he speaks of sleeping and railing as of the two sides of his normal condition. We have the Duke throughout by his side as a healthy contrast. The Duke did not seek the artificial life of the forest, though when driven to it by the stubbornness of fortune he can translate it to a quiet and sweet style : Jaques is repelled by his comrades' life as soon as it turns fortunate, and voluntarily flies from dancing measures to get
v. iv, from 186.
pleasure out of a dethroned convertite. So with regard to the dying stag : the Duke's pity is accidental, rising naturally out of surrounding circumstances—that the brute as a native burgher of the forest should be slaughtered in his own confines. Jaques pours out his pathos as an indulgence ; to borrow a word from the vocabulary of funeral sermons, he 'improves' the stag's dying agonies (having first found a comfortable position from which he can watch them) with a
ii. i.
thousand ingenious similes, and is so left by his companions weeping and commenting. Similar is Jaques' connection with the celebrated simile of the stage : the brilliant working out of this idea must not blind us to the morbid tone of mind of which it is the outcome. The Duke's reflection which
ii. vii. 136.
gives rise to the speech is cheerful, inviting to resignation because others have to endure. His accidental use of dramatic imagery is seized upon by Jaques as an opportunity for harping on the hollowness of everything human ; it is that *all the world* is no more than a stage, and the men and women *merely* players, which makes the attraction of the theme to Jaques' mind, and his ingenuity catches the lowest

view of every phase of life—the mewling and puking infant, Cʜ. XV.
the sighing and woeful young man, he characterises a soldier   ———
as quick in quarrel, reputation as a bubble, he distinguishes
the justice by his creature comforts, old age by its leanness
and childish treble, until he reaches a congenial climax in
'sans everything.'

Yet that melancholy is not the real object of this apostle of
melancholy some minor touches show.   Amiens sings a song
in praise of melancholy, Jaques at once turns it into ridicule, ii. v.
for to morbid humour its own pet affectation becomes objectionable when put forward by another.   In fact he must
have his melancholy to himself, as he is betrayed by Rosalind
into avowing—

> I have neither the scholar's melancholy, which is emulation ; nor the iv. i. 10.
> musician's, which is fantastical ; nor the courtier's, which is proud ; nor
> the soldier's, which is ambitious ; nor the lawyer's, which is politic ;
> nor the lady's, which is nice ; nor the lover's, which is all these : but it
> is a melancholy of mine own, compounded of many simples, extracted
> from many objects, and indeed the sundry contemplation of my travels,
> in which my often rumination wraps me in a most humorous sadness.

It is thus egotism that is at the root of his morbid humour,
which is no outcome of social life, but a constant attempt at
self-exaltation by the mode of differing from others.   He ii. v.
snubs modest excuses for a ragged voice, and compares
compliments to the encounter of two dog-apes.   He mocks
again at 'burdens' and 'stanzos,' and similar technical terms :
for your egotist both despises what everybody does as com-
mon-place, and equally regards any distinctive peculiarity he
does not share as silly pedantry.   Similarly with Jaques' objection to the Duke as too 'disputable': the natural course
for one who has information being to impart it, the morbid
mind affects reserve ; he 'thinks of as many things as others,
but gives Heav'n thanks, and makes no boast'—making thus
his powers one more difference between himself and his
fellow-men.   It must not however be supposed that there is
no exception to this universal depreciation.   Morbid egotism

shows its exaltation above ordinary pleasures by a selection of its own, and by vehemence of admiration in proportion as admiration is unexpected. Not only is Jaques merry on hearing a melancholy song, but—like an æsthete with a sunflower—he is raised to a delirious ecstasy by meeting a professional Fool.

ii. vii. 12.
> A fool, a fool! I met a fool i' the forest,
> A motley fool; a miserable world!
> As I do live by food, I met a fool.

As the Fool follows his profession of railing Jaques' lungs begin to crow like chanticleer, and he laughs sans intermission an hour by the dial.

It is abundantly clear that malevolence is the inspiration of Jaques' humour. His moralisings on the dying stag are, as ii. i. 44. the courtiers point out, 'invectively' conceived : he hits the landowners in his reflection on the stag weeping tears into the brook, giving his sum of more to that which has too much; the court come in for their share in the proverb of misery parting the flux of company, and the city when the herd is upbraided for forsaking the broken bankrupt. He envies the ii.vii, from 42. Fool's motley for the sake of the Fool's unfettered liberty of attack; and when the Duke points out how ill Jaques is qualified for the Jester's office of good-natured censor, his answer shows that Jaques believes the world to be as bad as he wishes to paint it. If Rosalind's humour is a tribute to the delightful oddities of things in general, and Touchstone's humour is a tribute to his professional office, Jaques' morbid humour is a tribute only to himself.

Into these three contrasted types has the simple humour of *Love's Labour's Lost* been expanded. On the other hand, for the elaborate and varied artificialities of that play we have *Pastoral Life the great conventionality in the play.* substituted one single conventionality which has maintained its ground in the world of imagination from Theocritus to Watteau—Pastoral Life. The traditional life of the old eclogues is lived again in the forest of Arden by the banished

Duke and his followers: with no worse ill than Adam's CH. XV.
penalty, the seasons' difference; with hunting of the stag for
enterprise, and presentation of him who killed the deer for
triumph; with feasts *al fresco*, and songs under the green-
wood tree. The simplicity of bucolic life is sufficiently
represented in William and Audrey; and, if pastoral lovers
are wanted, Phœbe for the fair unkind, Silvius as the de-
spairing lover, with Corin as the Old Shepherd to soothe him,
are types that the Sicilian Muses could not surpass. To the
end of time, I suppose, shepherd life will be the traditional
form in which the more elementary moods of the quiet
passions will be enshrined, and Shakespeare is paying his
footing as a universal poet when he makes the middle acts of
As You Like It a dramatised idyl.

Upon this accepted and most unmitigated conventionality *The three*
the three founts of humour in the drama are continually *humours in*
playing. To draw out in detail the resulting effects would be *with the*
to turn into dull prose half the play. Rosalind is pitted *pastoral*
mainly against the pastoral lovers, and for the soft and sleepy *ality.*
tenderness of such love there can be no more wholesome
tonic than the bright audacity and overwhelming flood of
high spirits that belong to our heroine.

> What though you have no beauty,—   iii. v. 37.
> As, by my faith, I see no more in you
> Than without candle may go dark to bed—
> Must you be therefore proud and pitiless?
> . . . . Od's my little life,
> I think she means to tangle my eyes too! . . .
> I pray you, do not fall in love with me,
> For I am falser than vows made in wine:
> Besides, I like you not.

Moreover, Rosalind in disguise is a humorous situation
embodied; and this applied to the hopeless suit of Silvius
draws out for the spectators a lengthened irony which finds a
happy climax in reconciled impossibilities.

Ch. XV.

ii. iv. 34.

Touchstone also has his fling at the pastoral lovers. When the unhappy Silvius paints the true idyllic passion—

> If thou remember'st not the slightest folly
> That ever love did make thee run into,
> Thou hast not loved—

the professional Fool seconds him with instances:

> I remember, when I was in love I broke my sword upon a stone and bid him take that for coming a-night to Jane Smile; and I remember the kissing of her batlet and the cow's dugs that her pretty chopt hands had milked . . . We that are true lovers run into strange capers; but as all is mortal in nature, so is all nature in love mortal in folly.
>
> *Rosalind.* Thou speakest wiser than thou art ware of.
>
> *Touchstone.* Nay, I shall ne'er be ware of mine own wit till I break my shins against it.

iii. iii; v. i.

iii. ii.

But Touchstone's license roams more widely over all the denizens of the woodland. He woos the rustic Audrey with folly, with folly he frightens away his rival William; he plays a match with Corin of court folly against pastoral wit, and when this model Shepherd, getting the worse, falls back upon his dignity—

> Sir, I am a true labourer: I earn that I eat, get that I wear, owe no man hate, envy no man's happiness, glad of other men's good, content with my harm, and the greatest of my pride is to see my ewes graze and my lambs suck—

Touchstone swoops upon this dyllic picture with a demonstration in theology that Corin's occupation is a simple sin involving him in a parlous state:

> If thou beest not damned for this, the devil himself will have no shepherds.

Finally the Fool gets an opportunity for one of his set discourses on this theme of the pastoral life:

> Truly, shepherd, in respect of itself, it is a good life; but in respect that it is a shepherd's life, it is naught. In respect that it is solitary, I like it very well; but in respect that it is private, it is a very vile life. Now, in respect it is in the fields, it pleaseth me well; but in

respect it is not in the court, it is tedious. As it is a spare life, look you, it fits my humour well; but as there is no more plenty in it, it goes much against my stomach.

If the conventionalities of pastoral poetry are to be taken literally, I do not know that the merits of that phase of existence could be more profoundly summed up.

As to the third type of humour, I have in describing it indicated sufficiently how the morbid melancholy of Jaques is turned upon every element of the life around him. But when, by expansion of the treatment in the earlier play, three distinct humours have been brought to bear upon the conventional, a further effect is still possible—the three humours can be brought into conflict with one another.

The three humours in conflict with one another.

Touchstone is the comrade and firm friend of Rosalind and her set, and if he chaffs them, it belongs to his office, and they readily join in the game. But when the folly is sprung upon them by surprise it is possible for them to be disconcerted. Celia believes herself alone as she comes reading the lover's verses, which endow her friend with the ' quintessence of every sprite '—

iii. ii. 133.

> Helen's cheek, but not her heart,
> Cleopatra's majesty,
> Atalanta's better part,
> Sad Lucretia's modesty.

Touchstone [1] startles her dreaming away—

> O most gentle pulpiter! what tedious homily of love have you wearied your parishioners withal, and never cried, ' Have patience, good people ! '
> *Celia.* How now! back, friends! Shepherd, go off a little. Go with him, sirrah.

---

[1] The editions give this speech to Rosalind (iii. ii. 163). But this is surely impossible. Not only is Celia's reproof addressed to Touchstone, and he in retiring treats it as such, but when he is gone Celia asks Rosalind, ' Didst thou hear these verses ? '—which would be absurd if Rosalind had spoken the words of satire on them.

Ch. XV. Celia is clearly 'out' in this game of wit, for she has answered pettishly; Touchstone feels he has scored:

> Come, shepherd, let us make an honourable retreat; though not with bag and baggage, yet with scrip and scrippage.

iii. ii, from 93. A precisely similar encounter takes place with Rosalind: but though surprised she rallies to the game, and puts the Fool himself out. She is indulging in the pastoral to her own praise—

> From the east to western Ind
> No jewel is like Rosalind.
> Her worth, being mounted on the wind,
> Through all the world bears Rosalind.
> All the pictures fairest lined
> Are but black to Rosalind.

The Fool breaks in, offering to rhyme her so for eight years together, dinners and suppers and sleeping-hours excepted: for such false gallop of verses is no more than the right butter-woman's rank to market.

> If a hart do lack a hind,
> Let him seek out Rosalind.
> If the cat will after kind,
> So be sure will Rosalind.
> Winter garments must be lined,
> So must slender Rosalind, &c.

Our heroine is disconcerted, but alert enough to exchange thrust and cut.

> *Rosalind.*   Peace, you dull fool! I found them on a tree.
> *Touchstone.*   Truly, the tree yields bad fruit.
> *Rosalind.*   I'll graff it with you, and then I shall graff it with a medlar: then it will be the earliest fruit i' the country; for you'll be rotten ere you be half ripe, and that's the right virtue of the medlar.

For once the professional Jester is unable to come up to time, and he has no repartee ready.

> *Touchstone.*   You have said; but whether wisely or no, let the forest judge.

Similarly, although Jaques patronises Touchstone, takes Сн. XV.
the Fool for his model and his ambition, snubs other
discourse in order to draw out his folly, and calls upon others
to enjoy it, yet a conflict between the morbid and the
professional humours is possible, when Touchstone descends
so far from the dignity of his office as to contemplate the
step of marrying. Jaques will assist his protégé's insane act
by giving Audrey away, but must at all events sneer at the
parson. iii. iii, from
72.

> Will you, being a man of your breeding, be married under a bush
> like a beggar? . . . . this fellow will but join you together as they join
> wainscot; then one of you will prove a shrunk panel, and, like green
> timber, warp, warp.

Touchstone is equal to a reply in his most professional
style.

> I am not in the mind but I were better to be married of him than of
> another: for he is not like to marry me well; and not being well
> married, it will be a good excuse for me hereafter to leave my wife.

Professional humour then has clashed with genuine,
morbid with professional. The treatment is complete when
the unhealthiness of humour in Jaques is accentuated by
his being brought into contact with humour that is sound.
When the man of melancholy crosses swords with the lover
Orlando he does not come off victorious. iii. ii, from
268.

> *Jaques.* God be wi' you: let 's meet as little as we can.
> *Orlando.* I do desire we may be better strangers.
> *Jaques.* I pray you, mar no more trees with writing love-songs in
> their barks.
> *Orlando.* I pray you, mar no more of my verses with reading them
> ill-favouredly.
> *Jaques.* Rosalind is your love's name?
> *Orlando.* Yes, just.
> *Jaques.* I do not like her name.
> *Orlando.* There was no thought of pleasing you when she was
> christened.
> *Jaques.* What stature is she of?

Orlando. Just as high as my heart.

Jaques. You are full of pretty answers. Have you not been acquainted with goldsmiths' wives, and conned them out of rings ?

Orlando. Not so ; but I answer you right painted cloth, from whence you have studied your questions.

Jaques admires the nimble wit, and proposes to sit down and rail in duet against ' our mistress the world, and all our misery.' Orlando takes up the position—unintelligible to a being like Jaques—of caring to rail at none but himself, against whom he knows most faults. Jaques retires in disgust.

Jaques. By my troth, I was seeking for a fool when I found you.

Orlando. He is drowned in the brook : look but in, and you shall see him.

Jaques. There I shall see mine own figure.

Orlando. Which I take to be either a fool or a cipher.

Jaques. I 'll tarry no longer with you : farewell, g od Signior Love.

Orlando. I am glad of your departure : adieu, good Monsieur Melancholy.

But the supreme touch of delineation for morbid humour is given by the mere contact of Jaques with the essence of health and brightness in the disguised Rosalind. Like evil spirits compelled by the touch of Ithuriel's spear to show themselves in their true shapes, Jaques seems drawn on by Rosalind's presence to call attention to his peculiar qualities with almost infantile complacency :—how he loves melancholy more than laughing, and thinks it good to be sad and say nothing (like a post, Rosalind interjects), and how, in detail, his melancholy has been compounded out of the scholar, the musician, the courtier, and all others he has met on his travels. So far Rosalind seems to have been looking at him quietly, as a curiosity : in the last sentence she finds the clue to understanding him.

Esp. **iv.** i. init.

Rosalind. A traveller ! By my faith, you have great reason to be sad : I fear you have sold your own lands to see other men's ; then, to have seen much and to have nothing, is to have rich eyes and poor hands.

Jaques. Yes, I have gained my experience.

Rosalind.   And your experience makes you sad : I had rather have a
fool to make me merry than experience to make me sad ; and to travel
for it too !

Jaques appears suddenly to wake up to the sort of impression
he is making on the attractive youth, and he seizes the first
opportunity for retreating in disgust, with the woman's last
word following him down the glade.

PART SECOND.

SURVEY OF

DRAMATIC CRITICISM

AS AN INDUCTIVE SCIENCE.

XVI.

TOPICS OF DRAMATIC CRITICISM.

I N the Introduction to this book I pleaded that a regular
inductive science of literary criticism was a possibility.
In the preceding fifteen chapters I have endeavoured to exhibit
such a regular method at work on the dramatic analysis of
leading points in Shakespeare's plays. The design of the
whole work will not be complete without an attempt to
present our results in complete form, in fact to map out a
Science of Dramatic Art. I hope this may not seem too pretentious an undertaking in the case of a science yet in its
infancy; while it may be useful at all events to the young
student to have suggested to him a methodical treatment with
which he may exercise himself on the literature he studies.
Moreover the reproach against literary criticism is, not that
there has not been plenty of inductive work done in this department, but that the assertion of its inductive character has
been lacking; and I believe a critic does good service by
throwing his results into a formal shape, however imperfectly
he may be able to accomplish his task. It will be understood
that the survey of Dramatic Science is here attempted only
in the merest outline: it is a glimpse, not a view, of a new
science that is proposed. Not even a survey would be possible within the limits of a few short chapters except by confining the matter introduced to that previously laid before the
reader in a different form. The leading features of Dramatic
Art have already been explained in the application of them
to particular plays: they are now included in a single view,

Purpose:
to survey
Dramatic
Criticism
as an in-
ductive
science.

CH. XVI. so arranged that their mutual connection may be seen to be building up this singleness of view. Such a survey, like a microscopic lens of low power, must sacrifice detail to secure a wider field. Its compensating gain will consist in what it can contribute to the orderly product of methodised enquiry which is the essence of science, and the interest in which becomes associated with the interest of curiosity when the method has been applied in a region not usually acknowledging its reign.

Definition of Dramatic Criticism: The starting-point in the exposition of any science is naturally its definition. But this first step is sufficient to divide inductive criticism from the treatment of literature mostly in vogue. I have already protested against the criticism which starts with the assumption of some 'object' or 'fundamental purpose' in the Drama from which to deduce binding canons. Such an all-embracing definition, if it is possible at all, will come as the final, not the first, step of investigation. Inductive criticism, on the contrary, will seek *as to its field and its method.* its point of departure from outside. On the one hand it will consider the relation of the matter which it proposes to treat to other matter which is the subject of scientific enquiry; on the other hand it will fix the nature of the treatment it proposes to apply by a reference to scientific method in general. That is to say, its definition will be based upon differentiation of matter and development in method.

Stages of development in the inductive method. To begin with the latter. There are three well-marked stages in the development of sciences. The first consists in the mere observation of the subject-matter. The second is distinguished by arrangement of observations, by analysis and classification. The third stage reaches systematisation—the wider arrangement which satisfies our sense of explanation, or curiosity as to causes which is the instinct specially developed by scientific enquiry. Astronomy remained for long ages in the first stage, while it was occupied with the observation of the heavenly bodies and the naming of the

constellations. It would pass into the second stage with
division of labour and the study of solar, lunar, planetary, and
cometary phenomena separately. But by such discoveries as
that of the laws of motion, or of gravitation, the great mass
of astronomical knowledge was bound together in a system
which at the same time satisfied the sense of causation, and
astronomy was fully developed as an inductive science. Or
to take a more modern instance : comparative philology has
attained completeness in our own day. Philology was in its
first stage at the Renaissance, when 'learning' meant the
mere accumulation of detailed knowledge connected with the
Classical languages ; Grimm's Law may illustrate the second
stage, a classification comprehensive but purely empiric ; the
principle of phonetic decay with its allied recuperative processes has struck a unity through the laws of philology which
stamps it as a full-grown science. Applying this to our *Dramatic*
present subject, I do not pretend that Literary Criticism has *Criticism*
reached the third of these three stages : but materials are *termediate*
ready for giving it a secure place in the second stage. In
time, no doubt, literary science must be able to explain the
modus operandi of literary production, and show how different
classes of writing come to produce their different effects.
But at present such explanation belongs mostly to the region
of speculation ; and before the science of criticism is ripe
for this final stage much work has to be done in the way of
methodising observation as to literary matter and form.

Dramatic Criticism, then, is still in the stage of provisional
arrangement. Its exact position is expressed by the technical *or 'topical'*
term 'topical.' Where accumulation of observations is great *stage.*
enough to necessitate methodical arrangement, yet progress
is insufficient to suggest final bases of arrangement which
will crystallise the whole into a system, science takes refuge
in 'topics.' These have been aptly described as intellectual
pigeon-holes—convenient headings under which materials
may be digested, with strict adherence to method, yet only as

a provisional arrangement until further progress shall bring more stable organisation. This topical treatment may seem an unambitious stage in scientific advance, the goal and reward of which is insight into wide laws and far-reaching systematisations. Still it is a stage directly in the line of sound method : and the judicious choice of main and subordinate topics is systematisation in embryo. The present enquiry looks no further than this stage in its analysis of Dramatic Art. It endeavours to find convenient headings under which to set forth its observations of Shakespeare's plays. It also seeks an arrangement of these topics that will at once cover the field of the subject, and also carry on the face of it such an economy of mutual connection as may make the topics, what they ought to be, a natural bridge between the general idea which the mind forms of Drama and the realisation of this idea in the details of actual dramatic works.

Continuous differentiation of scientific subject-matter. But the definition of our subject involves further that we should measure out the exact field within which this method is to be applied. Science, like every other product of the human mind, marks its progress by continuous differentiation : the perpetual subdivision of the field of enquiry, the rise of separate and ever minuter departments as time goes on. Originally all knowledge was one and undivided. The name of Socrates is connected with a great revolution which separated moral science from physics, the study of man from the study of nature. With Aristotle and inductive method the process became rapid : and under his guidance ethics, as the science of conduct, became distinct from mental science ; and still further, political science, treating man in his relations with the state, was distinguished from the more general science of conduct. When thought awoke at the Renaissance after the sleep of the Dark Ages, political science threw off as a distinct branch political economy; and by our own day particular branches of economy, finance, for example, have practically become independent sciences. This characteristic of science in general, the perpetual tendency to CH. XVI.

separate more confined from more general lines of investigation, will apply in an especial degree to literature, which
covers so wide an area of the mind and is the meeting-
ground of so many separate interests. Thus Shakespeare is
a poet, and his works afford a field for considering poetry in
general, both as a mode of thought and a mode of expression.
Again, no writer could go so deeply into human nature as
Shakespeare has done without betraying his philosophy and
moral system. Once more, Shakespeare must afford a speci-
men of literary tendencies in general, and that particular
modification of them we call Elizabethan; besides that
the language which is the vehicle of this literature has an
interest of its own over and above that of the thought which
it conveys. All this and more belongs properly to ' Shakespeare-Criticism': but from Literary Criticism as a whole a
branch is being gradually differentiated, Dramatic Criticism,
and its province is to deal with the question, how much of
the total effect of Shakespeare's works arises from the fact of
his ideas being conveyed to us in the form of dramas, and
not of lyric or epic poems, of essays or moral and philosophical treatises. It is with this branch alone that the present
enquiry is concerned.

Dramatic Criticism branches off on the one side from the wider Literary Criticism :

But more than this goes to the definition of Dramatic
Criticism. Drama is not, like Epic, merely a branch of
literature : it is a compound art. The literary works which
in ordinary speech we call dramas, are in strictness only
potential dramas waiting for their realisation on the stage.
And this stage-representation is not a mere accessory of
literature, but is an independent art, having a field where
literature has no place, in dumb show, in pantomime, in
mimicry, and in the lost art of Greek ' dancing.'

on the other side from the allied art of Stage-Repre-sentation.

The question arises then, what is to be the relation of Dramatic Criticism to the companion art of Stage-Representation?
Aristotle, the father of Dramatic Criticism, made Stage-Repre-

CH. XVI.   sentation one of the departments of the science; but we shall
———   be only following the law of differentiation if we separate the
two.   This is especially appropriate in the case of the Shakespearean Drama.   The Puritan Revolution, which has played
such a part in its history, was in effect an attack rather on
the Theatre than on the Drama itself.   No doubt when the
movement became violent the two were not discriminated,
and the Drama was made a 'vanity' as well as the Stage.
Still the one interest was never so thoroughly dropped by the
nation and was more readily taken up again than the other;
so that from the point of view of the Stage our continuity with
the Elizabethan age has been severed, from the point of view
of the literary Drama it has not.   The Shakespearean Drama
has made a field for itself as a branch of literature quite
apart from the Stage; and, however we may regret the
severance and look forward to a completer appreciation of
Shakespeare, yet it can hardly be doubted that at the present
moment as earnest and comprehensive an interest in our
great dramatist is to be found in the study as in the
theatre.

Dramatic Criticism, then, is to be separated, on the one
side, from the wider Literary Criticism which must include a
review of language, ethics, philosophy, and general art; and,
on the other hand, from the companion art of Stage-Repre-
Drama and   sentation.   But here caution is required: it may be con-
its Repre-
sentation   venient to make Literary Drama and Stage-Representation
separate in   separate branches of enquiry, it is totally inadmissible and
exposition,
not in idea.   highly misleading to divorce the two in idea.   The literary
play must be throughout read *relatively* to its representation.
In actual practice the separation of the two has produced
the greatest obstacles in the way of sound appreciation.
Amongst ordinary readers of Shakespeare, Character-Interest,
which is largely independent of performance, has swallowed
up all other interests; and most of the effects which depend
upon the connection and relative force of incidents, and on

the compression of the details into a given space, have been
completely lost. Shakespeare is popularly regarded as supreme in the painting of human nature, but careless in the
construction of Plot : and, worst of all, Plot itself, which it
has been the mission of the English Drama to elevate into
the position of the most intellectual of all elements in literary
effect, has become degraded in conception to the level of
a mere juggler's mystery. It must then be laid down
distinctly at the outset of the present enquiry that the Drama
is to be considered throughout relatively to its acting. Much
of dramatic effect that is special to Stage-Representation will
be here ignored : the whole mechanism of elocution, effects
of light, colour and costume, the greater portion of what
constitutes *mise-en-scène*. But in dealing with any play the
fullest scope is assumed for ideal acting. The interpretation
of a character must include what an actor can put into it ; in
dealing with effects regard must be had to surroundings
which a reader might easily overlook, but which would be
present to the eye of a spectator ; and no conception of the
movement of a drama will be adequate which has not
appreciated the rapid sequence of incidents that crowds the
crisis of a life-time or a national revolution into two or three
hours of actual time. The relation of Drama to its acting
will be exactly similar to that of Music to its performance,
the two being perfectly separable in their exposition, but
never disunited in idea.

Dramatic Art, then, as thus defined, is to be the field of *Funda-*
our enquiry, and its method is to be the discovery and *mental di-*
vision of
arrangement of topics. For a fundamental basis of such *Dramatic*
analysis we shall naturally look to the other arts. Now all *Criticism*
into Hu-
the arts agree in being the union of two elements, abstract *man Inter-*
and concrete. Music takes sensuous sounds, and adds a *est and Ac-*
tion.
purely abstract element by disposing these sounds in har-

monies and melodies; architecture applies abstract design to a concrete medium of stone and wood; painting gives us objects of real life arranged in abstract groupings; in dancing we have moving figures confined in artistic bonds of rhythm; sculpture traces in still figures ideas of shape and attitude. So Drama has its two elements of *Human Interest* and *Action*: on the one hand life 'presented in action'—so the word 'Drama' may be translated; on the other hand the action itself, that is, the concurrence of all that is presented in an abstract unity of design. The two fundamental divisions of dramatic interest, and consequently the two fundamental divisions of Dramatic Criticism, will thus be Human Interest and Action. But each of these has its different sides, the distinction of which is essential before we can arrive at an arrangement of topics that will be of practical

Twofold division of Human Interest. value in the methodisation of criticism. The interest of the life presented is twofold. There is our interest in the separate personages who enter into it, as so many varieties of the *genus homo*: this is Interest of *Character*. There is again our interest in the experience these personages are made to undergo, their conduct and fate: technically, Interest of *Passion*.

$$\text{Human Interest} \begin{cases} \text{Character.} \\ \text{Passion.} \end{cases}$$

Threefold division of Action. It is the same with the other fundamental element of art, the working together of all the details so as to leave an impression of unity: while in practice the sense of this unity, say in a piece of music or a play, is one of the simplest of instincts, yet upon analysis it is seen to imply three separate mental impressions. The mind, it implies, must be conscious of a unity. It must also be conscious of a complexity of details without which the unity could not be perceptible. But the mere perception of unity and of complexity would not give the art-pleasure it does give unless the unity were seen to be *developed* out of the complexity, and this brings in a third idea of progress and gradual *movement*.

Action $\begin{cases} \text{Unity.} \\ \text{Complexity.} \\ \text{Development, Succession, Movement.} \end{cases}$

Now if we apply the threefold idea involved in Action to the *Applica-* twofold idea involved in Human Interest we shall get the *tion of the* natural divisions of dramatic analysis. One element of *division of* Human Interest was Character: looking at this in the three-*Action to* fold aspect which is given to it when it is connected with *division of* Action we shall have to notice the interest of single charac-*Human* ters, or *Character-Interpretation*, the more complex interest *Interest.* of *Character-Contrast*, and in the third place *Character-Development*. Applying a similar treatment to the other side of Human Interest, Passion, we shall review single elements of Passion, that is to say, *Incidents and Effects*; the mixture of various passions to express which the term *Passion-Tones* will be used; and again the succession of these, or *Tone-Movement*. But Action has an interest of its own, considered in the abstract and as separate from Human Interest. This is *Plot*; and it will lend itself to the same triple treatment, falling into the natural divisions of *Single Action, Complex Action,* and that development of Plot which constitutes dramatic *Movement* in the most important sense. At this point it is possible only to name these leading topics of Dramatic Criticism: to explain each, and to trace them further into their lesser ramifications, will be the work of the remaining three chapters.

The Literary Drama $\begin{cases} \text{Character} \begin{cases} \text{Single Character-Interest, or} \\ \quad \textit{Character-Interpretation.} \\ \text{Complex Character-Interest, or} \\ \quad \textit{Character-Contrast.} \\ \textit{Character-Development.} \end{cases} \\ \\ \text{Passion} \begin{cases} \text{Single Passion-Interest, or} \\ \quad \textit{Incident and Effect.} \\ \text{Complex Passion-Interest, or} \\ \quad \textit{Passion-Tone.} \\ \textit{Tone-Movement.} \end{cases} \\ \\ \text{Plot (or Pure Action)} \begin{cases} \textit{Single Action.} \\ \textit{Complex Action.} \\ \textit{Plot-Movement.} \end{cases} \end{cases}$

Elementary Topics of Dramatic Criticism.

Ch. XVI.   These are the topics of Dramatic Criticism strictly so-called,
————   resting on the fundamental conception of it as a branch of
science.   Before passing on to the general exposition of
them in the chapters that follow, it is right to notice that
there are other topics belonging to the Drama in common
with other branches of art, though varying in part with the
Mechanical varieties of medium in which they are applied.   These may
Construc- be classed under the general term *Mechanical Construction*:
tion com-
mon to they are dependent, not on anything special to Drama, but
Drama and
other arts. upon our general interest in art, and in the operations of the
dramatist considered as a workman.   Examples of these
topics have been fully discussed in various parts of the
studies that have preceded: a brief enumeration will be
Reduction sufficient here.   One of them is the *Reduction of Difficulties*
of Difficul- in the construction of a story and the presentation of its
ties.
page 58.   matter.   Specially prominent amongst devices used for this
page 246.   purpose are *Rationalisation* and *Derationalisation*: both
&c.   illustrated in *The Tempest*, where the standing difficulty of
realising the supernatural is met by at once derationalising
the surroundings in which the enchantment is to appear,
and rationalising the supernatural element itself.   Again,
the sense of economy, which in so many ways enters into
Construc- dramatic art, is gratified in *Constructive Economy*, by which
tive Econo- personages and details introduced for mechanical purposes,
my.
that is to assist other effects, are also utilised for effects of
pages 75,   their own.   This has been fully illustrated in *The Merchant*
282.   *of Venice*; in *The Tempest* it has been further shown how
such personages can be faintly affected by the movement
of the play, and assist, though with a slightness proportioned
to their mechanical character, in reflecting the central
General idea.   Besides these, any *Constructive Processes* may be
Construc- enrolled amongst the topics of Dramatic Art, if they are
tive Pro-
cesses. prominent enough to present an interest in themselves, apart
from their bearing on the drift of the play.   Such a Con-
page 247.   structive Process is the maintenance throughout *The Tempest*

of a *Dramatic Background* of nature artistically in harmony
with the enchantment of the play [1]. Previous studies have
also noticed the *Dramatic Hedging,* by which unpleasant
elements in the characters of Shylock and Brutus are met
by another treatment bringing out peculiarities in the position
of these personages which restores them to our sympathy.
As a third example of Constructive Processes may be mentioned *Preparation*: by this the final effect to which a whole
play is leading up is anticipated in a modified form at an
early stage of the action ; as when the grand example of
providential control in Prospero's treatment of his human
friends and foes is, so to speak, rehearsed in the deliverance
of Ariel and the judgment on Caliban.

In general literary history *Conventionalities of Construction*
have played a great part,—arbitrary limitations prescribed
by literary fashion as problems of construction, chiefly interesting as feats of skill, like that of a violinist playing upon
one string. An example of such conventionality is the
Scenic Unities of Place and Time, discussed in the review
of *The Tempest.* By the Unity of Place, the arrangement
of the story is so limited that the scene shall always suggest
itself as the same—though (as in the case of the enchanted
island) different parts of this uniform scene may be exhibited in the various scenes. By the Unity of Time the
story is so arranged as not to require any intervals to be
supposed between consecutive scenes, the duration of the
action being, roughly, the same as the duration of the performance. The time taken up by the course of events in
The Tempest is, in so many words, limited to six hours ; and
the suggestion is that Prospero concludes his scheme at
Ariel's intercession earlier than he intended. Such unities
seem peculiarly suitable to a story of enchantment, as har-

CH. XVI.
———
pages 60,
176.

page 270.

*Construc-
tive Con-
vention-
alities.*

page 269.

i. ii.

v. i. 20.

---

[1] This should be distinguished from the case of Dramatic Background of nature in *Julius Cæsar* (above, p. 192), which changes with the
movement of the play, and is thus a dramatic motive (below, p. 393).

Ch. XVI. monising with the circumscribed area and duration of a
————   magician's power. In the case of *The Tempest*, as is usual
with classical plays, the observation of these unities carries
with it *Unity Devices*, such as the presentation of Prospero's
story, and other important incidents anterior to the opening
of the play, by means of narrative, or narrative dialogue.

Construc-   But the interest of Mechanical Construction which stands
tive Unity. out from all others is where the dramatist suggests to our
sense of analysis a grasp of the unity which binds together
his work into a single whole. That a play should impress
itself upon our minds as a unity is only another way of
saying that it is a work of art : it is a different thing when
this impression of unity seems to be analysable, and can be,
Dramatic   wholly or partially, formulated in words. The term *Dramatic*
Colouring. *Colouring* may be used where some unity of impression
extends to so large a proportion of the whole mass of matter
in a play as to give it a distinctive and recognisable individuality. It has been argued above that *The Tempest* is
thus coloured with enchantment; and the passion of Jealousy
has a similar prominence in *Othello*. It has been often
remarked how the play of *Macbeth* is coloured by the superstition and violence of the Dark Ages. The world of this
drama seems given over to the powers of darkness who can
read, if not mould, destiny ; witchcraft appears as an instrument of crime and ghostly agency of punishment. We have
rebellion without any suggestion of cause to ennoble it, ter-
minated by executions without the pomp of justice ; we have
a long reign of terror in which massacre is a measure of daily
administration and murder is a profession. With all this
there is a total absence of relief in any picture of settled
life : there is no rallying-point for order and purity. The
very agent of retribution gets the impulse to his task in a
compare   reaction from a shock of bereavement that has come down
iv. iii. 26, upon him as a natural punishment for an act of indecisive
and iv. ii.
1–22.   folly.

Such Dramatic Colouring is, however, a thing of general impression; there is a constructive unity going beyond this in the *Central Idea*, which will bear the test of the fullest analysis as to its connection with the whole matter of a drama, characterisation, passion, and plot being all duly related to it. I am chiefly concerned to maintain that the theory of Central Ideas is a matter which admits of accurate examination, and to urge that the term should not be lightly used. A Central Idea, to be worthy of the name, should be shown to embrace all the details of the play, it must be sufficiently distinctive to exclude other plays, while the distribution of the separate parts of the play should appear to agree with their direct or indirect bearing on this central and fundamental notion. I have in previous chapters suggested, with detailed justification, such Central Ideas for *The Tempest* and for *Love's Labour's Lost.*

It is obvious that these last two topics, Dramatic Colouring and Central Ideas, are closely connected with one another. Their mutual relation is well illustrated by the fact, noted above, that the Central Idea claimed for *Love's Labour's Lost* —namely, the conflict of humour with the conventional— is also found to colour large parts of *As You Like It*, in the central scenes of which the traditional conventionality of Pastoral Life is being played upon by three different types of humour in succession.

Mechanical Construction
- Reduction of Difficulties: especially, *Rationalisation* and *Derationalisation*.
- Constructive Economy: utilisation of mechanical personages and details.
- Constructive Processes: *Dramatic Background, Dramatic Hedging, Preparation*.
- Constructive Conventionalities: especially, the *Scenic Unities* of Place and Time.
- Constructive Unity: *Dramatic Colouring, Central Ideas*.

INTEREST OF CHARACTER.

CH. XVII.

———

*Unity ap-
plied to
Character :
Character-
Interpre-
tation.*

O F the main divisions of dramatic interest Character stands first for consideration : and we are to view it under the three aspects of unity, complexity, and movement. The application of the idea unity to the idea character suggests at once our interest in single personages. This interest becomes more defined when we take into account the medium through which the personages are presented to us : characters in Drama are not brought out by abstract discussion or description, but are presented to us concretely, self-pourtrayed by their own actions without the assistance of comments from the author.

Accordingly, the leading interest of character is *Interpretation*, the mental process of turning from the concrete to the abstract : out of the most diverse details of conduct and impression Interpretation extracts a unity of conception which we call a character. Interpretation when scientifically handled must be, we have seen, of the nature of an hypothesis, the value of which depends upon the degree in which it explains whatever details have any bearing upon the character. Such an hypothesis may be a simple idea : and we have seen at length how the whole portraiture of Richard precipitates into the notion of Ideal Villainy, ideal on the subjective side in an artist who follows crime for its own sake, and on the objective side in a success that works by fascination. But the student must beware of the temptation to grasp at epigrammatic labels as

sufficient solutions of character. In the great majority of
cases Interpretation can become complete only by recognising and harmonising various and even conflicting elements; and a practical illustration of this principle has
been given above in an elaborate discussion of the difficult
character of Jaques in *As You Like It.*

Incidentally we have noticed some of the principles govern- *Canons of*
ing careful Interpretation. One of these principles is that it *Interpre-*
tation.
must take into consideration all that is presented of a per- *It must be*
sonage. It is unscientific on the face of it to say (as is *exhaustive.*
repeatedly said) that Shakespeare is 'inconsistent' in ascrib-
ing deep musical sympathies to so thin a character as
Lorenzo. Such allegation of inconsistency means that the
process of Interpretation is unfinished; it can be paralleled
only by the astronomer who should complain of eclipses as
'inconsistent' with his view of the moon's movements. In
the particular case we found no difficulty in harmonising the
apparent conflict: the details of Lorenzo's portraiture fit
in well with the not uncommon type of nature that is so
deeply touched by art sensibilities as to have a languid interest in life outside art. Again: Interpretation must look
for *indirect* evidence of character, such as the impression a *It must take*
personage seems to have made on other personages in the *in indirect*
evidence ;
story, or the effect of action outside the field of view. It
is impatient induction to pronounce Bassanio unworthy of
Portia merely from comparison of the parts played by the
two in the drama itself. It happens from the nature of the
story that the incidents actually represented in the drama
are such as always display Bassanio in an exceptional and
dependent position; but we have an opportunity of getting
to the other side of our hero's character by observing the
attitude held to him by others in the play, an attitude
founded not on the incidents of the drama alone, but upon
the sum total of his life and behaviour in the Venetian
world. This gives a very different impression ; and when we

CH. XVII. take into consideration the force with which his personality sways all who approach him, from the strong Antonio and the intellectual Lorenzo to giddy Gratiano and the rough common sense of Launcelot, then the character comes out in its proper scale. As a third principle, it is perhaps too

and the de- obvious to be worth formulating that Interpretation must *gree to which the* allow for the degree to which the character is displayed by *character is* the action: that Brutus's frigid eloquence at the funeral of *displayed.* Cæsar means not coldness of feeling but stoicism of public

Interpre- demeanour. It is a less obvious principle that the very *tation re-* details which are to be unified into a conception of cha-*acting on* *the details.* racter may have a different complexion given to them when they are looked at in the light of the whole. It has been noticed how Richard seems to manifest in some scenes a slovenliness of intrigue that might be a stumbling-block to the general impression of his character. But when in our view of him as a whole we see what a large part is played by the invincibility that is stamped on his very demeanour, it becomes clear how this slovenliness can be interpreted by the analyst, and represented by the actor, not as a defect of power, but as a trick of bearing which measures his own sense of his irresistibility. Principles like these flow naturally from the fundamental idea of character and its unity. Their practical use however will be mainly that of tests for suggested interpretations: to the actual reading of character in Drama, as in real life, the safest guide is sympathetic insight.

Complexity The second element underlying all dramatic effect was *applied to* complexity; when complexity is applied to Character we *Character.* get Character-Contrast. In its lowest degree this appears in

Character- the form of *Character-Foils*: by the side of some prominent *Foils.* character is placed another of less force and interest but cast in the same mould, or perhaps moulded by the influence of

its principal, just as by the side of a lofty mountain are Ch. XVII.
often to be seen smaller hills of the same formation. Thus
beside Portia is placed Nerissa, beside Bassanio Gratiano,
beside Shylock Tubal; Richard's villainy stands out by
comparison with Buckingham, Hastings, Tyrrel, Catesby,
any one of whom would have given blackness enough to an
ordinary drama. It is quite possible that minute examination may find differences between such companion figures:
but the general effect of the combination is that the lesser
serves as foil to throw up the scale on which the other is
framed. The more pronounced effects of Character-Contrast depend upon differences of kind as distinguished from
differences of degree. In this form it is clear how *Cha-* *Character-*
racter-Contrast is only an extension of Character-Interpre- *Contrast.*
tation: it implies that some single conception explains (that
is, gives unity to) the actions of more than one person. A
whole chapter has been devoted to bringing out such contrast in the case of Lord and Lady Macbeth: to accept
these as types of the practical and inner life, cast in such an
age and involved in such an undertaking, furnishes a conception sufficient to make clear and intelligible all that the
two say and do in the scenes of the drama. Character- *Duplica-*
Contrast is especially common amongst the minor figures of *tion.*
a Shakespearean drama. In the case of personages demanded
by the necessities of the story rather than introduced for
their own sake Shakespeare has a tendency to double the
number of such characters for the sake of getting effects of
contrast. We have two unsuccessful suitors in *The Merchant
of Venice* bringing out, the one the unconscious pride of
royal birth, the other the pride of intense self-consciousness;
two wicked daughters of Lear, Goneril with no shading in
her harshness, Regan who is in reality a degree more calculating in her cruelty than her sister, but conceals it under a
charm of manner, 'eyes that comfort and not burn.' Of
the two princes in *Richard III* the one has a gravity iii. i.

Ch. XVII.

i. iv, from
84.

110.

124–157.

167.

165.

263.
beyond his years, while York overflows with not ungraceful pertness. Especially interesting are the two murderers in that play. The first is a dull, ' strong-framed' man, without any better nature. The second has had culture, and been accustomed to reflect; his better nature has been vanquished by love of greed, and now asserts itself to prevent his sinning with equanimity. It is the second murderer whose conscience is set in activity by the word 'judgment'; and he discourses on conscience, deeply, yet not without humour, as he recognises the power of the expected reward over the oft-vanquished compunctions. He catches, as a thoughtful man, the irony of the duke's cry for wine when they are about to drown him in the butt of malmsey. Again, instead of hurrying to the deed while Clarence is waking he cannot resist the temptation to argue with him, and so, as a man open to argument, he feels the force of Clarence's un-expected suggestion :

> He that set you on
> To do this deed will hate you for the deed.

Thus he exhibits the weakness of all thinking men in a moment of action, the capacity to see two sides of a question ; and, trying at the critical moment to alter his course, he ends by losing the reward of crime without escaping the guilt.

Character-Grouping. Character-Contrast is carried forward into *Character-Grouping* when the field is still further enlarged, and a single conception is found to give unity to more than two person-ages of a drama. A chapter has been devoted to showing how the same antithesis of outer and inner life which made the conception of Macbeth and his wife intelligible would serve, when adapted to the widely different world of Roman political life, to explain the characters of the leading conspirators in *Julius Cæsar*, of their victim and of his avenger : while, over and above the satisfaction of Interpret-ation, the Grouping of these four figures, so colossal and so impressive, round a single idea is an interest in itself. It Сн. XVII. has been shown, again, how the principal personages in *Othello* can be grouped about the idea of Suspicious Jealousy. In *Love's Labour's Lost* the underplot is made up of two Character Groups: one, coloured by Euphuism, centering around Armado, while the other centers round Holofernes and is distinguished by Pedantry.

There are, then, two distinct effects that arise when complexity enters into Character-Interest. The complexity is one never separable from the unity which binds it together : in the first effect the diversity is stronger than the unity, and the whole manifests itself as Character-Contrast ; in Character-Grouping the contrast of the separate figures is an equal element with the unity which binds them all into a group.

When to Character-Interpretation, the formation of a *Movement* single conception out of a multitude of concrete details, the *applied to Character:* further idea of growth and progress is added, we get the *Character-* third variety of Character-Interest—*Character-Development.* *Development.* In the preceding chapters this has received only negative notice, its absence being a salient feature in the portraiture of Richard. For a positive illustration no better example could be desired than the character of Macbeth. Three features, we have seen, stand out clear in the general conception of Macbeth. There is his eminently practical nature, which is the key to the whole. And the absence in him of the inner life adds two special features: one is his helplessness under suspense, the other is the activity of his imagination with its susceptibility to supernatural terrors. Now, if we fix our attention on these three points they become three threads of development as we trace Macbeth through the stages of his career. His practical power developes as capacity for crime. Macbeth undertook his first crime only after a protracted and terrible struggle ; the murder of the

CH. XVII. grooms was a crime of impulse; the murder of Banquo
appears a thing of contrivance, in which Macbeth is a
deliberate planner directing the agency of others, while his
iii. ii. 40, dark hints to his wife suggest the beginning of a relish for
&c. such deeds. This capacity for crime continues to grow,
until slaughter becomes an end in itself—

iv. iii. 4.
> Each new morn
> New widows howl, new orphans cry:

and then a mania:

v. ii. 13.
> Some say he's mad; others that lesser hate him
> Do call it valiant fury.

We see a parallel development in Macbeth's impatience of
suspense. Just after his first temptation he is able to brace
himself to suspense for an indefinite period:

i. iii. 143.
> If chance will have me king, why, chance may crown me,
> Without my stir.

i. vii. On the eve of his great crime the suspense of the few hours
that must intervene before the banquet can be despatched
and Duncan can retire becomes intolerable to Macbeth, and
he is for abandoning the project. In the next stage it is
the suspense of a single moment that impels him to stab the
grooms. From this point suspense no longer comes by fits
iii. ii. 13, and starts, but is a settled disease: his mind is as scorpions;
36, &c. it is tortured in restless ecstasy. Suspense has undermined
his judgment and brought on him the gambler's fever—the
haunting thought that just one more venture will make him
safe; in spite of the opposition of his reason—which his
iii. ii. 45. unwillingness to confide the murder of Banquo to his wife
betrays—he is carried on to work the additional crime which
unmasks the rest. And finally suspense intensifies to a panic,
and he himself feels that his deeds

iii. iv. 140.
> must be acted ere they may be scann'd.

The third feature in Macbeth is the quickening of his sen-

sitiveness to the supernatural side by side with the deadening CH.XVII.
of his conscience. Imagination becomes, as it were, a pictorial conscience for one to whom its more rational channels
have been closed: the man who 'would jump the world to
come' accepts implicitly every word that falls from a witch.
Now this imagination is at first a restraining force in Macbeth: the thought whose image unfixes his hair leads him to i. iii. 134.
abandon the treason. When later he has, under pressure,
delivered himself again to the temptation, there are still signs
that imagination is a force on the other side that has to be
overcome :

> Stars, hide your fires;   i. iv. 50.
> Let not light see my black and deep desires:
> The eye wink at the hand.

Once passed the boundary of the accomplished deed he becomes an absolute victim to terrors of conscience in supernatural form. In the very first moment they reach so near ii. ii. 22–
the boundary that separates subjective and objective that a 46.
real voice appears to be denouncing the issue of his crime :

> *Macbeth.* Methought I heard a voice cry 'Sleep no more.' . . .
> *Lady M.* Who was it that thus cried?

In the reaction from the murder of Banquo the supernatural
appearance—which no eye sees but his own—appears more iii. iv.
real to him than the real life around him. And from this
point he *seeks* the supernatural, forces it to disclose its iv. i. 48.
terrors, and thrusts himself into an agonised vision of generations that are to witness the triumph of his foes.

INTEREST OF PASSION.

HUMAN Interest includes not only varieties of human nature, or Character, but also items of human experience, or Passion. Passion is the second great topic of Dramatic Criticism. It is concerned with the life that is lived through the scenes of the story, as distinguished from the personages who live it; not treating this with the abstract treatment that belongs to Plot, but reviewing it in the light of its human interest; it embraces conduct still alive with the motives which have actuated it—fate in the process of forging. The word 'passion' signifies primarily what is suffered of good or bad; secondarily the emotions generated by suffering, whether in the sufferer or in bystanders. Its use as a dramatic term thus suggests how in Drama an experience can be grasped by us through our emotional nature, through our sympathy, our antagonism, and all the varieties of emotional interest that lie between. To this Passion we have to apply the threefold division of unity, complexity, and movement.

Unity applied to Passion. When unity is applied to Passion we get a series of details bound together into a singleness of impression as an Incident, a Situation, or an Effect. The distinction of the three rests largely on their different degrees of fragmentariness. *Incident.* *Incidents* are groups of continuous details forming a complete interest in themselves as ministering to our sense of story. The suit of Shylock against Antonio in the course of which fate swings right round; the murder of Clarence with its long-drawn agony; Richard and Buckingham with the

Lord Mayor and Citizens exhibiting a picture of political Сн.ХVІІІ. manipulation in the fifteenth century ; the startling sight of a Lady Anne wooed beside the bier of her murdered husband's murdered father, by a murderer who rests his suit on the murders themselves ; Banquo's Ghost appearing at the feast at which Banquo's presence had been so vehemently called for ; Lear's faithful Gloucester so brutally blinded and so instantly avenged ; the outraged Brabantio at midnight impeaching before the Duke's throne the unnatural wooer of his daughter, and seeing all Venice draw to his adversary's side ; the chain of discovery forged by fate for the Celibates of Navarre by which each hoping to surprise the others is himself taken by surprise ; a mysterious concurrence of circumstances luring on Antonio and Sebastian to a deed of murder, and reversing itself to check them in the moment of action :—all these are complete stories presented in a single view, and suggest how Shakespeare's dramas are constructed out of materials which are themselves dramas in miniature.

In *Situation*, on the other hand, a series of details cohere *Situation.* into a single impression without losing the sense of incompleteness. The two central personages in *The Merchant of Venice*, around whom brightness and gloom have been revolving in such contrast, at last brought to face one another from the judgment-seat and the dock ; Lorenzo and Jessica wrapped in moonlight and music, with the rest of the universe for the hour blotted out into a background for their love ; Rosalind from under the shelter of her disguise enjoying the sport of dictating to her unsuspecting lover how he should woo her ; Margaret like an apparition of the sleeping Nemesis of Lancaster flashed into the midst of the Yorkist courtiers while they are bickering through very wantonness of victory ; Shylock pitted against Tubal, Jew against Jew, the nature not too narrow to mix affection with avarice, mocked from passion to passion by the nature only wide enough to take in greed; Richard waking on Bosworth morning, and miserably piecing together the wreck of his invincible will which a sleeping vision has shattered; Macbeth's moment of rapture in following the airy dagger, while the very night holds its breath to break out again presently into voices of doom; the panic mist of universal suspicion amidst which Malcolm blasts his own character to feel after the fidelity of Macduff; Edgar from his ambush of outcast idiocy watching the sad marvel of his father's love restored to him; Prospero surveying the unbroken range of his omnipotence in the very act of renouncing it:—all these brilliant Situations are fragments of dramatic continuity in which the fragmentariness is a part of the interest. Just as the sense of sculpture might seek to arrest and perpetuate a casual moment in the evolutions of a dance, so in Dramatic Situation the mind is conscious of isolating something from what precedes and what follows so as to extract out of it an additional impression; the morsel has its purpose in ministering to a complete process of digestion, but it gets a sensation of its own by momentary delay in contact with the palate.

Effect.   Of a still more fragmentary nature is *Dramatic Effect*— Effect strictly so called, and as distinguished from the looser use of the term for dramatic impressions in general. Such Effect seems to attach itself to single momentary details, though in reality these details owe their impressiveness to their connection with others: the final detail has completed an electric circle and a shock is given. No element of the Drama is of so miscellaneous a character and so defies analysis: all that can be done here is to notice three special Dramatic Effects.

Irony as an Effect.   *Dramatic Irony* is a sudden appearance of double-dealing in surrounding events: a dramatic situation accidentally starts up and produces a shock by its bearing upon conflicting states of affairs, both known to the audience, but one

of them hidden from some of the parties to the scene.
This is the special contribution to dramatic effect of Greek
tragedy. The ancient stage was tied down in its subject-
matter to stories perfectly familiar to the audience as sacred
legends, and so almost excluding the effect of surprise : in
Irony it found some compensation. The ancient tragedies
harp upon human blindness to the future, and delight to exhibit a hero speculating about, or struggling with, or perhaps
in careless talk stumbling upon, the final issue of events
which the audience know so well ;—Œdipus, for example,
through great part of a play moving heaven and earth to
pierce the mystery of the judgment that has come upon his
city, while according to the familiar sacred story the offender
can be none other than himself. Shakespeare has used to
almost as great an extent as the Greek dramatists this effect
of Irony. His most characteristic handling of it belongs to
the lighter plays, in which the touches of Irony will often be
so numerous as to amount to a Motive [1]; yet in the group of
dramas dealt with in this work it is prominent amongst his
effects. It has been pointed out how *Macbeth* and *Richard III*
are saturated with it. There are casual illustrations in
Julius Cæsar, as when the dictator bids his intended
murderer—

Be near me, that I may remember you ; **ii.** ii. 123.

or in *Lear*, when Edmund, intriguing guiltily with Goneril, in
a chance expression of tenderness unconsciously paints the
final issue of that intrigue :

Yours in the ranks of death ! **iv.** ii. 25.

The pathos of Desdemona's position in the latter part of
Othello produces some wonderful strokes of Irony. One has
been pointed out in the chapter on that play ; another is
where in all her simplicity she turns to the author of her
ruin :
O good Iago,
What shall I do to win my lord again ?

[1] See below, page 388 note.

Ch.XVIII.

iv. i. 282. A comic variety of Irony occurs in the Trial Scene of *The Merchant of Venice*, when Bassanio and Gratiano in their distracted grief are willing to sacrifice their new wives if this could save their friend—little thinking these wives are so near to record the vow.   The doubleness of Irony is one which attaches to a situation as a whole : the effect however is iii. ii. 60–
73. especially keen when a scene is so impregnated with it that the very language is true in a double sense.

> *Catesby*. 'Tis a vile thing to die, my gracious lord,
> When men are unprepared and look not for it.
> *Hastings*. O monstrous, monstrous ! and so falls it out
> With Rivers, Vaughan, Grey: *and so 'twill do*
> *With some men else, who think themselves as safe*
> *As thou and I.*

Nemesis as an Effect.   *Nemesis*, though usually extending to the general movement of a drama, and so considered below, may sometimes be only an effect of detail—a sign connecting very closely retribution with sin or reaction with triumph.   Such a nemesis may be v. iii. 45. seen where Cassius in the act of falling on his sword recognises the weapon as the same with which he stabbed Cæsar.

Dramatic Fore-shadowing.   Another special variety of effect is *Dramatic Foreshadowing*—mysterious details pointing to an explanation in the sequel, a realisation in action of the saying that coming events cast their shadows before them.   The unaccountable i. i. 1. 'sadness' of Antonio at the opening of *The Merchant of Venice* is a typical illustration.   Others will readily suggest iii. i. 68. themselves—the Prince's shuddering aversion to the Tower i. i. 39. in *Richard III*, the letter G that of Edward's heirs the v. i. 77–90. murderer should be, the crows substituted for Cassius's eagles on the morning of the final battle.   A more elaborate example is seen in *Julius Cæsar*, where the soothsayer's i. ii. 18. vague warning 'Beware the Ides of March'—a solitary voice that could yet arrest the hero through the shouting of the iii. i. 1. crowd—is found later on not to have become dissipated, but to have gathered definiteness as the moment comes nearer :

> *Cæsar.* The Ides of March are come.
> *Soothsayer.* Ay, Cæsar; but not gone.

And the supreme example of Dramatic Foreshadowing is the scene in *Othello* when Desdemona is retiring to bed on the **iv.** iii. fatal night, under an irresistible weight of boding. She bids her marriage sheets be laid on the bed, and adds:

> If I do die before thee, prithee, shroud me
> In one of those same sheets.

Her mother's maid Barbara, who died of love, comes persistently into her mind, and when she tries to talk of other topics, the wailing burden of Barbara's song keeps reviving. The shadow of the murder has already enveloped her.

These three leading effects may be sufficient to illustrate a branch of dramatic analysis in which the variety is endless.

We are next to consider the application of complexity to *Complexity* Passion, and the contrasts of passion that so arise. Here *applied to* care is necessary to avoid confusion with a complexity of *Passion.* passion that hardly comes within the sphere of dramatic criticism. In the scene in which Shylock is being teased by **iii.** i. Tubal it is easy to note the conflict between the passions of greed and paternal affection: such analysis is outside dramatic criticism and belongs to psychology. In its dramatic sense Passion applies to experience, not decomposed into its emotional elements, but grasped as a whole by our emotional nature: there is still room for complexity of such passion in the appeal made *to different sides of our emotional nature, the serious and the gay.* In dealing with this element of dramatic *Passion-* effect a convenient technical term is *Tone.* The deep insight *Tone.* of metaphorical word-coining has given universal sanction to the expression of emotional differences by analogies of music: our emotional nature is exalted with mirth and depressed with sorrow, we speak of a chord of sympathy, a

CH.XVIII. strain of triumph, a note of despair; we are in a serious mood, or pitch our appeal in a higher key. These expressions are clearly musical, and there is probably a half association of music in many others, such as a theme of sorrow, acute anguish, and profound despair, response of gratitude, or even the working of our feelings. Most exactly to the purpose is a phrase of frequent occurrence, the 'gamut of the passions,' which brings out with emphasis how our emotional nature in its capacity for different kinds of impressions suggests a *scale* of passion-contrasts, not to be sharply defined but shading off into one another like the tones of a musical scale—Tragic, Heroic, Serious, Elevated, Light, Comic, Farcical. It is with such complexity of tones that Dramatic Passion is concerned.

Scale of Passion-Tones.

Mixture of Tones:

Now this *Mixture of Tones*, or inclusion of different tones in the field of the same play, is for the Shakespearean drama a most important department of dramatic interest. In *The Merchant of Venice*, as often in plays of Shakespeare, every tone in the scale is represented. When Antonio is enduring through the long suspense, and triumphant malignity is gaining point after point against helpless friendship, we have travelled far into the Tragic; the woman-nature of Portia calling Venetian justice from judicial murder to the divine prerogative of mercy throws in a touch of the Heroic; a great part of what centres around Shylock, when he is crushing the brightness out of Jessica or defying the Christian world, is pitched in the Serious strain; the incidents of the unsuccessful suitors, the warm exuberance of Oriental courtesy and the less grateful loftiness of Spanish family pride, might be a model for the Elevated drama of the English Restoration; the infinite nothings of Gratiano, prince of diners-out, the more piquant small talk of Portia and Nerissa when they criticise the man-world from the secrecy of a maiden-bower—these throw a tone of Lightness over their sections of the drama; Launcelot is an incarnation of the

iv. i.

iv. i. 184.

ii. v; iii. i, &c.

ii. i, vii; ii. ix.

i. i, &c. i. ii.

ii. ii, iii; iii. v, &c.

conventional Comic serving-man, and his Comedy becomes CH.XVIII.
broad Farce where he teases the sand-blind Gobbo and draws ii. ii, from
him on to bless his astonishing beard.   Such Mixture of 34.
Tones can be appreciated from contrast with the Classical *a distinc-*
Drama, where it was found impossible.   The exclusive and *tion of the*
uncompromising spirit of antiquity carried caste into art *modern*
itself, and their Tragedy and Comedy were kept rigidly *Drama.*
separate, and indeed were connected with different rituals.
The spirit of modern life is marked by its comprehensive-
ness and reconciliation of opposites; and nothing is more
important in dramatic history than the way in which
Shakespeare and his contemporaries created a new departure
in art, by seizing upon the rude jumble of sport and earnest
which the 'mob loved, and converting it into a source of
stirring passion-effects.   For a new faculty of mental grasp
is generated by this harmony of tones in the English Drama.
If the artist introduces every tone into the story he thereby
gets hold of every tone in the spectator's emotional nature;
the world of the play is presented from every point of view
as it works upon the various passions, and the difference
this makes is the difference between simply looking down
upon a surface and viewing a solid from all round:—the
mixture of tones, so to speak, makes passion of three
dimensions.   Moreover it brings the world of fiction nearer
to the world of nature, which has never yet evolved an
experience in which brightness was dissevered from gloom:
half the pleasure of the world is wrung out of others' pain;
the two jostle in the street, house together under every roof,
share every stage of life, and refuse to be sundered even in
the mysteries of death.

Complexity of Passion arises in its most pronounced form *Tone-*
when opposing tones of passion *clash* in the same incident *Clash.*
and are *fused* together.   These terms are, I think, scarcely
metaphorical: as a physiological fact we see our physical
susceptibility to pleasurable and painful emotions drawn into

CH.XVIII. conflict with one another in the phenomena of hysteria, and
their mental analogues must be capable of much closer
union.　As examples of these effects resting upon an appeal
to opposite sides of our emotional nature at the same time
may be instanced the flash of comic irony, already referred to
more than once, that starts up in the most pathetic moment
iv. i. 288, of Antonio's trial by his friend's allusion to his newly wedded
&c. wife.　Of the same double nature are the strokes of pathetic
iii. iii. 32. humour in this play; as where Antonio describes himself so
worn with grief that he will hardly spare a pound of flesh to
his bloody creditor; or again his pun,

iv. i. 280.
> For if the Jew do cut but deep enough
> I'll pay it presently with all my heart!

A play upon the same word, more elaborate and in equally
pathetic circumstances, is found in Antony's lament over
Cæsar's body :—
iii. i. 204.
> Here wast thou bay'd, brave hart;
> Here didst thou fall; and here thy hunters stand,
> Sign'd in thy spoil, and crimson'd in thy lethe.
> O world, thou wast the forest to this hart;
> And this indeed, O world, the heart of thee.

Shakespeare seems to regard the pun as the established form
for expression of these hysterical stages of emotion; for
the pun is distinguished by the clashing between sound and
sense, and so is fitted to be an outward symbol for clashings
of emotion where grief unnaturally laughs, and laughter
grows to tears.

Humour
the climax
of Tone-
Clash.

　　But these casual and isolated clashings of Passion-Tones are
swallowed up in the wider Humour, the most volatile and
unanalysable of all varieties of dramatic effect.　Humour
cannot exist without some conflict of opposites, or of
things incongruous ; and the more the incongruity the greater
is the humour.　If, by a change of metaphor, the various
Passion-Tones be regarded as different colours, then Humour
is the white light made by their fusion or rapid alternation.

Humour is thus the climax of Tone-Clash; and it is no- CH.XVIII.
where clearer to the eye of analysis than in the two plays of
Love's Labour's Lost and *As You Like It*, in which, as two
chapters have been devoted to showing, the dominant effect
is the perpetual clashings between humour and things which
are its antipathetic, resulting in tours-de-force of comic
brilliance.

Tone-Clash rises into Tone-Storm in such rare climaxes *Tone-*
as the centre-piece of *Lear*, where, against a tempest of *Storm.*
nature as a fitting background, we have the conflict of
three madnesses—the madness of fury, of idiocy and of
folly: each in itself is a fusion of several passion-tones, but
here we have them bidding against one another, and in-
flaming each other's wildness into an inextricable whirl of
frenzy.   A comic counterpart to this may be found in *As
You Like It*, where, as already pointed out, the three types of
natural, professional and morbid humour, besides playing
upon the various conventionalities and affectations of the
story, are in some of the central scenes pitted against one
another, and thus throw up the middle part of this comedy
with a perfect tempest of humorous passion.

Not only is dramatic interest susceptible to these varied *Movement*
tones of passion in a play, but it catches a further effect from *(or Suc-*
their alternation and succession.   We here reach the appli- *cession)*
cation to Passion of the third element in action—movement, *applied to*
development, succession.   The new type of dramatic interest *Passion.*
is most simply illustrated from the companion art of music,
where we are accustomed to find an adagio and an allegro, a
fantastic scherzo and a pompous march, included within the
same symphony or sonata, though in separate movements.
Such alternations may be technically described as Tone-Play
or Tone-Relief.

Tone-Play is made by simple variety and alternation of *Tone-Play.*

Ch.XVIII. light and serious passions. It has been pointed out in a previous chapter what a striking example of this is *The Merchant of Venice*, in which scene by scene two stories of youthful love and of deadly feud alternate with one another as they progress to their climaxes, until from the

iii. ii. 221. rapture of Portia united to Bassanio we drop to the full realisation of Antonio in the grasp of Shylock; and again the cruel anxiety of the trial and its breathless shock of deliver-

iv. i. 408. ance are balanced by the mad fun of the ring trick and the joy

v. i. of the moonlight scene which Jessica feels is too deep for mer-

Tone-Re-lief. riment. A slight variation of this is *Tone-Relief*: in an action which is cast in a uniform tone the continuity is broken by a brief spell of a contrary passion, the contrast at once relieving and intensifying the prevailing tone. One of the best examples (notwithstanding its coarseness) is the introduction

ii. iii. 1. in *Macbeth* of the jolly Porter, who keeps the impatient nobles outside in the storm till his jest is comfortably finished, making each furious knock fit in to his elaborate conceit of Hell-gate. This tone of broad farce, with nothing else like it in the whole play, comes as a single ray of common daylight to separate the agony of the dark night's murder from the

iii. i, ii, iii. agony of the struggle for concealment. A not dissimiliar effect is in *Othello*, where the terrible Suggestion Scenes —carrying on the action of the drama from the first request of Cassio for Desdemona's assistance up to the point where the ruin of both is vowed by Othello and Iago on their knees—are fringed off from the rest of the play by two morsels of farce from the Clown. In the first he chaffs the musicians and conveys the general's orders to cease playing, unless they happen to have some music that is inaudible; in the second he will not obey Desdemona's order to call Cassio without a word-combat over the double sense of the word 'lie.' And these make the only appearance of the Clown in the whole play.

　　Such word-play as that of this Clown seems to be re-

cognised by Shakespeare as a regular dramatic weapon, Cʜ.XVIII.
useful for tone-relief and other purposes; and in *Love's*
Labour's Lost I have illustrated[1] how, where the interest of
the story stands still for a moment, the interval is filled up
with this other interest of mental fencing. But Shakespeare
has another device in his repertoire, of the highest literary
importance, capable of marking the most delicate changes of
tone in his scenes. This is the alternation between prose
and verse, or between different styles of verse.

Devices of Tone-Relief: Word-play, and alternation of Verse and Prose.

This Shakespearean usage is not one that stands by itself:
it has its parallels in other divisions of the universal drama.
A leading feature of ancient classical dramas is the subtle
play of emotions they express by changes from iambics—
the Greek form of blank verse—to lyric measures. I am not
alluding to the purely lyric odes sung by the Chorus between
the scenes, but to the alternations between iambs and lyric
measures in the episodes on the stage. So in the late
Romantic Drama, such as Goethe's *Faust*, every possible
variation of measure, including prose as non-measure, is made
use of to fit in with variations of feeling to be expressed.
And when we come to Shakespeare himself, there are signs
in his earlier plays (notably in *Midsummer Night's Dream*) of
an attempt to use the variation between blank verse and
rhyme as a means of conveying changes in tone. But this
was abandoned as he followed his original genius more and
more; and the bolder device of variation between blank verse
and prose took more and more hold on him.

The point to be emphasised is, not that any particular class
of emotions is associated with any particular metrical form,
but that *changes* of tone are reflected in *changes* between
metre and metre, or metre and prose. Of course it will
usually happen that the more elevated tone or more agitated
passion will have verse rather than prose for its medium.
But this is not universally the case. In the finale of Goethe's

[1] See page 288.

CH.XVIII. *Faust* the awakening from the dissipation of the Walpurgis
Night to the full agony of knowing Margaret's fate is marked
by a sudden drop to prose; and no device could better
convey the shock of awakening.   In *Macbeth*, where nearly
the whole play is in blank verse, prose is reserved for the
climax of the Sleep-walking Scene.   So in the great Suggestion Scenes of *Othello*, the hero's passion has mounted in
iv. i. 34.   intensity until at the breaking pitch he changes from verse
to prose just before he falls down in a fit.

A very late play, *The Tempest*, illustrates the delicate changes
or varieties Shakespeare is able to suggest by this means.
i. i.   The bustle of the Shipwreck is conveyed in rough prose; but
when the courtiers realise that death is before them the
language rises to verse.

> *Gon.*   The king and prince at prayers! let's assist them,
> For our case is as theirs.

But after a while Gonzalo is unable to keep down his native
sense of humour, and there is a change back to prose.

> Now would I give a thousand furlongs of sea for an acre of barren
> ground. . . . The wills above be done! but I would fain die a dry
> death.

i. ii.   Then a change to mellifluous verse exquisitely conveys our
passing within the magic circle of the Enchanted Island.   A
ii. i.   later scene is a conversation between the whole party of
courtiers; Gonzalo essaying to console the bereaved King
keeps up the main thread of conversation in verse, while
Sebastian and Antonio, chaffing Gonzalo in an undertone,
use prose.   But when Gonzalo can no longer ignore their
20.   interruptions he turns on them in prose, and the conversation
becomes general, prose being spoken until the King elevates
106.   the tone, when he breaks silence, and pours out his sorrows
in verse.   The talk has now to be addressed to the King;
and even Sebastian and Antonio use verse.   Gonzalo, to
143.   divert the King from painful subjects, puts (in verse) his

project for a golden age, and Sebastian and Antonio resume CH.XVIII.
in prose their comments in an undertone. But at last the   ——
King is irritated by Gonzalo's well-meant but tiresome loqua-
ciousness, and expresses his irritation in prose : this checks 171.
altogether the elevated tone of the conversation, and Gonzalo
turns to exchange prose sarcasms with his tormentors, till the
main bulk of the party fall asleep under the charm of Ariel.
The startling suddenness of this drives the King into verse, 191.
and, when he too has joined the sleepers, the hideous
suggestiveness of the situation to the traitors keeps them at
the white heat of verse all through their conspiracy to the
end of the scene.

In the case of Caliban, fine dramatic effects are got out of
the variations between prose and verse. In his first ap- i. ii. 321.
pearance the scene is an exchange of fierce passion between
himself and his master, and is in verse throughout.   He next ii. ii. 1.
enters pouring out the passion of the previous scene in curses
of blank verse.   Then Trinculo and Stephano enter, and the
total change of tone is marked by change to prose; until
Stephano pours liquor from his bottle down Caliban's throat. 97.
The effect of liquor on Caliban is to make him worship the
drunken butler as a god ; and this effect is finely opened by
Caliban's first words rising into verse :   121.

> These be fine things, an if they be not sprites.
> That's a brave god, and bears celestial liquor.

So to the end of the scene (except a single morsel of musical 130.
prose) Caliban addresses his god in verse—the tone sharply
contrasting with the speeches of Trinculo and Stephano in
prose. When the party reappear the general situation is iii. ii.
continued : but here a very subtle transition is to be noted.
Caliban, his eyes 'set in his head' with drunken worship of
Stephano, can hardly be induced to speak at all; when
compelled, he addresses his god in a line of musical verse :   26.

> How does thy honour? Let me lick thy shoe—

CH.XVIII. but in the very next line drops to prose to express his
———   attitude to Trinculo, whom he does not worship:

> I'll not serve him; he's not valiant.

A quarrel ensues, and breaks the serene tone of worship,
prose continuing to the beginning of Caliban's tale; when
the interruption, *Thou liest*, drives Caliban to passion and to
52.   blank verse—which he maintains through his prayer and his
joy at its acceptance to the end of the scene, Stephano and
Trinculo, of course, continuing to talk in prose. When we
iv. i. 194.   next see the party the relations of the three are maintained;
and the contrast of tone between Caliban, intent on his
treason now all but consummated, and his companions too
drunk to be kept quiet though a sound may ruin all, is
admirably conveyed by the alternations between the verse of
Caliban and the prose of the other two. In the Finale
v. i. 261.   Caliban is confronted by his master, and the sight of a new
civilisation, and speaks his repentance in verse [1].

---

[1] I may here remark, anticipating the subject of a later chapter, that
alternations between verse and prose are also used by Shakespeare to
emphasise changes in dramatic 'movement'; though not (so far as I
have observed) in the plays reviewed in this book. One example is in
Measure for Measure. A great note of Shakespeare's action is his
contrivance of a central turning-point to the movement—somewhere in
the middle Act, and often at its exact centre. In *Measure for Measure*
the passion of the *complication* reaches its height in the terrible scene
between Claudio and his sister (**iii. i.**). Where the agony is at its
highest enters the (disguised) Duke (152), whom the audience recognise
(being in the secret of his disguise from **i. iii.**) as representing the
resolving force of the plot: and the Duke at once draws Isabella aside,
and commences with her the intrigue which proves the resolution of the
whole play. Now this central turning-point, or passage from the complication to the resolution, is emphasised by a change from verse to
prose: and every one must feel how the shock of this change gives
additional effect to the turn in the movement.

A precisely parallel case is *Winter's Tale*. In no play is the passage
from complication to resolution so clearly marked as here. In the course
of the middle Act (**iii. iii.** 58), Antigonus deposits the infant, and exit,
pursued by a bear—the complication which is connected with Sicilia is

The extension of this usage by which variations between one metre and another are added to variations between metre and prose, as devices for conveying changes of tone, is characteristic, as has been already remarked, of Shakespeare's early plays. In his later works it has left only slight traces. Every reader is familiar with the use of a rhymed couplet at the close of a scene. Akin to this is the indication by a rhymed couplet of a resolution formed, or the termination of a train of thought. A fine example of this is to be found in Macbeth's rhymed soliloquy breaking a scene of blank verse.

Ch.XVIII.

*Alter-
nations
between one
metre and
another.*

> The Prince of Cumberland! that is a step
> On which I must fall down, or else o'erleap,
> For in my way it lies. Stars, hide your fires;
> Let not light see my black and deep desires:
> The eye wink at the hand; yet let that be,
> Which the eye fears, when it is done, to see.

i. iv. 48;
compare
iii. 146.

It is, again, only natural that the more artificial measure should be used to convey what is consciously artificial language; thus, when Desdemona, to fill up a moment of waiting, calls upon Iago for an exercise in praising her, he puts his praises of women in rhyme, till he reaches the famous conclusion :

> She was a wight, if ever such wight were—
> To suckle fools, and chronicle small beer.

One of the plays treated in this book, *Love's Labour's Lost*, has claims to be considered Shakespeare's earliest original play, and it is found to be the one in which his metrical repertoire is most varied. We may erect a metrical scale, at the bottom of which is prose; next in order comes blank verse; rhymed couplets are a degree more elevated; and

played out. Then the Shepherd and Clown enter and discover the child—the resolution of the plot and the Bohemian side of the story begin. This change from complication to resolution is marked by a change from verse to prose.

CH.XVIII. at the top come measures more lyrical than the couplet,
———   such as alternate rhyming, or even trochaic and anapæstic
rhythms[1]. The alternation of these three metrical styles is
iv. iii.   well illustrated in the central scene of the play, where the
perjured celibates discover one another. Biron is the first on
the ground, and his soliloquy is in prose. The scene can
hardly be said to have commenced until the arrival of another
of the band, to be followed at intervals by the rest, each to
expose in fancied solitude the perjury which is to be over-
26.   heard. From this point the scene may be said to be in the
medium measure of rhymed couplets, broken by brief drops
e.g. 21, 48, to prose or irregular verse where the different parts of the
&c.   scene join on to one another, and rising to climaxes of the
elaborate lyrics. Thus three of the lovers read amatory
effusions in lyrics[2]; the comments on these are in couplets,
45-6, 85-6, and often a line of comment from one place of concealment
&c.   is, to the ear of the audience, capped by a rhyme from another.
Where the lovers spring in succession from their concealment
the battle still rages in couplets, until a great change is made
in the spirit of the scene by Biron, who abandons his
214.   annoyance at being discovered for justification of his perjury
on the ground that his Rosaline surpasses the mistresses of all
the rest. This change is reflected in a change to alternate
rhyming, and in this metre the climax of the scene continues.
284.   At last another break in the scene comes when the king
proposes to take things as they are and boldly justify them,
and he calls on Biron for reasons, such as may serve to cheat
the devil. Biron responds, and his immensely long speech is
in blank verse, here heard for the first time in the scene.

---

[1] Trochaics in **iv**. iii. 101–20; anapæstics **ii**. i. from 217 to end.
The Globe edition marks a good deal of the talk between Holofernes
and Sir Nathaniel as verse: but it is verse such as these pedants alone
could scan and classify. [E.g. **iv**. ii.]

[2] A piece of lyrics in alternate rhyme regularly closes with rhymed
couplets; e.g. Longaville's effusion, 60–73.

This continues to the end, except that a scene of such CH.XVIII.
metrical varieties cannot be wound up with merely the
ordinary couplet, but has for its coda a couple of couplets
followed by a quatrain of alternate rhymes.

Bir. For revels, dances, masks and merry hours
　　　Forerun fair Love, strewing her way with flowers.
King. Away, away! no time shall be omitted
　　　That will betime, and may by us be fitted.
Bir. Allons! allons! Sow'd cockle reap'd no corn;
　　　And justice always whirls in equal measure:
　　　Light wenches may prove plagues to men forsworn;
　　　If so, our copper buys no better treasure.

XIX.

INTEREST OF PLOT: STATICS.

WE now come to the third great division of Dramatic Criticism—Plot, or the purely intellectual side of action. Action itself has been treated above as the mutual connection and inter-weaving of all the details in a work of art so as to unite in an impression of unity. But we have found it impossible to discuss Character and Passion entirely apart from such action and interworking: the details of human interest become dramatic by being permeated with action-force. When however this mutual relation of all the parts is looked at by itself, as an abstract interest of design, the human life being no more than the material to which this design is applied, then we get the interest of Plot. So defined, I hope Plot is sufficiently removed from the vulgar conception of it as sensational mystery, which has done so much to lower this element of dramatic effect in the eyes of literary students. If Plot be understood as the extension of design to the sphere of human life, threads of experience being woven into a symmetrical pattern as truly as varicoloured threads of wool are woven into a piece of woolwork, then the conception of it will come out in its true dignity. What else is such reduction to order than the meeting-point of science and art? Science is engaged in tracing rhythmic movements in the beautiful confusion of the heavenly bodies, or reducing the bewildering variety of

external nature to regular species and nice gradations of life.
Similarly, art continues the work of creation in calling ideal
order out of the chaos of things as they are. And so the
tangle of life, with its jumble of conflicting aspirations, its
crossing and twisting of contrary motives, its struggle and
partnership of the whole human race, in which no two individuals are perfectly alike and no one is wholly independent of the rest—this has gradually in the course of ages
been laboriously traced by the scientific historian into some
such harmonious plan as evolution. But he finds himself
long ago anticipated by the dramatic artist, who has touched
crime and seen it link itself with nemesis, who has transformed passion into pathos, who has received the shapeless
facts of reality and returned them as an ordered economy of
design. This application of form to human life is Plot:
and Shakespeare has had no higher task to accomplish than
in his revolutionising our ideas of Plot, until the old critical
conceptions of it completely broke down when applied to
his dramas. The appreciation of Shakespeare will not be
complete until he is seen to be as subtle a weaver of plots as
he is a deep reader of the human heart.

As with Character and Passion, so Plot is to be considered
in its three aspects of unity, complexity and movement. But
the last is at once of special importance in itself, and different
in nature from the other two. It has been already noted how
the analysis which traces unity and complexity treats the
drama as a finished whole, and may piece together into one
elements of effect drawn from different parts of the play;
movement, on the contrary, is tied to the succession of
incidents as they stand in the story. The difference is
parallel to the difference between the two sides of mechanical
science: Statics treating matter in repose, and Dynamics
considering matter in relation to motion. It will be convenient in the present treatment to separate movement from
the other two divisions: the present Chapter will deal with the

CH. XIX.   interest of Plot which is Statical[1], and the Dynamics of Plot
——   will be left to the following Chapter.

Unity ap-
plied to
Plot.   The simplest element of Plot is the *Single Action*, which
may be defined as any train of incidents in a drama which
The Single can be conceived as a separate whole.   Thus a series of
Action.
details bringing out the idea of a crime and its nemesis will
constitute a Nemesis Action, an oracle and its fulfilment will
make up an Oracular Action, a problem and its solution a
Problem Action.   Throughout the treatment of Plot the root
idea of *pattern* should be steadily kept in mind: in the case
of these Single Actions—the units of Plot—we have as it were
the lines of a geometrical design, made up of their details as
Forms of   a geometrical line is made up of separate points.   The *Form*
Dramatic
Action.   of a dramatic action—the shape of the line, so to speak—will
be that which gives the train of incidents its distinctiveness:
the nemesis, the oracle, the problem.   An action may get its
distinctiveness from its tone as a Comic, a Tragic or a Humorous Action; or it may be a Character Action, when a
series of details acquire a unity in bringing out the character
of Hastings or Lady Macbeth; an action may be an Intrigue,
or the Rise and Fall of a person, or simply a Story like the
Caskets Story; it may be a Motive Action, bringing about, as
it progresses, the general changes in the fortunes of the
story; or it may be a Stationary Action that is kept entirely
outside the dramatic movement.   Finally, an action may
combine several different forms at the same time, just as a
geometrical line may be at once, say, an arch and a spiral.
The action that traces Macbeth's career has been treated as
exhibiting a triple form of Nemesis, Irony, and Oracular
Action; further, it is a Tragic Action in tone, it is a Character
Action in its contrast with the career of Lady Macbeth, and

———

[1] I borrow these terms from an able article by Mr. F. Ryland on the
Morte d'Arthur (in the *English Illustrated Magazine* for October,
1888).   Mr. Ryland uses the term 'statical' somewhat differently.

it stands in the relation of Main Action to others in the CH. XIX.
play [1].

Now what I have called Single Action constituted the *Complexity*
whole conception of Plot in ancient Tragedy; in the *applied to*
Action: a
Shakespearean Drama it exists only as a unit of Complex *distinction*
Action. The application of complexity to action is ren- *of Modern*
Drama.
dered particularly easy by the idea of pattern, patterns which
appeal to the eye being more often made up of several lines
crossing and interweaving than of single lines. Ancient
tragedy clung to 'unity of action,' and excluded such matter
as threatened to set up a second interest in a play. Modern
Plot has a unity of a much more elaborate order, perhaps
best expressed by the word *harmony*—a harmony of distinct
actions, each of which has its separate unity. The illustration of harmony is suggestive. Just as in musical harmony each part is a melody of itself, though one of them
leads and is *the* melody, so a modern plot draws together
into a common system a Main Action and other inferior yet
distinct actions. Moreover the step from melody alone to
melody harmonised, or that from the single instruments of
the ancient world to the combinations of a modern orchestra,
marks just the difference between ancient and modern art
which we find reflected in the different conception of Plot
held by Sophocles and by Shakespeare. Shakespeare's
plots are federations of plots: in his ordering of dramatic
events we trace a common self-government made out of
elements which have an independence of their own, and
at the same time merge a part of their independence in
common action.

---

[1] A Sub-Action is either an action distinctly subordinate to another
action (*Merchant of Venice*), or of inferior importance in the general
scheme of the play (*Love's Labour's Lost*); or it is so called because its
course is confined to a part and not the whole of the movement (*Julius
Cæsar*). See Tabular Analysis, pages 399-416.

CH. XIX.   The foundation of critical treatment in the matter of Plot
_____   is the *Analysis* of Complex Action into its constituent Single[1]
Analysis of
Action.   Actions.   This is easy in such a play as *The Merchant of
Venice.*   Here two of the actions are stories, a form of
unity readily grasped, and in this case the stories had an
independent existence outside the play.   These identified and
separated, it is easy also to see that Jessica constitutes a
fresh centre of interest around which other details gather
themselves; that the incidents in which Launcelot and
Gobbo are concerned are separable from these; while the
matter of the rings constitutes a distinct episode of the
Caskets Story: already the junction of so many separate
stories in a common working gratifies our sense of design.
In other plays where the elements are not stories the individuality of the Single Actions will not always be so positive: all would readily distinguish the Lear Main plot from
the Underplot of Gloucester, but in the subdivision of these
difference of opinion arises.   In an Appendix I have suggested schemes of Analysis for each of the nine plays treated
Canons of   in this work: I may here add four remarks.   (1) Any series
Analysis.   of details which can be collected from various parts of a drama
*Analysis
tentative,*   to make up a common interest may be recognised in Analysis
not posi-   as a separate action.   It follows from this that there may be
tive.   very different modes of dividing and arranging the elements
of the same plot: such Analysis is not a matter in which we
are to look for right or wrong, but simply for better or worse.
No scheme will ever exhaust the wealth of design which
reveals itself in a play of Shakespeare; and the value of Analysis
as a critical process is not confined to the scheme it produces,
but includes also the insight which the mere effort to analyse a
Design as   drama gives into the harmony and connection of its parts.
the test of   (2) The essence of Plot being design, that will be the best
Analysis.   scheme of Analysis which best brings out the idea of symmetry
Analysis   and design.   (3) Analysis must be exhaustive: every detail in
exhaustive.
                        [1] See note on page 74.

the drama must find a place in some one of the actions.
(4) The constituent actions will of course not be mutually
exclusive, many details being common to several actions :
these details are so many meeting-points, in which the lines
of action cross one another.—With these sufficiently obvious
principles I must leave the schemes of analysis in the
Appendix to justify themselves.

In the process of analysis we are led to notice special
forms of action : in particular, the *Enveloping Action.* This
interesting element of Plot may be described as the fringe,
or border, or frame, of a dramatic pattern. It appears when
the personages and incidents which make up the essential
interest of a play are more or less loosely involved with
some interest more wide-reaching than their own, though
more vaguely presented. It is seen in its simplest form
where a story occupied with private personages connects
itself at points with public history : homely life being thus
wrapped round with life of the great world ; fiction having
reality given to it by its being set in a frame of accepted
fact. We are familiar enough with it in prose fiction.
Almost all the Waverley Novels have Enveloping Actions,
Scott's regular plan being to entangle the fortunes of individuals, which are to be the main interest of the story, with
public events which make known history. Thus in *Wood-
stock* a Cavalier maiden and her Puritan lover become, as
the story proceeds, mixed up in incidents of the Commonwealth and Restoration ; or again, the plot of *Redgauntlet,*
which consists in the separate adventures of a pair of Scotch
friends, is brought to an issue in a Jacobite rising in
which both become involved. The Enveloping Action is a
favourite element in Shakespeare's plots. In the former part
of the book I have pointed out how the War of the Roses
forms an Enveloping Action to *Richard III* ; how its connection with the other actions is close enough for it to catch
the common feature of Nemesis ; and how it is marked

with special clearness by the introduction of Queen Margaret and the Duchess of York to bring out its opposite sides. In *Macbeth* there is an Enveloping Action of the super-natural centring round the Witches: the human workings of the play seem to be wrapped in a deeper working out of destiny, with prophetic beings to keep it before us. More simply, the supernatural gives to *The Tempest* an Enveloping Action of Enchantment. *Julius Cæsar*, as a story of political conspiracy and political reaction, is furnished with a loose Enveloping Action in the passions of the Roman mob: this is a vague power outside recognised political forces, appearing at the beginning to mark that uncertainty in public life which can drive even good men to conspiracy, while from the turning-point it furnishes the force the explosion of which is made to secure the conspirators' downfall.

A typical example is to be found in *Lear*, all the more typical from the fact that it is by no means a prominent interest in the play. The Enveloping Action in this drama is the French War. The seeds of this war are sown in the opening incident, in which the French King receives his wife i. i. 265. from Lear with scarcely veiled insult: it troubles Gloucester i. ii. 23. in the next scene that France is ' in choler parted.' Then we get, in the second Act, a distant hint of rupture from ii. ii. 172. the letter of Cordelia read by Kent in the stocks. In the other scenes of this Act the only political question is of ii. i. 11. ' likely wars toward ' between the English dukes; but at the beginning of the third Act Kent directly connects these quarrels of the dukes with the growing chance of a war with iii. i. 19–34. France: the French have had intelligence of the ' scattered kingdom,' and have been ' wise in our negligence.' In this iii. iii. Act Gloucester confides to Edmund the feeler he has re-ceived from France, and his trustfulness is the cause of his iii. iii. 22. downfall; Edmund treacherously reveals the confidence to iii. vi. 95–108. Cornwall, and makes it the occasion of his rise. Gloucester's measures for the safety of Lear have naturally a connection

with the expected invasion, and he sends him to Dover to Cʜ. XIX.
find welcome and protection. The final scene of this Act,
devoted to the cruel outrage on Gloucester, shows from its iii. vii. 2, &c.
very commencement the important connection of the Enveloping Action with the rest of the play : the French army
has landed, and it is this which is felt to make Lear's escape
so important, and which causes such signal revenge to be
taken on Gloucester. Throughout the fourth Act all the
threads of interest are becoming connected with the invading
army at Dover ; if this Act has a separate interest of its own
in Edmund's intrigues with both Goneril and Regan at once,
yet these intrigues are possible only because Edmund is iv. ii. 11,
hurrying backwards and forwards between the princesses in 15; iv. v. 12, 30, &c.
the measures of military preparation for the battle. The
fifth Act has its scene on the battlefield, and the double
issue of the battle stamps itself on the whole issue of the
play : the death of Lear and Cordelia is the result of the
French defeat, while, on the other hand, all who were to
reap the fruits of guilt die in the hour of victory. Thus v. iii. 238,
this French War is a model of Enveloping Action :—outside 256.
the main issues, yet loosely connecting itself with every
phase of the movement ; originating in the incident which is
the origin of the whole action ; the possibility of it developed
by the progress of the Main story, alike by the cruelty
shown to Lear and by the rivalry between his daughters ;
the fear of it playing a main part in the tragic side of the
Underplot, and the preparation for it serving as occasion for
the remaining interest of intrigue ; finally, breaking out as a
reality in which the whole action of the play merges.

In no play is this device of the Enveloping Action carried *The Frame*
so far as in *As You Like It*. The matter of this play analyses *in As You Like It.*
into two distinct systems of related actions [1]. One of these
is a system of love stories developed and carried to a happy

---

[1] See Tabular Analysis, below, page 415.

CH. XIX.   conclusion in the Forest of Arden.   But machinery has to be
———   set in motion to bring the personages of these love stories
into the forest world, where they are to meet and feel one
another's influence : the portions of the whole play devoted
to this purpose thus constitute a Frame in which the main
interest is enclosed.   But when this Frame comes to be
itself analysed, it is found to be a system of four distinct
Enveloping Actions, one inside another, like Chinese boxes.
The outermost belongs to the widest world of politics, the
Civil War of the Dukes, which has driven the good Duke into
exile and so set up the outlaw life of Arden forest.   One
degree less wide than Civil War are the dissensions of great
families, and the Feud in the De Boys family makes our
second Enveloping Action.   It appears to be loosely involved
i. ii, from   in the first, since the reigning Duke seems about to extend his
233.   protection to the oppressed Orlando, until he hears that he is
the son of his enemy, and then not only Orlando has to fly,
but the persecutor Oliver is made responsible for him and
driven from his estate.   These two Enveloping Actions are
accountable for the Woodland Life in the forest of Arden, and
the presence there of the lovers.   But this Woodland Life
itself makes another Enveloping Action, wrapping round all
the incidents of the love plot with its pastoral spirit.   And
there is yet one more effect of the same kind ; for this
Woodland Life has (before the commencement of the main
plot) attracted the morbid Jaques as a region favourable for
moralising, and his humour of melancholy makes an atmosphere in which the lovers are to move and breathe.   All
this complex system is no more than a Frame to the love
passages which make up the main plot.   But a Frame that
is so prominent will not unnaturally be allowed some share in
the movement of the play, and we get a very striking bit of
plot handling at the end.   The marriage of Celia and Oliver
v. ii. init.   terminates the Feud of the De Boys brothers, Oliver proposing
to estate upon Orlando all his father's revenues.   At the

marriage feast news comes of how the Duke, marching after
Oliver's flight against the Forest of Arden and its inmates,
had been smitten with penitence, and resigned his government
to the rightful ruler.   Accordingly the Woodland Life of the
Arden outlaws ceases with the occasion that brought it into
existence.   And, for a final touch, Jaques finds no longer any v. iv. 1 6.
attraction in his companions thus made happy, but goes to
the more congenial region of the penitent 'convertite.'   The
consummation of the love plot is thus made coincident with
the termination of the actions constituting the enclosing Frame,
which thus seems to drop to pieces, like a scaffold which has
served its purpose and been taken down.

From Analysis we pass naturally to *Economy.*   Considered *Economy: supplementary to Analysis.*
in the abstract, as a phase of plot beauty, Economy may be
defined as that perfection of design which lies midway between incompleteness and waste.   Its formula is that a play
must be seen to contain all the details necessary to the
unity, no detail superfluous to the unity, and each detail
expanded in exact proportion to its bearing on the unity.
In practice, as a branch of treatment in Shakespeare-
Criticism, Economy, like Analysis, deals with complexity of
plot.   The two are supplementary to one another.   The one
resolves a complexity into its elements, the other traces the
unity running through these elements.   Analysis distinguishes
the separate actions which make up a plot, while Economy
notes the various bonds between these actions and the way
in which they are brought into a common system: it
being clear that the more the separateness of the different
interests can be reduced the richer will be the economy of
design.

It will be enough to note three Economic Forms.   The *Economic Forms. Connection*
first is simple *Connection*:   the actual contact of action
with action, the separate lines of the pattern meeting at
various points.   In other words, the different actions have
details or personages in common.   Bassanio is clearly a

bond between the two main stories of *The Merchant of Venice*, in both of which he figures so prominently; and it has been pointed out that the scene of Bassanio's successful choice is an incident with which all the stories which enter into the *and Link-* action of the play connect themselves. There are *Link ing. Personages*, who have a special function so to connect stories, and similarly *Link Actions*: Gloucester in the play of *Lear* and the Jessica Story in *The Merchant of Venice* are examples. Or Connection may come by the interweaving of stories as they progress: they alternate, or fill, so to speak, each other's interstices. Where the Story of the Jew halts for a period of three months, the elopement of *from ii. i. to* Jessica comes to occupy the interval; or again, scenes *iii. ii. 319.* from the tragedy of the Gloucester family separate scenes from the tragedy of Lear, until the two tragedies have become mutually entangled. Envelopment too serves as a kind of Connection: the actions which make up such a play as *Richard III* gain additional compactness by their being merged in a common Enveloping Action.

Depend- Another Form of Economy is *Dependence*. This term ex-
ence. presses the relation between an underplot and main plot, or between subactions and the actions to which they are subordinate. The fact that Gloucester is a follower of *compare* Lear—he would appear to have been his court chamber-
i. i. 35, 191. lain—makes the story of the Gloucester family seem to spring out of the story of the Lear family; that we are not called upon to initiate a fresh train of interest ministers to our sense of Economy. In *The Tempest*, where the action is mainly occupied with enchantment, it has been shown that the underplot assists this fundamental idea by bringing forward phases of actual life allied to enchantment. Here also the relation of the underplot to the mainplot may be described as dependence: the term fairly covers such constructive support, just as in architecture buttresses at once lean against and support the main mass.

But in the Shakespearean Drama the most important
Economic Form is *Symmetry* : between different parts of a
design symmetry is the closest of bonds.   A simple form of
Symmetry is the *Balance* of actions, by which, as it were,
the mass of one story is made to counterpoise that of another.   If the Caskets Story, moving so simply to its goal
of success, seems over-weighted by the thrilling incidents of
the Jew Story, we find that the former has by way of compensation the Episode of the Rings rising out of its close,
while the elopement of Jessica and her reception at Belmont transfers a whole batch of interests from the Jew side
of the play to the Christian side.   Or again, in a play such
as *Macbeth*, which traces the Rise and Fall of a personage,
the Rise is accompanied by the separate interest of Banquo
till he falls a victim to its success ; to balance this we have
in the Fall Macduff, who becomes important only after
Banquo's death, and from that point occupies more and
more of the field of view until he brings the action to a close.
Similarly in *Julius Cæsar* the victim himself dominates the
first half ; Antony, his avenger, succeeds to his position for
the second half.

Symmetry :
Balance,

More important than Balance as forms of Symmetry are
Parallelism and *Contrast* of actions.   Both are, to a certain
extent, exemplified in the plot of *Macbeth* : the triple form of
Nemesis, Irony, and Oracular binding together all the elements
of the plot down to the Enveloping Action illustrates Parallelism, and Contrast has been shown to be a bond between
the interest of Lady Macbeth and of her husband.   But Parallelism and Contrast are united in their most typical forms in
Lear, which is at once the most intricate and the most symmetrical of Shakespearean dramas.   A glance at the scheme
of this plot shows its deep-seated parallelism.   A Main story
in the family of Lear has an Underplot in the family of
Gloucester.   The Main plot is a problem and its solution, the
Underplot is an intrigue and its nemesis.   Each is a system of

*Parallel-
ism and
Contrast.*

CH. XIX. four actions: there is the action initiating the problem with the three tragedies which make up its solution, there is again the action generating the intrigue and the three tragedies which constitute its nemesis. The threefold tragedy in the Main plot has its elements exactly analogous, each to each, to the threefold tragedy of the Underplot: Lear and Gloucester alike reap a double nemesis of evil from the children they have favoured, and good from the children they have wronged; the innocent Cordelia has to suffer like the innocent Edgar; alike in both stories the gains of the wicked are found to be the means of their destruction. Even in the subactions, which have only a temporary distinctness in carrying out such elaborate interworking, the same

e.g. i. iv. Parallelism manifests itself. They run in pairs: where Kent
85-104; has an individual mission as an agency for good, Oswald
ii. ii, &c. runs a course parallel with him as an agency for evil; of the

e. g. iv. ii. two heirs of Lear, Albany, after passively representing the
29; good side of the Main plot, has the function of presiding
v. iii, from over the nemesis which comes on the evil agents of the
59. Underplot, while Cornwall, who is active in the evil of the

iii. vii. Main plot, is the agent in bringing suffering on the good
iv. ii; iv. victims of the Underplot; once more from opposite sides
v; v. iii. of the Lear story Goneril and Regan work in parallel in-
238. trigues to their destruction. Every line of the pattern runs parallel to some distant line. Further, so fundamental is the symmetry that we have only to shift the point of view and the Parallelism becomes Contrast. If the family histories be arranged around Cordelia and Edmund, as centres of good and evil in their different spheres, we perceive a sharp antithesis between the two stories extending to every detail: though stated already in the chapter on *Lear*, I should like to state it again in parallel columns to do it full justice.

In the MAIN PLOT a Daughter,

- Who has received nothing but Harm from her father,
- Who has had her position unjustly torn from her and given to her undeserving elder Sisters,
- Nevertheless sacrifices herself to save the Father who *did* the injury from the Sisters who *profited by* it.

In the UNDERPLOT a Son,

- Who has received nothing but Good from his father,
- Who has, contrary to justice, been advanced to the position of an innocent elder Brother he had maligned,
- Nevertheless is seeking the destruction of the Father who *did* him the unjust kindness, when he falls by the hand of the Brother who *was wronged* by it.

The play of Lear is itself sufficient to suggest to the critic that in the analysis of Shakespeare's plots he may safely expect to find symmetry in proportion to their intricacy.

INTEREST OF PLOT: DYNAMICS.

WE now reach the Dynamics of Plot: the important department of dramatic interest which comprehends the effects dependent upon the actual progress of the story, as distinguished from those which imply the selection and comparison of its various parts. This interest of Movement falls under two heads—*Motive Form* and *Motive Force*. The first is made by a succession of incidents acting upon our sense of design. But motion implies force: and the second type of interest is in watching the underlying causes or principles which the current of incidents reveals. The first addresses itself to our sense of symmetry, the second to our sense of economy. They will be considered separately.

Motive Form.

Simple Movement: the Line of Action a straight line.

Complicated Movement: the Line of Action a curve.

Motive Form is the impression of design left by the succession of incidents in the order in which they actually stand. The succession of incidents may suggest progress to a goal, as in the Caskets Story. This is Simple [1] Movement: the Line of Action becomes a straight line. We get the next step by the variation that is made when a curved line is substituted for a straight line: in other words, when the succession of incidents reaches its goal, but only after a diversion. This in its most prominent form is what is known as *Complication and Resolution*. A train of events is obstructed and diverted from what appears its natural course, which gives the interest of Complication: after a time the obstruction is removed and the natural course is restored,

---

[1] See note on page 74.

which is the Resolution of the action : the Complication, like CHAP. XX.
a musical discord, having existed only for the sake of being
resolved. No clearer example could be desired than that of
Antonio, whose career when we are introduced to it appears
to be that of leading the money-market of Venice and extending patronage and protection all around; by the entanglement of the bond this career is checked and Antonio
turned into a prisoner and bankrupt ; then Portia cuts the
knot and Antonio becomes all he has been before. Or again,
the affianced intercourse of Portia and Bassanio begins with iii. ii. 173.
an exchange of rings ; by the cross circumstances connected
with Antonio's trial one of them parts with this token, and iv. ii.
the result is a comic interruption to the smoothness of lovers'
life, until by Portia's confession of the ruse the old footing is v. i. 266.
restored.

Complicated Movement as so stated belongs to the Action *Action-*
side of dramatic effect. It rests upon design and the inter- *Movement distin-*
working of details ; its interest lies in obstacles interposed to *guished*
be removed, doing for the sake of undoing, entanglement for *from Pas-sion-Move-*
its own sake; in its total effect it ministers to a sense of *ment.*
intellectual satisfaction, like that belonging to a musical
fugue, in which every opening suggested has been sufficiently
followed up. We get a movement which is at once different,
and yet a counterpart, when the sense of design is inseparable
from effects of passion, and the movement is, as it were, traced
in our emotional nature. In this case a growing strain is put
upon our sympathy which is not unlike Complication. But
no Resolution follows : the rise is made to end in fall, the
progress leads to ruin ; in place of the satisfaction that
comes from restoring and unloosing is substituted a fresh
appeal to our emotional nature, and from agitation we pass
only to the calmer emotions of pity and awe. There is
thus a *Passion-Movement* distinct from *Action-Movement* ;
and, analogous to the Complication and Resolution of the
latter, Passion-Movement has its *Strain and Reaction.* The

Line of Passion has its various forms.   A chapter has been

devoted to illustrating one form of Passion-Movement, which
may be called the *Regular Arch*—if we may found a technical term on the happy illustration of Gervinus.   The
example was taken from the play of *Julius Cæsar*, the
emotional effect in which was shown to pass from calm
interest to greater and greater degree of agitation, until after
culminating in the centre it softens down and yields to the
different calmness of pity and acquiescence.   The movement

of *Richard III, Othello*, and many other dramas more resembles the form of an *Inclined Plane*, the turn in the emo-

tion occurring long past the centre of the play.   Or again,

there is the *Wave Line* of emotional distribution, made by
repeated alternations of strain and relief.   This is a form
of Passion-Movement that nearly approaches Action-Movement, and readily goes with it in the same play ; in *The
Merchant of Venice* the union of the two stories gives such
alternate Strain and Relief, and the Episode of the Rings
comes as final Relief to the final Strain of the trial.

*For
‘ Comedy,’,
‘ Tragedy,’
substitute,
in the case
of Shake-
speare,*   The distinction between Action-Movement and Passion-
Movement is of special importance in Shakespeare-Criticism,
inasmuch as it is the real basis of distinction between the
two main classes of Shakespearean dramas.   Every one
feels that the terms Comedy and Tragedy are inadequate,
and indeed absurd, when applied to Shakespeare.   The distinction these terms express is one of Tone, and they were
quite in place in the Ancient Drama, in which the comic
and tragic tones were kept rigidly distinct and were not
allowed to mingle in the same play.   Applied to a branch of
Drama of which the leading characteristic is the complete
Mixture of Tones the terms necessarily break down, and the
so-called ‘ Comedies ’ of *The Merchant of Venice* and *Measure
for Measure* contain some of the most tragic effects in
Shakespeare.   The true distinction between the two kinds
of plays is one of Movement, not Tone.   In *The Merchant*

of Venice the leading interest is in the complication of An- CHAP. XX.
tonio's fortunes and its resolution by the device of Portia.
In all such cases, however perplexing the entanglement of
the complication may have become, the ultimate effect of
the whole lies in the resolution of this complication ; and
this is an intellectual effect of satisfaction. In the plays
called Tragedies there is no such return from distraction to
recovery : our sympathy having been worked up to the emotion of agitation is relieved only by the emotion of pathos or
despair. Thus in these two kinds of dramas the impression
which to the spectator overpowers all other impressions, and
gives individuality to the particular play, is this sense of intellectual or of emotional unity in the movement : is, in other
words, Action-Movement or Passion-Movement. The two *'Action-*
may be united, as remarked above in the case of *The Mer-* *Drama,'*
chant of Venice ; but one or the other will be predominant *'Passion-*
and will give to the play its unity of impression. The *Drama.'*
distinction, then, which the terms Comedy and Tragedy
fail to mark would be accurately brought out by sub-
stituting for them the terms Action-Drama and Passion-
Drama.

With complexity of action comes complexity of movement. *Compound*
Compound Movement takes in the idea of the relative motion *Movement.*
amongst the different actions into which a plot can be
analysed. A play of Shakespeare may present a system of
wheels within wheels, like a solar system in motion as a whole
while the separate members of it have their own orbits to
follow. The nature of Compound Movement can be most *Its three*
simply brought out by describing its three leading Modes of *Modes of*
Motion. In *Similar Motion* the actions of a system are *Similar*
moving in the same form. The plot of *Richard III*, for *Motion,*
example, is a general rise and fall of Nemesis made up of
elements which are themselves rising and falling Nemeses.
Such Similar Motion is only Parallelism looked at from the
side of movement. A variation of it occurs when the form

CHAP. XX. of one action is distributed amongst the rest: the main action of *Julius Cæsar* is a Nemesis Action, the two sub-actions are the separate interests of Cæsar and Antony, which put together amount to Nemesis.

Contrary Motion: Counter-Action,

Of *Contrary Motion* the simplest form is Counter-Action: where (as in *The Tempest*) an intrigue which serves as the original Complicating Action of the play has pitted against it a Resolving Action which undoes it. The difference between Contrary and Similar Motion is well illustrated in this play[1]. Its scheme involves three systems of Actions: a Main Plot, an Underplot, and a crowd of Mechanical Personages, who faintly reflect the general movement of the play. These three systems move in Similar Motion, all being included in a common complication and resolution. But the separate Actions of which each system is made up move in directions contrary from one another. The Complicating Action of the Main Plot has for Sub-Action an intrigue which is met by a like Sub-Action attached to the Resolving Action: these two Sub-Actions counteract one another. The Resolving Action of the Main Plot has two Sub-Actions, outside the scenic unity, and serving as preparation for the main movement. One of them is Prospero's judgment on Caliban, which prepares for that amount of further complication which is usually the task of a Resolving Action before it proceeds to resolve; the other, the work of mercy done to Ariel, prepares for the resolving side of Prospero's task: thus this pair of Sub-Actions also move in opposition to one another as Judgment and Mercy. Again, of the two Link Actions which constitute the Underplot one, the story of Ferdinand and Miranda, moves in the direction of their ultimate union; the other, the conspiracy of Caliban and the sailors, tends towards their ultimate separation, Caliban awaking in the universal restoration to the deception under which he has laboured:

[1] See Tabular Analysis, pages 411-2.

> What a thrice-double ass
> Was I, to take this drunkard for a god
> And worship this dull fool!

Even amongst the Mechanical Personages the group of Sailors and the group of Courtiers, so far as they have any share in the action of the play, seem to move in an opposition reflected in the humorous antagonism of their leaders, the Boatswain and Gonzalo, who are sparring with one another at the point of death, and resume their sparring as soon as they meet in the final enchantment. The whole play is a beautiful study for complexity of dramatic movement, exhibiting three systems of Actions moving together in Similar Motion, while the individual Actions of which each system is made up move forward in mutual antagonism. i. i. and v. i. 217.

Another variety of Contrary Motion is Interference, when the separate actions as they move on interfere with one another; as the Touchstone Action, or the Jaques Action, in *As You Like It*, with their professional or morbid humour, is continually clashing with the Main Action of Rosalind and Orlando, which is animated throughout by genuine humour. A more pronounced form of Interference between actions is where each acts as complicating force to the other, turning it out of its course; in reality they are helping one another's advance, seeing that complication is a step in dramatic progress. *The Merchant of Venice* furnishes an example. The Caskets Story progresses without check to its climax; in starting it complicates the Jew action—for before Bassanio can get to Belmont he borrows of Antonio the loan which is to entangle him in the meshes of the Jew's revenge; then the Caskets Story as a result of its climax resolves this complication in the Story of the Jew—for the union of Portia with Bassanio provides the deliverer for Bassanio's friend. But in thus resolving the Story of the Jew the Caskets Story, in the new phase of it that has commenced *Interference.*

with the exchange of betrothal rings, itself suffers complication—the circumstances of the trial offering the suggestion to Portia to make the demand for Bassanio's ring. Thus of the two actions moving on side by side the one interferes with and diverts the other from its course, and again in restoring it gets itself diverted. This mutual interference makes up Contrary Motion.

Convergent Motion. A third mode of Compound Movement is *Convergent Motion*, by which actions, or systems of actions, at first separate, become drawn together as they move on, and assist one another's progress. This has been described at length in the chapter on *Othello*. The play of *Lear* again furnishes a typical example. This play, it will be recollected, includes two distinct systems of actions tracing the story of two separate families. Moreover the main story after its opening incident presents, so far as movement is concerned, three different sides, according as its incidents centre around Lear, Goneril, or Regan. The first link between these diverse actions is Gloucester, the central personage of the whole

i. i. 35, 191. plot. Gloucester has been the King's chamberlain and his
ii. i. 93. close friend, the King having been godfather to his son. Accordingly, in the highly unstable political condition of a kingdom divided equally between two unprincipled sisters, Gloucester represents a third party, the party of Lear : he holds the balance of power, and the effort to secure him draws the separate interests together. Thus as soon as
i. v. i. Lear and Goneril have quarrelled Lear sends Kent to Gloucester, and our actions begin to approach one another.
ii. i. 9. Before this messenger can arrive we hear of 'hints and ear-kissing arguments' as to rupture between the dukes, and we see Regan and her husband making a hasty journey—
ii. i. 121. 'out of season threading dark-eyed night'—in order to be
ii. iv. 192. the first at Gloucester's castle ; when Goneril in self-defence follows all the separate elements of the main plot have found a meeting-point. But this castle of Gloucester in

which they meet is the seat of the underplot, and the two CHAP. XX.
systems become united in the closest manner by this central
linking. Regan arrives in time to use her authority in fur- ii. i. 88–
thering the intrigue against Edgar as a means of recom- 131, esp.
112.
mending herself to the deceived Gloucester; the other intrigue of the underplot, that against Gloucester himself, is iii. v, &c.
promoted by the same means when Edmund has betrayed to
Regan his father's protection of Lear; while the meeting of
both sisters with Edmund lays the foundation of the mutual
intriguing which forms the further interest of the entanglement between underplot and main story. All the separate
lines of action have thus moved to a common centre, and
their concentration in a common focus gives opportunity
for the climax of passion which forms the centre-piece
of the play. Then the Enveloping Action comes in as a
further binding force, and it has been pointed out above
how throughout the fourth and fifth Acts all the separate
actions, whatever their immediate purpose, have an ultimate
reference to Dover as the landing-place of the invading army:
in military phrase Dover is the common *objective* on which
all the separate trains of interest are concentrating. In this
way have the actions of this intricate plot, so numerous
and so separate at first, been found to converge to a
common centre and then move together to a common *dénouement.*

The distinction of movement from the other elements of *Turning-
points.*
Plot leads also to the question of *Turning-points*, an idea
equally connected with movement and with design. In the
movement of every play a Turning-point is implied: movement could not have dramatic interest unless there were a
change in the direction of events, and such change implies a
point at which the change becomes apparent. Changes of
a kind may be frequent through the progress of a play, but
one notable point will stand out at which the ultimate issues
present themselves as decided, the line of action changing

CHAP. XX.

The Cata-strophe: or Focus of Movement.

The Centre of Plot.

iv. i. 305.

iii. ii.

iv. ii. 45.

iii. iii. 15.

iii. iv. 20.

iii. iv. 49;
v. viii. 13.

from complication to resolution, the line of passion from strain to reaction. Such a point is technically a *Catastrophe*: a word whose etymological meaning suggests a turning round so as to come down. In Shakespeare's dramatic practice we find a not less important Turning-point in relation to the design of the plot. That is at the exact centre [1]—the middle of the middle Act—and serves as a balancing point about which the plot may be seen to be symmetrical: it is a *Centre of Plot* as the Catastrophe is a *Focus of Movement*. The Catastrophe of *The Merchant of Venice* is clearly Portia's judgment in the Trial Scene, by which in a moment the whole entanglement is resolved. In an earlier chapter it has been pointed out how the union of Portia and Bassanio—at the exact centre of the play—is the real determinant of the whole plot, uniting the complicating and resolving forces, and constituting a scene in which all the four stories find a meeting-point. In *Richard III*, while the Catastrophe comes in the hero's late recognition of his own nemesis, yet there has been, before this and in the exact centre, a turn in the Enveloping Action, which includes all the rest, shown by the recognition that Margaret's curses have now begun to be fulfilled. The exact centre of *Macbeth*, as pointed out above, marks the hero's passage from rise to fall, that is from unbroken success to unbroken failure: the corresponding Catastrophe in this play is double,

---

[1] The play of *Love's Labour's Lost* is only an apparent exception. For some reason I do not understand the numbering of the scenes is exceptional in this play: the second and third acts are very short, and the fifth act includes nearly half the play (ten twenty-fifths). Measured by lines the centre of the play falls within **iv**. iii : and this is obviously the Centre of Plot. In some plays the centring of the plot seems to be distributed evenly through the scenes of the middle Act. In *The Tempest*, for example, the different Actions reach their full complexity in the successive scenes of the third Act; in scene i, the Ferdinand and Miranda Action; in scene ii, the Caliban and Stephano Action; in scene iii, the Main Plot (including the Motive Sub-Actions: compare lines 10–17).

a first appearance of Nemesis in Banquo's ghost, its final CHAP. XX.
stroke in the revelation of Macduff's secret of birth. *Julius* ————
Cæsar presents the interesting feature of the Catastrophe
and Central Turning-point exactly coinciding, in the trium- iii. i. 122.
phant appeal of the conspirators to future history. A Centre
of Plot and a Catastrophe have already been pointed out in
Othello [1]. In *As You Like It* Orlando meets the disguised
Rosalind for the first time in the central scene; the dropping
of the disguise in the fifth act makes a Catastrophe. *Lear*,
according to the scheme of analysis suggested in this work,
has its Catastrophe at the close of the initial scene, by
which time the problem in experience has been set up in
action, and the tragedies arising out of it thenceforward
work on without break to its solution. A Centre of Plot is
found for this play where, in the middle Scene of the middle iii. iv. 45.
Act, the third of the three forms of madness is brought into
contact with the other two and makes the climax of passion
complete. This regular union by Shakespeare of a marked
catastrophe, appealing to every spectator, with a subtle
dividing-point, interesting to the intellectual sense of analysis,
illustrates the combination of force with symmetry, which is
the genius of the Shakespearean Drama : it throughout presents a body of warm human interest governed by a mind of
intricate design.

It may be added that in plots where the Enveloping Action *Further*
is prominent Shakespeare usually gives a Further Resolution, *Resolution.*
after the action of the play itself has been regularly wound
up; and a Further Resolution implies a third Turning-Point.
The most marked case is *Love's Labour's Lost*, where, after the v. ii. 723.
Complication set up by the French Princess's visit has
worked itself out to complete Resolution, a shock is given
by the news of the king of France's death, and a Further
Resolution of the action takes place which converts comic

[1] See above, page 240. Compare in all cases the Tabular Analysis
on pages 399–416.

into serious. So (as pointed out above) when the plot of *As You Like It* has been wound up in a quadruple marriage, the entrance of Jaques de Boys with his news makes a fresh Turning-point, which has the effect of dissipating the Frame Actions that have held the play together. And in *The Tempest*, where the Enveloping Action is Enchantment, Prospero after bringing the plot to a complete consummation makes a Further Resolution by laying his Enchantment down.

*Motive
Force.*

From Motive Form we pass to Motive Force. In fiction, just as much as in real life, the course of events is perpetually suggesting to us underlying causes or controlling forces,— whether these be Law, or some higher Will, or Chance; or, at the very least, the particular succession of incidents finds explanation in their combining to advance some common purpose. What are the purposes, or underlying principles, or technically, Motives, which thus carry forward the movement of the Shakespearean drama?

*Providence
as a
Dramatic
Motive.*

To begin with, Providence is itself a Motive Force in fiction, the analyst finding the same interest in tracing meaning and design in the action of a story that the thinker finds in discovering a Moral Providence in the issues of real life. It has been argued in a previous chapter that, to understand the term Dramatic Providence aright, it is necessary to recognise how all principles which the thinker sees in the actual universe, alike those which assist and those which disturb our notions of moral order, have a right to a place in the dramatic picture of the world. One of the plays reviewed stands alone in relation to this topic: *The Tempest* is a study of Personal Providence. By a device not uncommon in prose fiction [1] we are in this play enabled to see an individual

---

[1] The most familiar example is *The Count of Monte-Cristo*, by Alexander Dumas. The plot of this novel brings its hero, by a con-

will elevated into a controlling destiny. Enchantment is,
within its circle and during the influence of its auspicious star,
equivalent to omnipotence ; by such omnipotence of enchantment Prospero knows all that happens in his island, and
irresistibly controls the issues of all events : the dramatist, by
keeping us in continuous sympathy with Prospero, is working
out for our benefit a conception of Personal Providence.
But this is necessarily an exceptional case ; in the great mass
of plays the matter is confined to the experience of ordinary
life, nor will the action be allowed to display the ruling mind
of the universe to any greater degree than it presents itself
in the actual thinking of mankind. In general, then, the
Motive Forces handled by the dramatist will be such as he
can artistically associate with the course of events in real
life.

One of the great determinants of fate in the Drama is *Poetic Jus-*
Poetic Justice. What exactly is the meaning of this term ? It *tice a form*
of art-
is often understood to mean the correction of justice, as if *beauty.*
justice in poetry were more just than the justice of real life.
But this is not supported by the facts of dramatic story. An
English judge and jury would revolt against measuring out to

currence of extraordinary circumstances, consisting partly in personal
discipline, and partly in vast accessions of wealth and social power,
into the position of an Earthly Providence to the world of the French
capital, enabling him to execute irresistible designs on his friends and
foes. A more direct treatment still is Eugene Sue's *Mysteries of Paris.*
Here we have a hero actuated, not by sense of wrong, as in *Monte-Cristo,*
but by pure benevolence, raising himself into a providential director of
circumstances ; and he incites others to do the same. But the most
interesting variation of the theme is *The Wandering Jew* of the same
author. In this work a family, distinguished by a vast inheritance that
is to descend to the surviving members after generations of accumulation,
are displayed as placed between *two* opposing Earthly Providences :
the Jesuits (who, as a society, never die) are treated by the author as a
malignant Providence, seeking through a series of criminal intrigues to
secure the treasure for themselves ; while the ' Wandering Jew ' and his
sister (cursed, according to the legend, with immortality on earth, but
repentant) counteract these machinations.

Shylock the justice that is meted to him by the court of Venice, though the same persons beholding the scene in a theatre might feel their sense of Poetic Justice satisfied; unless indeed, which might easily happen, the confusion of ideas suggested by this term operated to check their acquiescence in the issue of the play. A better notion of Poetic Justice is to understand it as the modification of justice by considerations of art. This holds good even where justice and retribution do determine the fate of individuals in the Drama; in these cases our dramatic satisfaction still rests, not on the high degree of justice exhibited, but on the artistic mode in which it works. A policeman catching a thief with his hand in a neighbour's pocket and bringing him to summary punishment affords an example of complete justice, yet its very success robs it of all poetic qualities; the same thief defeating all the natural machinery of the law, yet overtaken after all by a questionable ruse, would be to the poetic sense far more interesting.

Nemesis as a dramatic motive. Treating Poetic Justice, then, as the application of art to morals, its most important phase will be *Nemesis*, which we have already seen involves an artistic link between sin and retribution. The artistic connection may be of the most *Varieties of Nemesis.* varied description. There is a Nemesis of perfect equality, Shylock reaping measure for measure as he has sown. When Nemesis overtook the Roman conspirators it was partly its *compare* suddenness that made it impressive: within fifty lines of their *iii. i. 118 and 165.* appeal to all time they have fallen into an attitude of deprecation. For Richard, on the contrary, retribution was delayed to the last moment: to have escaped to the eleventh hour is shown to be no security.

> Jove strikes the Titans down
> Not when they first begin their mountain piling,
> But when another rock would crown their work.

Nemesis may be emphasised by repetition and multiplication; in the world in which Richard is plunged there appears to be

no event which is not a nemesis. Or the point may be the CHAP. XX.
unlooked-for source from which the nemesis comes; as when
upon the murder of Cæsar a colossus of energy and resource
starts up in the time-serving and frivolous Antony, whom the
conspirators had spared for his insignificance. Or again, ii. i 165.
retribution may be made bitter to the sinner by his tracing
in it his own act and deed : from Lear himself, and from no
other source, Goneril and Regan have received the power
they use to crush his spirit. Nay, the very prize for which
the sinner has sinned turns out in some cases the nemesis
fate has provided for him ; as when Goneril and Regan use
their ill-gotten power for the state intrigues which work their iii. iii. 53-
death. In the great crisis of *The Tempest* the whole universe 82.
seems to resolve itself into nemesis upon a single crime.
And most keenly pointed of all comes the nemesis that is
combined with mockery: Macbeth, if he had not essayed
the murder of Banquo as an *extra* precaution, might have iii. i. 49.
enjoyed his stolen crown in safety ; his expedition against
Macduff's castle slays all *except* the fate-appointed avenger ; iv. iii. 219.
Richard disposes of his enemies with flawless success until
the last, Dorset, escapes to his rival. iv. ii. 46.

Such is Nemesis, and such are some of the modes in
which the connection between sin and retribution may be
made artistically impressive. Poetic Justice, however, is a *Poetic*
wider term than Nemesis. The latter implies some offence, *Justice*
other than
as an occasion for the operation of judicial machinery. But, *Nemesis.*
apart from sin, fate may be out of accord with character, and
the correction of this ill distribution will satisfy the dramatic
sense. But here again the practice of dramatic providence
appears regulated, not with a view to abstract justice, but to
justice modified by dramatic sympathy : Poetic Justice extends to the exhibition of fate moving in the interests of those
with whom we sympathise and to the confusion of those
with whom we are in antagonism. This gives point, we
have seen, to the episode of Ferdinand and Miranda in *The*

Chap. XX.   *Tempest.*   Again, viewed as a piece of equity the sentence on
iv. i. 346– Shylock—a plaintiff who has lost his suit by an accident of
363.   statute-law—seems highly questionable.   On the other hand,
this sentence brings a fortune to a girl who has won our
sympathies in spite of her faults ; it makes provision for those
for whom there is a dramatic necessity of providing ; above
all it is in accord with our secret liking that good fortune
should go with the bright and happy, and sever itself from
the mean and sordid.   Whether this last is justice, I will not
discuss : it is enough that it is one of the instincts of the
imagination, and in creative literature justice must pay tribute
to art.

Pathos as a   But however widely the term be stretched, justice is only
dramatic   one of the determinants of fate in the Drama, and perhaps
motive.   this principle is never more clearly seen than in *Love's
Labour's Lost*, where, as has been pointed out [1], the fortune of
the various personages is determined for better or worse
simply according to the sense of humour which each possesses.
Confusion on this point has led to many errors of criticism.
The case of Cordelia is in point.   Because she is involved in
the ruin of Lear it is felt by some commentators that a
consideration of justice must be sought to explain her death :
they find it perhaps in her original resistance to her father ;
or the ingenious suggestion has been made that Cordelia, in
her measures to save her father, invades England, and this
breach of patriotism needs atonement.   But this is surely
twisting the story to an explanation, not extracting an
explanation from the details of the story.   It would be a
violation of all dramatic proportion, needing the strongest
evidence from the details of the play, if Cordelia's ' most small
iv. iv. 27. fault' betrayed her to dramatic execution.   And as to the sin
ii. ii. 170– against patriotism, the whole notion of it is foreign to the play
177*; iii. itself, in which the truest patriots, such as Kent and Gloucester,
i, v.

---

[1] See above, page 291.

* The text in this passage is regarded as difficult by many editors, and

are secretly confederate with Cordelia and look upon her as CHAP. XX.
the hope of their unhappy country; while even Albany himself, however necessary he finds it to repel the invader, yet iv. ii. 2–
distinctly feels that justice is on the other side. The fact is 10 (com-
that in Cordelia's case, as in countless other cases, motives pare 55, 95); v. i.
determine fate which have in them no relation to justice; 21–27.
fiction being in this matter in harmony with real life, where
in only a minority of instances can we recognise any element
of justice or injustice as entering into the fates of individuals.
When in real life a little child dies, what consideration of justice is there that bears on such an experience? Nevertheless
there is an irresistible sense of beauty in the idea of the fleeting
child-life arrested while yet in its completeness, before the
rude hand of time has begun to trace lines of passion or
hardness; the parent indeed may not feel this in the case of
his own child, but in art, where there is no mist of individual

is marked in the Globe Edition as corrupt. I do not see the difficulty
of taking it as it stands, if regard be had to the general situation, in
which (as Steevens has pointed out) Kent is reading the letter in disjointed snatches by the dim moonlight. Commentators seem to me to
have increased the obscurity by taking 'enormous' in its rare sense of
'irregular,' 'out of order,' and making it refer to the state of England.
Surely it is used in its ordinary meaning, and applies to France; the
clause in which it occurs being part of the *actual words* of Cordelia's
letter, who naturally uses 'this' of the country from which she writes.
Inverted commas would make the connection clear.

> Approach, thou beacon to this under globe,
> That by thy comfortable beams I may
> Peruse this letter!—'Nothing almost sees miracles'—
> 'But misery'—I know 'tis from Cordelia,
> Who hath 'most fortunately been inform'd'
> Of my 'obscured course, and shall find time
> From this enormous state'—'seeking to give
> Losses their remedies,' &c.

I. e. Cordelia promises she will find leisure from the oppressive cares of
her new kingdom to remedy the evils of England. Kent gives up the
attempt to read; but enough has been brought out for the dramatist's
purpose at that particular stage, viz. to hint that Kent was in corre-
spondence with Cordelia, and looked to her as the deliverer of England.

feeling to blind, the sense of beauty comes out stronger than the sense of loss. It is the mission of the Drama thus to interpret the beauty of fate : it seeks, as Aristotle puts it, to purify our emotions by healthy exercise. The Drama does with human experience what Painting does with external nature. There are landscapes whose beauty is obvious to all; but it is one of the privileges of the artist to reveal the charm that lies in the most ordinary scenery, until the ideal can be recognised everywhere, and nature itself becomes art. Similarly there are striking points in life, such as the vindication of justice, which all can catch : but it is for the dramatist, as the artist in life, to arrange the experience he depicts so as to bring out the hidden beauties of fate, until the trained eye sees a meaning in all that happens;—until indeed the word ' suffering' itself has only to be translated into its Greek equivalent, and *pathos* is recognised as a form of beauty. Accumulation of Pathos then must be added to Poetic Justice as a determinant of fate in the Drama. And our sensitiveness to this form of beauty is nowhere more signally satisfied than when we see Cordelia dead in the arms of Lear : fate having mysteriously seconded her self-devotion, and nothing, not even her life, being left out to make her sacrifice complete.

As the Accumulation of Pathos is a determining purpose in one class of dramas, so for plays of the opposite type a leading motive is the Accumulation of Humour. *Love's Labour's Lost* is a clear example, the plot of which has been seen to be a contrivance for bringing together two opposites, the conflict of which will continually explode in humour. In Comedy generally Fun plays the part of Fate.

The Super-natural as a dramatic motive.   There remains a third great determinant of fate in the Drama—the Supernatural. Here, as in the discussion of Dramatic Providence, *The Tempest* must be placed in a category by itself: where the whole story is elevated out of the natural into the region of enchantment the Supernatural may

be said to vanish [1]. The supernatural element that can be
treated as a dramatic motive must be one that interferes in a
world of reality. I have in a former chapter pointed out
how in relation to this topic the modern Drama stands in
a different position from that of ancient Tragedy. In the
Drama of antiquity the leading motive forces were supernatural, either the secret force of Destiny, or the interposition
of supernatural beings who directly interfered with human
events. We are separated from this view of life by a *The Super-*
revolution of thought which has substituted Providence for *natural*
rational-
Destiny as the controller of the universe, and absorbed the *ised in*
supernatural within the domain of Law. Yet elements that *modern*
Drama :
had once entered so deeply into the Drama would not be
easily lost to the machinery of Passion-Movement; supernatural agency has a degree of recognition in modern thought,
and even Destiny may still be utilised if it can be stripped of
antagonism to the idea of a benevolent Providence. To begin
with the latter: the problem for a modern dramatist is to
reconcile Destiny with Law. The characteristics which made
the ancient conception of fate dramatically impressive—its irresistibility, its unintelligibility, and its suggestion of personal
hostility—he may still insinuate into the working of events :
only the destiny must be rationalised, that is, the course of
events must at the same time be explicable by natural causes.

First : Shakespeare gives us Destiny acting objectively, as *As an ob-*
an external force, in the form of *Irony*, already discussed in *jective force*
in Irony ;
connection with the standard illustration of it in *Macbeth*.
In the movement of this play Destiny appears in the most
pronounced form of mockery : every difficulty and check
being in the issue converted into an instrument for furthering

[1] Even in this case the principle that distinguishes the action of enchantment in *The Tempest* agrees with that laid down in the text for
Shakespeare's general treatment:—the supernatural intensifies, rather
than determines, human action, leading Antonio and Sebastian along
a path chosen by themselves, and bringing repentance only to those to
whom before repentance was possible. [Above, pages 273, 278.]

CHAP. XX. the course of events.   Yet this mockery is wholly without any suggestion of malignity in the governing power of the universe ; its effect being rather to measure the irresistibility of righteous retribution.   This Irony makes just the difference between the ordinary operations of Law or Providence and the suggestion of Destiny : yet each step in the action is sufficiently explained by rational considerations.   What more

i. iv. 37.   natural than that Duncan should proclaim his son heir-apparent to check any hopes which too successful service might excite ?   Yet what more natural than that this loss of

i. iv. 48.   Macbeth's remote chance of the crown should be the occasion of his resolve no longer to be content with chances ?

ii. iii. 141.   What more natural than that the sons of the murdered king should take flight upon the revelation of a treason useless to its perpetrator as long as they were living ?   Yet what again more natural than that the momentary reaction consequent

ii. iv. 21–
41.   upon this flight should, in the general fog of suspicion and terror, give opportunity to the object of universal dread himself to take the reins of government ?   The Irony is throughout no more than a garb worn by rational history [1].

As a sub-
jective
force in In-
fatuation.   Or, again, Destiny may be exhibited as a subjective force in *Infatuation* or *Judicial Blindness* : ' whom the gods would destroy they first blind.'   This was a conception specially impressive to ancient ethics ; the lesson it gathered from almost every great fall was that of a spiritual darkening which hid from the sinner his own danger, obvious to every other eye, till he had been tempted beyond the possibility of retreat.

> Falling in frenzied guilt, he knows it not ;
>   So thick the blinding cloud
> That o'er him floats ; and Rumour widely spread
> With many a sigh repeats the dreary doom,
>   A mist that o'er the house
>   In gathering darkness broods.

---

[1] In comic stories the Irony of Circumstances is a counterpart to the tragic Irony of Fate.   Rosalind's disguise converts the principal scenes of *As You Like It* into a prolonged Irony.

Such Infatuation is very far from being inconsistent with the idea of Law; indeed, it appears repeatedly in the strong figures of Scriptural speech, by which the ripening of sin to its own destruction—a merciful law of a righteously-ordered universe—is suggested as the direct act of Him who is the founder of the universe and its laws. By such figures God is represented as hardening Pharaoh's heart; or, again, an almost technical description of Infatuation is put by the fervour of prophecy into the mouth of God:—

> Make the heart of this people fat, and make their ears heavy, and shut their eyes; lest they see with their eyes, and hear with their ears, and understand with their heart, and convert, and be healed.

In the case of Macbeth the judicial blindness is maintained to the last moment, and he pauses in the final combat **v. viii. 13.** to taunt Macduff with certain destruction. Yet, while we thus get the full dramatic effect of Infatuation, it is so far rationalised that we are allowed to see the machinery by which the Infatuation has been brought about: we have heard the Witches arrange to deceive Macbeth with false oracles. **iii. v. 16.** A very dramatic, but wholly natural, example of Infatuation appears at the turning-point of Richard's career, where, when he has just discovered that Richmond is the point from which the storm of Nemesis threatens to break upon him, prophecies throng upon his memory which might have **iv. ii. 98,** all his life warned him of this issue, had he not been blind **&c.** to them till this moment. Again, Antonio's challenge to **i. iii. 131.** Shylock to do his worst is, as I have already pointed out, an outburst of *hybris*, the insolence of Infatuation: but this is no more than a natural outcome of a conflict between two implacable temperaments. In Infatuation, then, as in all its other forms, Destiny is exhibited by Shakespeare as harmonised with natural law.

Besides Destiny the Shakespearean Drama admits direct *Super-* supernatural agencies—witches, ghosts, apparitions, as well *natural* as portents and violations of natural law. It appears to *agencies :*

me idle to contend that these in Shakespeare are not really supernatural, but must be interpreted as delusions of their victims. There may be single cases, such as the appearance of Banquo to Macbeth, where, as no eye sees it but his own, the apparition may be resolved into an hallucination. But to determine Shakespeare's general practice it is enough to point to the Ghost in *Hamlet,* which, as seen by three persons at once and on separate occasions, is indisputably objective : and a single instance is sufficient to establish the assumption in the Shakespearean Drama of supernatural beings with a real existence. Zeal for Shakespeare's rationality is a main source of the opposite view; but for the assumption of such supernatural existences the responsibility lies not with Shakespeare, but with the opinion of the age he is pourtraying. A more important question is how far Shakespeare uses such supernatural agency as a motive force in his plays ; how far does he allow it to enter into the working of events, for the interpretation of which he is responsible? On this point Shakespeare's usage is clear and subtle : he uses the agency of the supernatural to intensify and to illuminate human action, not to determine it.

Intensify-
ing human
action ;
Supernatural agency intensifying human action is illustrated in *Macbeth.* No one can seriously doubt the objective existence of the Witches in this play, or that they are endowed with superhuman sources of knowledge. But the question is, do they in reality turn Macbeth to crime? In one of the chapters devoted to this play I have dwelt on the importance of the point that Macbeth has been already meditating treason in his heart when he meets the Witches on the heath. His secret thoughts—which he betrays in his
i. iii. 51. guilty start—have been an invitation to the powers of evil, and they have obeyed the summons: Macbeth has already ventured a descent, and they add an impulse downward. To bring this out the more clearly, Shakespeare keeps Banquo side by side with Macbeth through the critical stages of the

temptation : Banquo has made no overtures to temptation,
and to him the tempters have no mission. It is noticeable
that where the two warriors meet the Witches on the heath
it is Banquo who begins the conversation.

> *Banquo.* How far is 't called to Forres?

No answer. The silence attracts his attention to those he is
addressing.

> What are these
> So wither'd and so wild in their attire,
> That look not like the inhabitants o' the earth,
> And yet are on 't ?

Still no answer.

> Live you? or are you aught
> That man may question ?

They signify in dumb show that they may not answer.

> You seem to understand me,
> By each at once her chappy finger laying
> Upon her skinny lips : you should be women,
> And yet your beards forbid me to interpret
> That you are so.

Still he can draw no answer. At last Macbeth chimes in :—

> Speak, if you can : what are you?

The tamperer with temptation has spoken, and in a moment
they break out, 'All hail, Macbeth !' and ply their supernatural task. Later on in the scene, when directly challenged
by Banquo, they do respond and give out an oracle for him.
But into his upright mind the poison-germs of insight into
the future fall harmlessly; it is because Macbeth is already
tainted that these breed in him a fever of crime. In the
second incident of the Witches, so far from their being the
tempters, it is Macbeth who seeks them and forces from
them knowledge of the future. Yet, even here, what is
the actual effect of their revelation upon Macbeth? It is,
like that of his air-drawn dagger, only to marshal him
along the way that he is going. They bid him beware Mac-

CHAP. XX. duff : he answers, 'Thou hast harp'd my fear aright.'
They give him preternatural pledges of safety : are these a
help to him in enjoying the rewards of sin ? On the contrary, as a matter of fact we find Macbeth, in panic of sus-
iv. ii. 4, picion, seeking security by means of daily butchery ; the
&c. oracles have produced in him confidence enough to give
agony to the bitterness of his betrayal, but not such confidence as to lead him to dispense with a single one of the
natural bulwarks to tyranny. The function of the Witches
throughout the action of this play is exactly expressed by a
phrase Banquo uses in connection with them : they are only
i. iii. 124. 'instruments of darkness,' assisting to carry forward courses
of conduct initiated independently of them. Macbeth has
made the destiny which the Witches reveal.

Illuminat-   Again, supernatural agency is used to illuminate human
ing human action : the course of events in a drama not ceasing to obey
action.   natural causes, but becoming, by the addition of the super-
The Ora- natural agency, endowed with a new art-beauty. The great
cular Ac- example of this is the *Oracular Action*. This important
tion.   element of dramatic effect—how it consists in the working
out of Destiny from mystery to clearness, and the different
forms it assumes—has been discussed at length in a former
chapter. The question here is, how far do we find such
superhuman knowledge used as a force in the movement of
events ? As Shakespeare handles oracular machinery, the
conditions of natural working in the course of events are
not in the least degree altered by the revelation of the
future. The actor's belief (or disbelief) in the oracle may be
one of the circumstances which have influenced his action—
as it would have done in the real life of the age—but to the
spectator, to whom the Drama is to reveal the real governing forces of the world, the oracular action is presented not
as a force but as a light. It gives to a course of events the
illumination that can be in actual fact given to it by History,
the office of which is to make each detail of a story interesting

in the light of the explanation that comes when all the
details are complete.   Only it uses the supernatural agency to
project this illumination into the midst of the events themselves, which History cannot give till they are concluded;
and also it carries the art-effect of such illumination a stage
further than History could carry it, by making it progressive
in intelligibility, and making this progress keep pace with the
progress of the events themselves.   Fate will allow none but
Macduff to be the slayer of Macbeth.   True : but Macduff
(who moreover knows nothing of his destiny) is the most
deeply injured of Macbeth's subjects, and as a fact we find
it needs the news of his injury to rouse him to his task; as **iv.** iii.
he approaches the battle he feels that the ghosts of his wife **v.** vii. 15.
and children will haunt him if he allows any other to be the
tyrant's executioner.   Thus far the interpretation of History
might go : but the oracular machinery which Shakespeare
has introduced points dimly to Macduff before the first
breath of the King's suspicion has assailed him, and the
suggestiveness becomes clearer and clearer as the convergence of events carries the action to its climax.   The natural
working of human events has been undisturbed: only the
spectator's mind has been endowed with a special illumination for receiving them.

In another and very different way we have supernatural *The Super-*
agency called in to throw a peculiar illumination over *natural as*
                                                        Dramatic
human events.   In dealing with the movement of *Julius* *Back-*
Cæsar I have described at length the *Supernatural Back-* *ground.*
ground of storm, tempest, and portent, which assist the emotional agitation throughout the second stage of the action.
These are clearly supernatural in that they are made to suggest a mystic sympathy with, and indeed prescience of, mutations in human life.   Yet their function is simply that of
illumination : they cast a glow of emotion over the spectator
as he watches the train of events, though all the while the
action of these events remains within the sphere of natural

CHAP. XX. causes. In narrative and lyric poetry this endowment of nature with human sympathies becomes the commonest of poetic devices, personification; and here it never suggests anything supernatural because it is so clearly recognised as belonging to expression. But ' expression ' in the Drama extends beyond language, and takes in presentation; and it is only a device in presentation that tumult in nature and tumult in history, each perfectly natural by itself, are made to have a suggestion of the supernatural by their coincidence in time. After all there is no real meaning in storm any more than in calm weather, only that contemplative observers have transferred their own emotions to particular phases of nature: it would seem, then, a very slight and natural reversal of the process to call in this humanised nature to assist the emotions which have created it.

In these various forms Shakespeare introduces supernatural agency into his dramas. In my discussion of them it will be understood that I am not in the least endeavouring to explain away the reality of their supernatural character. My purpose is to show for how small a proportion of his total effect Shakespeare draws upon the supernatural, allowing it to carry further or to illustrate, but not to mould or determine a course of events. It will readily be granted that he brings effect enough out of a supernatural incident to justify the use of it to our rational sense of economy.

Motive Force as a part of Design. When all these special Dramatic Motives have been considered there still remains an interest of Motive Force belonging to a plot considered purely as a piece of design. In the adaptation of means to ends, which is one phase of design, it is clear that our sense of economy is gratified when we see single devices producing multiplicity of effects; when the successive incidents do not appear dependent upon any arbitrary will of the author, but, on the contrary, it is only necessary to assume a few postulates, and the rest of the story seems to follow from these of itself. It is a function,

then, of plot analysis to discover the main motive force of any CHAP. XX.
play. Sometimes this is found in a Motive Personage:
great part of the action in *Othello* is carried forward directly *Motive Personages.*
by the energy of Iago, and in *As You Like It* by the activity
of Rosalind. In the latter case we can go further, and
point to a distinct Motive Circumstance—Rosalind's disguise *Motive*
—as responsible for the larger proportion of the dramatic *Circumstance.*
entanglement. In connection with the *Merchant of Venice*, it
was pointed out how one of the actions—the Caskets Story *Motive*
—motives all the rest, the hero serving to complicate, the *Action.*
heroine to resolve. *Love's Labour's Lost* gives us at the outset
a Motive Situation: Biron in the first scene sees how the *Motive*
proclamation of celibacy, taken in conjunction with the for- *Situation.*
gotten circumstance of the Princess's visit, constitutes a sort
of unstable equilibrium in social relations, and the working
from this back to nature constitutes the whole plot. The
same description applies to *Lear*, except that Lear himself
creates the unstable situation by his false distribution of
power; and thus the first act generates what all the rest of
the play has to work out. In *The Tempest*, one personage, *Complicat-*
Antonio, has been the source of the complication, while *ing and Re-*
another, Prospero, by his power of enchantment is the sole *Personages.*
contriver of the Resolution. Often in Passion Movement
the Fall and the Rise seem natural parts of a single action. *Rise and*
Precisely as the effort which throws a ball into the air seems *Fall a*
to the eye all that is responsible for the ball's eventually *tive.*
turning round and descending, so when the conspirators in
Julius Cæsar, or the hero in *Macbeth*, have risen by their
energy to a climax, they seem to fall by no other force than
the exhaustion of their original energy against a sort of
moral gravitation. This is true also of *Richard III*, with *The En-*
the exception that in this play the Enveloping Action—the *veloping*
feud of York and Lancaster—yields considerable part of the *source of*
Motive Force: Richard does much to carry forward the *Motion,*
progress of this war, but he is himself a product of it, and is

CHAP. XX. eventually swept by its momentum to destruction.   In most of the cases previously mentioned the Enveloping Action of the play is responsible for some part of the Motive Force : the Witches assist the career of Macbeth, though they do not alter its direction ; and the fickleness of the Roman mob counts for something in the sum of forces which produce the *and under-* downfall of the Republicans.   And such a consideration *going Motive re-* lends especial interest to the case of plays mentioned in a *action.* previous paragraph, where a further Revolution makes the Enveloping Action share the movement of the play ; and, in the particular case of *As You Like It*, the elaborate Frame which has brought into existence and supported the main actions of the play is by the consummation of these itself shattered and brought to an end.

Conclusion.   The plan laid down for this work has now been followed to its completion.   The object I have had in view throughout has been the *recognition* of inductive treatment in literary study.   For this purpose it was first necessary to distinguish the inductive method from other modes of treatment founded on arbitrary canons of taste and comparisons of merit, so natural in view of the popularity of the subject-matter, and to which the history of Literary Criticism has given an unfortunate impetus.   This having been done in the Introduction, the body of the work has been occupied in applying the inductive treatment to some of the masterpieces of Shakespeare.   The practical effect of such exposition has been, it may be hoped, to intensify the reader's appreciation of the poet, but also to suggest that the detailed and methodical analysis which in literary study is usually reserved for points of language is no less applicable to a writer's subject-matter and art.   But to entitle Dramatic Criticism to a place in the circle of the inductive sciences it has further appeared necessary to lay down a scheme for the study as a

whole, that should be scientific both in the relation of its
parts to one another, and in the attainment of a completeness proportioned to the area to which the enquiry was
limited and the degree of development to which literary
method has at present attained. The proper method for
the nascent science was fixed as the enumeration and arrangement of topics; and by analogy with the other arts
a simple scheme for Dramatic Criticism was found, in which
all the results of the analysis performed in the first part of
the book could be readily distributed under one or other of
the main topics—Character, Passion and Plot. Incidentally
the discussion of Shakespeare has again and again reminded
us of just that greatness in the modern Drama which judicial criticism with its inflexibility of standard so persistently
missed. Everywhere early criticism recognised our poet's
grasp of human nature, yet its almost universal verdict of
him was that he was both irregular in his art as a whole,
and in particular careless in the construction of his plots.
We have seen, on the contrary, that Shakespeare has
elevated the whole conception of Plot, from that of a mere
unity of action obtained by reduction of the amount of
matter presented, to that of a harmony of design binding
together concurrent actions from which no degree of complexity was excluded. And, finally, instead of his being a
despiser of law, we have had suggested to us how Shakespeare and his brother artists of the Renaissance form a
point of departure in legitimate Drama so important as amply
to justify the instinct of history which named that age the
Second Birth of literature.

TOPICS OF DRAMATIC SCIENCE.

Character
- Single Character-Interest or Character-Interpretation
  - Interpretation as an hypothesis
  - Canons of Interpretation
- Complex Character-Interest
  - Character-Contrast and Duplication
  - Character-Grouping
- Character-Development

Passion
- Single Passion-Interest
  - Incident and Situation
  - Effect
    - Irony
    - Nemesis
    - Dramatic Foreshadowing
- Complex Passion-Interest or Passion-Tone
  - Mixture of Tones
  - Tone-Clash, Humour, Tone-Storm
- Tone-Movement
  - Tone-Play and Tone-Relief
  - Metrical Alternation

Plot
- Single Action
  - General conception of Single Actions
  - Forms of Dramatic Action
- Complex Action
  - General conception of Complex Action
  - Analysis of Complex Action into Single Actions, with Canons of Analysis
  - Economy
    - Connection
      - Contact and Linking
      - Interweaving
      - Envelopment
    - Dependence
    - Symmetry
      - Balance
      - Parallelism and Contrast
- Movement [Motive Form]
  - Simple Movement: the Line of Motion a straight line
  - Action-Movement or Complication and Resolution: the Line of Motion a curve
  - Passion-Movement or Strain and Reaction: the Line of Passion a
    - Regular Arch
    - Inclined Plane
    - Wave Line
  - Compound (or Relative) Movement
    - Similar Motion
    - Contrary Motion
    - Convergent Motion
  - Turning-points
    - Catastrophe: or Focus of Movement
    - Centre of Plot
    - Further Resolution
- Movement [Motive Force]
  - Dramatic Providence
  - Poetic Justice: or Retribution as a form of Art-beauty
  - Pathos: or [unretributive] Fate as a form of Art-beauty
  - The Supernatural
    - Destiny rationalised
      - Objectively in Irony
      - Subjectively in Infatuation
    - Supernatural Agency
      - Intensifying human action
      - Illuminating human action
        - The Oracular
        - Supernatural Background

Mechanical Construction
- Reduction of Difficulties: especially, Rationalisation and Derationalisation.
- Constructive Economy: utilisation of mechanical persons and details.
- Constructive Processes: Dramatic Background, Dramatic Hedging, Preparation, etc.
- Constructive Conventionalities: especially, Scenic Unities of Place and Time.
- Constructive Unity
  - Dramatic Colouring
  - Central Ideas

APPENDIX.

TECHNICAL ANALYSIS OF PLOTS.

THE MERCHANT OF VENICE

AN ACTION-DRAMA

Scheme of Actions

Main Plot.
{
First Main **Cross Nemesis** Action : Story of the Jew : complicated and resolved.

Under-plot.
{
Sub-Action to First Main, also Link Action : Jessica and Lorenzo : simple movement.
Comic Relief Action : Launcelot : stationary .
Sub-Action to Second Main : Episode of the Rings : complicated and resolved.
}

Second Main **Problem** Action : Caskets Story : simple movement.
}

External Circumstance [2] : The (rumoured) Shipwrecks.

Economy

Two Main Actions connected by Common Personage [Bassanio] and by Link Action [Jessica].

General Interweaving.

Balance. The First Main Action, which is complicated, balances the Second, which is simple, by the additions to the latter of the Jessica interest transferred to it, and the Episode of the Rings generated out of it. [Pages 82, 88.]

Movement

Action-Movement : with Contrary Motion between the two Main Actions. The First Main complicated and resolved by the Second

---

[1] Stationary, as having no place in the movement of the plot : its separateness from the rest of the Jessica Action only for purposes of Tone-effect, as Comic Relief.

[2] 'External' as not included in any action, 'Circumstance' because it presents itself as a single detail instead of the series of details necessary to make up an Action. An External Circumstance is analogous to an Enveloping Action : outside the other Actions, yet in contact with them at certain points.

Main [hero of Second, Bassanio, is Complicating Force ; heroine of Second, Portia, is Resolving Force], the Complication assisted by the External Circumstance of the Shipwrecks—in process of resolving the First generates a Complication to the Second in the form of the Episode of the Rings, which is self-resolved. [Pages 66, 375.]

Motive Force : The Second Main Action thus serves as Motive Action to the rest : assisted by the Motive Circumstance of the Shipwreck.

Turning-Points

Centre of Plot : Scene of Bassanio's Choice (**iii.** ii.) in which the Complicating and Resolving Forces are united and all the Four Actions meet. [Pages 67-8.]

Catastrophe : Portia's Judgment in the Trial (**iv.** i, from 299).

RICHARD THE THIRD

A PASSION-DRAMA

Scheme of Actions

Main **Nemesis** Action : Life and Death of Richard.

CLARENCE has betrayed the Lancastrians for the sake of the House of York :

He falls by a treacherous death from the KING of the House of York. — To this the QUEEN and her kindred have been assenting parties [**ii. ii.** 62–5] :

The shock of Clarence's death as announced by Gloster kills the King (**ii. i.** 131), leaving the Queen and her kindred at the mercy of their enemies. — Unseemly Exultation of their great enemy HASTINGS :

Underplot : System of **Cross Nemesis** Actions connecting Main with YORK side of Enveloping Action.

The same treachery step by step overtakes Hastings in his Exultation [**iii. iv.** 15–95). — In this treacherous casting off of Hastings when he will no longer support them BUCKINGHAM has been a prime agent [**iii.** i, from 157; **iii.** ii. 114] :

By precisely similar treachery Buckingham himself is cast off when he hesistates to go further with Richard [**iv.** ii. and **v.** i].

Link **Nemesis** Action connecting Main with Lancaster side of Enveloping Action : Marriage of Richard and Anne (page 113).

Enveloping **Nemesis** Action : The War of the Roses [the Duchess of York introduced to mark the York side, Queen Margaret to mark the Lancastrian side].

Economy

All the Actions bound together by the Enveloping Action of which they make up a phase.

Parallelism : the common form of Nemesis.

Central Personage : Richard.

Movement

Passion-Movement, with Similar Motion [form Nemesis repeated throughout (page 373)].

Motive Force : The Enveloping Action and Richard as Motive Personage. [Page 395.]

Turning-points

Centre of Plot : Realisation of Margaret's Curses [turn of Enveloping Action] in **iii. iii. 15.**

Catastrophe : Realisation of Nemesis in the Main Action : **iv. ii,** from **45.**

MACBETH

A Passion-Drama

Scheme of Actions

{ Main **Character** Action : Rise and Fall of Macbeth.
{ **Character** Counter-Action: Lady Macbeth.

{ **Character** Sub-Action: covering and involved in the Rise:
  Banquo.
{ **Character** Sub-Action : covering and involving the Fall :
  Macduff. [Pages 129, 142.]

Enveloping **Supernatural** Action : The Witches.

Economy

Parallelism : Triple form of Nemesis, Irony and Oracular Action
extending to the Main Action, to its parts the Rise and Fall
separately, and through to the Enveloping Action.

Contrast as a bond between the Main and Counter-Action.

Balance : the Rise by the Fall, the Sub-Action to the Rise by the
Sub-Action to the Fall. [Page 367.]

Movement

Passion-Movement, with Similar Motion between all.

Motive Force : The Main Action—partly assisted by Enveloping
Action. [Pages 387, 396.]

Turning-points

Centre of Plot : Change from unbroken success to unbroken
failure : **iii.** iii. 18. [Page 127.]

Catastrophe : Divided : First Shock of Nemesis : Appearance of
Banquo's Ghost (**iii.** iv).

Final Accumulation of Nemesis : Revelation of Macduff's birth (**v.** viii. 12).

JULIUS CÆSAR

A Passion-Drama

Scheme of Actions

> Main **Nemesis** Action : Rise and Fall of the Republican Con-
> spirators.
>> { Sub-Action to the Rise [**Character-decline**] : The Victim
>> Cæsar.
>> Sub-Action to the Fall [**Character-rise**] : The Avenger An-
>> tony.
> Enveloping Action : the Roman Mob.

Economy

> Balance about the Centre : the Rise by the Fall, the Sub-Action to
> the Rise by the Sub-Action to the Fall.

Movement

> Passion-Movement, with Similar Motion between the Main and
> Sub-Actions. [The form of the Main is distributed between the
> two Sub-Actions : compare page 374.]
> Motive Force : The Main Action, slightly assisted by the Envelop-
> ing Action. (Page 396.)

Turning-points

> The Centre of Plot and Catastrophe coincide : **iii.** i. between 121
> and 122.

KING LEAR

A Passion-Drama

Scheme of Actions

Main Plot: a **Problem** Action: Family of Lear: falling into

Generating Action: Lear's unstable settlement of the kingdom,
[the Problem]. power transformed from the good to the bad.

System of Tragedies
[the Solution].

⌈ **Double Nemesis** Action: Lear receiving good from the injured and evil from the favoured children.

Tragic Action: Cordelia: Suffering of the innocent.

Tragic Action: Goneril and Regan: Evil passions endowed with power using it to work their own destruction. ⌊

Underplot: an **Intrigue** Action: Family of Gloucester: falling into

Generating Action: Gloucester deceived into reversing the
[the Intrigue]. positions of Edgar and Edmund.

System of Tragedies
[its Nemesis].

⌈ **Double Nemesis** Action: Gloucester receiving good from the injured and evil from the favoured child.

Tragic Action: Edgar: Suffering of the innocent.

Tragic Action: Edmund: Power gained by intrigue used for the destruction of the intriguer. ⌊

Central Link Personage between Main Plot and Underplot: Gloucester (page 376).

Sub-Actions, linking Main and Underplot, or different elements of the Main together.

First Pair:
- From the good side of the Main: Kent.
- From the evil side of the Main: Oswald.

Crossing & complicating one another.

Second Pair:
- From the good side of the Main assisting Nemesis on Evil Agent of the Underpiot: Albany.
- From the evil side of the Main assisting Nemesis on Good Victim of the Underplot: Cornwall.

Third Pair: Cross Intrigues between the Evil sides of Main and Underplot
{ Goneril and Edmund } culminating in
{ Regan and Edmund }
destruction of all three (v. iii. 96, 221-7, and compare 82 with 160).

Farcical Relief Action: The Fool: Stationary.

Enveloping Action: The French War: originating ultimately in the Initial Action and becoming the Objective of the dénouement. [Page 377.]

Economy

The Underplot dependent to the Main (page 366).
Especially: Parallelism and Contrast (page 367-9).
Central Linking by Gloucester.
Interweaving: Linking by Sub-Actions, &c., and movement to a common Objective.
Envelopment in common Enveloping Action.

Movement

Passion-Movement, with Convergent Motion between the Main and Underplot, and their parts: the Lear and Gloucester systems by the visit to Gloucester's Castle drawn to a Central Focus and then moving towards a common Objective in the Enveloping Action. [Pages 376-7.]
Motive Force: The Motive Situation set up by the Generating Actions.

Turning-points

Catastrophe: at the end of the Initial Action, the Problem being set up in practical action (page 205).
Centre of Plot: the summit of emotional agitation when three madnesses are brought into contact (page 223).

OTHELLO

A Passion-Drama

Scheme of Actions

Three **Tragic** Actions:

1. Bianca's illicit liaison with Cassio—culminates in her being arrested as his murderer (**v.** i. fin.).
2. Roderigo's pursuit of Desdemona—culminates in his murder.
3. True love of Othello and Desdemona—ends in jealousy, murder, suicide.

Four **Intrigues** centering in Iago:

4. Iago *versus* Roderigo: to get money out of him and then get rid of him (**v.** i. 14).—[Succeeds.]
5. Iago *versus* Cassio: to get his place. [Arising out of Cassio's appointment (**i.** i.)—successful (**iii.** iii. fin.).]
6. Iago *versus* Cassio: to destroy him. [Arises out of general hatred (**v.** i. 19) and marriage jealousy (**ii.** i. 316).—Partially fails and assists the Reaction.]
7. Iago *versus* Othello: to make him the victim of his own jealousy. [Arises out of general hatred (**i.** i. init.) and marriage jealousy (**ii.** i. 304, &c).—Succeeds.]

Reaction:

8. Nemesis upon Iago.—[All his Intrigues recoil on him: see page 239.]

Faint Enveloping Action: The Turkish War.

Economy and Movement

The main Economy of the plot lies in the Convergent Motion of all the Actions to a common Culmination with Reaction. Chiefly through a series of Link Devices:

By the device of making Cassio the object of Othello's jealousy (i. iii. 400):

Nos. 6 and 7 are merged in one action.

By the device of making Cassio in his repentance utilise Desdemona (ii. iii. 319):

No. 3 is made to work in with Nos. 6 and 7.

By the device of making Cassio the object of Roderigo's jealousy (ii. i. from 220)—and the device of utilising the Commission (iv. ii. 220):

No. 2 is made to co-operate with Nos. 6 and 7, and at the same time with No. 4:

Thus Nos. 2, 3, 4, 5, 6, 7 are now merged in one action.

By the device of the handkerchief (iii. iii. 321):

No. 1 is worked in to No. 7:

Thus all the actions are united in one common movement.

Motive Force: Iago is the Motive Personage of the plot: source of the Intrigues, and of the convergence of the Actions, and object of the Reaction.

Turning-points

Catastrophe: **v.** ii. 140: First hint of the Reaction.

Centre of Plot: **iii.** iii. 90: Climax of Main Action (No. 3) before its Fall begins.

THE TEMPEST

An Action-Drama

Constructed in the Scenic Unities of the Classical Drama[1].

Scheme of Actions

Main Plot: A pair of **Motive** Counter-Actions.

Complicating **Intrigue** Action: *Conspiracy of Antonio and Sebastian against Prospero.*

Motive Sub-Actions.
{ Sub-Action to the Complicating Action: Intrigue of Sebastian and Antonio against Alonso.
Sub-Action to the Resolving Action: Ariel and the invisible music.

Resolving **Providence** Action: Prospero on the Island.

Preparation Sub-Actions.
{ *On the Complicating side* [*Judgment*]: *Caliban and Prospero* (i. ii).
On the Resolving side [*Mercy*]: *Ariel's deliverance* (i. ii).

Underplot: A pair of Dependent Link Actions, motived with the Main Plot.

{ Love of Ferdinand and Miranda : linking the children of the two sides of the play.
Conspiracy of Caliban and Stephano : linking the servants of the two sides of the play.

Mechanical Personages, outside the strict movement yet faintly motived with the Main and Underplot (see page 261).

{ The Crowd of Sailors, led by Boatswain.
The Crowd of Courtiers, led by Gonzalo.

Enveloping **Supernatural** Action: Enchantment.

---

[1] Actions outside the scenic unity are printed in italics.

Economy

Dependence and Linking between Main and Underplot.

Parallelism between separate parts of Underplot and Mechanical Personages.

Common Envelopment.

Movement

Action-Movement. Counter-Action between the two main Actions: the Resolving Action further complicates the opening complication, and finally resolves it (**v**. i. 20)—Similar Motion between Main and Underplot (and Mechanical Personages)—Contrary Motion between the separate members of each—all the actions Convergent by the link Prospero to the final scene of universal restoration.

Motive Force. Two Motive Personages: Antonio of the Complication, Prospero (with the aid of the Enveloping Action) of the Resolution.

Turning-Points

Centre of Plot: In Act **iii** the different Actions successively reach their full complication.   [See page 378 note.]

Catastrophe: The change from Judgment to Mercy: **v**. i. 20.

Further Resolution: The Resolving Force demotived: Prospero renouncing his enchantment (**v**. i. 51).

LOVE'S LABOUR'S LOST

An Action-Drama

Scheme of Actions

Main **Humour** Action: The Celibate Scheme disconcerted by
the French Embassy: rises in complication out of the initial
situation and self-resolved.—Falls into two phases:

> Artificial attitude of Celibates to one another—breaks down
> (**iv.** iii) and abandoned.
> Artificial attitude of Celibates to ladies: gradually abandoned
> (from **iv.** iii).

Underplot.

> Two **Character-Groups:**
>
> (*a*) Armado: set off by Moth, Custard, Jaquenetta, &c.
> [Euphuism.]
>
> (*b*) Holofernes: set off by Nathaniel and Dull. [Pedantry.]
>
> Out of which rise two Sub-Actions:
>
> (A) **Intrigue** Sub-Action of Armado and Jaquenetta—setting
> off first phase of main Action and Complications.
>
> (B) **Farcical** Sub-Action: Pageant of the Worthies—setting
> off second phase of the Main Action and Resolution.

Enveloping **Motive** Action: The king of France's illness [generat-
ing the Complication] and Death [bringing about a Further
Resolution].

Economy

Common Envelopment.
The Underplot and Main by Dependence.

Movement

>Action-Movement of Complication and Resolution [with Further Resolution by a turn in the Enveloping Action: page 297-8].
>—Similar Motion between Main and Underplot.

>Motive Force: The whole movement comes from the Initial Motive Situation (page 395): this from the Enveloping Action in conflict with the Complicating Circumstance of the Vow of Celibacy.— The Further Resolution motived by the Enveloping Action.

Turning-points

>Centre of Plot: The Discovery Scene (**iv.** iii).   See page 378 note.

>Catastrophe: **v.** ii. 522: the Representatives of conventionality join in ridiculing their own pageant.

>Further Resolution: **v.** ii. 723: Entrance of Mercade with news of the king of France's death.

AS YOU LIKE IT

An Action-Drama

Scheme of Actions

Frame: A System of Enveloping Actions, one within another (pages 363-5):
Outer Enveloping Action : Civil War of the Dukes.
Inner Enveloping Action : Feud in the De Boys family.
Woodland Action : Life in Arden Forest.
Humour Action: Melancholy of Jaques.

These form a setting to

Main Plot : A System of Four **Love** Actions:

1. Love and (Genuine) Humour : Orlando and Rosalind: initiated in complication out of the Enveloping Action and self-resolved.
2. Love at first sight : Oliver and Celia: initiated out of the Frame and consummated.
3. Conventional Pastoral Love : Silvius and Phœbe : rises out of the Frame, complicated and resolved by No. 1.
4. Love and (Professional) Humour : initiated out of the Frame Actions and consummated.

[Half-developed **Character** Sub-Action : Adam—ignored after second act.]

Economy
Actions united by Common Envelopment and Movement.

Movement

Action-Movement : with Convergent Motion between separate Actions up to a common Culmination : dropping of Rosalind's disguise. Interference of the three Humour Actions with the rest and with one another. [Pages 307, 309.]

Motive Force.

(1) The Frame Actions initiate the Actions of the Main system, assisting their complication and [arrival of Oliver] resolution : then are self-destroyed coincidently with consummation of the Main System. [Pages 364-5.]

(2) Rosalind serves as further Motive Personage.

Turning-points

Centre of Plot : **iii. ii.** 313 : Orlando and the disguised Rosalind meet for the first time.

Catastrophe : **v. iv.** 113 : Rosalind drops her disguise.

Further Resolution : **v. iv.** 156 : Entrance of Jaques de Boys with news.

INDEXES

GENERAL INDEX.

₊ *For particular Characters or Scenes see under their respective plays.*

Abbott, Dr., quoted 15.
Academy, French 18.
Achilles and the River-god 193.

Action a fundamental element of Drama 323–5—its threefold division 324—Plot as pure Action 325—or the intellectual side of Action 356.
Action, Analysis of: 360–5—canons of Analysis 360–1.
'Action-Drama' as substitute for 'Comedy' 372–3.
Action, Economy of: 365–9. General notion and connection with Analysis 365—Economic Forms 365–6—Connection and Linking 365–6—Dependence 366—Symmetry 366–9—Balance 367—Parallelism and Contrast 367–9—Economy in Technical Analyses of the plays 401–16.
Action, Enveloping 361–5—Illustrations: *Richard III* 361—111–2—*Macbeth* 362—*Julius Cæsar* 362—*King Lear* 362–3—*As You Like It* 363–5.
Actions, focussing of: 209.
Action, Forms of Dramatic: 358–9, 125, 202.
Action, Schemes of in Technical Analyses, 401–16.
Action, Single and Complex 324, 357, &c.
Action, Systems of: 108, 110, 208.
Action, Unity of: 14, 324, 358–9—unity of action in Modern Drama becomes harmony 359.
Actions, **Varieties** of: Character-

Action 358; Comic Action 358, 401; Enveloping 361–5; Farcical 408; Generating 407; Humorous 358, 413; Initial and Resultant 208; Intrigue 358, 207; Irony 358; Link 81, 208; Main and Subordinate 359; Motive 358; Nemesis 358, &c.; Oracular 358, &c.; Problem 358, 202; Providence 411; Relief 401, 408; Rise and Fall 358, 119, 127; Stationary 401; Story 358; Supernatural 411; Tragic 358, 407; Triple 358, 125, 142.

Actor, Acting 98, 321. [*See* Stage-Representation.]
Addison: on scientific progress 5—his Critique of *Paradise Lost* 16—his list of English poets 16—his *Cato* 17, 19—on rules of art 20—on Rymer 21.
Affectations attacked by Humour the Central Idea of *Love's Labour's Lost* 285—compare *As You Like It* 300.
Analysis as a stage in scientific development 318.
Analysis, Dramatic: 360. [*See* Action, Analysis of.]
Ancient Drama 125, 387—Mixture of Tones an impossibility 345—the Supernatural its leading Motive 387—its unity of action different from that of the Modern Drama 359.
Ancient Thought, points of difference from Modern: 44, 125–7, 137.
Antigone and Poetic Justice 267.

example of Dramatic Background of Nature 192.

Johnson, Dr.: on Shakespeare 10–11, 20—on Milton's minor poems 11 — on Blank Verse 14 — on Metaphysical Poetry 16—on Addison's *Cato* 19—on the Unities 20.

Jonson, Ben: 2–4—his Dramatic Satires 3—his Blank Verse 13—his *Catiline* 17.

Journalism: its influence on critical method 5—place of Reviewing in literary classification 21–2.

Judicial Blindness 201, 388. [*See* Infatuation.]

Julius Cæsar, Play of: 168–201, Chapters VIII and IX. As an example of Character-Grouping 168 and Chapter VIII, 334—as a study of Passion and Movement 185 and Chapter IX.

Julius Cæsar, Characters in: Antony balances Cæsar 129—spared by the Conspirators 171—contrasted by Cæsar with Cassius 179–80 — his general character 182–3—its culture 179–80—self-seeking 182—affection for Cæsar 183, 199—his position in the group of characters 183, 184—peculiar tone of his oratory 198—dominant spirit of the reaction 198—upspringing of a character in him 198—his ironical conciliation of the conspirators 199—his oration 199–200—Antony's servant 198. Artemidorus 196.

Brutus: general character 171–6—its equal balance 171–5—its force 171—softness 173—this concealed under Stoicism 173, 174–5, 183 — his culture 173—relations with his Page 173–4—with Portia 173–4—with Cæsar 175—slays Cæsar for what he might become 175—position in the State 176—relations with Cassius 172, 173, 182—overrules Cassius in council 172—his general position in the Grouping 183.

Cæsar: a balance to An-

tony 129—general discussion of his character 176–81—its difficulty and contradictions 176–8—his vacillation 176–7—explained by the antithesis of Practical and Inner Life 178—Cæsar pre-eminently the Practical man 178–9—strong side of his character 176-7—lacking in the Inner Life 178–9—compared with Macbeth 178—a change in Cæsar and his world 180–1—his superstition 180–1—position in the Grouping 183—different effect of his personality in the earlier and later half of the play 188, 195, 197. Calpurnia 194–5. Casca 172, 194, 195. Cassius: his relations with Brutus 172, 182—brings out the defective side of Cæsar 179—contrasted by Cæsar with Antony 179–80—his character discussed 181–2—Republicanism his grand passion *ib.*—a professional politician 182 —his tact 182—his position in the Grouping 183–4—his relish for the supernatural portents 195—his nemesis 342 —Cassius and the eagles 342. Decius 181, 195. Ligarius 172. Page of Brutus 173-4, 201. Popilius Lena 172, 197. Portia 173, 174, 196. Roman Mob 188, 200. Soothsayer 196, 342. Trebonius 341.

Julius Cæsar, Incidents and Scenes: Capitol Scene 196–200—Conspiracy Scene 171, 172, 176, 181 —its connection with storm and portents 193–4—Incidents of the Fever and Flood 178, 179—Funeral and Will of Cæsar 175, 199–200, 332.

Julius Cæsar, Plot of: Technical Analysis 406.—Affords examples of Enveloping Action 362—Balance 367 — Regular Arch-Movement 372—Similar Motion 374—Turning-points 379—Rise and Fall a single motive 395. [*See* next paragraph.]

* The reader will remember that ' Single' is used as antithetical to ' Compound' or ' Complex,' and ' Simple' to ' Complicated.' See note to page 74.

---

* See Note on previous page.

pest: arbitrary causation 252—casual permeated by design *ib.*—barrier between mind and matter breaking down 253—passage from real to supernatural 253—supernatural agents 254—nature humanised 255.

Raw Material of the Romatic Drama 43.

Reaction 198. [*See* Passion-Strain.]

Reduction of Difficulties an element in Dramatic workmanship 58, 326, 329—illustrated: *Merchant of Venice* 58-66.

Relief 348. [*See* Tone.]

Renaissance and its influence on critical method 4, 18, 320—Shakespeare a type 397.

Representation 321. [*See* Stage.]

Resolution 67, 370 [*see* Complication]—Resolving Force 67.—Further Resolution 379-80, 398, and Tables 401-16.

Reviewing, the lyrics of prose 22.

Rhymed couplet 30—its usage by Shakespeare 135, 353-5.

Richard III, Play of: an example of the intimate relation between Character and Plot 107—treated from the side of Character 90 and Chapter IV—from the side of Plot 107 and Chapter V—affords examples of Situations 339—of Dramatic Foreshadowing 342.

Richard III, Character of: 90 and Chapter IV—Ideal Villainy 90-1, 330—in scale 91—development 91, 335—not explained by sufficient motive 92—an end in itself 93. Richard as an Artist in Villainy 93-6—absence of emotion 93—intellectual enjoyment of Villainy 95-6. His Villainy ideal in its success 96-103—fascination of irresistibility 97, 103—use of unlikely means 98—economy 99—imperturbability and humour 100-1—fairness 101—recklessness suggesting resource 101, 332—inspiration as

distinguished from calculation 102—his keen touch for human nature 102.

Ideal and Real Villainy 104—Ideal Villainy and Monstrosity 105. [Also called Gloster.]

Richard III, Characters in : Anne 94, 113, 115 [*see* Wooing Scene] —Buckingham 91, 96, 100, 109, 115, 118, 121, 333—Catesby 117, 333—Clarence 108, 114, 116—his Children 109—his Murderers 334—Derby 117—Dorset 120—Elizabeth 121—Ely 100, 121—Hastings 91, 98, 109, 114, 115, 117, 333, 342—King Edward IV 99, 108, 114, 117—King Edward V 100, 333-4, 342—Lord Mayor 99—Margaret 94, 112, 115, 339—Queen and her kindred 98, 108, 114, 115, 116—Richmond 120, 121—Stanley 117, 123—Tyrrel 94, 333—York 99, 333-4—Duchess of York 95, 111.

Richard III, Incidents and Scenes in : Wooing Scene 339—analysed 103-4—an example of fascination 94, 97—Richard's blunders 102, 332. Margaret and the Courtiers 94, 339—Reconciliation Scene 99, 117—Murder of Clarence 116, 334, 338.

Richard III, Plot of: 107 and Chapter V. How Shakespeare weaves Nemesis into History *ib.*—Its Underplot as a System of Nemeses 108—its Enveloping Action a Nemesis 111—further multiplication of Nemesis 112—special devices for neutralising the weakening effect of such multiplication 114-8—the multiplication needed as a background to the villainy 118—Motive Force of the whole a Nemesis Action 119. Fall of Richard 119-23—protracted not sudden 119, 382—Turning-point delayed 120—tantalisation and mockery in Richard's fate 121-4—Climax in sleep and the Apparitions 122—final stages 123—play begins and ends in peace 123.

rationalised in Modern Drama
387.   In an objec-
tive form as Irony 387-8—in a
subjective form as Infatuation
388-9.
Supernatural Agencies 389-94—
not to be explained as hallucinations 390—Shakespeare's usage of
Supernatural Agency : to intensify
human action 390-2—to illuminate human action 392-4—the
Oracular 392-3—the Dramatic
Background of Nature 393-4—its
difficulties, modes of reducing :
246, &c.—Derationalisation 247—
Rationalisation 252—Addition of
kindred Reality 259.   Illustrations : the Apparitions to Richard
122—the Ghost of Banquo 165-6
—the Apparitions in *Macbeth* 135,
&c.—the Witches 158, 390-2—
portents in *Julius Cæsar* 193-4—
the Ghost of Cæsar 201—omen of
Eagles to Cassius 201.
Symmetry as a dramatic element 68
—as a form of Economy 366-9.
    Illustrations: *Merchant of
Venice* 67-8 ; *King Lear* 207-9,
367-9.
Systematisation as a Stage of scientific progress 318, 319.

Table of Elementary Topics 325,
329—of general Topics 398.
Taste as condensed Experience 6.
[*See* Criticism.]

Tempest, Play of : as a drama of
Enchantment 246 and Chapter XII
—as a study in Dramatic Colouring 262 and Chapter XII—as a
study in Central Ideas 264 and
Chapter XIII—as a Study in Personal Providence 264 and Chapter
XIII—as a study in the Supernatural 386.   Dryden's alteration
of 10.   Its Dramatic Background
of Nature 247—Masque in 248—
Metrical Variations 350-2.
Tempest, Characters in : Alonso

277-8, 279.   Antonio 273, 277-8,
279, 339.   Ariel : as an
Elemental Being 256-8 — delivered by Prospero 270—Ariel's
Story 270—dismissed 281.
Boatswain 282.   Caliban : as
a Natural Savage 250—as an Elemental Being 258-9—his origin
258—his connection with Stephano and Trinculo 261—Caliban's story 271—his use of verse
and prose 351-2.   Ferdinand
250, 252, 260, 271.   Gonzalo :
248, 274, 279, 280—as a leading
Mechanical Personage 282—his
connection with the Boatswain
282—as a Chorus-leader 282—
his relations to Providence 283.
Miranda : as a Child of Nature
249—her connection with Ferdinand 260, 271, 281.   Prospero :
Chapter XII *passim*, Chapter XIII
passim [*see* under Providence,
Personal] — his story 270 — his
relations with Ariel 257, 262,
270, 279—his relations with Caliban 250, 271 — his connection
with Ferdinand and Miranda 260,
271 — his connection with the
comic personages 275—his connection with the climax 280, 340.
        Sebastian 273, 277-8, 279.
Stephano 261, 274.   Sycorax 258,
259.   Trinculo 261, 274.
Tempest, Incidents and Scenes in :
The Masque 248 — Quarrel of
Caliban and Prospero 250—Expulsion from Milan 252—Quarrel
of Ariel and Prospero 257—Opening Tempest 269—Ariel's Deliverance 270 — Caliban's revolt
271—Conspiracy of Antonio and
Sebastian 273, 339—Quarrel of
Trinculo and Stephano 274—
Nemesis Scene 276-8—Universal
Restoration 279—Prospero's Renunciation 280, 340.
Tempest, Plot of : Technical Analysis
411-2.—Its Underplot : Story of
Ferdinand and Miranda as a study
of love at first sight 260—connected with the Movement 271—

INDEX OF SCENES

ILLUSTRATED IN THE FOREGOING CHAPTERS.

₊ *Clarendon type is used where the passage referred to approaches the character of an analysis of the scene.*

THE END.

CATALOGUE OF DOVER BOOKS

Literature, History of Literature

ARISTOTLE'S THEORY OF POETRY AND THE FINE ARTS, edited by S. H. Butcher. The celebrated Butcher translation of this great classic faced, page by page, with the complete Greek text. A 300 page introduction discussing Aristotle's ideas and their influence in the history of thought and literature, and covering art and nature, imitation as an aesthetic form, poetic truth, art and morality, tragedy, comedy, and similar topics. Modern Aristotelian criticism discussed by John Gassner. lxxvi + 421pp. 5⅜ x 8. **T42 Paperbound $2.00**

INTRODUCTIONS TO ENGLISH LITERATURE, edited by B. Dobrée. Goes far beyond ordinary histories, ranging from the 7th century up to 1914 (to the 1940's in some cases.) The first half of each volume is a specific detailed study of historical and economic background of the period and a general survey of poetry and prose, including trends of thought, influences, etc. The second and larger half is devoted to a detailed study of more than 5000 poets, novelists, dramatists; also economists, historians, biographers, religious writers, philosophers, travellers, and scientists of literary stature, with dates, lists of major works and their dates, keypoint critical bibliography, and evaluating comments. The most compendious bibliographic and literary aid within its price range.

Vol. I. THE BEGINNINGS OF ENGLISH LITERATURE TO SKELTON, (1509), W. L. Renwick, H. Orton. 450pp. 5⅛ x 7⅞. **T75 Clothbound $4.50**

Vol. II. THE ENGLISH RENAISSANCE, 1510-1688, V. de Sola Pinto. 381pp. 5⅛ x 7⅞. **T76 Clothbound $4.50**

Vol. III. AUGUSTANS AND ROMANTICS, 1689-1830, H. Dyson, J. Butt. 320pp. 5⅛ x 7⅞. **T77 Clothbound $4.50**

Vol. IV. THE VICTORIANS AND AFTER, 1830-1940's, E. Batho, B. Dobrée. 360pp. 5⅛ x 7⅞. **T78 Clothbound $4.50**

EPIC AND ROMANCE, W. P. Ker. Written by one of the foremost authorities on medieval literature, this is the standard survey of medieval epic and romance. It covers Teutonic epics, Icelandic sagas, Beowulf, French chansons de geste, the Roman de Troie, and many other important works of literature. It is an excellent account for a body of literature whose beauty and value has only recently come to be recognized. Index. xxiv + 398pp. 5⅜ x 8. **T355 Paperbound $2.00**

THE POPULAR BALLAD, F. B. Gummere. Most useful factual introduction; fund of descriptive material; quotes, cites over 260 ballads. Examines, from folkloristic view, structure; choral, ritual elements; meter, diction, fusion; effects of tradition, editors; almost every other aspect of border, riddle, kinship, sea, ribald, supernatural, etc., ballads. Bibliography. 2 indexes. 374pp. 5⅜ x 8. **T548 Paperbound $1.85**

MASTERS OF THE DRAMA, John Gassner. The most comprehensive history of the drama in print, covering drama in every important tradition from the Greeks to the Near East, China, Japan, Medieval Europe, England, Russia, Italy, Spain, Germany, and dozens of other drama producing nations. This unsurpassed reading and reference work encompasses more than 800 dramatists and over 2000 plays, with biographical material, plot summaries, theatre history, etc. "Has no competitors in its field," THEATRE ARTS. "Best of its kind in English," NEW REPUBLIC. Exhaustive 35 page bibliography. 77 photographs and drawings. Deluxe edition with reinforced cloth binding, headbands, stained top. xxii + 890pp. 5⅜ x 8. **T100 Clothbound $6.95**

THE DEVELOPMENT OF DRAMATIC ART, D. C. Stuart. The basic work on the growth of Western drama from primitive beginnings to Eugene O'Neill, covering over 2500 years. Not a mere listing or survey, but a thorough analysis of changes, origins of style, and influences in each period; dramatic conventions, social pressures, choice of material, plot devices, stock situations, etc.; secular and religious works of all nations and epochs. "Generous and thoroughly documented researches," Outlook. "Solid studies of influences and playwrights and periods," London Times. Index. Bibliography. xi + 679pp. 5⅜ x 8. **T693 Paperbound $2.75**

A SOURCE BOOK IN THEATRICAL HISTORY (SOURCES OF THEATRICAL HISTORY), A. M. Nagler. Over 2000 years of actors, directors, designers, critics, and spectators speak for themselves in this potpourri of writings selected from the great and formative periods of western drama. On-the-spot descriptions of masks, costumes, makeup, rehearsals, special effects, acting methods, backstage squabbles, theatres, etc. Contemporary glimpses of Molière rehearsing his company, an exhortation to a Roman audience to buy refreshments and keep quiet, Goethe's rules for actors, Belasco telling of $6500 he spent building a river, Restoration actors being told to avoid "lewd, obscene, or indecent postures," and much more. Each selection has an introduction by Prof. Nagler. This extraordinary, lively collection is ideal as a source of otherwise difficult to obtain material, as well as a fine book for browsing. Over 80 illustrations. 10 diagrams. xxiii + 611pp. 5⅜ x 8. **T515 Paperbound $3.00**

CATALOGUE OF DOVER BOOKS

WORLD DRAMA, B. H. Clark. The dramatic creativity of a score of ages and eras — all in two handy compact volumes. Over ⅓ of this material is unavailable in any other current edition! 46 plays from Ancient Greece, Rome, Medieval Europe, France, Germany, Italy, England, Russia, Scandinavia, India, China, Japan, etc. — including classic authors like Aeschylus, Sophocles, Euripides, Aristophanes, Plautus, Marlowe, Jonson, Farquhar, Goldsmith, Cervantes, Molière, Dumas, Goethe, Schiller, Ibsen, and many others. This creative collection avoids hackneyed material and includes only completely first-rate works which are relatively little known or difficult to obtain. "The most comprehensive collection of important plays from all literature available in English," SAT. REV. OF LITERATURE. Introduction. Reading lists. 2 volumes. 1364pp. 5⅜ x 8.

Vol. 1, T57 Paperbound **$2.25**
Vol. 2, T59 Paperbound **$2.50**

MASTERPIECES OF THE RUSSIAN DRAMA, edited with introduction by G. R. Noyes. This only comprehensive anthology of Russian drama ever published in English offers complete texts, in 1st-rate modern translations, of 12 plays covering 200 years. Vol. 1: "The Young Hopeful," Fonvisin; "Wit Works Woe," Griboyedov; "The Inspector General," Gogol; "A Month in the Country," Turgenev; "The Poor Bride," Ostrovsky; "A Bitter Fate," Pisemsky. Vol. 2: "The Death of Ivan the Terrible," Alexey Tolstoy "The Power of Darkness," Lev Tolstoy; "The Lower Depths," Gorky; "The Cherry Orchard," Chekhov; "Professor Storitsyn," Andreyev; "Mystery Bouffe," Mayakovsky. Bibliography. Total of 902pp. 5⅜ x 8.

Vol. 1 T647 Paperbound **$2.00**
Vol. 2 T648 Paperbound **$2.00**

EUGENE O'NEILL: THE MAN AND HIS PLAYS, B. H. Clark. Introduction to O'Neill's life and work. Clark analyzes each play from the early THE WEB to the recently produced MOON FOR THE MISBEGOTTEN and THE ICEMAN COMETH revealing the environmental and dramatic influences necessary for a complete understanding of these important works. Bibliography. Appendices. Index. ix + 182pp. 5⅜ x 8. T379 Paperbound **$1.35**

THE HEART OF THOREAU'S JOURNALS, edited by O. Shepard. The best general selection from Thoreau's voluminous (and rare) journals. This intimate record of thoughts and observations reveals the full Thoreau and his intellectual development more accurately than any of his published works: self-conflict between the scientific observer and the poet, reflections on transcendental philosophy, involvement in the tragedies of neighbors and national causes, etc. New preface, notes, introductions. xii + 228pp. 5⅜ x 8. T741 Paperbound **$1.50**

H. D. THOREAU: A WRITER'S JOURNAL, edited by L. Stapleton. A unique new selection from the Journals concentrating on Thoreau's growth as a conscious literary artist, the ideals and purposes of his art. Most of the material has never before appeared outside of the complete 14-volume edition. Contains vital insights on Thoreau's projected book on Concord, thoughts on the nature of men and government, indignation with slavery, sources of inspiration, goals in life. Index. xxxiii + 234pp. 5⅜ x 8. T678 Paperbound **$1.65**

THE HEART OF EMERSON'S JOURNALS, edited by Bliss Perry. Best of these revealing Journals, originally 10 volumes, presented in a one volume edition. Talks with Channing, Hawthorne, Thoreau, and Bronson Alcott; impressions of Webster, Everett, John Brown, and Lincoln; records of moments of sudden understanding, vision, and solitary ecstasy. "The essays do not reveal the power of Emerson's mind . . . as do these hasty and informal writings," N.Y. Times. Preface by Bliss Perry. Index. xiii + 357pp. 5⅜ x 8. T477 Paperbound **$1.85**

FOUNDERS OF THE MIDDLE AGES, E. K. Rand. This is the best non-technical discussion of the transformation of Latin pagan culture into medieval civilization. Covering such figures as Tertullian, Gregory, Jerome, Boethius, Augustine, the Neoplatonists, and many other literary men, educators, classicists, and humanists, this book is a storehouse of information presented clearly and simply for the intelligent non-specialist. "Thoughtful, beautifully written," AMERICAN HISTORICAL REVIEW. "Extraordinarily accurate," Richard McKeon, THE NATION. ix + 365pp. 5⅜ x 8. T369 Paperbound **$2.00**

PLAY-MAKING: A MANUAL OF CRAFTSMANSHIP, William Archer. With an extensive, new introduction by John Gassner, Yale Univ. The permanently essential requirements of solid play construction are set down in clear, practical language: theme, exposition, foreshadowing, tension, obligatory scene, peripety, dialogue, character, psychology, other topics. This book has been one of the most influential elements in the modern theatre, and almost everything said on the subject since is contained explicitly or implicitly within its covers. Bibliography. Index. xlii + 277pp. 5⅜ x 8. T651 Paperbound **$1.75**

HAMBURG DRAMATURGY, G. E. Lessing. One of the most brilliant of German playwrights of the eighteenth-century age of criticism analyzes the complex of theory and tradition that constitutes the world of theater. These 104 essays on aesthetic theory helped demolish the regime of French classicism, opening the door to psychological and social realism, romanticism. Subjects include the original functions of tragedy; drama as the rational world; the meaning of pity and fear, pity and fear as means for purgation and other Aristotelian concepts; genius and creative force; interdependence of poet's language and actor's interpretation; truth and authenticity; etc. A basic and enlightening study for anyone interested in aesthetics and ideas, from the philosopher to the theatergoer. Introduction by Prof. Victor Lange. xxii + 265pp. 4½ x 6⅜. T32 Paperbound **$1.45**

Fiction

THE LAND THAT TIME FORGOT and THE MOON MAID, Edgar Rice Burroughs. In the opinion of many, Burroughs' best work. The first concerns a strange island where evolution is individual rather than phylogenetic. Speechless anthropoids develop into intelligent human beings within a single generation. The second projects the reader far into the future and describes the first voyage to the Moon (in the year 2025), the conquest of the Earth by the Moon, and years of violence and adventure as the enslaved Earthmen try to regain possession of their planet. "An imaginative tour de force that keeps the reader keyed up and expectant," NEW YORK TIMES. Complete, unabridged text of the original two novels (three parts in each). 5 illustrations by J. Allen St. John. vi + 552pp. 5⅜ x 8½.

T1020 Clothbound **$3.75**
T358 Paperbound **$2.00**

AT THE EARTH'S CORE, PELLUCIDAR, TANAR OF PELLUCIDAR: THREE SCIENCE FICTION NOVELS BY EDGAR RICE BURROUGHS. Complete, unabridged texts of the first three Pellucidar novels. Tales of derring-do by the famous master of science fiction. The locale for these three related stories is the inner surface of the hollow Earth where we discover the world of Pellucidar, complete with all types of bizarre, menacing creatures, strange peoples, and alluring maidens—guaranteed to delight all Burroughs fans and a wide circle of adventure lovers. Illustrated by J. Allen St. John and P. F. Berdanier. vi + 433pp. 5⅜ x 8½.

T1051 Paperbound **$2.00**

THREE MARTIAN NOVELS, Edgar Rice Burroughs. Contains: Thuvia, Maid of Mars; The Chessmen of Mars; and The Master Mind of Mars. High adventure set in an imaginative and intricate conception of the Red Planet. Mars is peopled with an intelligent, heroic human race which lives in densely populated cities and with fierce barbarians who inhabit dead sea bottoms. Other exciting creatures abound amidst an inventive framework of Martian history and geography. Complete unabridged reprintings of the first edition. 16 illustrations by J. Allen St. John. vi + 499pp. 5⅜ x 8½.

T39 Paperbound **$1.85**

TO THE SUN? and OFF ON A COMET!, Jules Verne. Complete texts of two of the most imaginative flights into fancy in world literature display the high adventure that have kept Verne's novels read for nearly a century. Only unabridged edition of the best translation, by Edward Roth. Large, easily readable type. 50 illustrations selected from first editions. 462pp. 5⅜ x 8.

T634 Paperbound **$1.75**

FROM THE EARTH TO THE MOON and ALL AROUND THE MOON, Jules Verne. Complete editions of two of Verne's most successful novels, in finest Edward Roth translations, now available after many years out of print. Verne's visions of submarines, airplanes, television, rockets, interplanetary travel; of scientific and not-so-scientific beliefs; of peculiarities of Americans; all delight and engross us today as much as when they first appeared. Large, easily readable type. 42 illus. from first French edition. 476pp. 5⅜ x 8.

T633 Paperbound **$1.75**

THREE PROPHETIC NOVELS BY H. G. WELLS, edited by E. F. Bleiler. Complete texts of "When the Sleeper Wakes" (1st book printing in 50 years), "A Story of the Days to Come," "The Time Machine" (1st complete printing in book form). Exciting adventures in the future are as enjoyable today as 50 years ago when first printed. Predict TV, movies, intercontinental airplanes, prefabricated houses, air-conditioned cities, etc. First important author to foresee problems of mind control, technological dictatorships. "Absolute best of imaginative fiction," N. Y. Times. Introduction. 335pp. 5⅜ x 8.

T605 Paperbound **$1.50**

SEVEN SCIENCE FICTION NOVELS, H. G. Wells. Full unabridged texts of 7 science-fiction novels of the master. Ranging from biology, physics, chemistry, astronomy to sociology and other studies, Mr. Wells extrapolates whole worlds of strange and intriguing character. "One will have to go far to match this for entertainment, excitement, and sheer pleasure . . . ," NEW YORK TIMES. Contents: The Time Machine, The Island of Dr. Moreau, First Men in the Moon, The Invisible Man, The War of the Worlds, The Food of the Gods, In the Days of the Comet. 1015pp. 5⅜ x 8.

T264 Clothbound **$4.50**

28 SCIENCE FICTION STORIES OF H. G. WELLS. Two full unabridged novels, MEN LIKE GODS and STAR BEGOTTEN, plus 26 short stories by the master science-fiction writer of all time. Stories of space, time, invention, exploration, future adventure—an indispensable part of the library of everyone interested in science and adventure. PARTIAL CONTENTS: Men Like Gods, The Country of the Blind, In the Abyss, The Crystal Egg, The Man Who Could Work Miracles, A Story of the Days to Come, The Valley of Spiders, and 21 more! 928pp. 5⅜ x 8.

T265 Clothbound **$4.50**

THE WAR IN THE AIR, IN THE DAYS OF THE COMET, THE FOOD OF THE GODS: THREE SCIENCE FICTION NOVELS BY H. G. WELLS. Three exciting Wells offerings bearing on vital social and philosophical issues of his and our own day. Here are tales of air power, strategic bombing, East vs. West, the potential miracles of science, the potential disasters from outer space, the relationship between scientific advancement and moral progress, etc. First reprinting of "War in the Air" in almost 50 years. An excellent sampling of Wells at his storytelling best. Complete, unabridged reprintings. 16 illustrations. 645pp. 5⅜ x 8½.

T1135 Paperbound **$2.00**

CATALOGUE OF DOVER BOOKS

THE PIRATES OF VENUS and LOST ON VENUS: TWO VENUS NOVELS BY EDGAR RICE BURROUGHS. Two related novels, complete and unabridged. Exciting adventure on the planet Venus with Earthman Carson Napier broken-field running through one dangerous episode after another. All lovers of swashbuckling science fiction will enjoy these two stories set in a world of fascinating societies, fierce beasts, 5000-ft. trees, lush vegetation, and wide seas. Illustrations by Fortunino Matania. Total of vi + 340pp. 5⅜ x 8½. T1053 Paperbound **$1.75**

A PRINCESS OF MARS and A FIGHTING MAN OF MARS: TWO MARTIAN NOVELS BY EDGAR RICE BURROUGHS. "Princess of Mars" is the very first of the great Martian novels written by Burroughs, and it is probably the best of them all; it set the pattern for all of his later fantasy novels and contains a thrilling cast of strange peoples and creatures and the formula of Olympian heroism amidst ever-fluctuating fortunes which Burroughs carries off so successfully. "Fighting Man" returns to the same scenes and cities—many years later. A mad scientist, a degenerate dictator, and an indomitable defender of the right clash— with the fate of the Red Planet at stake! Complete, unabridged reprinting of original editions. Illustrations by F. E. Schoonover and Hugh Hutton. v + 356pp. 5⅜ x 8½. T1140 Paperbound **$1.75**

RURITANIA COMPLETE: THE PRISONER OF ZENDA and RUPERT OF HENTZAU, Anthony Hope. The first edition to include in one volume both the continually-popular "Prisoner of Zenda" and its equally-absorbing sequel. Hope's mythical country of Ruritania has become a household word and the activities of its inhabitants almost a common heritage. Unabridged reprinting. 14 illustrations by Charles Dana Gibson. vi + 414pp. 5⅜ x 8. T69 Paperbound **$1.35**

FLATLAND, E. A. Abbott. A science-fiction classic of life in a 2-dimensional world that is also a first-rate introduction to such aspects of modern science as relativity and hyperspace. Political, moral, satirical, and humorous overtones have made FLATLAND fascinating reading for thousands. 7th edition. New introduction by Banesh Hoffmann. 16 illustrations. 128pp. 5⅜ x 8. T1 Paperbound **$1.00**

THE WONDERFUL WIZARD OF OZ, L. F. Baum. Only edition in print with all the original W. W. Denslow illustrations in full color—as much a part of "The Wizard" as Tenniel's drawings are for "Alice in Wonderland." "The Wizard" is still America's best-loved fairy tale, in which, as the author expresses it, "The wonderment and joy are retained and the heartaches and nightmares left out." Now today's young readers can enjoy every word and wonderful picture of the original book. New introduction by Martin Gardner. A Baum bibliography. 23 full-page color plates. viii + 268pp. 5⅜ x 8. T691 Paperbound **$1.50**

THE MARVELOUS LAND OF OZ, L. F. Baum. This is the equally enchanting sequel to the "Wizard," containing the adventures of the Scarecrow and the Tin Woodman. The hero this time is a little boy named Tip, and all the delightful Oz magic is still present. This is the book with the Animated Saw-horse, the Woggle-Bug, and Jack Pumpkinhead. All the original John R. Neill illustrations, 16 in full color. 287pp. 5⅜ x 8. T692 Paperbound **$1.50**

FIVE GREAT DOG NOVELS, edited by Blanche Cirker. The complete original texts of five classic dog novels that have delighted and thrilled millions of children and adults throughout the world with stories of loyalty, adventure, and courage. Full texts of Jack London's "The Call of the Wild"; John Brown's "Rab and His Friends"; Alfred Ollivant's "Bob, Son of Battle"; Marshall Saunders' "Beautiful Joe"; and Ouida's "A Dog of Flanders." 21 illustrations from the original editions. 495pp. 5⅜ x 8. T777 Paperbound **$1.75**

THE CASTING AWAY OF MRS. LECKS AND MRS. ALESHINE, F. R. Stockton. A charming light novel by Frank Stockton, one of America's finest humorists (and author of "The Lady, or the Tiger?"). This book has made millions of Americans laugh at the reflection of themselves in two middle-aged American women involved in some of the strangest adventures on record. You will laugh, too, as they endure shipwreck, desert island, and blizzard with maddening tranquility. Also contains complete text of "The Dusantes," sequel to "The Casting Away." 49 original illustrations by F. D. Steele. vii + 142pp. 5⅜ x 8. T743 Paperbound **$1.00**

GHOST AND HORROR STORIES OF AMBROSE BIERCE, Selected and introduced by E. F. Bleiler. 24 morbid, eerie tales—the cream of Bierce's fiction output. Contains such memorable pieces as "The Moonlit Road," "The Damned Thing," "An Inhabitant of Carcosa," "The Eyes of the Panther," "The Famous Gilson Bequest," "The Middle Toe of the Right Foot," and other chilling stories, plus the essay, "Visions of the Night" in which Bierce gives us a kind of rationale for his aesthetic of horror. New collection (1964). xxii + 199pp. 5⅜ x 8⅜. T767 Paperbound **$1.00**

BEST GHOST STORIES OF J. S. LE FANU, Selected and introduced by E. F. Bleiler. LeFanu is deemed the greatest name in Victorian supernatural fiction. Here are 16 of his best horror stories, including 2 nouvelles: "Carmilla," a classic vampire tale couched in a perverse eroticism, and "The Haunted Baronet." Also: "Sir Toby's Will," "Green Tea," "Schalken the Painter," "Ultor de Lacy," "The Familiar," etc. The first American publication of about half of this material: a long-overdue opportunity to get a choice sampling of LeFanu's work. New selection (1964). 8 illustrations. 5⅜ x 8⅜. T415 Paperbound **$1.85**

Art, History of Art, Antiques, Graphic Arts, Handcrafts

ART STUDENTS' ANATOMY, E. J. Farris. Outstanding art anatomy that uses chiefly living objects for its illustrations. 71 photos of undraped men, women, children are accompanied by carefully labeled matching sketches to illustrate the skeletal system, articulations and movements, bony landmarks, the muscular system, skin, fasciae, fat, etc. 9 x-ray photos show movement of joints. Undraped models are shown in such actions as serving in tennis, drawing a bow in archery, playing football, dancing, preparing to spring and to dive. Also discussed and illustrated are proportions, age and sex differences, the anatomy of the smile, etc. 8 plates by the great early 18th century anatomic illustrator Siegfried Albinus are also included. Glossary. 158 figures, 7 in color. x + 159pp. 5⅝ x 8⅜.　　　　T744 Paperbound **$1.50**

AN ATLAS OF ANATOMY FOR ARTISTS, F Schider. A new 3rd edition of this standard text enlarged by 52 new illustrations of hands, anatomical studies by Cloquet, and expressive life studies of the body by Barcsay. 189 clear, detailed plates offer you precise information of impeccable accuracy. 29 plates show all aspects of the skeleton, with closeups of special areas, while 54 full-page plates, mostly in two colors, give human musculature as seen from four different points of view, with cutaways for important portions of the body. 14 full-page plates provide photographs of hand forms, eyelids, female breasts, and indicate the location of muscles upon models. 59 additional plates show how great artists of the past utilized human anatomy. They reproduce sketches and finished work by such artists as Michelangelo, Leonardo da Vinci, Goya, and 15 others. This is a lifetime reference work which will be one of the most important books in any artist's library. "The standard reference tool," AMERICAN LIBRARY ASSOCIATION. "Excellent," AMERICAN ARTIST. Third enlarged edition. 189 plates, 647 illustrations. xxvi + 192pp. 7⅞ x 10⅝.　　　T241 Clothbound **$6.00**

AN ATLAS OF ANIMAL ANATOMY FOR ARTISTS, W. Ellenberger, H. Baum, H. Dittrich. The largest, richest animal anatomy for artists available in English. 99 detailed anatomical plates of such animals as the horse, dog, cat, lion, deer, seal, kangaroo, flying squirrel, cow, bull, goat, monkey, hare, and bat. Surface features are clearly indicated, while progressive beneath-the-skin pictures show musculature, tendons, and bone structure. Rest and action are exhibited in terms of musculature and skeletal structure and detailed cross-sections are given for heads and important features. The animals chosen are representative of specific families so that a study of these anatomies will provide knowledge of hundreds of related species. "Highly recommended as one of the very few books on the subject worthy of being used as an authoritative guide," DESIGN. "Gives a fundamental knowledge," AMERICAN ARTIST. Second revised, enlarged edition with new plates from Cuvier, Stubbs, etc. 288 illustrations. 153pp. 11⅜ x 9.　　　　T82 Clothbound **$6.00**

THE HUMAN FIGURE IN MOTION, Eadweard Muybridge. The largest selection in print of Muybridge's famous high-speed action photos of the human figure in motion. 4789 photographs illustrate 162 different actions: men, women, children—mostly undraped—are shown walking, running, carrying various objects, sitting, lying down, climbing, throwing, arising, and performing over 150 other actions. Some actions are shown in as many as 150 photographs each. All in all there are more than 500 action strips in this enormous volume, series shots taken at shutter speeds of as high as 1/6000th of a second! These are not posed shots, but true stopped motion. They show bone and muscle in situations that the human eye is not fast enough to capture. Earlier, smaller editions of these prints have brought $40 and more on the out-of-print market. "A must for artists," ART IN FOCUS. "An unparalleled dictionary of action for all artists," AMERICAN ARTIST. 390 full-page plates, with 4789 photographs. Printed on heavy glossy stock. Reinforced binding with headbands. xxi + 390pp. 7⅞ x 10⅝.　　　　T204 Clothbound **$10.00**

ANIMALS IN MOTION, Eadweard Muybridge. This is the largest collection of animal action photos in print. 34 different animals (horses, mules, oxen, goats, camels, pigs, cats, guanacos, lions, gnus, deer, monkeys, eagles—and 21 others) in 132 characteristic actions. The horse alone is shown in more than 40 different actions. All 3919 photographs are taken in series at speeds up to 1/6000th of a second. The secrets of leg motion, spinal patterns, head movements, strains and contortions shown nowhere else are captured. You will see exactly how a lion sets his foot down; how an elephant's knees are like a human's—and how they differ; the position of a kangaroo's legs in mid-leap; how an ostrich's head bobs; details of the flight of birds—and thousands of facets of motion only the fastest cameras can catch. Photographed from domestic animals and animals in the Philadelphia zoo, it contains neither semiposed artificial shots nor distorted telephoto shots taken under adverse conditions. Artists, biologists, decorators, cartoonists, will find this book indispensable for understanding animals in motion. "A really marvelous series of plates," NATURE (London). "The dry plate's most spectacular early use was by Eadweard Muybridge," LIFE. 3919 photographs; 380 full pages of plates. 440pp. Printed on heavy glossy paper. Deluxe binding with headbands. 7⅞ x 10⅝.　　　　T203 Clothbound **$10.00**

CATALOGUE OF DOVER BOOKS

SHAKER FURNITURE, E. D. Andrews and F. Andrews. The most illuminating study on what many scholars consider the best examples of functional furniture ever made. Includes the history of the sect and the development of Shaker style. The 48 magnificent plates show tables, chairs, cupboards, chests, boxes, desks, beds, woodenware, and much more, and are accompanied by detailed commentary. For all antique collectors and dealers, designers and decorators, historians and folklorists. "Distinguished in scholarship, in pictorial illumination, and in all the essentials of fine book making," Antiques. 3 Appendixes. Bibliography. Index. 192pp. 7⅞ x 10¾. T679 Paperbound **$2.00**

JAPANESE HOMES AND THEIR SURROUNDINGS, E. S. Morse. Every aspect of the purely traditional Japanese home, from general plan and major structural features to ceremonial and traditional appointments—tatami, hibachi, shoji, tokonoma, etc. The most exhaustive discussion in English, this book is equally honored for its strikingly modern conception of architecture. First published in 1886, before the contamination of the Japanese traditions, it preserves the authentic features of an ideal of construction that is steadily gaining devotees in the Western world. 307 illustrations by the author. Index. Glossary. xxxvi + 372pp. 5⅝ x 8⅜. T746 Paperbound **$2.00**

COLONIAL LIGHTING, Arthur H. Hayward. The largest selection of antique lamps ever illustrated anywhere, from rush light-holders of earliest settlers to 1880's—with main emphasis on Colonial era. Primitive attempts at illumination ("Betty" lamps, variations of open wick design, candle molds, reflectors, etc.), whale oil lamps, painted and japanned hand lamps, Sandwich glass candlesticks, astral lamps, Bennington ware and chandeliers of wood, iron, pewter, brass, crystal, bronze and silver. Hundreds of illustrations, loads of information on colonial life, customs, habits, place of acquisition of lamps illustrated. A unique, thorough-going survey of an interesting aspect of Americana. Enlarged (1962) edition. New Introduction by James R. Marsh. Supplement "Colonial Chandeliers," photographs with descriptive notes. 169 illustrations, 647 lamps. xxxi + 312pp. 5⅝ x 8¼. T975 Paperbound **$2.00**

CHINESE HOUSEHOLD FURNITURE, George N. Kates. The first book-length study of authentic Chinese domestic furniture in Western language. Summarises practically everything known about Chinese furniture in pure state, uninfluenced by West. History of style, unusual woods used, craftsmanship, principles of design, specific forms like wardrobes, chests and boxes, beds, chairs, tables, stools, cupboards and other pieces. Based on author's own investigation into scanty Chinese historical sources and surviving pieces in private collections and museums. Will reveal a new dimension of simple, beautiful work to all interior decorators, furniture designers, craftsmen. 123 illustrations; 112 photographs. Bibliography. xiii + 205pp. 5¼ x 7¾. T958 Paperbound **$1.50**

ART AND THE SOCIAL ORDER, Professor D. W. Gotshalk, University of Illinois. One of the most profound and most influential studies of aesthetics written in our generation, this work is unusual in considering art from the relational point of view, as a transaction consisting of creation-object-apprehension. Discussing material from the fine arts, literature, music, and related disciplines, it analyzes the aesthetic experience, fine art, the creative process, art materials, form, expression, function, art criticism, art and social life and living. Graceful and fluent in expression, it requires no previous background in aesthetics and will be read with considerable enjoyment by anyone interested in the theory of art. "Clear, interesting, the soundest and most penetrating work in recent years," C. J. Ducasse, Brown University. New preface by Professor Gotshalk. xvi + 248pp. 5⅝ x 8½. T294 Paperbound **$1.50**

FOUNDATIONS OF MODERN ART, A. Ozenfant. An illuminating discussion by a great artist of the interrelationship of all forms of human creativity, from painting to science, writing to religion. The creative process is explored in all facets of art, from paleolithic cave painting to modern French painting and architecture, and the great universals of art are isolated. Expressing its countless insights in aphorisms accompanied by carefully selected illustrations, this book is itself an embodiment in prose of the creative process. Enlarged by 4 new chapters. 226 illustrations. 368pp. 6⅛ x 9¼. T215 Paperbound **$2.00**

VITRUVIUS: TEN BOOKS ON ARCHITECTURE. Book by 1st century Roman architect, engineer, is oldest, most influential work on architecture in existence; for hundreds of years his specific instructions were followed all over the world, by such men as Bramante, Michelangelo, Palladio, etc., and are reflected in major buildings. He describes classic principles of symmetry, harmony; design of treasury, prison, etc.; methods of durability; much more. He wrote in a fascinating manner, and often digressed to give interesting sidelights, making this volume appealing reading even to the non-professional. Standard English translation, by Prof. M. H. Morgan, Harvard U. Index. 6 illus. 334pp. 5⅜ x 8. T645 Paperbound **$2.00**

THE BROWN DECADES, Lewis Mumford. In this now classic study of the arts in America, Lewis Mumford resurrects the "buried renaissance" of the post-Civil War period. He demonstrates that it contained the seeds of a new integrity and power and documents his study with detailed accounts of the founding of modern architecture in the work of Sullivan, Richardson, Root, Roebling; landscape development of Marsh, Olmstead, and Eliot; the graphic arts of Homer, Eakins, and Ryder. 2nd revised enlarged edition. Bibliography. 12 illustrations. Index. xiv + 266pp. 5⅜ x 8. T200 Paperbound **$1.65**

ANIMALS IN MOTION, Eadweard Muybridge. Largest, most comprehensive selection of Muybridge's famous action photos of animals, from his ANIMAL LOCOMOTION. 3919 high-speed shots of 34 different animals and birds in 123 different types of action: horses, mules, ⌐n, pigs, goats, camels, elephants, dogs, cats, guanacos, sloths, lions, tigers, jaguar⌐ ⌐- coons, baboons, deer, elk, gnus, kangaroos, many others, in different actions — wa⌐⌐ ⌐g, running, flying, leaping. Horse alone shown in more than 40 different ways. Photos taken against ruled backgrounds; most actions taken from 3 angles at once: 90°, 60°, rear. Most plates original size. Of considerable interest to scientists as a classic of biology, as a record of actual facts of natural history and physiology. "A really marvellous series of plates," NATURE (London). "A monumental work," Waldemar Kaempffert. Photographed by E. Muybridge. Edited by L. S. Brown, American Museum of Natural History. 74-page introduction on mechanics of motion. 340 pages of plates, 3919 photographs. 416pp. Deluxe binding, paper. (Weight 4½ lbs.) 7⅞ x 10⅝. **T203 Clothbound $10.00**

THE HUMAN FIGURE IN MOTION. Eadweard Muybridge. This new edition of a great classic in the history of science and photography is the largest selection ever made from the original Muybridge photos of human action: 4789 photographs, illustrating 163 types of motion: walking, running, lifting, etc. in time-exposure sequence photos of speeds up to 1/6000th of a second. Men, women, children, mostly undraped, showing bone and muscle positions against ruled backgrounds, mostly taken at 3 angles at once. Not only was this a great work of photography, acclaimed by contemporary critics as a work of genius, it was also a great 19th century landmark in biological research. Historical introduction by Prof. Robert Taft, U. of Kansas. Plates original size, full detail. Over 500 action strips. 407pp. 7¾ x 10⅝. Deluxe edition. **T204 Clothbound $10.00**

Psychology

THE PHYSICAL DIMENSIONS OF CONSCIOUSNESS, Edwin G. Boring. By one of the ranking psychologists of this century, a major work which reflected the logical outcome of a progressive trend in psychological theory—a movement away from dualism toward physicalism. Boring, in this book, salvaged the most important work of the structuralists and helped direct the mainstream of American psychology into the neo-behavioristic channels of today. Unabridged republication of original (1933) edition. New preface by the author. Indexes. 17 illustrations. xviii + 251pp. 5⅜ x 8. **S1040 Paperbound $1.75**

BRAIN MECHANISMS AND INTELLIGENCE: A QUANTITATIVE STUDY OF INJURIES TO THE BRAIN, K. S. Lashley. A major contemporary psychologist examines the influence of brain injuries upon the capacity to learn, retentiveness, the formation of the maze habit, etc. Also: the relation of reduced learning ability to sensory and motor defects, the nature of the deterioration following cerebral lesions, comparison of the rat with other forms, and related matters. New introduction by Prof. D. O. Hebb. Bibliography. Index. xxii + 200pp. 5⅜ x 8½. **T1038 Paperbound $1.75**

THE DYNAMICS OF THERAPY IN A CONTROLLED RELATIONSHIP, Jessie Taft. One of the most important works in the literature of child psychology; it describes and illustrates relationship or Rankian therapy, presenting the complete record of the author's contacts with 2 seven-year old children and elucidating the underlying theory involved. Discusses the time element in therapy, presents the case histories, and indicates the forces that make for therapy. Unabridged republication. New introduction by Dr. V. P. Robinson. xix + 269pp. 5⅜ x 8. **T325 Paperbound $1.75**

CONDITIONED REFLEXES: AN INVESTIGATION OF THE PHYSIOLOGICAL ACTIVITIES OF THE CEREBRAL CORTEX, I. P. Pavlov. Full, authorized translation of Pavlov's own survey of his work in experimental psychology reviews entire course of experiments, summarizes conclusions, outlines psychological system based on famous "conditioned reflex" concept. Details of technical means used in experiments, observations on formation of conditioned reflexes, function of cerebral hemispheres, results of damage, nature of sleep, typology of nervous system, significance of experiments for human psychology. Trans. by Dr. G. V. Anrep, Cambridge Univ. 235-item bibliography. 18 figures. 445pp. 5⅜ x 8. **S614 Paperbound $2.35**

ERROR AND ECCENTRICITY IN HUMAN BELIEF, Joseph Jastrow. From 180 A.D. to the 1930's, the surprising record of human credulity: witchcraft, miracle workings, animal magnetism, mind-reading, astral-chemistry, dowsing, numerology, etc. The stories and exposures of the theosophy of Madame Blavatsky and her followers, the spiritism of Helene Smith, the imposture of Kaspar Hauser, the history of the Ouija board, the puppets of Dr. Luy, and dozens of other hoaxers and cranks, past and present. "As a potpourri of strange beliefs and ideas, it makes excellent reading," New York Times. Formerly titled "Wish and Wisdom, Episodes in the Vagaries of Belief." Unabridged publication. 56 illustrations and photos. 22 full-page plates. Index. xv + 394pp. 5⅜ x 8½. **T986 Paperbound $1.85**

THE PRINCIPLES OF PSYCHOLOGY, William James. The full long course, unabridged, of one of the great classics of Western science. Wonderfully lucid descriptions of human mental activity, consciousness, emotions, reason, abnormal phenomena, and similar topics. Examines motor zones, sensory aphasia, phosphorus and thought, cerebral thermometry, neural process in perception, ideo-motor action—in short, the entire spectrum of human mental activity. "Standard reading . . . a classic of interpretation," PSYCHIATRIC QUARTERLY. 94 illustrations. Two volume set. Total of 1408pp. 5⅜ x 8.
T381 Vol I Paperbound **$2.50**
T382 Vol II Paperbound **$2.50**
The set **$5.00**

SELECTED PAPERS ON HUMAN FACTORS IN THE DESIGN AND USE OF CONTROL SYSTEMS, Edited by H. Wallace Sinaiko. Nine of the most important papers in this area of increasing interest and rapid growth. All design engineers who have encountered problems involving man as a system-component will find this volume indispensable, both for its detailed information about man's unique capacities and defects, and for its comprehensive bibliography of articles and journals in the human-factors field. Contributors include Chapanis, Birmingham, Adams, Fitts and Jones, etc. on such topics as Theory and Methods for Analyzing Errors in Man-Machine Systems, A Design Philosophy for Man-Machine Control Systems, Man's Senses as Informational Channels, The Measurement of Human Performance, Analysis of Factors Contributing to 460 "Pilot Error" Experiences, etc. Name, subject indexes. Bibliographies of over 400 items. 27 figures. 8 tables. ix + 405pp. 6⅛ x 9¼.
S140 Paperbound **$2.75**

YOGA: A SCIENTIFIC EVALUATION, Kovoor T. Behanan. A complete reprinting of the book that for the first time gave Western readers a sane, scientific explanation and analysis of yoga. The author draws on controlled laboratory experiments and personal records of a year as a disciple of a yoga, to investigate yoga psychology, concepts of knowledge, physiology, "supernatural" phenomena, and the ability to tap the deepest human powers. In this study under the auspices of Yale University Institute of Human Relations, the strictest principles of physiological and psychological inquiry are followed throughout. Foreword by W. A. Miles, Yale University. 17 photographs. Glossary. Index. xx + 270pp. 5⅜ x 8.
T505 Paperbound **$1.75**

THE ANALYSIS OF SENSATIONS, Ernst Mach. Great study of physiology, psychology of perception, shows Mach's ability to see material freshly, his "incorruptible skepticism and independence." (Einstein). Relation of problems of psychological perception to classical physics, supposed dualism of physical and mental, principle of continuity, evolution of senses, will as organic manifestation, scores of experiments, observations in optics, acoustics, music, graphics, etc. New introduction by T. S. Szasz, M. D. 58 illus. 300-item bibliography. Index. 404pp. 5⅜ x 8.
S525 Paperbound **$1.75**

BEYOND PSYCHOLOGY, Otto Rank. The first work in English by the great psychologist, psychoanalyst, sociologist, teacher. Contains the results of lifelong thought and research about man's essential nature. He explores the ultimates of human existence—fear of death, desire for immortality, sexuality, basis of personality, social organization, need for love, creativity, irrationality and rationality. Detailed critiques of rational psychologies. A work of grand scope and lasting significance. 1 photo. Bibliography of author's works. Preface, forward. 291pp. 5⅜ x 8.
T485 Paperbound **$2.00**

SEX IN PSYCHO-ANALYSIS (formerly CONTRIBUTIONS TO PSYCHO-ANALYSIS), Sandor Ferenczi. Translated by Ernest Jones. A classic of modern psychology by Freud's associate, covering such topics as impotence, transference in the healing process, analysis and children, obscene words, dream analysis, masturbation and male homosexuality, paranoia, the sense of reality, the origin of symbols, pathological interest in money, hypnotism, etc. A wealth of illustrative material and case studies. Simple, non-technical treatment understandable to the lay reader. Also includes full text of THE DEVELOPMENT OF PSYCHO-ANALYSIS, by Ferenczi and Otto Rank. Two books bound together as one. Total of 406pp. 5⅜ x 8.
T324 Paperbound **$1.85**

EXPLANATION OF HUMAN BEHAVIOUR, F. V. Smith. An important intermediate-level critical introduction to 8 systems of the psychology of human behavior. Emphasizes methodology and theoretical principles. Part I is an analysis of the problems involved in the attempt to explain behavioral processes. Parts II and III present thorough expositions of the theories of McDougall, Allport, Lewin the Gestalt and Freudian aproaches, and the behavioristic systems of Watson, Hull, and Tolman. Biographical notes. Bibliography of over 800 items. 2 indices. 38 figures. xii + 460pp. 5½ x 8¾.
T253 Clothbound **$6.00**

PRINCIPLES OF ANIMAL PSYCHOLOGY, N. R. F. Maier and T. C. Schneirla. The definitive treatment of the development of animal behavior and the comparative psychology of all animals. This edition, corrected by the authors and with a supplement containing 5 of their most important subsequent articles, is a "must" for biologists, psychologists, zoologists, and others. First part of book includes analyses and comparisons of the behavior of characteristic types of animal life—from simple multicellular animals through the evolutionary scale to reptiles and birds, tracing the development of complexity in adaptation. Two-thirds of the book covers mammalian life, developing further the principles arrived at in Part I. New preface by the authors. 153 illustrations and tables. Extensive bibliographic material. Revised indices. xvi + 683pp. 5⅜ x 8½.
S1120 Paperbound **$3.00** (tentative)

Language Books and Records

GERMAN: HOW TO SPEAK AND WRITE IT. AN INFORMAL CONVERSATIONAL METHOD FOR SELF STUDY, Joseph Rosenberg. Eminently useful for self study because of concentration on elementary stages of learning. Also provides teachers with remarkable variety of aids: 28 full- and double-page sketches with pertinent items numbered and identified in German and English; German proverbs, jokes; grammar, idiom studies; extensive practice exercises. The most interesting introduction to German available, full of amusing illustrations, photographs of cities and landmarks in German-speaking cities, cultural information subtly woven into conversational material. Includes summary of grammar, guide to letter writing, study guide to German literature by Dr. Richard Friedenthal. Index. 400 illustrations. 384pp. 5⅜ x 8½.
T271 Paperbound **$2.00**

FRENCH: HOW TO SPEAK AND WRITE IT. AN INFORMAL CONVERSATIONAL METHOD FOR SELF STUDY, Joseph Lemaitre. Even the absolute beginner can acquire a solid foundation for further study from this delightful elementary course. Photographs, sketches and drawings, sparkling colloquial conversations on a wide variety of topics (including French culture and custom), French sayings and quips, are some of aids used to demonstrate rather than merely describe the language. Thorough yet surprisingly entertaining approach, excellent for teaching and for self study. Comprehensive analysis of pronunciation, practice exercises and appendices of verb tables, additional vocabulary, other useful material. Index. Appendix. 400 illustrations. 416pp. 5⅜ x 8½.
T268 Paperbound **$2.00**

DICTIONARY OF SPOKEN SPANISH, Spanish-English, English-Spanish. Compiled from spoken Spanish, emphasizing idiom and colloquial usage in both Castilian and Latin-American. More than 16,000 entries containing over 25,000 idioms—the largest list of idiomatic constructions ever published. Complete sentences given, indexed under single words—language in immediately useable form, for travellers, businessmen, students, etc. 25 page introduction provides rapid survey of sounds, grammar, syntax, with full consideration of irregular verbs. Especially apt in modern treatment of phrases and structure. 17 page glossary gives translations of geographical names, money values, numbers, national holidays, important street signs, useful expressions of high frequency, plus unique 7 page glossary of Spanish and Spanish-American foods and dishes. Originally published as War Department Technical Manual TM 30-900. iv + 513pp. 5⅜ x 8.
T495 Paperbound **$1.75**

SPEAK MY LANGUAGE: SPANISH FOR YOUNG BEGINNERS, M. Ahlman, Z. Gilbert. Records provide one of the best, and most entertaining, methods of introducing a foreign language to children. Within the framework of a train trip from Portugal to Spain, an English-speaking child is introduced to Spanish by a native companion. (Adapted from a successful radio program of the N. Y. State Educational Department.) Though a continuous story, there are a dozen specific categories of expressions, including greetings, numbers, time, weather, food, clothes, family members, etc. Drill is combined with poetry and contextual use. Authentic background music is heard. An accompanying book enables a reader to follow the records, and includes a vocabulary of over 350 recorded expressions. Two 10″ 33⅓ records, total of 40 minutes. Book. 40 illustrations. 69pp. 5¼ x 10½.
T890 The set **$4.95**

AN ENGLISH-FRENCH-GERMAN-SPANISH WORD FREQUENCY DICTIONARY, H. S. Eaton. An indispensable language study aid, this is a semantic frequency list of the 6000 most frequently used words in 4 languages—24,000 words in all. The lists, based on concepts rather than words alone, and containing all modern, exact, and idiomatic vocabulary, are arranged side by side to form a unique 4-language dictionary. A simple key indicates the importance of the individual words within each language. Over 200 pages of separate indexes for each language enable you to locate individual words at a glance. Will help language teachers and students, authors of textbooks, grammars, and language tests to compare concepts in the various languages and to concentrate on basic vocabulary, avoiding uncommon and obsolete words. 2 Appendixes. xxi + 441pp. 6½ x 9¼.
T738 Paperbound **$2.45**

NEW RUSSIAN-ENGLISH AND ENGLISH-RUSSIAN DICTIONARY, M. A. O'Brien. Over 70,000 entries in the new orthography! Many idiomatic uses and colloquialisms which form the basis of actual speech. Irregular verbs, perfective and imperfective aspects, regular and irregular sound changes, and other features. One of the few dictionaries where accent changes within the conjugation of verbs and the declension of nouns are fully indicated. "One of the best," Prof. E. J. Simmons, Cornell. First names, geographical terms, bibliography, etc. 738pp. 4½ x 6¼.
T208 Paperbound **$2.00**

96 MOST USEFUL PHRASES FOR TOURISTS AND STUDENTS in English, French, Spanish, German, Italian. A handy folder you'll want to carry with you. How to say "Excuse me," "How much is it?", "Write it down, please," etc., in four foreign languages. Copies limited, no more than 1 to a customer.
FREE

Say It language phrase books

These handy phrase books (128 to 196 pages each) make grammatical drills unnecessary for an elementary knowledge of a spoken foreign language. Covering most matters of travel and everyday life each volume contains:

> Over 1000 phrases and sentences in immediately useful forms — foreign language plus English.
>
> Modern usage designed for Americans. Specific phrases like, "Give me small change," and "Please call a taxi."
>
> Simplified phonetic transcription you will be able to read at sight.
>
> The only completely indexed phrase books on the market.
>
> Covers scores of important situations: — Greetings, restaurants, sightseeing, useful expressions, etc.

These books are prepared by native linguists who are professors at Columbia, N.Y.U., Fordham and other great universities. Use them independently or with any other book or record course. They provide a supplementary living element that most other courses lack. Individual volumes in:

Russian 75¢	Italian 75¢	Spanish 75¢	German 75¢
Hebrew 75¢	Danish 75¢	Japanese 75¢	Swedish 75¢
Dutch 75¢	Esperanto 75¢	Modern Greek 75¢	Portuguese 75¢
Norwegian 75¢	Polish 75¢	French 75¢	Yiddish 75¢
Turkish 75¢		English for German-speaking people 75¢	
English for Italian-speaking people 75¢		English for Spanish-speaking people 75¢	

Large clear type. 128-196 pages each. 3½ x 5¼. Sturdy paper binding.

Listen and Learn language records

LISTEN & LEARN is the only language record course designed especially to meet your travel and everyday needs. It is available in separate sets for FRENCH, SPANISH, GERMAN, JAPANESE, RUSSIAN, MODERN GREEK, ITALIAN and HEBREW, and each set contains three 33⅓ rpm long-playing records—1½ hours of recorded speech by eminent native speakers who are professors at Columbia, New York University, Queens College.

Check the following special features found only in LISTEN & LEARN:

- **Dual-language recording. 812 selected phrases and sentences**, over 3200 words, spoken first in English, then in their foreign language equivalents. A suitable pause follows each foreign phrase, allowing you time to repeat the expression. You learn by unconscious assimilation.
- **128 to 206-page manual** contains everything on the records, plus a simple phonetic pronunciation guide.
- **Indexed for convenience. The only set on the market** that is completely indexed. No more puzzling over where to find the phrase you need. Just look in the rear of the manual.
- **Practical.** No time wasted on material you can find in any grammar. LISTEN & LEARN covers central core material with phrase approach. Ideal for the person with limited learning time.
- **Living, modern expressions**, not found in other courses. Hygienic products, modern equipment, shopping—expressions used every day, like "nylon" and "air-conditioned."
- **Limited objective.** Everything you learn, no matter where you stop, is immediately useful. You have to finish other courses, wade through grammar and vocabulary drill, before they help you.
- **High-fidelity recording.** LISTEN & LEARN records equal in clarity and surface-silence any record on the market costing up to $6.

"Excellent . . . the spoken records . . . impress me as being among the very best on the market," **Prof. Mario Pei,** Dept. of Romance Languages, Columbia University. "Inexpensive and well-done . . . it would make an ideal present," CHICAGO SUNDAY TRIBUNE. "More genuinely helpful than anything of its kind which I have previously encountered," **Sidney Clark,** well-known author of "ALL THE BEST" travel books.

UNCONDITIONAL GUARANTEE. Try LISTEN & LEARN, then return it within 10 days for full refund if you are not satisfied.

Each set contains three twelve-inch 33⅓ records, manual, and album.

SPANISH	the set $5.95	GERMAN	the set $5.95
FRENCH	the set $5.95	ITALIAN	the set $5.95
RUSSIAN	the set $5.95	JAPANESE	the set $5.95
PORTUGUESE	the set $5.95	MODERN GREEK	the set $5.95
MODERN HEBREW	the set $5.95		

Trubner Colloquial Manuals

These unusual books are members of the famous Trubner series of colloquial manuals. They have been written to provide adults with a sound colloquial knowledge of a foreign language, and are suited for either class use or self-study. Each book is a complete course in itself, with progressive, easy to follow lessons. Phonetics, grammar, and syntax are covered, while hundreds of phrases and idioms, reading texts, exercises, and vocabulary are included. These books are unusual in being neither skimpy nor overdetailed in grammatical matters, and in presenting up-to-date, colloquial, and practical phrase material. Bilingual presentation is stressed, to make thorough self-study easier for the reader.

COLLOQUIAL HINDUSTANI, A. H. Harley, formerly Nizam's Reader in Urdu, U. of London. 30 pages on phonetics and scripts (devanagari & Arabic-Persian) are followed by 29 lessons, including material on English and Arabic-Persian influences. Key to all exercises. Vocabulary. 5 x 7½. 147pp. Clothbound $1.75

COLLOQUIAL PERSIAN, L. P. Elwell-Sutton. Best introduction to modern Persian, with 90 page grammatical section followed by conversations, 35-page vocabulary. 139pp.
Clothbound $1.75

COLLOQUIAL ARABIC, DeLacy O'Leary. Foremost Islamic scholar covers language of Egypt, Syria, Palestine, & Northern Arabia. Extremely clear coverage of complex Arabic verbs & noun plurals; also cultural aspects of language. Vocabulary. xviii + 192pp. 5 x 7½.
Clothbound $2.50

COLLOQUIAL GERMAN, P. F. Doring. Intensive thorough coverage of grammar in easily-followed form. Excellent for brush-up, with hundreds of colloquial phrases. 34 pages of bilingual texts. 224pp. 5 x 7½. Clothbound $1.75

COLLOQUIAL SPANISH, W. R. Patterson. Castilian grammar and colloquial language, loaded with bilingual phrases and colloquialisms. Excellent for review or self-study. 164pp. 5 x 7½.
Clothbound $1.75

COLLOQUIAL FRENCH, W. R. Patterson. 16th revision of this extremely popular manual. Grammar explained with model clarity, and hundreds of useful expressions and phrases; exercises, reading texts, etc. Appendixes of new and useful words and phrases. 223pp. 5 x 7½.
Clothbound $1.75

COLLOQUIAL CZECH, J. Schwarz, former headmaster of Lingua Institute, Prague. Full easily followed coverage of grammar, hundreds of immediately useable phrases, texts. Perhaps the best Czech grammar in print. "An absolutely successful textbook," JOURNAL OF CZECHO-SLOVAK FORCES IN GREAT BRITAIN. 252pp. 5 x 7½. Clothbound $3.00

COLLOQUIAL RUMANIAN, G. Nandris, Professor of University of London. Extremely thorough coverage of phonetics, grammar, syntax; also included 70-page reader, and 70-page vocabulary. Probably the best grammar for this increasingly important language. 340pp. 5 x 7½.
Clothbound $2.50

COLLOQUIAL ITALIAN, A. L. Hayward. Excellent self-study course in grammar, vocabulary, idioms, and reading. Easy progressive lessons will give a good working knowledge of Italian in the shortest possible time. 5 x 7½. Clothbound $1.75

COLLOQUIAL TURKISH, Yusuf Mardin. Very clear, thorough introduction to leading cultural and economic language of Near East. Begins with pronunciation and statement of vowel harmony, then 36 lessons present grammar, graded vocabulary, useful phrases, dialogues, reading, exercises. Key to exercises at rear. Turkish-English vocabulary. All in Roman alphabet. x + 288pp. 4¾ x 7¼. Clothbound $4.00

DUTCH-ENGLISH AND ENGLISH-DUTCH DICTIONARY, F. G. Renier. For travel, literary, scientific or business Dutch, you will find this the most convenient, practical and comprehensive dictionary on the market. More than 60,000 entries, shades of meaning, colloquialisms, idioms, compounds and technical terms. Dutch and English strong and irregular verbs. This is the only dictionary in its size and price range that indicates the gender of nouns. New orthography. xvii + 571pp. 5½ x 6¼. T224 Clothbound $2.75

LEARN DUTCH, F. G. Renier. This book is the most satisfactory and most easily used grammar of modern Dutch. The student is gradually led from simple lessons in pronunciation, through translation from and into Dutch, and finally to a mastery of spoken and written Dutch. Grammatical principles are clearly explained while a useful, practical vocabulary is introduced in easy exercises and readings. It is used and recommended by the Fulbright Committee in the Netherlands. Phonetic appendices. Over 1200 exercises; Dutch-English, English-Dutch vocabularies. 181pp. 4¼ x 7¼. T441 Clothbound $2.25

Books Explaining Science and Mathematics

WHAT IS SCIENCE?, N. Campbell. The role of experiment and measurement, the function of mathematics, the nature of scientific laws, the difference between laws and theories, the limitations of science, and many similarly provocative topics are treated clearly and without technicalities by an eminent scientist. "Still an excellent introduction to scientific philosophy," H. Margenau in PHYSICS TODAY. "A first-rate primer . . . deserves a wide audience," SCIENTIFIC AMERICAN. 192pp. 5⅜ x 8. S43 Paperbound **$1.25**

THE NATURE OF PHYSICAL THEORY, P. W. Bridgman. A Nobel Laureate's clear, non-technical lectures on difficulties and paradoxes connected with frontier research on the physical sciences. Concerned with such central concepts as thought, logic, mathematics, relativity, probability, wave mechanics, etc. he analyzes the contributions of such men as Newton, Einstein, Bohr, Heisenberg, and many others. "Lucid and entertaining . . . recommended to anyone who wants to get some insight into current philosophies of science," THE NEW PHILOSOPHY. Index. xi + 138pp. 5⅜ x 8. S33 Paperbound **$1.25**

EXPERIMENT AND THEORY IN PHYSICS, Max Born. A Nobel Laureate examines the nature of experiment and theory in theoretical physics and analyzes the advances made by the great physicists of our day: Heisenberg, Einstein, Bohr, Planck, Dirac, and others. The actual process of creation is detailed step-by-step by one who participated. A fine examination of the scientific method at work. 44pp. 5⅜ x 8. S308 Paperbound **75¢**

THE PSYCHOLOGY OF INVENTION IN THE MATHEMATICAL FIELD, J. Hadamard. The reports of such men as Descartes, Pascal, Einstein, Poincaré, and others are considered in this investigation of the method of idea-creation in mathematics and other sciences and the thinking process in general. How do ideas originate? What is the role of the unconscious? What is Poincaré's forgetting hypothesis? are some of the fascinating questions treated. A penetrating analysis of Einstein's thought processes concludes the book. xiii + 145pp. 5⅜ x 8. T107 Paperbound **$1.25**

THE NATURE OF LIGHT AND COLOUR IN THE OPEN AIR, M. Minnaert. Why are shadows sometimes blue, sometimes green, or other colors depending on the light and surroundings? What causes mirages? Why do multiple suns and moons appear in the sky? Professor Minnaert explains these unusual phenomena and hundreds of others in simple, easy-to-understand terms based on optical laws and the properties of light and color. No mathematics is required but artists, scientists, students, and everyone fascinated by these "tricks" of nature will find thousands of useful and amazing pieces of information. Hundreds of observational experiments are suggested which require no special equipment. 200 illustrations; 42 photos. xvi + 362pp. 5⅜ x 8. T196 Paperbound **$2.00**

THE UNIVERSE OF LIGHT, W. Bragg. Sir William Bragg, Nobel Laureate and great modern physicist, is also well known for his powers of clear exposition. Here he analyzes all aspects of light for the layman: lenses, reflection, refraction, the optics of vision, x-rays, the photoelectric effect, etc. He tells you what causes the color of spectra, rainbows, and soap bubbles, how magic mirrors work, and much more. Dozens of simple experiments are described. Preface. Index. 199 line drawings and photographs, including 2 full-page color plates. x + 283pp. 5⅜ x 8. T538 Paperbound **$1.85**

SOAP-BUBBLES: THEIR COLOURS AND THE FORCES THAT MOULD THEM, C. V. Boys. For continuing popularity and validity as scientific primer, few books can match this volume of easily-followed experiments, explanations. Lucid exposition of complexities of liquid films, surface tension and related phenomena, bubbles' reaction to heat, motion, music, magnetic fields. Experiments with capillary attraction, soap bubbles on frames, composite bubbles, liquid cylinders and jets, bubbles other than soap, etc. Wonderful introduction to scientific method, natural laws that have many ramifications in areas of modern physics. Only complete edition in print. New Introduction by S. Z. Lewin, New York University. 83 illustrations; 1 full-page color plate. xii + 190pp. 5⅜ x 8½. T542 Paperbound **95¢**

Music

A GENERAL HISTORY OF MUSIC, Charles Burney. A detailed coverage of music from the Greeks up to 1789, with full information on all types of music: sacred and secular, vocal and instrumental, operatic and symphonic. Theory, notation, forms, instruments, innovators, composers, performers, typical and important works, and much more in an easy, entertaining style. Burney covered much of Europe and spoke with hundreds of authorities and composers so that this work is more than a compilation of records . . . it is a living work of careful and first-hand scholarship. Its account of thoroughbass (18th century) Italian music is probably still the best introduction on the subject. A recent NEW YORK TIMES review said, "Surprisingly few of Burney's statements have been invalidated by modern research . . . still of great value." Edited and corrected by Frank Mercer. 35 figures. Indices. 1915pp. 5⅜ x 8. 2 volumes. **T36 The Set, Clothbound $12.50**

A DICTIONARY OF HYMNOLOGY, John Julian. This exhaustive and scholarly work has become known as an invaluable source of hundreds of thousands of important and often difficult to obtain facts on the history and use of hymns in the western world. Everyone interested in hymns will be fascinated by the accounts of famous hymns and hymn writers and amazed by the amount of practical information he will find. More than 30,000 entries on individual hymns, giving authorship, date and circumstances of composition, publication, textual variations, translations, denominational and ritual usage, etc. Biographies of more than 9,000 hymn writers, and essays on important topics such as Christmas carols and children's hymns, and much other unusual and valuable information. A 200 page double-columned index of first lines — the largest in print. Total of 1786 pages in two reinforced clothbound volumes. 6¼ x 9¼. **The set, T333 Clothbound $17.50**

MUSIC IN MEDIEVAL BRITAIN, F. Ll. Harrison. The most thorough, up-to-date, and accurate treatment of the subject ever published, beautifully illustrated. Complete account of institutions and choirs; carols, masses, and motets; liturgy and plainsong; and polyphonic music from the Norman Conquest to the Reformation. Discusses the various schools of music and their reciprocal influences; the origin and development of new ritual forms; development and use of instruments; and new evidence on many problems of the period. Reproductions of scores, over 200 excerpts from medieval melodies. Rules of harmony and dissonance; influence of Continental styles; great composers (Dunstable, Cornysh, Fairfax, etc.); and much more. Register and index of more than 400 musicians. Index of titles. General Index. 225-item bibliography. 6 Appendices. xix + 491pp. 5⅝ x 8¾. **T705 Clothbound $10.00**

THE MUSIC OF SPAIN, Gilbert Chase. Only book in English to give concise, comprehensive account of Iberian music; new Chapter covers music since 1941. Victoria, Albéniz, Cabezón, Pedrell, Turina, hundreds of other composers; popular and folk music; the Gypsies; the guitar; dance, theatre, opera, with only extensive discussion in English of the Zarzuela; virtuosi such as Casals; much more. "Distinguished . . . readable," Saturday Review. 400-item bibliography. Index. 27 photos. 383pp. 5⅜ x 8. **T549 Paperbound $2.00**

ON STUDYING SINGING, Sergius Kagen. An intelligent method of voice-training, which leads you around pitfalls that waste your time, money, and effort. Exposes rigid, mechanical systems, baseless theories, deleterious exercises. "Logical, clear, convincing . . . dead right," Virgil Thomson, N.Y. Herald Tribune. "I recommend this volume highly," Maggie Teyte, Saturday Review. 119pp. 5⅜ x 8. **T622 Paperbound $1.25**

WILLIAM LAWES, M. Lefkowitz. This is the definitive work on Lawes, the versatile, prolific, and highly original "King's musician" of 17th century England. His life is reconstructed from original documents, and nearly every piece he ever wrote is examined and evaluated: his fantasias, pavans, violin "sonatas," lyra viol and bass viol suites, and music for harp and theorbo; and his songs, masques, and theater music to words by Herrick ("Gather Ye Rosebuds"), Jonson, Suckling, Shirley, and others. The author shows the innovations of dissonance, augmented triad, and other Italian influences Lawes helped introduce to England. List of Lawes' complete works and several complete scores by this major precursor of Purcell and the 18th century developments. Index. 5 Appendices. 52 musical excerpts, many never before in print. Bibliography. x + 320pp. 5⅜ x 8. **T706 Clothbound $10.00**

THE FUGUE IN BEETHOVEN'S PIANO MUSIC, J. V. Cockshoot. The first study of a neglected aspect of Beethoven's genius: his ability as a writer of fugues. Analyses of early studies and published works demonstrate his original and powerful contributions to composition. 34 works are examined, with 143 musical excerpts. For all pianists, teachers, students, and music-minded readers with a serious interest in Beethoven. Index. 93-item bibliography. Illustration of original score for "Fugue in C." xv + 212pp. 5⅝ x 8⅜. **T704 Clothbound $6.00**

CATALOGUE OF DOVER BOOKS

ROMAIN ROLLAND'S ESSAYS ON MUSIC, ed. by David Ewen. 16 best essays by great critic of our time, Nobel Laureate, discuss Mozart, Beethoven, Gluck, Handel, Berlioz, Wagner, Wolf, Saint-Saëns, Metastasio, Lully, Telemann, Grétry, "Origins of 18th Century 'Classic' Style," and musical life of 18th century Germany and Italy. "Shows the key to the high place that Rolland still holds in the world of music," Library Journal. 371pp. 5⅜ x 8.
T550 Paperbound **$1.50**

A GENERAL HISTORY OF THE SCIENCE AND PRACTICE OF MUSIC, Sir John Hawkins. Originally published in 1776, long regarded a genuine classic of musicology. Traces the origin and development of music theory, harmonic and contrapuntal processes, polyphony, musical notation, orchestration, instrumentation, etc. from earliest recorded evidence of music experiment to the author's own time, taking into account a score of musical forms—plainsong, motet, ballad, oratorio, opera, madrigal, canon, cantata, many more—and the particular contributions of various peoples. Still extremely valuable for its consideration of musical theorists and their work and detailed summaries and exact quotes from historically important works unavailable except in largest libraries. Biographical and critical information about hundreds of musicians undeservedly forgotten and now being rediscovered. A unique and significant work of music scholarship, prized by musicologists, composers, performers, historians of culture, and musical amateurs. Reproduction of 1853 edition. New introduction by Charles Cudworth, Curator, Pendlebury Library of Music, Cambridge, England. 315 illustrations; 60 full-page plates. 153 musical excerpts. 20 facsimiles of ancient manuscripts. Memoir of author. Index. Two volumes. Total of 1020pp. of text. 7⅞ x 10¾.
T1048-49 The set, Clothbound **$15.00**

THE GIFT TO BE SIMPLE, Edward Deming Andrews. Students of American history and culture, hymnologists, musicians, historians of religion, and anyone interested in reading about unusual peoples and customs will welcome this unique and authoritative account of Shaker music. Examines the origin of verses and of numerous Shaker dances; the rituals and gestures that accompanied singing; the unusual music theory developed by Shaker musicians and the melodies that were produced. Captures the spirit of an humble and devout people as expressed in many actual texts of hymns, dance songs, ritualistic songs, songs of humility, etc. Includes musical notations of about eighty melodies. A short introduction shows the development of the Shaker movement from its origins (about 1750), through the period of its greatest influence in the 1840's, to its post-Civil War decline. Index of first lines and melodies. Bibliography. 17 illustrations. ix + 170pp. 5⅜ x 8. T22 Paperbound **$1.50**

BEETHOVEN AND HIS NINE SYMPHONIES, George Grove, editor of Grove's Dictionary of Music and Musicians. In this modern middle-level classic of musicology Grove not only analyzes all nine of Beethoven's symphonies very thoroughly in terms of their musical structure, but also discusses the circumstances under which they were written, Beethoven's stylistic development, and much other background material. This is an extremely rich book, yet very easily followed; it is highly recommended to anyone seriously interested in music. Over 250 musical passages. Index. viii + 407pp. 5⅜ x 8. T334 Paperbound **$2.00**

AIDA BY GIUSEPPI VERDI, translated and introduced by Ellen H. Bleiler. Full handbook to the most popular opera of all; everything the operagoer (or listener) needs except the music itself. Complete Italian libretto, with all repeats, with new, modern English translation in parallel columns; biography of Verdi and librettists; background to composition of Aida; musical history; plot summary; musical excerpts; pictorial section of 76 illustrations showing Verdi, famous singers, famous performances, etc. Large clear type for easy reading. 147pp. 5⅝ x 8½. T405 Paperbound **$1.00**

LA BOHEME BY GIACOMO PUCCINI, translated and introduced by Ellen H. Bleiler. Complete handbook for the operagoer, with everything needed for full enjoyment except the musical score itself. Complete Italian libretto, with new modern English line-by-line translation—the only libretto printing all repeats; biography of Puccini; the librettists; background to the opera, Murger's La Boheme, etc.; circumstances of composition and performances; plot summary; and pictorial section of 73 illustrations showing Puccini, famous singers and performances, etc. Large clear type for easy reading. 124pp. 5⅜ x 8½. T404 Paperbound **$1.00**

Prices subject to change without notice.

Dover publishes books on art, music, philosophy, literature, languages, history, social sciences, psychology, handcrafts, orientalia, puzzles and entertainments, chess, pets and gardens, books explaining science, intermediate and higher mathematics, mathematical physics, engineering, biological sciences, earth sciences, classics of science, etc. Write to:

Dept. catrr.
Dover Publications, Inc.
180 Varick Street, N.Y. 14, N.Y.

MR

NEW VARIORUM SHAKESPEARE SERIES,
EDITED BY HORACE H. FURNESS

As You Like It, $2.25
Hamlet, Two volume set $4.50
King Lear, $2.25
Love's Labour's Lost, $2.25
Macbeth, edited by Horace H. Furness, Jr., $2.25
The Merchant of Venice, $2.25
A Midsummer Night's Dream, $2.25
Much Ado About Nothing, $2.25
Othello, $2.25
Romeo and Juliet, $2.25
The Tempest, $2.25
Twelfth Night, or What You Will, $2.25
The Winter's Tale, $2.25

Shakespeare
AS A DRAMATIC ARTIST

by Richard G. Moulton
Late Professor of English, University of Chicago

Despite an abundance of critical works on Shakespeare, few studies have dealt adequately with the structure of his plays. Though Shakespeare's poetry and his understanding of human nature have been universally admired, certain schools of criticism have held that he was weakest in his handling of plot. Setting his plays against the classical French tradition of the "well-made" play, some critics have apologized for the "formlessness" of Shakespeare's work; others have ignored the problem of construction altogether. This well-known classic study is the only major critical work to give a stimulating and satisfactory discussion of the subject.

Denying that Shakespeare was merely an intuitive genius who did not know what he was doing, the author carefully examines the structure of a number of Shakespeare's plays. His thorough and penetrating analyses of "The Merchant of Venice," "Richard III," "Macbeth," "Julius Caesar," "King Lear," "Othello," "The Tempest," "Love's Labour's Lost," and "As You Like It" reveal Shakespeare's extraordinary skill at dramatic composition; his remarkable interweaving of major story plots and subplots, the blending of light and serious stories, the technique of dramatic hedging, the use of character groupings and other dramatic devices which enabled him to adroitly avoid or reduce the difficulties inherent in his source plots. Topics that Professor Moulton covers include: varying concepts of Fate, the concept of Nemesis as a dramatic idea, the problem of judgment by appearances, the antithesis of the outer and inner life, passion and movement as elements of dramatic effect, the institution of the court fool, word play as a dramatic weapon, etc. There is also a provocative discussion of dramatic criticism in general, in which deductive and inductive theories are explained and contrasted.

In his introduction to this Dover reprint, Eric Bentley hails Moulton's work as "the only notable book on Shakespeare's handling of plot . . . one of the most valuable of all books on Shakespeare to the student of today." Written in 1885, this book is still an arresting volume, indispensable to all who would like to understand and appreciate the construction of Shakespeare's plays.

Unabridged and unaltered republication of 3rd revised and enlarged 1893 edition. Author's prefaces. New introduction by Eric Bentley. Appendix. Subject Index. Index of Scenes. xviii + 443pp. 5⅜ x 8.

T1546 Paperbound $2.00

A DOVER EDITION DESIGNED FOR YEARS OF USE!

We have made every effort to make this the best book possible. Our paper is opaque, with minimal show-through; it will not discolor or become brittle with age. Pages are sewn in signatures, in the method traditionally used for the best books, and will not drop out, as often happens with paperbacks held together with glue. Books open flat for easy reference. The binding will not crack or split. This is a permanent book.